DATE DUE

FEB 1 0 1994	MAR 2 6 1996
	APR 1 0 1996
FEB 2 4 1994	OCT 3 1 1996
MAR - 3 1994	MAR 1 1997
MAR 2 4 1994	APR 2 9 1997
APR 3 1994	NOV 1 7 1997
OCT 1 3 1994	NOV 2 8 1998
OCT 1 9 1994	NOV 1 8 1999
NOV 2 2 1994	NOV 2 9 1999
DEC - 6 1994	
JAN 3 0 1995	
FEB 1 8 1995 MAR 1 3 1995	
MAR 3 0 1995 NOV - 2 1995	
NOV 1 7 1995	
DEC - 3 1995	
FEB - 7 1996	
Feb. 21	

BRODART   Cat. No. 23-221

EATING
DISORDERS

Also by Hilde Bruch

Don't Be Afraid of Your Child

The Importance of Overweight

Studies in Schizophrenia

EATING DISORDERS

*Obesity,
Anorexia Nervosa,
and the Person Within*

HILDE BRUCH M.D.

PROFESSOR OF PSYCHIATRY

Baylor College of Medicine / Houston, Texas

Basic Books, Inc., Publishers

NEW YORK

© 1973 by Basic Books, Inc.
Library of Congress Catalog Card Number: 72–89189
ISBN: 0–465–01784–3 (cloth)
ISBN: 0–465–01782–7 (paper)
Manufactured in the United States of America
DESIGNED BY VINCENT TORRE
10 9 8 7 6 5

TO THE MEMORY OF

Rudolf, Auguste, AND *Selma*

VICTIMS OF NAZI ATROCITIES

AND TO

Richard Alexander AND THE FUTURE

Acknowledgments

This book is based on studies that have extended over nearly 40 years and that were possible only through the continuous and active collaboration and support of many. There is probably no one among my professional and personal friends and acquaintances who has not contributed in some form or another. Some shared with me their personal habits, concerns, and secret indulgences; others listened to my efforts to formulate my evolving concepts and confirmed or challenged them. I wish it were possible to acknowledge my gratitude to all of them individually.

My greatest indebtedness is to those who extended to me the use of the clinical and research facilities under their directorship. I wish to express my gratitude to Dr. Rustin McIntosh, Dr. Leo Kanner, Dr. John C. White-horn, Dr. Lawrence C. Kolb, Dr. Shervert H. Frazier, and Dr. Alex Pokorny who were in charge of the various services where these studies were carried out, at the College of Physicians and Surgeons (Columbia University), the Johns Hopkins Hospital, and Baylor College of Medicine. I also wish to thank the professional staffs of these institutions for their active help—the nurses, psychologists, social workers, occupational therapists, and many others, though I shall mention by name only Ms. Grace Touraine who opened up the field of family investigation during the early part of the obesity study, and Ms. Winifred Winikus whose tact and unflagging interest made contact possible, up to the present, with even the most difficult anorexic families.

I wish to acknowledge the contributions of the many physicians who referred their difficult patients for consultation or extended psychotherapy and who reported in detail about their own observations. It would be impossible to be complete, and I apologize to those whose names are not mentioned; their contribution is not valued any the less. I record here only the names of those whose information on individual patients' background or treatment histories has been used in the text, though in a disguised form, and express my thanks to Drs. Henry Aranow, Jr., Anny Baumann, Harold Brown, Stuart L. Brown, Thomas M. Cassidy, Alfred E. Leiser, Harry S. Lipscomb, Ephraim T. Lisansky, Alvin M. Mesnikoff, Robert Michels, Marc Moldawer, John Money, Peter A. Olsson, Stanley R. Palombo, Richard B. Pessikoff, Clifton Rhead, James S. Robinson, Howard P. Roffwarg, John A. Talbott, and Lucia E. Tower.

The work would not have been possible without the continuous painstaking help of my secretaries during these years. Here again I can mention only one, Ms. Jacqueline Reasoner, who labored untiringly through the various drafts of this book.

H.B.

Contents

PART IV
Treatment

PART I

General Aspects

1

Orientation and Point of View

This book will concern itself with individuals who misuse the eating function in their efforts to solve or camouflage problems of living that to them appear otherwise insoluble. Food lends itself readily to such usage because eating, from birth on, is always closely intermingled with interpersonal and emotional experiences, and its physiological and psychological aspects cannot be strictly differentiated. For normal people, too, food is never restricted to the biological aspects alone. There is no human society that deals rationally with food in its environment, that eats according to the availability, edibility, and nutritional value alone. Food is endowed with complex values and elaborate ideologies, religious beliefs, and prestige systems. Social and group organizations may center around food. It is these aspects that give to eating habits and food traditions their special cultural and national character, and to the food habits of one's background and family the emotional connotation of warmth and home.

The people to be discussed in this book are characterized by the abnormal amounts they eat, and they show this by becoming conspicuous in their appearance. They may eat excessively and grow fat, or they may restrict their intake to the point of becoming dangerously emaciated. Clinically these conditions are known as obesity and anorexia nervosa, one prevalent, the other exceedingly rare, but they are closely related through common underlying problems.

As to obesity, I shall deal with the exceptions rather than the rule. Incidence of overweight and obesity in the United States has been estimated to be as high as 30% or more, suggesting that there are 60 to 70 million people or more whose weight is above the statistical average. About the majority of these people little or nothing is known because they have not been studied except for appearing in statistics. Those who seek medical attention or apply to insurance companies supposedly are willing and able to follow advice, adhere to the prescribed program, and lose the undesirable weight. There must be countless others who follow the reducing diets so lavishly offered through the mass media and never get fat, or who readily shed any extra weight. Others go in large numbers to self-help groups and lose the unwanted weight. About all these easy and successful reducers, I know little or nothing.

The individuals who have come to my attention are those who have repeatedly tried these widely propagandized and readily available roads, and have failed or had temporary success and relapsed, or have become acutely disturbed or depressed during such attempts at reducing. Extended contact with such difficult individuals has led me to conclude that, as handicapping as overweight is, there are people who function better with the extra weight. Obesity, although a faulty adaptation, may serve as a protection against more severe illness; it represents an effort to stay well or to be less sick. These individuals, overweight or otherwise, cannot function unless the underlying problems are clarified and resolved. For such people the actual weight loss must be considered a secondary question. Paradoxical as it may sound, for them reducing is not the cure of their problems. At best, as they are improving, dieting may become possible, a signal that the underlying problems are less disturbing and capable of a more rational solution.

No figures are available about the incidence, whether rare or frequent, of obesity associated with such severe personality problems. However large or small a percentage they represent in relation to the enormous number of overweight people, they are frequent enough to constitute the "problem" cases who keep physicians and nutritionists puzzled and dissatisfied with their recommendations. They are often discounted in reports of treatment results because they are "uncooperative." Little is known about the frequency of such failures, except that the number of overweight people does not seem to decrease in spite of all the propaganda to make them change their ways. In talking about obesity, whatever other subdivisions one chooses to apply, there is need to differentiate between two basic groups: those who can follow a diet and function well while doing so, and the others who encounter serious difficulties or find it intolerable. It is with these troublesome cases of obesity that this book is concerned.

The other condition, anorexia nervosa, the relentless pursuit of thinness through self-starvation, even unto death, is rare indeed, but the medical interest in it has always been great, quite out of proportion to its infrequent occurrence. The continued fascination with this rare condition is probably evoked by the tragedy of seeing a young person, in the bloom of youth, seeking solution to life's problems through this bizarre method of voluntary starvation, something that runs counter to all human experience. Though anorexia nervosa deserves to be defined as a special clinical syndrome, one may also conceive of it as a counterpart to obesity. In a way, it represents a caricature of what will happen when the common recommendation that reducing will make you slim, beautiful, and happy is taken too literally and carried out to the extreme. A better understanding of obesity has come from the study of its grotesque mirror image. The very intensity of the preoccupation with food and weight in anorexia nervosa permits a clearer definition of the basic problems in weight disturbances, including obesity, and of their association with personality and emotional problems. Gradually it has become evident that the very organization of awareness of hunger and of other bodily needs is the outcome of reciprocal transactional processes within the interpersonal field, and not something inherent in the individual organism. I wish to offer here the hypothesis that obesity and anorexia nervosa are related to faulty hunger awareness, that "hunger" is not innate knowledge; learning is necessary for its organization into recognizable patterns.

During these extended studies it was gradually recognized that neither obesity nor anorexia nervosa is a uniform condition; they represent various different symptom complexes which cannot be explained by one simple mechanism. They are neither purely physiochemical nor physiological in some other way, nor due to psychological or social factors alone, but rather they develop as an expression of disturbances in the interaction of these various forces. When the first observations were reported it required careful, even apologetic statements that such a complex approach was also scientific. During the past 30 years a definite change has occurred, in some ways amounting to a revolution, in our concepts of what constitutes scientific inquiry. Such marginal, formerly even suspect, phenomena, like emphasis on social and psychological factors in physical illness, have gained increasing recognition. The old-style biology was characterized by assumptions of linearity, of uniform causal logic, of determinancy. This applies to earlier psychoanalytic and psychological thinking as well as to organic biological studies. The older studies are not conceived of as wrong, but they are rated in modern biological thinking only as parts of wider systems.

The trend in biological inquiries has been away from deterministic questions, away from reducing the complexities of biological events, specifically of human behavior, to simple problems of isolated incidents of cause and effect, the "bits and pieces" image of the world that in its very concept violates the true nature of the organism. Emphasis is increasingly on the constant feedback processes whereby "parts" and "whole" interact. With recognition of the inadequacy of the mechanistic model for understanding of major areas of biological and psychological facts, a great shift in the life sciences has come about. There is less concern with the transmission of *energy*; the movement is toward models in which it is transmission of *information* and *meaning* that matters most.

The new science of biology has room for the large variety and complexity of individual response. In his extensive biological studies Rene Dubos has emphasized that each person is unique, unprecedented, and unrepeatable (1).

Some of these mechanisms (resulting in this behavioral singularity) have their roots deep in the evolutionary past of the human race itself and have similar effects in all human beings. Other mechanisms derive from the peculiarities of the genetic endowment of each person, and still others—these are perhaps the most important—concern the relationships that make each individual respond to his total environment and be modified in an irreversible manner by these responses.

Early influences in an individual's life have profound and lasting effects not only on his mental and emotional characteristics but also upon the *anatomic, physiologic, and metabolic characteristics* of the adult.

· With these changes in theoretical approach, a multitude of discrete observations are being organized in various conjectural designs of immense complexity, and these demand new conceptual tools. The new scientific concepts are diffusing into general literacy, and in recent years such terms as "general system theory," "cybernetics," "feedback," "interface," "information," "coding," etc., have filtered through from their specialized mathematically formalized usage into the speech of biologists and behavioral and social scientists. I can do no more here than refer to the modern developments which make it possible to consider multiple, isolated facts and findings under the concept of the total pattern of the many activities in an organism. System theory has attracted particular interest in psychiatry because of its apparent ability to accommodate complex interactions involving a variety of levels. But just enumerating the complexities of such problems is not general system theory; in the study of the family the word "system" has acquired a nearly magical quality. I shall present my own data with the orientation under which they were collected, though the newer vocabulary might provide at times a clearer or a more convenient way of describing the complexities of the various interactions with which I am here concerned.

It is amazing how little of this increasing awareness of complex biological transactions is reflected in the clinical literature on obesity and anorexia nervosa, though in psychosomatic medicine in general a shift can be recognized from the linear model of causality toward a cyclic model in which illness is viewed as resulting from interrelated factors in the physiological, psychological, and environmental experiences of an individual. Though it is now common to speak of the multiple factors that are involved in the development of obesity, with the exception of a few reports coming from the basic sciences, the majority of papers continue to focus on one or other aspects as the "cause" of the condition. The more an investigator is convinced of the importance of his own theory, the more he is inclined to use his particular findings as explanation for the whole picture.

Even interdisciplinary conferences, with the goal of and opportunity for becoming familiar with diverging or opposing views, seem to have little effect in changing anybody's convictions. As Kubie has pointed out in his examination of factors interfering with the flow of communication in multidisciplinary conferences and research teams, scientific disciplines can compare and reconcile their theoretical assumptions, their methods, and their findings only if they can translate their respective languages, both colloquial and technical, into symbols which all can understand (2). Unhappily, representatives from different disciplines find it unexpectedly difficult to communicate with one another, and not infrequently may even deny the reality of the complex data of others. The obesity literature abounds with examples of ignoring well-documented findings of workers from different disciplines. Psychological observations in particular suffer this fate. The somatic approach has been so long in the foreground that it is often the only one that is considered as giving hard scientific data; to many the psychological approach continues to appear suspect. Kubie speaks of "psychophobic organicists" and "organophobic psychologists" who behave and act as if problems in both domains could not be operative in the same individual and influence each other. With the experimentalist's search for simplicity in his investigations, it is all too easy for him to deny the complexities of clinical phenomena; this holds particularly true in the organicist's appraisal of psychiatric phenomena.

In my use of the literature I shall be highly selective. I shall not quote any publication, however important, just for the sake of historical completeness, or for conducting something along the lines of a public opinion poll of diversified views, or to demonstrate that I have been diligent and have read everything published. I have read many, many contributions, and if only a few of them are mentioned, it is not for lack of appreciation of their value, but mainly to avoid a simple enumeration of a series of names, and also in order not to become involved in arguments about different viewpoints concerning details of psychiatric theory. I shall refer mainly to publications that I have found helpful in developing my own point of view or, conversely, to those who approach the problem from such an opposite angle that they can lead to a sharper delineation of the issues by contrast.

I shall try to present my own views in as simple language as possible, and forego the impulse toward scholarliness with step-by-step documentation of how each point agrees or differs from that of others, though I shall make some overall comparisons. I shall also forego the temptation of using the conventional psychoanalytic vocabulary, though I regret that this will deprive my presentation of some picturesque and lively imagery.

My observations were made over more than 35 years, and a certain change in style and orientation will be recognized. Since reports on long-range outcome are practically nonexistent in the obesity literature and highly unsatisfactory in anorexia nervosa, I felt it would be of value to report on the long-range development of patients who were seen during the early part of my study, though some of my concepts and my treatment approach have changed considerably in the interval. My goal is to illustrate how many factors and influences interact in the development of abnormal eating patterns which need to be understood for their correction. John

Muir, the naturalist, is credited with the saying: "When we try to pick out anything by itself, we usually find it hitched to everything else in the universe." This quality of being hitched to everything else can be recognized in the various functions in eating disorders.

BIBLIOGRAPHY

1. Dubos, R., Deep are the roots: The biological basis of individuality, Bull. Assn. Psychoanal. Med., 8:43–45, 1969.
2. Kubie, L. S., Problems of multidisciplinary conferences, research teams, and journals, Perspec. Biol. Med., 13:405–427, 1970.

2

Historical and Sociocultural Perspectives

The oldest representation of the human form, dating back to the Paleolithic period 20,000 to 30,000 B.C., was found in a village on the shores of the Danube and is named the "Venus of Wilendorf." It is the statue of an extremely obese woman with large breasts and an enormous abdomen. Other paleontological figurines represent similar fat women, often with steatopygia in addition. The taste for obesity in women persisted into the Neolithic period. Prehistoric Greek, Babylonian, and Egyptian sculptures, too, indicate preference or artistic admiration for women with large pregnant abdomens and heavy hips and thighs.

It is not known whether the archeological "Venuses" are realistic representations or whether they reflect an artistic ideal or convention, symbolizing a dream of abundance and fertility at a period in human history when famine was an ever-present possibility and threatened mankind as the greatest disaster that could befall it. Fear of starvation has played a decisive role in determining the actions and the attitudes of men. The history of man has been called the chronicle of his quest for food. In every age and in every land people have starved, and the twentieth century is no exception. Obesity has been conceived of as a defense against the dreaded fate of starvation.

Famine and Fasting

The "Stele of Famine" carved on a granite tomb on an island in the First Cataract of the Nile is among the earliest authentic records of history. Its exact antiquity is unknown but there is evidence to show that it was chiseled about 2000 years before the story of Abraham. Its legend reads:

I am mourning on my high throne for the vast misfortune, because the Nile flood in my time has not come for seven years! Light is the grain; there is lack of crops and of all kinds of food. Each man has become a thief to his neighbor. They desire to hasten and cannot walk. The child cries, the youth creeps along, and the old man; their souls are bowed down, their legs are bent together and drag along the ground, and their hands rest in their bosoms. The counsel of the great ones in the court is but emptiness. Torn open are the chests of provisions, but instead of content there is air. Everything is exhausted (18).

This tale of woe from the remote past dramatically conveys the extreme misery and physical and moral deterioration of starving people, and in the course of history it has been repeated over and over. The Old Testament has many references to starvation and famine. The immediate origin of famines in early records was crop failure from droughts, excessive rain, unseasonable frosts, or other natural disasters.

At the time of Joseph the development of granaries had progressed so that food control was possible. It was of immense political consequence and could be used to reduce a people to slavery. There are also numerous records of starvation due to war, usually on a local scale in the actual zone of battle or immediately along the march of an army, and particularly in besieged cities. An appalling combination of crop failure and callous political mismanagement resulted in The Great Hunger in Ireland during the 1840's, reducing the population by several millions (32). Withholding of food for punishment or subjugation has a long history, but starvation as a political weapon was probably never used on as large a scale as during Hitler's regime in concentration and extermination camps in Germany, and as a means of subjugation in occupied countries. Millions suffered death by starvation during the 900 Days of the Siege of Leningrad. In 1970 a shocked world could observe on television how starving people, in their frantic need, ran and fought for the food brought in by helicopters in the aftermath of the typhoon and tidal wave in East Pakistan.

In an extensive study Keys and his co-workers reviewed the documents of starvation in historical times and the experiences of explorers and wartime observers (18). All reports and observations tell with monotonous repetition the same tale, how hunger becomes completely overpowering, inciting every kind of baseness in human behavior. There is an extraordinary similarity in the reactions to hunger of all human beings, regardless of time and place. There have been few exceptions where individuals with high motivation and spiritual strength have risen above the brutal demoralization by hunger, though there was no escape from the suffering.

Two phases stand out in the course of starvation: an immediate reaction to being deprived of food, and a final picture when emaciation has become extreme. In the early phase, there is a relentless preoccupation with food, loss of sexual desire, a coarsening of all emotional responses, and increasing selfishness with complete loss of other human considerations.

Wiesel (31) re-creates the ultimate despair in his dialogues of pious Jews in concentration camps. "*And what about ideas? Ideals? All the great dreams of man imposing his will on the universe?* . . . You may have them all for one crust of bread." The final stage is characterized by inactivity, apathy, and withdrawal from life, and by heightened irritability over any disturbance. During recovery, the desire for food seems to be insatiable, and preoccupation with food and fear of not getting enough persists long after the body has made a physiologic recovery.

Even without such drastic experiences, fear of starvation and anxiety about loss of body substance may be aroused. I have been impressed by how often fat patients react as if they were threatened by dangerous starvation, long before any significant loss of body weight has been achieved. Conversely, in anorexia nervosa, complete denial of the severe emaciation and of the accompanying fatigue and other symptoms appears to be characteristic.

Observations of animals have suggested two types of feeding behavior, both of which are also available to humans (2). In one, each searches for himself, ranging freely, taking small items of food here and there. In the other type, commensalism, there is a hierarchy or rank whereby the highest ranking male is accorded the privilege of satisfying himself first. Snacking or vagabond feeding is appropriate behavior when catastrophic starvation reigns, when living on scraps picked up here and there as one moves about restlessly is the only solution. This type of snack feeding is considered the more primitive, original type of feeding—and has recently been suggested for correction of obesity. With higher organization of societies the pattern has been established whereby the family sits down at the dinner table according to rank and remains together for a considerable time. Bilz has suggested that anorexia nervosa may be a throwback to the vagabond type of feeding, a flight from the feudal organization of the family table, with the patients avoiding regular meals but living on secret snacks, obtaining their food here and there, sometimes even resorting to stealing.

With the haunting specter of starvation hanging over mankind, deliberate refusal of food is a complex, rather "unnatural" phenomenon. Voluntary abstinence from food is a prescribed ritual in many religious traditions, an effort to liberate oneself from selfish and materialistic concerns, and to purify body and soul. Whether such ascetic denial could lead to enlightenment and salvation was put to the test by Buddha (12).

Certain of the absurd vanities (of the Yogis), he practiced them to the most extreme degree in his extraordinary fast, eating only one grain of jujube, then only one grain of rice, and finally one grain of millet a day. Then with greater and greater self control, he refused all food. We do not have to guess the effects that these privations had on his physical being, for artists and writers have shown and described them to us. . . .
Gautama's limbs became like knotty sticks and his spine which could be grasped from the front through the flabby skin of his abdomen was like the rough weave of a braid. His protruding thorax was like the ribbed shell of a

crab, and his emaciated head was like a gourd that had been plucked too soon and had withered, dried up well. Even though the Bodhisattva was only skin and bones he still charmed the eye the way a new moon, however slight, delights the lotus. . . .

This image of extreme starvation is preserved in a sculpture, "The Fasting Bodhisattva," dating back to the second or third century, A.D.

At this point he was ready to proclaim that "this was not a road which led to enlightenment in order to end birth, old age and death." His whole organism needed to be restored. Therefore the first step was to break his fast. Legend would have it that at that moment certain gods, guessing his desire, came to propose a secret vital insufflation through his pores. The Bodhisattva indignantly refused to lend himself to such a fraudulent trick. He was, in the eyes of the peasants, a total abstainer and he would fail them completely if he seemed to remain so and yet secretly received food by supernatural means. Since it seemed necessary to do so, he had to take food honestly, in sight of all.

In the Far East the idea of fasting as a means of impressing others has a long tradition. A man could humiliate an enemy in ancient Japan by "fasting against him," or literally starving on his doorstep. Voluntary abstinence from food has also been used in the West in the form of hunger strikes, as a political weapon against imprisonment and unjust authority. Well known are the hunger strikes of the British suffragettes, which forced the "Cat and Mouse Act" on the authorities so that a political prisoner who starved herself was released from jail and permitted to disappear quietly. The final outcome was that women did get the vote.

In India a similar means of calling attention to grievances is called "sitting dharna," and seventeen such fasts "to the death" were undertaken by Gandhi in his long struggle for the independence of India. Erikson examined the motivation of Gandhi's decision to fast, and also why he came to regret it as not quite worthy of his cause (10).

It should be clear that there cannot really be any "pure" decision to starve one's self to death, for such determination can only emerge from a paradoxical combination of a passionate belief in the absolute vitality of certain living issues and the determination to die for them: thus one "lives up" to a principle by dying for it. A martyr, too, challenges death, but at the end he forces others to act as his executioners. The decision to let one's self die is of a different and admittedly more obscure order.

Gandhi insisted that the fasting person must be prepared to the end to discover or to be convinced of a flaw in his position, and then to terminate the fast.

Many others have followed Gandhi's example, though their reasons have often been impulsive, vindictive, or faddish. Gandhi, at one time, urged any individual or authority that was "fasted against" and which considered the fast to be blackmail "to refuse to yield to it, even though the refusal may result in the death of the fasting person."

Fasting as a means of coercion is effective only in relation to a responsive partner. During the Irish struggle for independence the British did not

sting prisoners and two of them died after holding out for 74 and
he longest prison fast on record. During the Nazi terror, too, it is
able that noneating political prisoners would have been granted
their freedom, or been given any other special consideration.

Fear of hunger is so universal that undergoing it voluntarily arouses
admiration, awe, and curiosity—and publicity seekers have exploited this.
During the fifteenth and sixteenth centuries, before anorexia nervosa had
been described, so-called "Miracle Maidens" attracted much public attention and also stimulated learned medical discussions because they al-
legedly stayed alive without food and drink (28). In some cases it was
discovered that they took food secretly, and judgment of their deceit was
so severe that they were executed. More recently, in the beginning of this
century when there was much interest in oddities of behavior and endur-
ance, hunger artists, locked in cages, would exhibit themselves and show
to an awed public that they cheerfully and artistically endured hunger,
fading away before their very eyes. This professional fasting has gone out
of style. Kafka, in one of his short stories, "The Hunger Artist," revealed
the basic futility of this pursuit, and showed that however long a man
fasted the feeling persisted that he could do it one day longer (16). The
story ends finally, when, at the threshold of death, the hero confesses, " 'I
have to fast, I can't help it, because I couldn't find the food I liked. If I
had found it, believe me, I should have made no fuss and stuffed myself
like you or anyone else.' These were his last words, but in his dim eyes
remained the firm, though no longer proud persuasion that he was still
continuing to fast."

Self-inflicted starvation as a psychiatric disorder, as an individual's expression of his psychological affliction, was recognized only fairly recently,
in contrast to the long history of obesity in medical thinking. Whatever its
purpose and meaning, food refusal would be an ineffectual tool in a setting
of poverty and food scarcity. To all anorexic patients with whom I am
familiar, even to those of lower economic background, food was available
in abundance, and its refusal had an enormously disorganizing effect on
their families. No reports on anorexia nervosa have come from underdeveloped countries where there is still danger of widespread starvation or
famine. It is worth mentioning that in the United States anorexia nervosa
has not been reported in Negroes or members of other underprivileged
groups. A disproportionately large percentage of patients with anorexia
nervosa come from upper-class backgrounds, a few from the ranks of the
super-rich. In other words, self-starvation is observed only under conditions of adequate or abundant food supply.

Obesity

Even more remarkable is the paradox that in affluent societies obesity is commonly associated with poverty and lower-class status. Availability of food is of course a prerequisite for the development of obesity, and in underdeveloped countries it occurs only among the privileged few. When I sought to learn the attitudes of different primitive people toward obesity and eating, in the anthropological index at the Institute for Human Relations at Yale University, I was informed that the index did not contain references to obesity because it was so rare among primitive people. There are reports, though, that in some of the Polynesian peoples it was considered the sign of greatest distinction to be so well-nourished as to become fat. It has also been recorded that Malayan kings were very large and fat. They were treated with special massages and exercises to keep them in good health.

Anthropologists have observed in their field studies of pre-literate tribal societies that a major part of all activities is concerned with the production of food—food gathering, hunting, fishing, agriculture, raising cattle, or some combination of these activities. I quote from Hortense Powdermaker (27):

Tools were crude—a wooden hoe and a stone ax. The only means of transportation was by foot or canoe. . . . Strenuous physical activity was the norm for men and for women, whatever the type of economy. But although everyone worked hard and long in the production of food, hunger was a common experience. Famines and periods of scarcity were not unusual. . . . It is, therefore, not difficult to understand that gluttony, one of the original sins in our society, was an accepted and valued practice for these tribal peoples whenever it was possible. In anticipating a feast a Trobriand Islander in the Southwest Pacific says, "We shall be glad, we shall eat until we vomit." A South African tribal expression is, "We shall eat until our bellies swell out and we can no longer stand."

Another author, Cloete, describes the attitude of the typical South African who works for the white man: ". . . and what is his heart's desire? Fat above all things. To be fat himself, to have a fat wife and children and fat cattle. This is the native's dream, the Biblical dream of plenty in a starving land" (8).

Even before modern anthropologists made their detailed studies, ancient travelers had reported the curious customs of primitive cultures. In many parts of the African continent young girls at puberty were sent to fattening houses to make them ready for marriage. The fatter a girl grew the more beautiful she was considered, in marked contrast to what was expected for men, which was to remain athletic and slim. The royal women, the king's mother and his wives, vied with each other as to who should be the stoutest. They took no exercise, but were carried in litters when going from place to place. From talking to African students at

American colleges, I learned that this custom is still practiced in certain rural districts where it is almost a necessity; many girls were so undernourished, scrawny, and skinny that it took this special preparation and indulgence to get them ready for adult life, pregnancy, and motherhood.

Commenting on these old practices and comparing them to her own observations in a modern mining community in the copperbelt of Northern Rhodesia during the 1950's, Powdermaker cites a popular song of young men:

> "Hullo, Mama, the beautiful one, let us go to the town;
> You will be very fat, you girl, if you stay with me."

She adds that the standard of beauty for women at that time was not extreme fatness but rather a moderate plumpness (27).

A primitive desire for fatness was expressed by the mothers of a large group of obese children of lower- and middle-class background who attended an obesity clinic in New York City during the 1930's. Many of these women had been poor immigrants who had suffered hunger during their early lives. They did not understand why anyone should object to a child's being big and fat, which to them indicated success and freedom from want (4).

Several authors who grew up under such immigrant conditions have given vivid accounts of the attitude toward food. I quote from Harry Golden's *Ess, Ess, Mein Kindt*, which translates literally as *Eat, Eat, My Child* (13).

But it means much more. Its meaning is profound. Ess, ess, mein kindt is not only an expression of the love of a mother for her child. Along the lower East Side of New York it was a rallying cry of survival.

Food, of course, is literally—survival. Among the immigrant Jews in the tenement districts of New York, Philadelphia, and Chicago, there was somehow always more than enough food. The poorest managed to eat—big. I was never hungry, nor were my sisters and brothers, nor were any of our friends or neighbors. All of us were sometimes cold, sometimes ragged, sometimes overworked, but not hungry.

Alfred Kazin describes similar joy in the abundance of food, experienced a decade or so later, in his *A Walker in the City* (17).

As I went down Belmont Avenue, the copper-shining herrings in the tall black barrels made me think of the veneration of food in Brownsville families. I can still see the kids pinned down to the tenement stoops, their feet helplessly kicking at the pots and pans lined up before them, their mouths pressed open with a spoon while the great meals are rammed down their throats. "Eat, Eat! May you be destroyed if you don't eat. What sin have I committed that God should punish me with you! Eat! What will become of you if you don't eat! Imp of darkness, may you sink ten fathoms into the earth if you don't eat! Eat!"

We never had a chance to know what hunger meant. At home we nibbled all day long as a matter of course. On the block we gorged ourselves continually on "Nestles," "Hersheys," gumdrops, poppy seeds, nuts, chocolate-covered cherries, charlotte russe, and ice cream. . . . The hunger for sweets, jellies, and soda water raged in us like a disease; during the grimmest punchball game, in the middle of a fist fight, we would dash to the candy store to get down two-cent blocks of chocolate and "small" three-cent glasses of cherry soda; or calling "upstairs" from the street, would have flung to us, or carefully hoisted down at the end of a clothesline, thick slices of rye bread smeared with chicken fat.

A child who was heavy in this setting was not called fat, but was admired for being "solid" or "hefty." Golden relates the emphasis on food, among other things, to the fear of tuberculosis, which was endemic among the ghetto sweatshop workers of those days.

The immigrant mother learned that one of the first symptoms was loss of weight. And so they watched their men and their children. The mothers thought as long as they all ate heartily there was no danger. You may have weighed one hundred and forty pounds at the age of twelve and the kids on the block were calling you "Fatty," but if you once dawdled over your food, your mother was terribly distressed—"Look at him, nothing but skin and bones—eat, eat, my child, do you want to get sick?" The first question relatives and friends asked when someone returned from a vacation was, "How much did you gain?"

Now we didn't eat simply to ward off tuberculosis. Actually the offering of food by the mother of the household was the offering of her love. When her food was not eaten it was as if her love was rejected. Guests who may have just left their own dinner table valiantly ate everything the hostess offered. It would have been an insult to do otherwise (13).

Many of these immigrants' children have become successful and prominent and have adopted with their accomplishments the middle- and upper-class style of life. Yet many continue their early food habits—or conduct a strenuous, often futile struggle against them. Harry Golden confesses: "I, too, was a husky kid and when I worried about it my mother consoled me with the observation, 'In America, the fat man is the boss and the skinny man is the bookkeeper.'" He describes himself as "No longer so young, but hefty still," and adds: "One of the American phenomena which I have sedulously avoided is a diet. I find it easy to avoid dieting. All one has to do is avoid scales."

I should like to add a clinical observation of my own: a middle-aged physician of ghetto background had suffered a coronary attack and knew that it was urgent for him to reduce. He was discouraged because he found it impossible to do so. As we discussed his problems, it became apparent that deep down he felt that his real failure was not that he lacked the will power to stay on a diet, but that he did not have the courage to be as fat as he felt he was meant to be. His outstanding memory about his early life was his mother's urging him to eat, always with a stern invocation: "Ess, ess, ich sterbe weg" (Eat, eat, or I will die). These words came to his mind and the feeling that he would hurt his mother (who had been dead for many years) whenever he went on a diet persisted in adult life and was stronger than his rational knowledge that his excess weight represented a danger to his own health.

Obesity as a widespread condition of the poor can occur only when there is ample and relatively inexpensive food for everybody, combined with release from toil and effort through mechanization. This condition has probably never existed on such a large scale as in present-day affluent countries like the United States and certain European countries.

Changing Attitudes toward Obesity in History

Concern about obesity is not new, and the privileged classes of the Western world have been preoccupied through the ages with the question of how to stay slim in the face of abundance. The ancient Greeks envied their cultural predecessors, the Cretans, for having known of a drug that permitted them to stay slim while eating as much as they wanted. The old Spartans were stern and punitive in their attitude toward obesity. Young people were looked over in the nude once a month and those who had gained extra weight were forced to exercise to keep from becoming fat. The Athenians, too, frowned upon being fat though some outstanding Greeks were stout. We know that Socrates danced every morning in order to keep slim, and the Greeks forgave Plato his fatness only on account of his mental brilliance. Hippocrates described obesity in great detail and made a number of observations that are still pertinent today (5).

The Romans disliked obesity as much as the Greeks, and it seems that the Roman ladies, at least at the time of the Empire, had to suffer as much as, if not more than, our modern young girls in order to keep slim. They were literally starved to make them slim as reeds. The Romans are also known for the invention of the vomitorium that permitted them to indulge in excessive eating and then to relieve themselves, a method reinvented by modern college girls. Yet, as in Greece, there were also famous Romans who were fat, and exact descriptions have been preserved of some of their eating habits. It is known that Marius, the defender of Rome, enjoyed enormous quantities of food. Horace, the poet, in contrast, was a gourmet who was famous for the extraordinary variety and elegant preparation of his meals.

It is not known whether in ancient cultures, with their scorn for obesity, there was also a class distinction, or whether, under the socioeconomic conditions of antiquity, the poor did not have access to abundant and cheap food. The old slogan of "pane and circenses," implying bread distribution and passive entertainment, suggests that obesity may well have been a characteristic of the lower classes in Ancient Rome.

During the Middle Ages various views were held on obesity. On the one hand, gluttony, together with pride and lust, was counted among the venal sins. But obesity was also considered a sign of the "Grace of God." An interesting document of the moralistic attitude toward obesity is Lochner's painting, "The Last Judgment"; the sinners who are being dragged to Hell are heavy and stout, whereas the blessed ones who are led into Paradise are slender (20).

A rich literature exists on the occurrence of obesity in different societies and at different times, and on the many outstanding individuals who have been fat. Clauser and Spranger reviewed the many national and folk ideas and artistic representations of obesity and leanness, which indicate the prevalence of popular psychological interpretations of these conditions and an awareness of class distinctions (7).

William Wadd, in the early nineteenth century, introduced his booklet *Cursory Remarks on Corpulence* with the sentence: "If the increase of wealth and refinement of modern times have tended to banish plague and pestilence from our cities, they have probably introduced the whole train of nervous disorders, and increased the frequence of corpulence" (30). Ebstein, in a book published in 1884, divided obesity into three stages, known respectively as the enviable, the comical, and the pitiable (9). A vivid description of the hostile social attitude was given by Banting in his *Letter on Corpulence, Addressed to the Public*, published in 1864 (1). He complained:

No man laboring under obesity can be quite insensitive to the sneers and remarks of the cruel and injudicious in public assemblies, public vehicles, or the ordinary street traffic. . . . Therefore he naturally keeps away as much as possible from places where he is likely to be made the object of the taunts and remarks of others.

Even in modern Western society there have been marked fluctuations in attitudes about obesity. It was not too long ago when gourmandizing and display of its consequences was a sign of success, of newly won riches, of "conspicuous consumption." M. F. K. Fisher (11) describes in vivid terms that:

. . . each of us has in him a trait of gluttony, potential or actual. . . . I pity anyone who has not permitted himself this sensual experience (of stuffing himself to the bursting point) if only to determine what his own private limitations are, and where for himself alone, gourmandism ends and gluttony begins. . . .
Probably this country will never again see so many fat, rich men as were prevalent at the end of the last century, copper kings and railroad millionaires and suchlike literally stuffing themselves to death in imitation of Diamond Jim, whose abnormally large stomach coincided so miraculously with the period. . . . It is interesting to speculate on what his influence would be today, when most of the robber barons have gastric ulcers and lunch on crackers and milk at their desk.

A French clinician, Heckel, complained in 1911 that at times fashion interfered with weight reducing programs:

One must mention here that aesthetic errors of a worldly nature to which all women submit, may make them want to stay obese for reasons of fashionable appearance (14). It is beyond a doubt that in order to have an impressive décolleté each woman feels herself duty bound to be fat around the neck, over the clavicle and in her breasts. Now it happens that fat accumulates with greatest difficulty in these places and one can be sure, even without examining such a woman, that the abdomen and the hips, and the lower members are hopelessly fat. As to treatment, one cannot obtain weight reduction of the abdomen without the woman sacrificing in her spirits the upper part of her body. To her it is a true sacrifice because she gives up what the world considers beautiful.

This sounds to us like something from an entirely different era, and it is difficult to believe that it was written in Paris during this century and relates to women's desire to look fashionable.

During the 1930's, Ogden Nash (23) expressed his concern about American women and their eternal dieting, saying, "All ladies think that they weigh too much," and he closed his poem with words of regret:

> So I think that it is very nice for ladies to be lithe and lissome,
> But not so much so that you cut yourself if you happen
> to embrace or kissome.

Slenderness at that time was a far cry from what has been proclaimed as the standard of beauty and propagated as the height of fashion during the last decade, when a malnourished waif, "Twiggy" (5'7", 92 lbs), was held up as a model for thousands of normally developing adolescents. It made them concentrate their mental energies on achieving a similar starved appearance even at the sacrifice of their health. In this decade, with the greater activity of minority groups fighting against discrimination, over-weight people are beginning to revolt against unjust public pressure and prejudice.

Sociological Studies

Systematic inquiries into sociological and psychological aspects of obesity have confirmed the old popular knowledge about its social rating and standing. In the 1950's, a survey of 1600 adults living in a central residential area of New York City revealed that obesity occurred seven times more frequently among women of the lowest socioeconomic level than among those of the highest level; among men the same relationship existed, although to a lesser degree (21). The study of white school children, 5 to 18 years of age, in 3 eastern cities, revealed that by age 6, 29% of lower-class girls were rated obese as compared with only 3% of upper-class girls (29). The differences continued through age 18. Similar, though less striking differences were found between boys of upper and lower socioeconomic status. The data suggest that early life experiences have a lasting influence on factors involved in weight regulation, and that the socioeconomic status in which a person is born is almost as closely linked with obesity as his current socioeconomic status. In Sweden the weight of women in the upper classes was found to be lower and less variable than that of women of poorer economic background (3). However, men in the lower sociological group in Sweden did not tend to be overweight.

A German sociological study gave a somewhat different picture (26).

In a group of independent farmers and small business people obesity was observed at approximately the same frequency in men and women. In the highest and lowest social class, the sex distributions went in opposite directions. Obesity was more frequent in women of the lowest, and in men of the highest, socioeconomic class. It seems that under the special conditions of German culture, obesity in men has an entirely different sociological significance from that in women; in men it seems to add to their sense of power and prestige.

According to these reports, the figures for which were collected during the 1950's, lower-class people express little concern about being fat. It would be of interest to repeat these surveys now, after a whole generation of lower-class children has grown up exposed to television which promotes as a beauty ideal the image of a slender or even too slim figure. It would not be surprising to find that the new generation of lower-class adults is less complacent about being obese than has been reported for the past generation. The pressures to which obese adolescents are exposed in our slimness-conscious society are reflected in the results of projective tests which showed that upper-class obese girls suffer from heightened sensitivity to and obsessive preoccupation with the state of being fat; combined with this is a tendency to be passive and isolated from the group, with the feeling of being victims of intense prejudice (22). The attitudes of obese college students and of obese youngsters attending a nutrition clinic were studied and it was observed that the obese teen-ager feels discriminated against but comes to accept this treatment as just; he feels unable to escape his condition, becomes timidly withdrawn, eager to please, and tolerant of abuse (6).

Some of the sociological studies suffer from a tendency to draw generalized conclusions beyond the evidence at hand, and to contrast these findings with biological and psychological observations, as if these different approaches were mutually exclusive. This they are not. Psychological problems are attributed entirely to the social disgrace of being fat, as being secondary to the stigma of obesity or to being a member of a despised minority. Or, conversely, in view of the high frequency of obesity in the lower socioeconomic groups, it is concluded that obesity is "normal" for poor people. This reasoning is about as sound as if 50 years ago rickets or pellagra had been declared "normal" in the poorer populations because they were so prevalent. A recent study on mental illness and obesity in lower-class women reflects the confusion resulting from such generalizations. It was hypothesized that the degree of obesity and degree of psychiatric disturbances would show a direct relationship (15). This assumption runs contrary to everything that has been reported on psychological problems and obesity. If a generalized statement is possible at all, then it is that the overeating and excess weight may have a stabilizing effect in a precarious overall adjustment, and that even severe depression may not be manifest as long as the excess weight persists. Not unexpectedly, the findings did not support the erroneous hypothesis. Unjustifiably, it was concluded that obesity in lower-class women can no longer be called abnormal, since lower-class women do no incur the social disfavor which middle- and upper-class women suffer.

The climate of social disapproval is only one aspect of the problem. Though an obese individual of upper-class background is more likely to be pressured into becoming thin than one of lower-class standing, this does not imply that all upper-class youngsters who are obese are emotionally disturbed, or that obesity in a lower-class individual may not be an expression of serious emotional difficulties. It is as misleading to deny inner psychological problems as to underrate damage from group pressure. The ability to respond to social demands in a constructive way or to be defeated by them is itself an expression of the range of a person's adaptability, competence, and self-respect.

There are many factors in lower-class life that appear to be related to the higher incidence of obesity. One is the simple economic fact that "fattening" foods, such as starches and sweets, are cheaper and more readily available than "diet" foods, such as meat and other proteins and fresh fruit and vegetables. The pursuit of athletics and other recreational activities, too, is expensive, and demands skills and an expenditure of time not readily available to poor people, least of all to lower-class women, those with the highest incidence of obesity.

Attitudes and personality characteristics that develop under conditions of deprivation and poverty may predispose to obesity. Lower-class mothers have been described as being more often authoritarian and controlling in their attitudes, and having less time for distinct individual interaction with their child. The families are also said to be mother-centered. There has even been talk of a "culture of poverty," which is conceived of as a subculture of the Western social order (19). Part of the dominant value system, but not of the poverty subculture, is emphasis on appearance, with slenderness as the only valued body configuration. Children raised under the conditions of poverty absorb the basic attitudes and values of their subculture, though there is also awareness of middle-class values. Individuals growing up under these conditions have strong feelings of fatalism, helplessness, dependence, and inferiority. Other traits have been described as weak ego, orality, and confusion of sexual identification. These personality traits are amazingly similar to what is observed in individuals with an early onset of obesity (developmental obesity), in whom "no will power," lack of mastery, submission to fate, and readiness to give up in the face of difficulties are characteristic features. These traits may develop in a child of any social class when he fails to receive encouragement toward initiative and self-sufficiency, not for reasons of poverty and the hardship it entails, but due to the particular features and deprivations that characterize his upbringing and determine his early experiences.

Most studies of deprived children have focused on the problems in relation to education, the apparent deficit in cognitive functioning. As will be discussed in Chapter 4, a deficit in discriminating hunger awareness and in the capacity to discriminate between biological urges and emotional needs, and a lack of the sense of control from within are part of the pattern of development that predisposes to obesity. An inability to control and regulate food intake is an outstanding characteristic of obese people regardless of their social class. The conditions of lower-class life seem to encourage such developmental deficits, hence the higher incidence of obesity. The lack of interest in losing weight in contrast to the excessive concern with slimness of upper-class individuals reflects only a secondary aspect of the problem, and has little to do with the development of the potential for obesity.

My first observations of the psychological factors in obesity were made in a pediatric clinic attended by patients of lower-middle- and lower-class background, whose economic plight had been greatly aggravated by the depression of the 1930's. Details about the patterns of family interaction will be given in Chapter 5, and their long-range development in Chapter 8. Subsequent experiences in private practice taught me that it is unjustified and erroneous to draw generalized conclusions about mental health or ill health from the social class or ethnic background of a patient. Not that these aspects do not deserve to be considered; on the contrary, without knowledge of the background factors it is difficult to grasp an individual's problems and needs, and to outline a meaningful treatment program for a fat person or for anybody else; but social factors alone do not explain a condition.

That individual emotional experiences, not social conditions, are involved in the development of obesity, is described with brilliant psychological awareness in two novels by Joyce Carol Oates. In *Expensive People* (24), the hero, Richard, had murdered his mother when he was 11 years old. When he tried to confess no one would believe him; finally he resigned himself to this and stopped saying anything at all. "I sleepwalked my way through the years, and as I slept I ate, and as I walked I ate, because there was this peculiar hollowness inside me that I had to fill." And, "I am being carried along on the wave of a most prodigious hunger. All I ask is the strength to fill the emptiness inside me, to stuff it once and for all!" The book represents his memoirs, written when he was 18 years old, of his mother and of himself as a child murderer. He describes himself:

I am not well. I weigh two hundred and fifty pounds and I am not well. . . . How old am I? Did I stop growing on the day when "it" happened, note the shrewd passivity of that phrase, as if I hadn't made "it" happen myself, or did I maybe freeze into what I was, and outside of that shell layers and layers of fat began to form?

In the other novel, *Them* (25), Maureen tried to escape her home's dismal poverty by becoming a prostitute. When she was discovered in this by her stepfather, who gave her a severe beating, she withdrew to her room, her bed, and complete inactivity. Her brother is shocked when he sees her sitting up in bed and staring at him.

The covers were drawn up around her though the room was warm. Her hair had grown long and straggly . . . her face had a puffed, plump, shiny look to it. It had been about a month since he had seen her last and in that short time she had put on a lot of weight. . . . Her eyes were large and drugged. He could not believe, glancing at this heavy, ugly girl, that she was the same girl who had been his sister.

She did not respond when he tried to talk to her, but she reached greedily for the cake which he offered and ate it quickly. Maureen's eating was what maintained her mother's morale and she reassured herself, "She eats everything I make for her, so she is all right." And so the months passed, "Maureen lying in bed, forever lying in bed and stuffing her face with coffee cake and cookies and whatever sweet crap Loretta gave her, so that her face had broken out, her body grown disgusting."

When she finally recovered she lost weight quickly:

Those days I liked to fast; to make up for the days I ate so much, so I got dizzy sometimes at night. I ate crackers and some bread after work and a banana or orange or something, that was all. I liked to feel my stomach ache with hunger, knowing that I was hungry and not filled up, not fat anymore.

Nadine, the girl from the wealthy home, reacted differently when she ran away from the involvement of a love affair.

I had to get out and leave you. I had to escape. I am sorry. . . . I called home. They both flew down to get me. . . . I couldn't sleep or eat. I kept crying all the time. All I could think about was you. I tried to starve myself. I felt sorry for myself, and I wanted to punish my parents. . . . I wrote long letters for you, crazy things. They put me in a kind of hospital. . . . A place for people sick in the head. We all carried ourselves like glass, we were very breakable.

BIBLIOGRAPHY

1. Banting, W., *Letter on Corpulence, addressed to the public,* 4th edition, Mohun, Ebbs and Hough, New York, 1864.
2. Bilz, R., Anorexia nervosa, Bibl. Psychiat., 147:219–244, 1971.
3. Bjurulf, P., and Lindgren, G., A preliminary study on overweight in the south of Sweden, pp. 9–15, in *Occurrences, Causes and Prevention of Overnutrition,* ed. G. Blix, Almqvist & Wiksell, Uppsala, 1964.
4. Bruch, H., Obesity in childhood. III. Physiologic and psychologic aspects of the food intake of obese children, Amer. J. Dis. Child., 58:738–781, 1940.
5. Bruch, H., The cultural frame, Chapter 3, pp. 35–59, in *The Importance of Overweight,* W.W. Norton & Co., Inc., New York, 1957.
6. Cahnman, W. J., The stigma of obesity, Soc. Quart., 283–299, Summer, 1968.
7. Clauser, G., and Spranger, J., Hinweise auf die Aetiologie der Fett-und Magersucht aus Volkstum, Kunst, Medizingeschichte und Wissenschaft, München. Med. Wschr., 99:53–58, 1957.
8. Cloete, S., I speak for the African, *Life,* 34:111, 1953.

9. Ebstein, W., *Die Fettleibigkeit und ihre Behandlung nach physiologischen Grundsaetzen*, Bergman, Wiesbaden, 1882.
10. Erikson, E. H., *Gandhi's Truth*, W. W. Norton & Co., Inc., New York, 1969.
11. Fisher, M. F. K., *An Alphabet for Gourmets*, Viking Press, New York, 1949.
12. Foucher, A., *The Life of the Buddha*, trans. S. B. Boas, Wesleyan University Press, Middletown, Conn., 1962.
13. Golden, H., *Ess, Ess, Mein Kindt* (Eat, Eat, My Child), G. P. Putnam's Sons, New York, 1963. Reprinted with permission.
14. Heckel, F., *Les grandes et petites obésités*, Masson et Cie, Paris, 1911.
15. Holland, J., Masling, J., and Copley, D., Mental illness in lower class normal, obese, and hyperobese women, Psychosom. Med., 32:351–357, 1970.
16. Kafka, F., The Hunger Artist, in *The Penal Colony: Stories and Short Pieces*, Schocken Books, New York, 1948.
17. From *A Walker in the City*, 1951, by Alfred A. Kazin. Reprinted by permission of Harcourt Brace Jovanovich, Inc., New York.
18. Keys, A., Brozek, J., Henschel, A., Mickelsen, O., and Taylor, H. L., *The Biology of Human Starvation*, Vols. 1 & 2, University of Minnesota Press, Minneapolis, 1950.
19. Lewis, O., The culture of poverty, Sci. Amer., 215:19–25, 1966.
20. Lochner, S., "Das Weltgericht", painting in Wallraf-Richartz Museum, Nr. 66, Cologne.
21. Moore, M. E., Stunkard, A., Srole, L., Obesity, social class, and mental illness, JAMA, 181:962–966, 1962.
22. Monello, L. F., and Mayer, J., Obese adolescent girls: unrecognized minority group? Amer. J. Clin. Nutr., 13:35–38, 1963.
23. Nash, O., lines from "Curl Up And Diet" in *I'm A Stranger Here Myself*. Copyright 1935, by Ogden Nash. This poem originally appeared in *The New Yorker*. Reprinted with permission of Little, Brown & Co., Boston.
24. Oates, J. C., *Expensive People*, Vanguard Press, Inc., New York, 1968.
25. Oates, J. C., *Them*, Vanguard Press, Inc., New York, 1969.
26. Pflanz, M., Medizinisch-soziologische Aspekte der Fettsucht, Psyche (Stuttgart), 16:579–591, 1963.
27. Powdermaker, H., An anthropological approach to the problem of obesity, Bull. NY Acad. Med., 36:286–295, 1960.
28. Schadewaldt, H., Medizingeschichtliche Betrachtungen zum Anorexie-Problem, pp. 1–14, in *Anorexia Nervosa*, J.-E. Meyer and H. Feldmann, eds., Georg Thieme Verlag, Stuttgart, 1965.
29. Stunkard, A, d'Aquili, E., Fox, S., and Filion, R. D. L., The influence of social class on obesity and thinness in children, JAMA, 221: 579–584, 1972.
30. Wadd, W., *Cursory Remarks on Corpulence*: or obesity considered as a disease, with a critical examination of ancient and modern opinions relative to its causes and cure, 3rd edition, I. Callow, London, 1816.
31. Wiesel, E. *One Generation After*, Random House, New York, 1972.
32. Woodham-Smith, C., *The Great Hunger*, Harper & Row, Inc., New York, 1964.

3

Biological Basis of
Eating Disorders

Obesity and anorexia nervosa are such obvious somatic conditions that it is not surprising that research has mainly been directed toward uncovering abnormalities in the underlying physiological mechanisms or some other organic factors. There has been decided progress during the last few decades, with more precise knowledge of metabolic functions, neurological pathways, and morphological constituents.

It would go beyond the scope of this book, and also my range of competence, to present in detail the complexities of the biochemical, neurophysiological, and other investigations underlying modern concepts of disturbed weight regulation. I can discuss here only certain changes and trends, and I do so with full awareness that some exciting recent discoveries, such as the biological role of neurohormones and the new regulating agent, cyclic AMP, have not yet been applied to obesity research at the time of this writing, though they may well lead to far-reaching changes in our understanding and approach to the problem.

More important than any one individual finding are the underlying fundamental changes in biological research. Though many investigators continue to proceed as if all cases of weight excess were identical, and attempt to explain these complex conditions by reducing the whole pathology to one outstanding deviation, there is definite evidence of beginning convergence of opinion with emphasis on the complexity of interactional patterns, away from the old point-by-point explanation of one symptom through one isolated cause. In modern biological thinking, a living organism is conceived of as a nodal point in an extremely complex network of interactions, relations, and transactions. Part of this causal network is internal: the biochemical and physiological processes by which the body keeps alive and active. Part is external, concerned with the interaction between the organism and other members of the living world, and with the nonliving factors of the environment. Environmental stresses, such as interpersonal experiences and over- or undernutrition, are only part of this elaborate system, though at times of great importance. There is also beginning application of modern methodological and conceptual tools, such as are offered in general system theory through which "systems" are studied as entities rather than as conglomerates of parts. Particularly important for the understanding of the living organism is the fact that it is an *open* system, with matter and information being introduced from the outside.

Though I report ongoing studies under different headings, I do so with full awareness of the dynamic interaction of multivariable systems.

Genetic Factors

The old adage, "obesity runs in families," is still the strongest support for the assumption of genetic factors in human obesity. In spite of marked progress, with clearer definition of the objectives of genetic investigations (namely uncovering disturbances in the informational code of the DNA molecule, or correlating microcellular changes with certain clinical symptoms) the case for heredity in obesity continues to be made on the basis of indirect evidence, such as the high family incidence, or by analogy with known hereditary syndromes also associated with obesity, though distinctly different from ordinary obesity.

There are numerous older studies which are quoted with monotonous repetition in every survey, showing the high incidence of obesity in the offspring of obese parents, particularly high when there is obesity on both sides of the family (11, 13, 30). The figures vary somewhat, with an incidence of about 40% if only one parent is obese and of over 70% in the offspring of two obese parents. Such studies are based on the often unreliable statements of patients, and the inability to record the potentially obese and the actually obese phenotypes makes interpretation of their significance even more difficult, as was pointed out by Angel (2). His own data do not fit any simple hypothesis. Whatever the genetic determinants, he feels, they are complicated by the effects of environmental factors, the family eating habits, psychic influences, and traumatic events.

There is no doubt that obesity is a condition with a high familial incidence; probably higher than any figures record (4). Weight control has been propagandized so extensively that there are many potentially obese people, particularly in middle- and upper-class families, who to all outer appearances are slender, even skinny. Unless one questions every member in detail, the figures in the ordinary case history are apt to be too low. Deliberate dieting may have gone on through several generations, with the grandparents, too, reported as slim. A fat youngster will then stand out even more as an embarrassing branch of the family tree. Yet some of the most severe cases of obesity I have observed came from families where even detailed inquiry failed to reveal obesity in other members.

Having followed fat children and adolescents into adulthood I can state with equal definiteness that whatever the transmitted genetic potential, their offspring are not doomed to becoming obese. Not one of the severely obese and also emotionally disturbed adolescents who had been in psychiatric treatment raised an obese child, though some of their spouses had also been plump. They had learned to avoid the errors of their own parents, namely overemphasizing food; instead, they permitted their children free choice of what and how much to eat. Several of these second generation children have now grown into young adults without having become fat.

These observations do not contradict the existence of hereditary factors. They illustrate, however, the fallacy of speaking of obesity as due to genetic rather than to environmental factors. The genetic potential of an organism is set at the moment of conception, but the extent to which this potential develops depends upon its interaction with the environment. Some genotypes will flourish in one type of environment and not in another, or a particular environment may increase certain manifestations and inhibit others.

Another approach cites certain rare syndromes of inherited abnormalities associated with obesity, as evidence of genetic factors causing obesity in general. This reasoning is about as logical as if one were to explain nutritional anemia by citing the genetic patterns of sickle-cell anemia or some other well-defined form. In anemia, there are many other ways for distinguishing between different types, whereas in obesity weight excess is often the only objective measurement. To quote just one example: in 1929, Christiansen (8) described an unusual form of obesity named "macrosomia adiposa congenita." The progeny of two sisters showed extraordinary universal growth, enormous appetite from birth on, and excessive deposition of fat. Five of the seven children with the syndrome died within the first year of life. In spite of its rarity, this syndrome continues to be quoted as evidence of hereditary factors for obesity in general. In the same way, inbred experimental animals are described in great detail to make the case for heredity in human obesity. The description by Danforth (10) of hereditary adiposity in mice, in 1927, was an exciting event, but no comparable form has been discovered in humans. This strain has been extensively studied, and so have other strains of mice with different hereditary obese syndromes (25).

These extensive studies are important for the understanding of human obesity because they have helped to elucidate various mechanisms and pathways through which the obese state may develop, and have also shown that different forms may be associated with different complications. At the same time they illustrate the most important shortcoming of genetic studies of human obesity thus far, namely that of not differentiating between different types. Many of the old clinical arguments and contradictions lose their meaning once it is recognized that there are different forms

sity, even though the study of such discrete physiological mecha-
in human obesity lags behind that of animal observations, and there
o evidence that any of the animal obesities has a counterpart in
humans.

Even in animals not genetically predisposed, manipulation of the environment may create obesity. Even "social" factors may exert such an influence under strictly experimental conditions. A normal mouse sharing the cage with a hypothalamic obese mouse, will gain more weight than its litter mates not associated with a fat mouse, though not as much as the fat mouse itself (22).

Litters of rats were separated at birth and given different feeding experiences (17). One group had access to food only during 2 hours, whereas the litter mates had free access to food throughout the 24-hour day. The deprived infant rats, after initial weight loss, soon learned to gulp their food so fast and to process it in such a way that they outgained their litter mates and became obese. This was associated with metabolic changes and increased lipogenesis. Their abnormal feeding patterns persisted and they remained obese even with free access to food throughout the day. This cycle could be interrupted through a period of starvation.

In another experiment litter size of rats was manipulated. Some mother rats had to provide nourishment for only 2 or 3 pups, whereas 10 to 12 infant rats were assigned to other mothers (16). Those with the ample food supply outgrew and outweighed their relatively deprived litter mates, and developed larger fat deposits, with an increased fat cell count. If the experiment was carried out over 21 days, the rats which had been deprived as infants remained permanently smaller, with a low fat tissue cell count which was not corrected by free access to ample food supply later on. Laboratory-raised infant baboons on a self-feeding device for their formula diet, with continuous access to nourishment, outgained those where the nourishment was offered periodically (35). By 4 months the weight excess had reached 60% and necessitated interruption of the self-feeding.

These various examples illustrate that the traditional way of asking whether environment or heredity causes obesity does not clarify the problem. Hereditary and environmental factors are not opposed but interact and influence each other. The question needs to be restated as "how much is biologically given and how much is framed by experience?" and, more important, "how do these two aspects interact?"

Thermodynamic Approach

Equally limited is the approach that insists that obesity is "simply" the result of a disturbed energy balance, that since the law of conservation of energy must be preserved, obesity is the outcome of a food intake in excess of energy output. There is no doubt that this is so, but this statement does not say anything about the underlying reasons for this disequilibrium. Even this approach has not been undisputed. At the height of the popularity of endocrine explanations, it was not uncommon to read that a patient had grown fat on very little food. Recently arguments have been over the relative importance of overeating or inactivity for the development of obesity. Much of the contradiction is explained by the way data are collected. Information based on questionnaires, however detailed, is singularly inaccurate. I have yet to see an obese person who would not lose weight on the amount of food he reports he eats. There is also a need to differentiate between the active and stationary phase of obesity. Overeating is conspicuous only during the phase of active weight increase; the amounts needed to maintain the high weight may not be too different from normal intake or may even be small when associated with inactivity. This may be rather extreme, seen not so much by absence of participation in athletics but in the daily habits, the sheer immobility, the reduction in the small fidgeting or adjusting movements normal people make.

For decades the scientific approach to obesity required measuring the "basal metabolism," the amount of calories used to maintain the vital functions, which were compared to a standard; the difference between the actual measurement and this norm was reported as "basal metabolic rate." In obese subjects it was usually reported as "low," and was interpreted as indicating thyroid deficiency. The whole procedure rested on the erroneous assumption that fat tissue was metabolically inert and should be discounted in the computation (5). Unavoidably, the heavier the person the lower the reported rate. The myth of low basal metabolism and of hypothyroidism in obesity was finally laid to rest when thyroid function could be measured more directly.

Obesity has also been explained as related to disturbances in thermal regulation. According to this assumption, the metabolism of some obese people will not accelerate on exposure to cold. In contrast, thin people depend on metabolic acceleration for maintenance of body temperature. It has been postulated that body weight may slowly increase as a result of such ongoing differences in metabolic expenditure. Observations in Antarctic stations have shown that these stressful conditions lead to an enormous increase in appetite and food consumption, with weight gain not unusual.

It is now generally recognized that the abnormal patterns of food intake and energy expenditure are expressions of underlying disturbances. Yet whatever the theoretical concepts about the etiology of obesity, as far as therapy goes, little has been changed and the thermodynamic approach dominates the field with the age old prescription of "eat less and exercise more."

Endocrine and Biochemical Factors

Modern investigation of the metabolic aspects of obesity focuses on the biochemical processes through which foodstuffs are assimilated into the body or become available for use as fuel. The metabolic breakdown of carbohydrates has been understood much longer than that of fats, and thus the older obesity literature focuses nearly exclusively on aberrations in carbohydrate metabolism. As long as the breakdown of the fatty acids was not understood, fat was considered an inert mass, passively deposited in the connective tissues. Two scientific breakthroughs during the late 1930's dramatically changed these old concepts. Schoenheimer's pioneer investigations (32), with the aid of isotopes, of the intermediary metabolism of fatty acids proved wrong the old premise that fat tissue was metabolically inert. "Contrary to the general idea of the slow metabolism of fat tissues, all experiments point to the fact that the fat stores are very actively involved in the conversion processes characteristic of life."

The other great discovery was the elucidation of the details of the various steps in the oxidation of carbohydrates and fatty acids, which were integrated into a theory known as the Krebs cycle, a fruitful working hypothesis for visualizing metabolic activities as occurring in a continuous wheel-like process with two carbon units (acetic acid derived from carbohydrates, fat, or amino acids) serving as the common currency in energy production (21). The cycle plausibly describes the "converting one form of energy into another—like man-made machines which require one specific form of energy." The steps in the conversion of carbohydrates to the form in which they enter the oxidation cycle have been analyzed in practically complete detail. The exciting aspect of this discovery is the recognition that the intermediary products which occur in the advanced stages of the oxidation of fatty acids are identical with the breakdown products that are finally derived from the oxidation of carbohydrates and also proteins. (It had been known empirically that carbohydrates could be converted into fat, and that fat deposits could be utilized to fulfill the body's energy requirements.)

These exceedingly complex processes, which have gradually been elucidated, give, in the final analysis, a simple picture of how the same chemical compounds, though derived from different foodstuffs, can compete or substitute for each other in metabolic processes. The individual steps of this breakdown are very complex, involving different specific enzymes and co-enzymes for each reaction. It is also assumed, although not yet proved, on the basis of the study of the function of co-enzyme A that most, if not all, reactions are reversible. However, it is still virtually unknown whether the metabolic deviations in obesity are caused by possible differences in the inherited enzymes, or whether the weakness in the enzymatic apparatus has been induced by the continuous overeating and abnormal inactivity.

Concepts of hormonal interaction with metabolic processes have become much more complex since the early reports with their naive enthusiasm in making an endocrine diagnosis on superficial evidence, and of therapeutic overoptimism that attempted to correct complex conditions with some glandular substance of, at best, dubious efficacy. This resulted in the rejection of simplistic assertions about endocrine functions, the fallacy of which was proved over and over again. Modern endocrine research focuses on their discrete role in the internal metabolism.

Characteristic of obesity are defective glucose metabolism, hyperinsulinism, and water retention. Glucose, when available, is more readily oxidized than any other energy source, and fat cells metabolize glucose more rapidly than other cells. Fixation of fatty acids in the adipose tissue for storage depends upon a continuous supply of glucose, and, inasmuch as insulin is required for utilization of this glucose, it is obvious that control of fat metabolism is mediated by glucose and insulin. Stated in other words, the storage of body fat becomes impossible unless glucose is simultaneously metabolised. The implication of this interrelationship is that the excess storage of fat, as in obesity, might be associated with, or is the result of, an overproduction of insulin and excessive intake of carbohydrate food, or both. A wide diversity of physiological circumstances may exert, by various mechanisms operating through the glucose fatty acid cycle, a carbohydrate-saving action. Due to the defective glucose oxidation the obese person converts large amounts of carbohydrates into fat and stores it.

The constant stimulation of an obese person's pancreatic islets by large amounts of dietary glucose and amino acids results in hyperinsulinism. The association between obesity and hyperinsulinism prompted investigation of possible causal connections. There are suggestions that obesity is a causal factor, since hyperinsulinism is observed in extremely obese people, and disappears when weight is reduced to normal. Though much of the evidence points toward the excess insulin being the result of continuous overeating, the lurking suspicion continues that it may have a primary causal role. The same applies to enzymatic activity and other hormones which may show abnormality due to some slight innate weakness, or which may become exhausted as a consequence of continuous nutritional abuse.

Other modern investigations of hormonal disturbances deal with the increased production and excretion of certain adrenal steroids, high level of plasma antidiuretic hormone, lowered glomerulo filtration, and reduced renal clearance of water and decreased ability to excrete sodium.

With all the detailed work, much of which comes from laboratory observations on pure bred animal strains and which is suggestive of a primary metabolic or enzymatic disorder, studies of human obesity are not yet able to differentiate between factors that are the cause of obesity, or the result of it.

It is completely outside the range of this presentation to go into more detail except to state that there is increasing evidence that many of the metabolic processes tend toward increased lipogenesis and inhibition of lipolysis. Several recent symposiums have reviewed the topic in detail (1, 14).

Neuro-Regulatory Mechanisms

Since the early part of this century a controversy has raged over whether lesions at the base of the brain lead to obesity through endocrine or neurological pathways. Gradually the hypophysis was displaced from its position as "the master gland" by the hypothalamus. Studies of the hypothalamus have been so rewarding, with investigation of various cell groups that were isolated as "centers," that for a while it was considered, through the "appestat," to be the center of eating behavior and weight regulation and also of emotions. With the change in basic biological thinking during the past decade, it became increasingly apparent that there are no "locations" for any specific behavior in any hypothalamic "compartments," and that there is a need for an integrative approach to the functioning of the nervous system. I shall follow here a recent review by Morgane and Jacobs (28) who, on the basis of their extensive work on hunger and thirst, have come to the conclusion that "the general system approach to several interrelated brainstem areas seems a more useful one in understanding brain functioning than does pin-point localization of so-called 'centers' which are in reality only components of a larger system." In modern thinking the hypothalamus is conceived of as embedded in the limbic forebrain, limbic mid-brain circuits, and reticular activities.

Though these considerations remove the hypothalamus from the pinnacle on which it was held for some time, it does not diminish the importance of the detailed studies that have been carried out in the past, which were ably summarized by Mayer (26). Extensive animal experiments during the last 20 or 30 years showed that primary signals related to the need to eat involved central neural regulation; production of stereotaxic or chemical (gold thioglucose) lesions suggested the localization of certain regulatory mechanisms. It has been assumed that messages from the periphery would stimulate these so-called feeding centers, and that these stimuli were either metabolic or sensory. Several possibilities have been considered as signals for hunger and satiety. There is agreement that some combination of metabolic signals, as a consequence of food intake or its absence, is involved in the control of food intake. The thermostatic theory is based on the known sensitivity of the hypothalamus to changes in blood temperature, and the fact that animals eat to keep warm and stop eating if they get too hot. Mayer introduced a general distinction between "regulatory" obesity, with primary impairment of the central mechanisms regulating food intake, and the "metabolic" obesities with primary impairment in an acquired or inborn error in tissue metabolism. More recent works suggest that the surgically produced hypothalamic obesity is not a simple "regulatory" obesity but rather involves other disturbances, with indication that neural lesions may directly produce "metabolic" disturbances mediated either by nervous pathways or neuro-humeral release mechanisms.

Kennedy (19) pointed out that the obesity caused by stereotaxic operations in the rat was never exclusively a disorder of appetite, but that inactivity was an etiological factor of equal importance. Hypothalamic obese rats also showed defects of motivation. Though these various components can be isolated, they are so frequently disturbed together and the hypothalamic controls are so interrelated that they can hardly be considered independent. Miller and his co-workers (27) found that rats with destruction of the hypothalamic "satiety centers" ate more than normal controls only when the food was readily available. When various types of work impediments were interposed between rats and the food source, the rats with the hypothalamic lesions ate less than normal rats.

There is little doubt that decreased motor activity influences the rate of fat accumulation, but it is still questionable whether decreased motor activity associated with ventromedial hypothalamic lesions is the cause or the consequence of the obesity. Other studies have shown that rats who have been trained to consume their daily ration in a single meal developed enhanced lipogenesis with an increase in adipose tissue. Increased lipogenesis has also been demonstrated in the liver of hypothalamic hyperphagic mice. These experiments tend to indicate the possibility that "metabolic" effects may result from ventromedial hypothalamic lesions but which effects are primary and which are secondary to feeding habits and the developing obesity remains unsettled.

Lesions in the lateral hypothalamic area may have a drastic effect on the rate of weight loss showing something like metabolic decay. This more drastic defect in feeding and drinking behavior produced by the far lateral lesions seems to evolve direct "metabolic effects" and not purely regulatory ones. These mid-lateral hypothalamic lesions produce a defect more related to the "motivation" to feed and are easily reversible by special feedings, whereas a defect in the far-lateral area is more severe and involves more than mere failure to eat and drink.

Physiological studies have tended to neglect or even deny a role to the sensory components of food, at least as part of the physiological system of regulating intake. Unlesioned rats and those in the dynamic phase of obesity were much less discriminative than fat animals. The hyperphagia following operation appears to represent a primitive, unconditioned urge to eat that normally is inhibited by the hypothalamic "satiety" mechanism. Damage to the hypothalamus appears to release this type of hunger from inhibition but also allows discrimination to play a greater part in determining food intake.

Taste, flavor, and other sensory qualities have been studied by an almost independent group of investigators, and for different reasons. These studies have shown that the sensory properties of food, taste, and flavor are necessary to discriminate food objects and choices. Sensory cues can control intake via simple taste preferences in animals, and by complex emotional factors, attitudes, and social conditioning in human beings. The precision of food choices and patterning over the long run comes from the pairing of sensory cues with metabolic effects. Learning becomes increasingly important in all behavior modifications, including sensory signals as guides to caloric value of food in higher animals and certainly in humans. There seems to be some evidence to suggest that sensory signals may play an innate as well as a learned role in food intake, and should be considered biologically as well as psychologically.

Morgane and Jacobs emphasize in their review that there is much specialization within the brain, but highly integrative functions involving the organism as a whole (that is, global behavior) involve complex interaction between the various levels of the neuro-axis. The brain is not a "mosaic" of functional centers each residing and functioning unto itself. The hypothalamus is only one link within the framework of neural functioning, and the hypothalamic mechanisms themselves can only be understood in the light of the total neuronal system of which they are an interacting component. There are no feeding and satiety centers in the brain, nor are there any other "centers"; rather, the very concept of integrative action of the nervous system implies reciprocal activities between various elements of nervous functioning. Behavior is not just a consequence of the widespread neuronal interaction. It does not yet appear likely that the brain as a whole will be studied, but when brain mechanisms are related to behavior and the "hardware" of the nervous system is to be united with the "software" of the nervous system, the psychological processes, it can more likely be accomplished by recognizing and comprehending operations within a broad system complex.

These extensive neurophysiological studies have contributed to our knowledge of the mechanisms of eating and emotionality. The very complexity of the brain function permits the integration of psychological and experiential data with observations on neurophysiological mechanisms. MacLean (24) defined psyche as *information*, not matter or energy; in the light of present knowledge, it may be inferred that the central nervous system derives information on the basis of changing patterns of neuronal activity. The patterns themselves are without substance, but they depend on physiochemical processes within the nervous tissue, with behavior as the physical correlate of information.

There is also increasing evidence that the brain is not a passive receiver of information or stimulation, but an active participant in this process. Pribram (29) spoke of the servo-mechanism type of neural organization and concluded that a simple stimulus-response-association model of brain behavior organization has become untenable. Based on his own experiments and those of others, he suggested that the organism's input is influenced by the most recently developed portion of the central nervous system and, further, that two reciprocally acting mechanisms of control exist, and that feedback is ubiquitous in the organization of the nervous system. In discussing theories of emotions, he pointed out that they fall into two major groups, the social-behavioral or "intrapsychic," and the biological, which includes the physical, chemical, and the neurological. Terms are all too often taken from one frame of reference and applied to another in a haphazard and uncritical fashion. He considers it essential "to keep the two universes of discourse clear." Morgane has made the same point: "If the same neural events are in principle observable at two 'levels,' the neurological and the psychological, closing the gap between observable behavior and neurophysiological processes will not be made any more possible by 'installing *microhomunculi*' in the brain."

For the understanding of the brain mechanisms underlying emotions and motivation, Pribram proposed a model that is memory-based rather than drive-based or viscerally based; that means that the traces of past and ongoing experiences enter into the organization of patterns. This model assumes a base line of organzied stability and its potential perturbation. The base line is established by the process of *habituation of the orienting reaction*, which in turn is related to the formation of a "neuronal model," a configuration against which subsequent input of the organism is matched. His proposal is both neurobehavioral and neurocybernetic in its conception.

In the following chapter I shall discuss how hunger awareness develops out of the reciprocal feedback patterns of interaction between mother and child. Such a concept is in agreement with Pribram's model of brain function of dual control, of the importance of external as well as of internal determinants, an *autonomy vs. externally controlled* dimension.

The Adipose Tissue System

The adipose tissue has been the neglected substance in obesity research; it was assigned a passive role as nothing more than the nonspecific accumulation of excess lipids in the loose connective tissue cells pervading the entire body. In spite of repeated challenges to this concept, it is only recently that studies have resulted in the recognition of adipose tissue as a highly specialized tissue. The possibility of disturbances in fat metabolism and fat storage in obesity had not been entirely overlooked in the older European literature where repeated references to the special qualities of the adipose tissue are found (3).

There have been repeated efforts to define the morphological aspects of the adipose tissue. The whole topic, including the question of whether feedback mechanisms exist between adipose tissue and regulatory mechanisms for food intake, has recently been reviewed by Liebelt (23). Utilizing the chick embryo, he demonstrated that localized masses of adipose tissue developed consistently in specific anatomical sites and at relatively specific times of development, and persisted throughout the adult life of the bird. The data support the concept that adipose tissue is distributed through the chick body as discrete anatomical structures which have the morphological and functional attributes of individual organs. On the other hand, the lipid content of these fat depots showed a relationship to body weight, fluctuating with the nutritional status of the host. It seems that distribution and location of the lipid-free components occur according to hereditary principles; the accumulation of fat globules in this adipose tissue is determined by many other factors.

In pure bred mice the patterns of lipid deposition are in part under the control of genetic factors which are characteristic for a given strain. If grafts of adipose tissue from genetically "obese" mice and from genetically "lean" mice are implanted in the right and left ear, respectively, of a single hybrid host, and thus exposed to an identical physiological environment in terms of ingested calories, hormonal milieu, and energy expenditure, the two genetically distinct adipose tissues will reflect their parental origin in that the graft derived from the "obese" parent will deposit a significantly greater amount of lipid than those from the "lean" parent. This suggests that for these two strains the adipose tissue per se appears to be the site of gene action.

In gold thioglucose obesity, fat organs will become much larger in one location than in another, but they remain proportional to the total body lipid content, suggesting some form of interaction mediated on a systemic basis. These studies suggest also that increased lipid deposition occurs initially in existing fat cells, but when they are "saturated" new fat cells are formed to accommodate the increasing lipid content. Hirsch (15), utilizing a technique of counting and sizing isolated fat cells, concluded that human obesity of early onset is accompanied by an increase in the number of adipose cells. He also demonstrated that excessive feeding early in infancy is accompanied by an increase in the number of fat cells and felt that this would predispose an individual toward obesity throughout life. My own observations are only partially in agreement with this, as will be discussed in the chapter on Obesity in Childhood. Formerly fat infant baboons, when given unlimited food supply at 2½ years of age, did not outgain their controls who were also exposed to unlimited food (7).

Feedback mechanisms between adipose tissue and food intake suggest that the adipose tissue mass is in some manner functionally integrated. The maintenance of a relatively constant body weight, despite variations in caloric intake and energy expenditure, suggests that the body mass is probably controlled by homeostatic mechanisms which regulate the metabolism of adipose tissue. Various hormones or physiological tracer substances have been considered, such as gonadal and adrenal steroids, changes in the growth hormone, or some hypothetical humoral factor not identical with classically defined hormones. As the functional and organizational components of the adipose tissue system become better understood, it will be possible to integrate them with those from the relatively well-defined body systems. "Thus, in effect, attempts to define the 'internal ecosystem' of the organism, i.e., the interaction of the constituent body systems with ingested nutrients, will provide a clearer perspective of the integrative workings involved in food intake regulation."

Comment

Most of the reported research has been carried out on experimental animals. In ordinary human obesity, problems are rarely as clear-cut, with definite lesions or distinct hereditary patterns. However, in operational terms, as possibilities of patterns of abnormal functioning and interactions, the evidence coming from these various studies has definite value. The rich and diversified isolated findings gain their meaning through integration into cycles of interactional and feedback patterns.

Once different forms of human obesity are defined and studied individually, it is to be expected that various patterns of abnormalities will be recognized. Even then it will probably remain a difficult task to differentiate primary factors from those secondary to the obese state. Most clinical studies have been done on people with long-standing obesity and its complications, not on those with unstable weight, with rapid increases and dramatic weight losses. They are the ones frequently referred for psychiatric evaluation and treatment. All patients who had been referred to me had been studied with the current laboratory methods in renowned medical centers, but in no instance have physiological deviations been discovered that might have explained the severe weight fluctuations, or offered some information relevant for treatment. Hopefully, some substances will eventually be defined that might interrupt this cycle of gaining or losing, or prevent the progressive obesity of middle age. If they cannot effect a cure, treatment efforts might become less stressful, the way metabolic disturbances in diabetes are ameliorated by insulin. What such substances might be is a matter of speculation; it might be necessary to replace a missing or defective enzyme, or hormone, or there might be some way of influencing abnormal neurological mechanisms, or something that makes the excessive fat cells melt away may be discovered. It certainly will not be one miracle substance that would be effective in all cases.

Somatic Aspects of Anorexia Nervosa

In anorexia nervosa, too, opinion has fluctuated widely about the importance of somatic factors. The name, anorexia nervosa, implies that the early authors considered mental stress as its cause. The whole discussion was thrown into a new focus when Simmonds, a pathologist, reported in 1914 that destructive processes in the anterior pituitary gland were related to cachexia (33). For the next two or three decades the condition was explained in endocrine terms, and treatment was attempted through administration of endocrine substances, and even by implantation of pituitary glands. Subsequent clinical studies were directed toward differentiating a psychiatric syndrome from a glandular disorder. The whole question has recently been summarized by Russell (31).

In a condition as rare as anorexia nervosa it is difficult to assume genetic patterns of transmission and innate constitutional factors. Nevertheless, such factors have been considered. Crisp (9) feels that a high birth weight, excellent nutrition during childhood, and early puberty are expressions of a predisposing constitution. King (20), after outlining distinct behavior features, postulated that primary anorexia nervosa was an obscure organic disease, occurring in subjects of a particular constitution. Observations on monozygotic twins, with discordant occurrence of anorexia nervosa, do not support the assumption of a genetic or constitutional factor (6, 12).

The present tendency is to consider all functional symptoms of anorexia nervosa as secondary to the starvation; Russell has shown that though many of the actions of the anterior pituitary gland are preserved, there is a growing body of evidence that the release of gonadotropin is impaired. He considers the malnutrition only part of the cause of the gonadal failure that he assumes to be of primary endocrine origin, which in turn reflects a disturbance at the level of the hypothalamus. Refeeding and restoration of the lost body weight leads to increased excretion of gonadotropin and estrogens in the urine, but the recovery is not complete and does not include the cyclic variation preceding normal menstrual cycles. Studies extending over several months suggested that weight gain was one of the necessary factors for recovery, but not the only one. Studies in male patients showed a hormonal disorder analogous to that in females, with low urinary levels of gonadotropin, and low output of testosterone and gonadal hormones.

In any discussion of secondary amenorrhea it must be considered that there is probably no other function as vulnerable to emotional stress as the sexual cycle (18). The maintenance of the normal cycle is dependent upon the persistence of normal pituitary, ovarian, and endometrial function. Organic pathological changes are demonstrable only occasionally, but there are definite syndromes with disturbances in the endocrine interplay. Extensive studies of prisoners during and following World War II strongly suggest that amenorrhea is primarily due to the emotional concomitance of detention, and not to food deprivation. It occurred with greater frequency in the beginning of imprisonment, when nutrition was still adequate. In a study in Theresienstadt, women prisoners living under extreme conditions showed an incidence of amenorrhea of 54%, as compared to 25% in women living under relatively more favorable conditions. Many women resumed menstruation immediately after liberation, without undergoing any treatment and before refeeding.

Russell raises the question of whether the gonadal failure might not contribute to the loss of sexual interest which is such a common feature in anorexia nervosa, and speculates whether some faulty organization in the early stages of development in the nervous system might conceivably have some bearing on the abnormal attitudes and conflicts over the physical, sexual, and emotional development that occurs with puberty.

The loss of weight is mainly due to a rigid reduction of food intake; it may be accelerated through self-induced vomiting and purgation which, in turn, may lead to pernicious metabolic and electrolyte complications. These patients selectively avoid carbohydrates; though relatively high, the absolute intake of protein is also low and there is loss of body tissue. Many of the somatic symptoms, the susceptibility to cold, the cold and blue extremities, the hyperkeratosis and the increase in body hair, are considered consequences of the malnutrition. In many patients, particularly in those who use laxatives and frequently vomit, hypokalemia is a common complication. The serum level of sodium may also be reduced, with accompanying hypochloremia and alkalosis; this is most likely to happen when there are multiple sources of potassium loss from the body. These multiple roads of electrolyte loss lead to an increased secretion rate of aldesterone and worsening of the potassium depletion. Whatever the mechanism, hypokalemia is a complication which should be recognized; if chronic it may give rise to renal tubular vaculation and a reduced renal function.

Organic Pathology

In this brief and sketchy review of modern trends in research into disturbed eating functions the focus has been on the interaction of multiple biological as well as experiential factors that mutually influence each other and thus result in abnormal weight. It must not be overlooked, however, that there are also cases with a definable organic onset. There has been so much emphasis on psychological factors that I have repeatedly seen young patients referred for psychiatric evaluation in whom an encephalitic episode had been overlooked. I should like to give here two examples of weight disturbance with organic pathology in the central nervous system. The course of their disturbance is distinctly different from the histories of those in whom psychological and physiological factors interact.

A 20-year-old woman was seen in consultation, after a large weight loss, as a possible victim of anorexia nervosa. During the past 3 years she had developed progressive neurological symptoms which were assumed to belong to the multiple sclerosis area. She could walk only with support, suffered from double vision, had a weak hand grip, and her speech was occasionally slurred. She was remarkably cheerful and appeared to be quite unconcerned about her condition.

She came from a large family, but was the only fat member; she had weighed 100 lbs at age 6, and had crossed the 200-lb mark when 10 years old. She kept on gaining though she claimed that she had followed the prescribed diets and denied any problems due to her weight. From age 14 on she suffered from unexplained abdominal pain, and an exploratory laparotomy at age 17 revealed a large cyst which was removed. The first neurological symptoms were detected at that time, and the weight loss began.

She recites the outstanding figures with definite pride. Her highest weight had been 397 lbs, just before the operation at age 17; the lowest weight was 108 lbs, on admission. In 3 weeks her weight had risen to 135 lbs. She received intravenous feedings and would eat when food was offered with enough persuasion, though generally she was "not interested" in food. On questioning she expressed some concern about getting fat again, without anything like the frantic fear about weight gain that is characteristic of anorexia nervosa. She had lost more weight than any other patient I have seen but in her psychic attitude she was distinctly different from patients with anorexia nervosa, and she had accepted refeeding, with a gain of over 25 lbs, without objection or emotional reaction.

Two years later she was readmitted to the neurological service, with increased neurological deficits, generalized weakness, incoordination and irreflexia. She ate poorly, her diet consisting mainly of liquids, with an intake of approximately 500 calories per day, and her weight was down to 109 lbs. Extensive laboratory examinations failed to establish a metabolic disorder. Hypopituitarism and multiple sclerosis were considered as probable diagnoses.

The other case concerns an extremely obese (highest weight 430 lbs) 20-year-old man who had developed symptoms of congestive heart failure, increased pulmonary pressure, and polycythemia. He had been repeatedly hospitalized but each time regained the lost weight. At home he was completely inactive, socially withdrawn, sleeping most of the time. He was referred to the psychiatric service in the hope of helping him establish control over his eating.

He had been an active and bright boy until he became acutely sick at age 12 with abdominal pain and vomiting; then his legs began to stiffen and he became stuporous. He remained comatose for 4 days, with bulbar paralysis, and he was fed by a nasal gastric tube. Gradually the coma lightened and the paralysis of his legs and tongue diminished slowly. He was very hungry and thirsty upon awakening and he recalled the frustration he felt when people did not understand him when he asked for food. The diagnosis was epidemic encephalitis.

Following his illness marked changes in his personality and behavior were noted; having before been friendly and active he now became irritable, argumentative, and increasingly seclusive. He had an enormous craving for food and ate constantly, getting up at night and emptying the refrigerator. Within a year his weight rose from 120 to 200 lbs. He became self-conscious and disturbed because he was teased about his increasing weight. Things got worse when he entered high school; he lost all interest in his studies, feeling unable to concentrate. For a while he had a private tutor and seemed to do somewhat better, but ultimately he dropped out of high school. Socially, too, things deteriorated and he spent all his time just sitting around, going to the movies, or watching TV. The food craving persisted. He became very nervous and keyed up when he felt deprived of food during hospitalizations.

This patient is included in Stunkard's study of eating patterns in obesity (34), as manifesting the "eating-without-satiation" pattern, characterized by a subject having difficulty stopping once he has started to eat, without relationship to periods of stress or periodicity, occurring in random manner throughout the day.

In my observation of this patient, which extended over several months, I felt that there was a certain relationship between his state of tension and his craving for food. During the first few months he felt happy because people were being considerate of him, and he was social and quite active. He did not encounter too many difficulties in adhering to the ordinary meal schedule. Psychological tests revealed evidence of moderately severe organic brain impairment, though there were no neurological signs. He lost weight to a low of 320 lbs, enjoyed feeling less heavy, and was rather proud that he could live on such small amounts on which "even a bird would die of starvation." However, he had little confidence that he himself would be able to control his eating; his only way of staying slim was to stay in the role of a patient.

His whole behavior changed when the possibility of discharge was discussed. His weight began to creep up again, at the rate of about 10 lbs per month; he ate again between meals and often secured food in devious ways. He withdrew from activities and appeared preoccupied with daydreams, which reflected extreme passivity and isolation. He dreamed of having a house in the woods, where there were no people around. This house had a glass roof and a creek would flow straight through the middle and keep it cool. He would sit in comfort and fish while watching television. He had no intent of sharing this ideal with anyone.

BIBLIOGRAPHY

1. Albrink, M. J., Guest Editor, Endocrine aspects of obesity, Amer. J. Clin. Nutr., 21:1395–1485, 1968.
2. Angel, J. L., Constitution in female obesity, Amer. J. Phys. Anthrop. N.S., 7:433–452, 1949.
3. Bruch, H., Obesity in childhood, III. Physiologic and psychologic aspects of the food intake of obese children, Amer. J. Dis. Child., 58:738–781, 1940.
4. Bruch, H., The case for heredity, Chapter 5, pp. 86–105, in *The Importance of Overweight*, W. W. Norton & Co., Inc., New York, 1957.
5. Bruch, H., Some basic facts on basal metabolism, Chapter 7, pp. 129–146, in *The Importance of Overweight*, W. W. Norton & Co., Inc., New York, 1957.
6. Bruch, H., The insignificant difference: Discordant incidence of anorexia nervosa in monozygotic twins, Amer. J. Psychiat., 126:123–128, 1969.
7. Bruch, H., and Voss, W. R., Hyperphagia and weight regulation in baboons with infantile obesity, to be published.
8. Christiansen, T., Macrosomia adiposa congenita, a new dysendocrine syndrome of familial occurrence, Endocrinology, 13:149, 1929.
9. Crisp, A. H., Reported birth weights and growth rates in a group of patients with primary anorexia nervosa (weight phobia), J. Psychosom. Res., 14:23–50, 1970.
10. Danforth, C. H., Hereditary adiposity in mice, J. Hered., 18:153, 1927.
11. Davenport, C. B., *Body-build and Its Inheritance*, Carnegie Institution of Washington Publication, Vol. 329, 1923.
12. Gifford, S., Murawski, B. J., and Pilot, M. L., Anorexia nervosa in one of identical twins, pp. 139–228, in *Anorexia Nervosa and Obesity*, C. V. Rowland, Jr., ed., Inter. Psychiat. Clin., Vol. 7, No. 1, Little, Brown & Co., Boston, 1970.
13. Gurney, R., The hereditary factor in obesity, Arch. Int. Med., 57:557, 1936.
14. Halpern, S. L., ed., Symposium on obesity, Med. Clin. N.A., 48:1283–1405, 1964.
15. Hirsch, J., and Gallian, E., Methods for the determination of adipose cell size in man and animals, J. Lipid Res., 9:110–119, 1968.
16. Hirsch, J., and Han, P. W., Cellularity of rat adipose tissue: effects of growth, starvation, and obesity, J. Lipid Res., 10:77–82, 1969.
17. Hollifield, G., and Parson, W., Metabolic adaptations to a "stuff and starve" feeding program, J. Clin. Invest., 41:245–250, 1962.
18. Kelley, K., Daniels, G. E., Poe, J., Easser, R., and Monroe, R., Psychological correlations with secondary amenorrhea, Psychosom. Med., 16:129–147, 1954.
19. Kennedy, G. C., The central nervous regulation of calorie balance. Proc. Nutr. Soc., 20:58–64, 1961.
20. King, A., Primary and secondary anorexia nervosa syndromes, Brit. J. Psychiat., 109:470–479, 1963.
21. Krebs, H. A., *The Tricarboxylic Cycle; Harvey Lectures*, 1948–49, Williams & Wilkins Co., Baltimore, 1949.
22. Liebelt, R. A., Response of adipose tissue in experimental obesity as influenced by genetic, hormonal, and neurogenic factors, Ann. NY Acad. Sci., 110 (Part II): 723–748, 1963.
23. Liebelt, R. A., Bordelon, C. B., and Liebelt, A. G., The adipose tissue system and food intake, in *Progress in Physiological Psychology*, V., E. Stellar, ed., in press.
24. MacLean, P. D., Contrasting functions of limbic and neocortical systems of the brain and their relevance to psychophysiological aspects of medicine, Amer. J. Med., 25:611–626, 1958.

25. Mayer, J., Genetic, traumatic and environmental factors in the etiology of obesity, Physiol. Rev., 33:472–508, 1953.
26. Mayer, J., Some aspects of the problem of regulation of food intake and obesity, New Eng. J. Med., 274:610–616; 662–673; 722–773, 1966.
27. Miller, N., Clark, J., and Stevenson, A., Decreased "hunger" but increased food intake resulting from hypothalamic lesions, Science, 112:256, 1950.
28. Morgane, P. J., and Jacobs, H. L., Hunger and satiety, World Rev. Nutr. Diet., 10:100–213, 1969.
29. Pribram, K. H., Toward a neuropsychological theory of person, pp. 150–160, in The Study of Personality, eds., E. Norbeck, D. Price-Williams and W. M. McCord, Holt, Rinehart and Winston, New York, 1968.
30. Rony, H. R., Obesity and Leanness, Lea & Febiger, Philadelphia, 1940.
31. Russell, G. F. M., Anorexia nervosa: Its identity as an illness and its treatment, pp. 131–164, Chapter 6, in Modern Trends in Psychological Medicine, J. H. Price, ed., Butterworths, Great Britain, 1970.
32. Schoenheimer, R., The Dynamic State of Body Constituents, Harvard University Press, Cambridge, Mass., 1942.
33. Simmonds, M., Ueber embolische Prozesse in der Hypophysis, Arch. Path. Anat., 217:226, 1914.
34. Stunkard, A. J., Eating patterns and obesity, Psychiat. Quart. 33:284–292, 1959.
35. Voss, W. R., Buss, D. H., and Carroll, L. W., A self-feeding device for infant baboon liquid diets, Lab. Anim. Sci., 21:901–903, 1971.

4

Hunger Awareness and
Individuation

Hunger is such a universal phenomenon, familiar to everybody through personal experiences, beginning as far back as one can remember, that it has always been taken for granted that hunger is an innate drive or sensation. In patients with severe eating disorders a basic disturbance can be recognized in the way the sensation of hunger is experienced. This is related to disturbances in many other areas of functioning, all with earmarks of having resulted from some errors in early experiences (5).

This functional deficit, not an organic defect, in the perceptual and conceptual awareness of hunger was recognized over a period of time during psychiatric and psychoanalytic treatment of a large number of severely disturbed obese and anorexic patients, mainly adolescents. At first the manifold symbolic meanings of the disturbed food intake were recognized, both in voracious uncontrolled intake as well as in rigid refusal to eat. Food may symbolically stand for an insatiable desire for unobtainable love, or as an expression of rage and hatred; it may substitute for sexual gratification or indicate ascetic denial; it may represent the wish to be a man and possess a penis, or the wish to be pregnant, or fear of it. It may provide a sense of spurious power and thus lead to self-aggrandizement, or it may serve as a defense against adulthood and responsibility. Preoccupation with food may appear as helpless, dependent clinging to parents, or as hostile rejection of them. On the basis of psychoanalytic investigation of obese patients, Hamburger also observed that the symbolic significance of food may carry an enormous variety of different, often contradictory connotations (9).

Fascinating as it was to unravel the unconscious symbolic motivation, the *why* of the disturbed eating patterns, the great diversity itself suggested the question of *how* it had been possible for a body function as essential and basic as food intake to develop in such a way that it could be misused so widely in the service of nonnutritional needs. Pursuit of this question, using a fact-finding therapeutic approach instead of the traditional interpretative one, led to the recognition that the experience of hunger is not innate, but something that contains important elements of learning. It gradually became apparent that something had gone wrong in the experiential and interpersonal processes surrounding the satisfaction of nutritional and other bodily needs of these later patients, and that incorrect and confusing early experiences had interfered with their ability to recognize hunger and satiation, and to differentiate "hunger," the urge to eat, from other signals of discomfort that have nothing to do with "food deprivation," and from emotional tension states aroused by the greatest variety of conflicts and problems.

Preoccupied as these patients are with eating or not eating, and in their use of the eating function as a pseudo-solution of personality problems, they have in common the inability to identify hunger correctly or to distinguish it from other states of bodily need or emotional arousal. It became gradually clear that the old charge against obese people of having "no will power" describes their not being discriminately aware of bodily sensations: they cannot exercise control over a function or need which is not even recognized.

Once the question was formulated in this way, evidence of a deficit in hunger awareness rapidly accumulated. Anorexic patients will spontaneously declare, "I do not need to eat" and seem to mean it literally; at other times they are overpowered by urges for food and then will gorge themselves to the point of spontaneous or induced vomiting.

Many fat patients, when questioned on this point, will answer, with an immediate sense of recognition, that all their lives they had suffered from such an inability. Often they admit being aware that they were not really hungry, saying, for example, "My stomach does not need it—but my mouth wants it," or in extreme passivity, "I find myself eating—but do not even know how I got into the restaurant." During eating binges they feel driven to eat against their wish not to gain more weight, and even consume food they ordinarily dislike. They experience neither hunger nor pleasure or satiation during this kind of eating. They may find temporary relief from the anxious and depressive feelings that have been mistakenly experienced as "need to eat," but it is short-lived and the cycle of "not feeling right" and unsatisfying eating is endlessly repeated.

The concept that an instinct or drive, hunger particularly, is not a truly innate or preformed function present at birth, but something that requires some sort of learning for its effective use appeared startling at first. However, when a strict distinction between the physiological state of nutritional deficiency and the psychological act of perceptual recognition of this deficiency as "hunger" is made, the importance of such learning and its complexity appears less debatable. Many studies in the past have overlooked that "hunger" is a rather complex concept with many different meanings. *Hunger* is used to refer to the *physiological state of nutritional depletion* or severe food deprivation, or to long-continued starvation, or to widespread famine. *Hunger* also denotes a *psychological experience*, namely the complex, unpleasant, and compelling sensation an individual feels when deprived of food, which results in searching, even fighting for food to relieve its torment. In a more pleasant form and as desire for a particular food it is called *appetite* and plays an important role in our enjoyment of food and the great variation and refinement of our eating habits.

Failure to make the distinction between the physiological and psychological aspects of hunger has also plagued the physiological studies of food deprivation. Historically there were two main theories concerning mechanisms responsible for hunger, the peripheral and the central. Proponents of the peripheral theory felt that hunger was modulated through sensory endings in the peripheral organs, most notably the stomach. Adherents to the central theory felt the hunger sensation originated in the brain itself, which secondarily affected peripheral organs. The old controversies have been resolved in the modern idea that the state of nutritional depletion is accompanied by various physiological changes throughout the body which come as "information" to the visceral brain centers, which in turn send messages to the neocortex which identifies the sensation as "hunger" and initiates action to mitigate this discomfort. For a study of psychological aspects it is of the utmost importance to separate the physiological state of nutritional need and the perception and conceptual awareness of this state.

Problems of similar complexity exist with regard to the concept of "pain," and they have been widely discussed by biologists and neurologists. Langer in *Mind: An Essay on Human Feeling*, brought the various observations together (14). She pointed out that this problem involves semantic as well as philosophical considerations. Confusion has arisen from efforts to detect the condition of the nerves which "give rise" to pain.

A state cannot "break through" to anything. But I think a neurophysiological process can be said to "break through to feeling," and how this can reasonably be said is the theme of my present chapter. That is a philosophical issue.

At what point the psychical phenomenon, feeling, begins to occur is a question of fact, i.e., a psychological question, difficult but not invalid. On the whole, the relation of mental events, i.e., felt impingements and activities—to the rest of nature is the subject matter of psychology, which demands studies in neurology, genetics, and also careful introspection and clinical protocol analysis for its systematic understanding. If we are indeed speaking of two "logical languages" and always tending to mix them, as recent immigrants in a new country mix its spoken language with their native tongue, we must settle on one or the other.

It soon becomes apparent, however, that it is not a choice of language that confronts us. If "psychophysical entities" occur in nature, the vocabulary of natural science must be able to designate them, and to accommodate itself to discourse about them; if this is not possible, it is not our language that is inadequate, but our basic assumptions.

There is a third way in which the word *hunger* is used, namely as a symbolic expression of a state of need in general, or as a simile for want in other areas. This, too, has led to confusion. An author using "hunger" symbolically for description of psychological experiences may suddenly switch and speak concretely about eating and food intake. In recent years, in the debate on poverty and malnutrition in America, the word "hunger" has acquired a highly emotional political meaning.

Case Study

I should like to present here a case study from which I first formulated these concepts in a lecture given in 1960 (2).

The case history I am going to present may sound to some of you like a dramatic exaggeration. It is not. On the contrary, I regret that my literary ability is not adequate to convey the full flavor of the grotesque atmosphere of mutual coercion and violence that surrounded the whole development of the patient whom I shall call Gail. She entered the New York State Psychiatric Institute in October, 1959, at the age of 20. Gail was a slim, well-groomed and fashionably dressed young lady. Her doctor had made arrangements for hospitalization several weeks earlier but Gail had refused to sign the application for voluntary admission. Her weight was 96 lbs, a sacred figure to which she had rigidly clung for the past 4 or 5 years. And thereby hangs the tale—how she had managed to maintain her weight.

Up to the age of 13 she had been plump, a fate for which she blamed her parents. Her weight had reached nearly 140 lbs and had earned her the nickname of Two-Ton Tilly. When Tilly was 11 years old the parents had sought help at a child guidance clinic because she was unmanageable at home. There was no improvement during a year of treatment of mother and child, and a boarding school with treatment facilities was recommended. Tilly went there under violent protest, saying her parents wanted to get rid of her. At the school she felt terrified and would not dare eat anything. Her fear of eating was so great that she thought if she took as little as a glass of water she might get out of hand and become even fatter. Instead a miracle happened—she began to grow thinner. When the weight loss became visible, she decided also to get rid of the much-ridiculed name Tilly, and choose for herself a new name, Gail. She continued to protest against being at the boarding school, talked about running away and wanted to go home. The parents finally gave in to her protestations, feeling guilty about the accusation of having gotten rid of her and believing her promise of better behavior. She came back weighing 96 lbs and was determined not to get fat again.

Her absolute insistence on remaining at this magic weight of 96 lbs led to her dominating the household with enforced rituals. Her parents were forced to shop three times a day because she would not permit food in the home between meals. Any food left over after a meal had to be thrown away, since she feared that she might succumb to the compulsion of eating it and thereby spoil her magic weight. She entered high school and obtained very good grades by studying religiously. In order to study she had to have absolute quiet around the home and her parents were not allowed to be there when she worked. The parents were unable to cope with the situation. They again sought psychiatric help and Gail consented to see a psychiatrist, though on her terms.

Things went along this way, with many outbursts of violence, until Gail's graduation from high school. She did not want her parents to come to the graduation and refused to get tickets for them. The mother insisted they would go just the same; Gail asked: "How? How?" When the mother refused to tell, Gail became more and more frantic in her questioning and finally grabbed a pair of scissors and attacked her mother, threatening to kill her. The mother ran out of the house to the father's store; they called the police and Gail was taken to a city hospital. She was cowed by the hospital experience and returned home with the best intentions but then was unable to control herself. She stayed at a private hospital for six months where she was kept quiet with medication; no effort at psychotherapy was made. After her return home she saw a psychiatrist regularly and became very dependent on him. She also began to work and was out of the home a good deal. For a year and a half she kept jobs as a salesgirl, lasting in any one place approximately three or four months.

Throughout this period her behavior at home was unchanged, and she still controlled the family with her demand for a restricted diet. The father suggested that now that she was earning money she should have an apartment of her own. Gail's response was: "You can't get rid of me that easily." She quit her job and just stayed home. Her behavior was so violent that within two months her parents moved out into a furnished room, the address of which they kept a strict secret. Even now, after Gail has been in the hospital for over a year, they have not moved back to their old apartment. The mother does not dare to live there; it reminds her of her daughter's violence with every piece of furniture and fixture marred and half destroyed from these battles. In fits of anger Gail had carved initials into the furniture, and the bedroom door was covered with hammer marks made when Gail had tried to invade her parents' room after they had locked themselves in in desperation. After the upholstery had been destroyed the mother had bought slipcovers but Gail had cut them into ribbons. She also had torn down the shades and drapes from the windows. The parents had put up with all this because Gail's psychiatrist implored them to be patient. The parents said that the doctor had complied with Gail's request not to talk about certain topics, for instance, the word *food* was absolutely forbidden. He also urged the parents never to talk about food, but just to obey the patient.

Gail only left the apartment to go to her doctor's office three times a week. She also had the privilege of phoning him whenever she felt anxious. Otherwise she kept entirely to herself, except for phoning the parents at the store to give them orders. This stage of affairs lasted one and a half years, the parents coming in three times a day and bringing her prepared food. This food had to be the exact amount that would keep Gail from gaining weight. If she gained as much as half a pound she would create a violent scene.

It became apparent that not only was no progress being made but that the whole situation had deteriorated, and Gail became more and more withdrawn. But she absolutely refused to enter the hospital as a voluntary patient. This was just one more of her parents' schemes to get rid of her. Things stayed in this stalemate until one day the mother reacted to her violence and began shouting and throwing things. This was so terrifying to Gail that she consented to hospitalization. "I did not know what was happening to my mother." She felt she must have done something wrong because she had caused this terrible outburst and felt she was no longer in control of her mother.

During the first few months at the hospital the effort to keep her weight under control remained her chief preoccupation. Since people in the hospital did not submit to her dietary demands, this was a strenuous task. She had brought her own scale and weighed herself every day and did not eat if she had gained an ounce. Things changed when an attractive young male patient spoke to her. This indicated to Gail that he was going to fall in love with her. She set out to accomplish this with all her manipulative skills, with the result that he fled and openly rebuffed her. Even now, many months later, she is indignant and bewildered that he did not want to love her even though she was at the perfect weight of 96 lbs and could be glamorous whenever she wanted. Actually she dressed up or was well-groomed only a few times during their brief relationship. Then she became conspicuously sloppy, expecting that since he knew she could be well-dressed if she wanted to be, he should admire her beauty even when she was dirty and neglected. Immediately after this rebuff she began to gain weight rapidly, reaching 150 lbs, within 2 or 3 months. She dressed now in maternity clothes with the expressed intent of creating the impression of being pregnant. This to her was less shameful and aroused less guilt than appearing fat. The idea of intercourse and pregnancy, however, was revolting to her. If it were not painful she would have had her uterus removed, just to be safe.

I became familiar with Gail only after her first physician had left this hospital. She had greeted her new physician with a sarcastic outburst: "I hate you already. You can never be Dr. X. I can see with one look that you are inexperienced, impervious and do not know much psychiatry." These accusations persisted through several treatment sessions. Her new doctor felt discouraged, and with justification. In spite of therapeutic efforts for eight or ten years, including one year at the Psychiatric Institute, the course had been downhill. He asked for help in evaluating the situation, for supervision if it was felt that anything could be done.

In reviewing the previous treatment approaches it became apparent that they had been conducted according to the principle of avoiding past errors, be it that of the parents or the previous psychiatrist, and of confronting the patient with her manipulative behavior and power struggle. The underlying conceptual delusions about herself and all human relatedness had *not* been recognized and therefore had remained unexplored and uncorrected. Actually Gail was unusually clear on this point—but the significance of her frequent statements had been missed. In a conference together with her parents she burst out: "I tried to remake my parents all through my life. I wanted to put them in a different role, make them warm and understanding so that they could raise me better. It is their fault that I am not a good child. What I am now, my parents have created. I'm the product of their creation. The reason that people don't like me is because I am no good; but that is because my parents did not know how to raise me. It is all their fault." There was a note of despair when she added: "Don't they see how much I suffer, don't they see how unhappy I am about being a brat, always fighting and arguing." Being thin was one way of being something in her own right, not quite her parents' product. They always had pushed food on her and wanted her to be fat. Now she is quite heavy and she is infuriated when her father greets her: "Oh, you look so much better now."

The patient was quite concrete in her assumptions (and her parents shared her delusion) that a child remains the parents' property and creation. The mother had been very devoted and attached to a little niece, Gail's five-year-old cousin. She had adored this child, a cuddly and plump baby. When Gail was born, the mother was dreadfully disappointed because her baby was long and stringy, not plump at all. She set out to change her into this dream child and it became her desperate life's work to make her skinny child plump and pleasant.

The result was this tragedy of mutual blame and guilt. I have called the interaction of this family the Frankenstein Theme. The daughter, conceived of as her parents' creation, had turned monster-like against her creators, but appearances notwithstanding, basically not in aggression but in a desperate effort to change her parents so that they would undo their errors and recreate her in a better mold. The deep conviction of her own helplessness was vividly acted out in the dieting arrangement, which in turn must be conceived of as a consequence of her inability to recognize correctly hunger or satiation; hence the urgency with which she demanded control over her own bodily needs through the parents.

It is too soon to say whether this new orientation toward her problems will be successful. There has been a decided change in her attitude toward treatment; there seems to be a glimmer of hope that she can become a better person without having to change her parents first.* I have reported on this patient, although I have many others whom I know more intimately, because she expressed with startling and dramatic directness what I have come to recognize as crucial issues in many patients with serious eating disorders, namely *the basic delusion of not having an identity of their own,* of not even owning their body and its sensations, with the *specific inability of recognizing hunger as a sign of nutritional need.* Whatever we know about regulatory centers in the midbrain, these patients act as if for them the regulation for food intake was outside their own bodies.

Discussion: I have emphasized two traits, the *inability to recognize hunger* and other bodily sensations, and *lack of awareness of living one's own life,* as being of fundamental significance for the development of severe eating disturbances. In my struggles to come to a more precise understanding of the processes that go on within a fat person and lead to his becoming disoriented about his body and its sensations, his self-awareness and social relations, I gradually became aware that the whole problem needed to be approached on a different level of complexity than that of analyzing the psychodynamic and motivational aspects of his problems and life situation. We are in the habit of using adult emotional terms in describing a child's development and how he must have felt as an infant or a child, and we often forget that we really do not know and cannot know how an infant or young child feels, or out of what motives he acts.

The same holds true for the use of language in our theoretical formulations. It took some time before I became aware that statements such as that people overeat because they feel frustrated, or substitute food for love and security really explain nothing. These and other pronouncements about the symbolic meaning of food, or of the large body size, have become very popular. The trouble is not that these statements are entirely in error (I could illustrate the above points readily with new examples), but they do not go far enough. They fail to explain what is wrong with these patients, what has happened in the course of their development so that they perceive, or misperceive, their bodily sensations so that *the nutritional function can be misused in the service of complex emotional and interpersonal problems.* Restating the problem as a question on a different level resulted in a decisive change in my theoretical concepts. Detailed information about early and also later eating experiences, both in obesity and anorexia nervosa, suggests that this important function needs to be learned and that the learning process can miscarry when the responses of the environment and the verbal and conceptual communication that accompanies it are confusing and misleading. Until then I had tacitly

---

* Details about her subsequent treatment will be given in Chapter 17.

assumed that the organism "knows" its bodily sensations and could recognize its "drives," and that on a primitive level of homeostatic regulation an unsatisfied need would lead to corrective behavior. If things go well a child will learn to identify his body needs correctly and to satisfy them in ways that are biologically appropriate and at the same time proper for his social and cultural setting. If the innate needs of the child and the environmental responses are poorly attuned to each other, a perplexing confusion in his conceptual awareness will result.

Such individuals do not recognize when they are hungry or satiated, nor do they differentiate need for food from other uncomfortable sensations and feelings. They need signals coming from the outside to know when to eat and how much; their own inner awareness has not been programmed correctly. In our clinical work we are not apt to ask for this type of information as long as we assume that human beings have an inborn knowledge of how their body feels. Nutrition is of course not the only function that is misperceived or misused in this way. Such people also have difficulties in identifying other bodily sensations or interpersonal situations. But since disturbances in eating are reflected in a changed body size we are in the habit of labeling people according to this conspicuous deviation. In patients with other problems, e.g., homosexuality, incorrect conceptualization of bodily states can also be detected.

The early histories often fail to give evidence of gross neglect, and the commonly used terms like rejection or lack of proper love, do not help us understand the problem. The details one usually learns are quite subtle; the important aspect is whether *the response to the child's need was appropriate, or was superimposed according to what the mother felt he needed*, often mistakenly.

Corroborative Experimental Evidence

When these theoretical deductions from clinical observations were first formulated there was little experimental work and few clinical observations by others to support them. Considering the fact that it is little more than 10 years since their publication the amount of confirming evidence is rather impressive.

In pursuit of this question Coddington and I designed an experimental situation whereby measured amounts of food were introduced into the stomach of 74 subjects of normal and abnormal weights (8). Marked individual differences were observed in their accuracy of recognizing whether or not, and how much, food had been received. Some healthy normal subjects were consistently accurate; others, though of normal weight, were less so. Obese and anorexic patients were significantly more inaccurate than subjects of normal weight.

In a study of the gastric motility of 8 anorexia patients and 10 matched controls, Silverstone and Russell (18) found that the gastric activity of anorexia patients was similar to that found in normal subjects; however, when questioned about their sensations of hunger, they usually denied feeling anything. After refeeding there was a slight but not significant reduction in gastric activity. The puzzling aspect of these observations is that patients who deny that they ever feel hungry can still sense contractions though they interpret them abnormally.

Similar observations had previously been reported by Stunkard (19). Fasting obese women usually failed to report awareness of hunger during the presence of stomach contractions, whereas nonobese women usually reported hunger during contractions of the empty stomach, and no hunger during the absence of such contractions. Stunkard interpreted this "denial of hunger" as an indication of some conflict over eating which obese subjects experienced in the face of social disapproval, and that this conflict altered a person's perception of visceral stimuli. In subsequent observations he could demonstrate that this error in the reporting of hunger during gastric motility was not due to an imperfect nervous apparatus, but contained strong elements of learned behavior. He was able to "teach" some of his obese subjects to detect gastric contractions and this learning persisted for some time (20). But the improvement in the ability to detect gastric contractions had no apparent effect on the ability to control body weight.

Further support for the assumption of a perceptual and conceptual disturbance came from a series of ingenious experiments by Schachter (17) in which external factors were manipulated and which showed that obese subjects are affected by external cues such as the sight of food, its availability, and apparent passage of time, whereas subjects of normal weight eat according to enteroceptive determinants. Schachter concluded that the set of bodily symptoms a subject labels as "hunger" differs for obese and normal subjects. While the manipulations had a major effect on the amounts eaten by normal subjects, nothing seemed to have a substantial effect on the amounts eaten by obese subjects.

Most of the subjects were college students who were included in the experiment on the basis of widely varying weight excess, ranging from 14% to 75%; no information is given as to how the difference in weight affected the test results. There is also no comment on the psychiatric or personality problems of these subjects, though their ability to function suggests that they were essentially healthy, in contrast to the "patients" on whom the clinical reports are based. The majority of his subjects were students, which suggests that they were young, representing juvenile obesity, and this leaves open the question of whether these findings apply also to middle-age obesity. These studies also fail to consider the importance of the multiple, individually different, internal, non-nutritional cues, such as frustration, depression, and anxiety, which play such a significant role in clinically obese patients who are often unresponsive to arousal of fear in to them irrelevant situations, as is done in an experimental setting. The findings give important support to the clinical observation that obese people differ from normal ones in being unable to recognize and to conceptualize such an important bodily need as hunger.

Recently, Cabanac and Duclaux (7) reported a series of experiments in which obese subjects differed from normal ones in their response to sucrose; normal subjects experienced the taste of glucose solutions as pleasant, but after being loaded for an hour with glucose solutions they experienced oral sucrose stimuli as unpleasant. In contrast, obese subjects did not change their responses to the sucrose stimulus from pleasant to unpleasant after they had been sated with glucose solution. The authors feel that these data lend support to the theory that obese people are unaware of internal signals for control of food intake, though the experiments do not indicate whether this phenomenon is a cause or a result of the obese state.

While these considerations are relatively new to clinicians, physiologists have been familiar with them for some time. When Hebb, in 1949, summarized his experiences and those of others in his book, *The Organization of Behavior*, he pointed out that the sensation of hunger was not inborn (11). Lack of food, the state of nutritional deprivation, is apt to be disruptive of behavior. Even in the rat certain learning knowledge must be acquired for appropriate feeding behavior. In man, with his much more complex brain structure, the ways of learning are also more complex. Hebb felt that in a phenomenon such as hunger the role of learning is often dismissed because the function has been traditionally conceived as an innate drive, as a basic part of the organism's physiological endowment, subject only to the most superficial modifications. Wolff's (22) observations on newborn infants go in the same direction, showing that in neonates hunger has a disorganizing effect on goal-directed activities after an initial augmenting phase.

Further support for the assumption that seemingly innate functions require learning experiences early in life comes from animal observations where experiments like raising animals in complete isolation can be carried out with an extreme degree of consistency not possible in experiments using humans. Probably best known are the observations by Harlow, who studied the effect on infant monkeys of complete isolation from the mothers in experiments that had been designed to clarify the development of "affectional systems." These infant monkeys were removed from their mothers at birth and were given free access to wire dummies (referred to as "mothers") to whom they could cling without restriction; some of these dummies were covered by soft terry cloth. It had been expected that monkeys with access to cloth covered dummies would grow up more affectionate and secure than the other group who had access only to raw wire dummies (10). This expectation was not fulfilled. On the contrary, when fully grown, both groups of monkeys were grossly abnormal, apathetic, stereotyped in their responses, suffering from abiding affectional deficiency, inadequate sex behavior (though having undergone normal physiological puberty), and exhibiting many bizarre mouthing habits. One may consider as the outstanding deficit in this setting the *absence of response*, confirming, reinforcing, or inhibiting, from a live mother monkey to behavior initiated by the infant. Thus these monkeys were deprived of learning experiences essential for the organization of usable and adaptive behavior.

Three of these isolated monkeys, who had been removed from their mothers within 24 hours of birth and raised in total isolation for the next 12 months, were studied in Mirsky's laboratory (15). The isolates were between 4 and 5 years old at that time and had spent the preceding 3 years in a group of monkeys. In conditioning experiments it was found that their capacity to acquire instrumental and cardiac responses to avoidance stimuli had not been affected. However, when paired for such studies with feral monkeys, the isolates were totally incapable of responding either physiologically or instrumentally to the nonverbal facial expressions of other monkeys, and were also seriously impaired in sending recognizable "messages" to others. This suggests that the ability to express normally or interpret accurately the social behavior of others of their species must be acquired by monkeys during early infancy.

During these experiments it was observed that the isolates ingested larger quantities of fluid than others (16). The question of their food intake was subsequently studied. Throughout their lives they had received the same amount of food as other members of their species and their weights were normal. When larger amounts were given their intake rapidly increased and the supply was always low or exhausted when checked, however much food had been offered. Laboratory-raised infant baboons who were fed through a self-feeding device became visibly fat and at age 4 months weighed 60% more than infant baboons who were raised on amounts leading to a normal weight increase (21). Isolation and absence of stimulation with others result in defective organization in humans, too, often with the inability to control food intake or to express pain in response to injury.

These studies and observations demonstrate beyond any doubt that seemingly innate functions, specifically hunger, require early learning experiences in order to become organized into distinct and useful behavior patterns.

Feeding, Feedback, and Personality

How does this learning occur and how is the disordered hunger awareness related to the severe personality problems, even schizophrenic disorganization, that handicap obese and anorexic patients? Certain common features could be recognized in their behavior in the treatment situation, their transactions with various members of their families, and from their interpersonal experiences in school, in work situations, and friendships: they experience themselves as not being in control of their behavior, needs, and impulses, as not owning their own bodies, as not having a center of gravity within themselves. Instead, they feel under the influence and direction of external forces. They act as if their body and behavior were the product of other people's influences and actions. From detailed reconstructions of their developmental histories, it could be recognized that they had certain distorting experiences in common, namely, absence or paucity of appropriate and confirming responses to signals indicating their needs and other forms of self-expression (4,5,6).

Expressed in the simplest possible language, I have formulated a model of child development that permits the integration of innate and experiential factors for a wide range of functions. Though immature, a newborn infant is not utterly helpless or completely dependent as has often been stated. The seeming helplessness is related to his functional immaturity, in particular his inability to move about. In spite of this the newborn infant is a remarkably capable organism from birth on. He can see, hear, and smell; he is sensitive to pain and touch and is able to suck the finger or the nipple when inserted into his mouth. He can thrash and kick his feet and can turn his head in the direction in which his cheek is touched. He can cry, cough, turn away, swallow, vomit, smack his lips, and chew his fingers. His cry is probably his most important tool, through which he can give cues and signals indicating his discomforts, wants, and needs. How the cries are responded to, fulfilled, or neglected appears to be the crucial point for his becoming aware of his needs. From birth on, *two* basic forms of behavior must be differentiated, namely behavior *initiated* in the infant, and behavior in *response* to stimuli from the outside. This distinction applies to both the biological and the social-emotional field, and also to pleasure or pain-producing states. The mother's behavior in relation to the child is either *responsive* or *stimulating*. The interaction between the environment and the infant can be rated as *appropriate* or *inappropriate*, depending on whether it serves his survival and development or disregards or distorts it. These elementary distinctions permit the dynamic analysis, irrespective of the specific area or content of the problem, of an amazingly large variety of different situations and events.

This theoretical frame goes beyond, or avoids, the traditional dichotomy of somatic and psychological aspects of development. An infant handicapped by genetic factors, or suffering from paranatal injuries or confusing earliest experiences, is apt to give clues to his needs that are weak, indistinct, or contradictory. It would be a difficult task for any mother to satisfy them appropriately, and will be completely confusing to a mother who herself is emotionally disturbed, preoccupied with her own problems, and impervious to expressions of a child's needs.

The biological preparation for each learning step must have a genetic determination. But this does not mean that the development of the genetic learning potential is independent of environmental influences. The newborn is no more a tabula rasa than a homunculus. The infant can learn certain things only at certain times, but it seems that these time periods are much longer than what has been recognized as "critical periods" in ethological studies. For feeding behavior this learning begins at the moment of birth.

Appropriate responses to clues coming from the infant, in the biological field as well as in the intellectual, social, and emotional field, are necessary for the child to organize the *significant building stones for the development of self-awareness and self-effectiveness.* If confirmation and reinforcement of his own initially rather undifferentiated needs and impulses have been absent, or have been contradictory or inaccurate, then a child will grow up perplexed when trying to differentiate between disturbances in his biological field and emotional and interpersonal experiences, and he will be apt to misinterpret deformities in his self-body concept as externally induced. Thus he will become an individual deficient in his sense of separateness, with "diffuse ego boundaries," and will feel helpless under the influence of external forces.

For healthy development, experiences in both modalities are essential: confirmation of clues originating in the child and his responses to outside stimuli. It must be assumed that this applies to all areas of development. How it operates can be observed in the eating function. When a mother offers food in response to signals indicating nutritional need, the infant will gradually develop the engram of "hunger" as a sensation distinct from other tensions or needs. If, on the other hand, a mother's reaction is continuously inappropriate, be it neglectful, oversolicitous, inhibiting, or indiscriminately permissive, the outcome for the child will be a perplexing confusion. When he is older he will not be able to discriminate between being hungry or sated, or between nutritional need and some other discomfort or tension. At the extremes of eating disorders, one finds the grotesquely obese person who is haunted by the fear of starvation, and the emaciated anorexic who is oblivious to the pangs of hunger and other symptoms characteristic of chronic undernourishment. Even more confusing to the child are the actions of a mother who is continuously preoccupied with herself; whatever a child does, it is interpreted as expressing something about the mother. In such a setting noneating may be equated with criticism of the mother, and eating as expressing happiness and love.

Correct or incorrect learning experiences are codified in the brain on various levels for conceptual representation, depending on the stage of brain maturation and the emotional state at the time of the experience. The learning process is not restricted to infancy but is continued throughout childhood. The content of this learning relates to the whole range of experiences that characterize human life. The larger the area of appropriate responses to the various expressions of a child's needs and impulses, the more differentiated will the child become in identifying his bodily experiences, and other sensations, thoughts, and feelings as arising within him, and as distinct from the human or nonhuman environment. In other words, he will grow into a person who, regardless of difficulties of living, feels essentially self-directed in his experiences. Failure of regular and persistent appropriate responses to his needs deprives the developing child of the essential groundwork for acquiring his own "body identity" with discriminating perceptual and conceptual awareness of his own functions.

A child growing up this way may acquire the facade of adequate functioning by robot-like submission to the environmental demands. The gross defect in initiative and active self-experience will become manifest when he is confronted with new situations for which the distorted routines of his background have left him unprepared. Puberty is frequently the time when this confrontation takes place, or leaving home, such as going to summer camp or college. Such an individual may feel helpless under the impact of his bodily urges, or he may feel controlled from the outside, *like not owning his own sensations and his own body*. The clinical impression may be that of defective regulation in the lower brain centers, which had been supplied with incorrect or contradictory information during the early developmental period.

In this theoretical model of child-mother interaction the emphasis has been on what fails to go right, and not on any particular traumatic event. The child is conceived as *an active participant* in this process of his own development, not just as responding to stimuli from within or without. His innate maturing processes are, of course, important, but *awareness* of himself as a separate individual evolves only through *experiences* and *continuous interaction* with the environment. In these transactions the infant himself gives the clues to his needs and the sense of adequacy and competence he achieves in his development is related to the appropriateness with which his needs are met. It is important whether they are fulfilled in a way that is attuned to the child's own expression, or whether they are disregarded, either completely neglected or fulfilled in a mechanical way, as, for instance, when the right amount of calories is rigidly given according to a prescribed fixed schedule.

In this model "good mothering," loving care, can be expressed in functional terms as providing careful and discriminating attention to a child's expression of biological needs, such as giving food when his cry indicates nutritional need. Thereby the mother will selectively strengthen certain aspects of his behavior and help him in establishing discriminating concepts about his inner states, such as being "hungry," or being "sated," or "having had enough." Thus the child gradually learns to differentiate between various bodily needs, and, with increasing maturity, becomes accurate in identifying and presenting his needs, and able to act in ways appropriate for their satisfaction. In contrast, when food is given as the great pacifier, without regard for the real reason for a child's discomfort, or as reward for "good" (that is compliant) behavior, and is withheld as punishment for undesirable or disapproved actions, he will grow up confused and unable to differentiate between various needs, feeling helpless in controlling his biological urges and emotional impulses.

A comment needs to be made on the different meanings of "learning." I have used the word here as indicating the achievement of discriminating mastery over and use of an innate but unpracticed potential, which becomes organized only through interactional experiences, such as learning to walk upright, or recognizing nutritional need as hunger. This usage is distinct from the way the word "learning" is used in behavioristic learning theories which conceive of the mind as more or less a blank on which an experimenter, through external conditioning such as reward or punishment, can imprint different capacities for performances which may be completely incongruent to an organism's needs.

Converging Clinical Evidence

Some recent studies of early development have focused directly on the patterns of the mother-child interaction in the early feeding experiences. Studying the sucking behavior of the neonate, Kron came to the conclusion that there were some hypothetical mechanisms by which constitutional and experiential factors collaborated in the earliest behavior development (13). The neonate's primary behavior is dominated by nonspecific appetitional responses which wax and wane with changes in his central nervous system arousal. During this period the mother provides reinforcing stimuli to the infant. To do so she must learn to detect the infant's cyclic changes in physiological state, and adjust the schedule accordingly.

In an extensive study of mother-child interaction in the first 3 months of life, Ainsworth and Bell focused on feeding situations, since the largest proportion of such interaction has reference to feeding (1). The study involved 26 babies of white, middle-class families who were under the care of pediatricians in private practice and on whose records overweight and underweight judgments were based.

The multiple features of the feeding interaction could be reduced to four chief aspects, the *timing of the feeding*, determination of the *amount of food ingested* and the end of feeding, the mother's handling of her *baby's preferences* in kind of food, and the *pacing of the rate* of the baby's intake. It was recognized that the factor of greatest importance was the *mother's response to the baby's signals*, her allowing the baby to determine the amount of food, her handling of rejection of new or disliked food, and whether her feeding was geared to the child's own rate, permitting him to slow down or to drowse, or whether she would let the milk come too fast.

In the patterns at the top of the list the *baby was an active partner* and the *mothers* showed themselves *highly sensitive to the signals* of their babies, in contrast to those toward the end of the list where the mothers were more and more dominant in their transactions. The sensitive mothers tended to establish a schedule with gentle nudging toward regulatory rather than rigid control, or a demand feeding with staving off in a sociable way intended to give the baby pleasure. *The prime emphasis was on gratifying the baby.*

Next to the sensitive mothers came those, both in the demand or schedule group, who tended to *overfeed* their babies, in *attempts to gratify them.* In another pattern, low in the grouping, the mothers *overstuffed* their babies with the intent of *making them sleep a long time* and thus demand little attention from them. The investigators felt that this distinction in intent was important. This is in agreement with clinical observations on obese children where one finds mothers who are loving and accepting of their child, though they continuously overfeed him, and others who basically reject the child but stuff him with food and are impervious to his other needs and efforts at self-expression. The mothers who would overfeed to gratify the baby tended to treat too broad a spectrum of cues and signals as if they indicated hunger. Consequently the babies were overfed, although both mother and baby seemed to enjoy the prolonged contact.

In the pattern of schedule with too much staving off, or of pseudo-demand with an impatient mother, the babies tended to be poorly nourished. These babies were not permitted to be active participants in the feeding situation, nor were they well-regulated in their rhythms in the first 3 months. The deliberately overstuffed babies belonged to this group. In the lowest group, that of rigid schedule by the clock or arbitrary feeding, the babies had unhappy feeding experiences. In the last group in particular, the mothers were often disturbed, detached, and insensitive to the baby's signals. The timing of feedings was erratic, but the most conspicuous feature was the forced nature of the feeding.

When rated at 12 months, the infants in whom the feeding interaction had been most appropriate to their needs, permitting them active participation, showed the strongest attachment to their mothers, with a clear-cut tendency to seek her proximity, and to express distress at her absence. They made active efforts to gain and maintain contact with her. In contrast babies with inappropriate feeding experiences, showed little or no tendency to seek proximity, interaction, or contact with the mother and little or no tendency to cling when picked up or to resist being released. They tended either to ignore the mother on her return, or to turn away or go away from her.

There was a third group which included the one of pseudo-demand with overfeeding, in which children were distressed by separation, but showed less ability to use the mother as a secure basis from which they could enjoy exploring the strange environment. They generally displayed more maladaptive behavior in relation to new and strange situations. This observation is in good agreement with what is learned in retrospective accounts of the early behavior of emotionally disturbed fat children, namely that of anxious clinging to the mother, extreme shyness, and fear of new situations and contacts. There were six overfed babies and two of the mothers themselves had weight problems, but the babies who were most overweight had mothers who were not plump. The babies maintained their overweight and the mothers persisted in overfeeding them.

An interesting example of pathogenic, nonappropriate transactional patterns between a mother and her two small children was described by Henry, in his naturalistic observations of families who had produced a hospitalized schizophrenic child (12). During this study he lived in a family in which there were younger children. He observed that there was no absence of "maternal love and affection" and the children turned to their mother for comfort. He described in detail, however, the problems surrounding the feeding of a 5-month-old girl and a 16-month-old boy. The mother appeared to be disoriented about time and modified the feeding schedule at will, with complete disregard for the children's urgent crying for food. His overall summation of her attitude toward the feeding of the children was that it was "biologically markedly inappropriate." The feeding records duplicated each other with monotonous sameness day in and day out. They showed a series of patterned elements, of the mother overpowering the children with food when they rejected it after they had been left to cry to a high pitch or exhaustion, or her disregarding the defensive maneuvers against this forced feeding, often of items that seemed inappropriate, such as solid food to the crying 5-month-old baby and baby food to the 16-month-old boy, and complete nonattention to expressed dislikes. The older child had learned to perceive the feeding complex as painful in part, but he did not dislike food. He engaged simultaneously in both avoidant and appetitive behavior in the presence of a gratifying stimulus and he perceived the stimulus simultaneously in contradictory ways. Henry generalized that every mother expresses her conception of what the child is in her feeding behavior, and in the long run she communicates this to the child. In this way, the manner of feeding becomes a message system telling the child what his mother thinks of him. Henry suggested the term "pathogenic metamorphosis" for the distorting process. Confusion about bodily states and bodily identity is commonly observed in schizophrenic patients.

As illustration of inappropriate responses of a mother to her child's needs I should like to cite the developmental history of an extremely fat and indolent boy, Saul, who at age 14 weighed nearly 300 lbs, at a height of 5'5". According to the first information he had "always" been an insatiable eater; then it was learned that his desire for food had been without limits only since he was 10 months old.

Saul was the third child in a family with two older sisters. In this orthodox Jewish family, the husband and father-in-law had prevailed upon the mother to have another child because they wanted a male child, but she had only reluctantly consented. The boy weighed only 5 lbs at birth, was a difficult feeder and would spit up the formula. The pattern of slow feeding and spitting continued for several months. The father was more patient than the mother and he would get up in the night and sit for as long as two hours holding the baby and feeding him. At 2½ months, Saul weighed 7½ lbs, and still needed to be coaxed while eating. When he was 3 or 4 months old, the mother developed a backache from which she has suffered recurrently and for which no organic cause has been discovered at any time. The backache made it impossible for her to lean over the crib or to lift the baby. When he was able to sit in a high chair the mother still could not lift him so he sat for long stretches and would become restless and cry. The mother discovered that she could keep him quiet by sticking a cookie into his mouth. This would not keep him quiet for very long and the number of cookies increased. Saul's weight was normal at 8 months, but he had become decidedly chubby by 10 months. The mother complained that no amount of food would keep him quiet, and as her rate of feeding increased so did his weight. By 2 years of age he weighed 65 lbs, and was taken for study to a renowned medical center. He was placed on a 500-calorie diet and lost some weight. The family felt Saul was becoming too weak and the caloric intake was increased. The grandfather, as well as the father, made light of the mother's concern about the rapidly increasing weight, and as Saul grew older he would visit his grandfather, who would cook for him all day long.

This history gives evidence of a grotesquely inappropriate learning experience: "food" was offered as a cure-all for whatever discomfort the baby's crying expressed. The mother had felt at all times that this child was "too much" for her and paid very little attention to him, except for keeping him quiet by stuffing him with food. This early "programming" of his regulatory centers became his permanent pattern. This "brainwashing" occurred at a time when infants begin to show differentiated perception, cognition, and outward-directed, exploring behavior, to which Saul's mother failed to respond in an encouraging way. Other modalities of his developmental needs were disregarded; there was no encouragement toward any physical activities, or expression of initiative and autonomy.

The early feeding histories of many fat and anorexic patients have been reconstructed in great detail. Often they are conspicuous by their blandness. The parents feel there is nothing to report: the child never gave any trouble, ate exactly what was put before him; the mother was the envy of her friends and neighbors because her child did not fuss about food, nor

was he negativistic during the classic "period of resistance." This goodness was reported for other areas too, like cleanliness, no rough play or
destructive behavior, and no disobedience or talking back. Several mothers of anorexic or fat schizophrenic patients reported with pride how they
had paraded their 3- or 4-year-old girls, white gloves on their little hands
and not a speck of dirt on their dresses, through the theater district in
hopes of arousing the interest of a producer who might discover her child
as an actress. Others would report how they always "anticipated" their
child's needs, never permitting him to "feel hungry." A generation ago
such mothers would report with much self-satisfaction that they waited for
exactly the minute for which the feeding was scheduled and made sure
that the child took every drop of the prescribed amount (6).

I have focused here mainly on the transactional patterns surrounding
the feeding situation as a nonverbal presymbolic communication. Frequently distorting feeding experiences occur together with continuous distortions in verbal communication, with direct mislabeling of a child's
feeling state, such as that he *must* be hungry (or cold, or tired), regardless
of the child's own experience. This mislabeling applies also to a child's
role in the family, and his mood. Specifically, he is not allowed to be
"unhappy" because this would imply an insult to the parents' conviction
of their superiority. Thus a child comes to mistrust the legitimacy of his
own feelings and experiences.

In order to maintain even the most unstable equilibrium with the persons in his environment on whom he is most dependent, such a child is
obliged to accept these distorted conceptions about his body and body
functions and thus is prevented from developing a clearly differentiated
body scheme and sense of competence. When his own needs are forced to
his attention, either through demands of the culture for self-reliance, or
through the outbreak into awareness of his own accumulated frustration,
he experiences his inability to understand and satisfy these needs as a
chaotic disintegration of the unity of body and self, and as his failure
in making contact with others with integrated body selves.

Hunger Awareness and Psychoanalytic Theory

These concepts of child development as reciprocal transactional processes
developed out of observations of patients in psychoanalytic treatment.
The study of what is usually called transference gave clues to the disturbances in self-concepts, including deficits in the sense of personal identity
and effectiveness and conceptual confusion about eating, and to the patterns of the past interpersonal experiences. To what extent does this formulation agree with, or differ from, the traditional psychoanalytic concepts? There is agreement on the fundamental issue, that personality
develops out of the dynamic interaction and experiences of the child with
the people in his environment. Psychoanalytic views on this interplay have
changed, and the concepts I have presented here are in better agreement
now, in the 1970's, with the increasing emphasis in psychoanalysis on ego

psychology, than they were during the 1950's when they were first formulated.

I consider the falsification in the perception of bodily states and the lack of awareness of the effectiveness of one's own thoughts and actions as of fundamental importance. The psychodynamic problems on which we usually focus may be considered efforts at compensating for these deficiencies. Lacking the essential tools for the subsequent developmental steps, a child is bound to be continuously bewildered and anxious, incapable of effective self-assertion in an incomprehensible world. Thus he may develop any one of the disturbed emotional reactions and defense mechanisms characteristic of the wide variety of psychiatric disorders.

The recognition of the intricate ways through which human factors impinge on all biological functions is Freud's great contribution to human understanding. He interpreted it as indicating that an erotic or "libidinal" component attached itself to the various bodily functions. One may conceive of this also in the reversed order. All body functions, including the sexual drive, are exposed to a variety of appropriate or inappropriate learning experiences, reinforcements, distortions, or even extinction due to the immaturity of the human neonate and the long period of dependency on others. They may develop normally, and then are available for use in the fulfillment of their proper function, or they may develop abnormally and then will be misused in the service of neurotic or psychotic conflicts.

The model of early development as reciprocal transaction is in good agreement with other recent studies; some of these were carried out by psychologists, others by child analysts. Discussions of and research into early psychological events have become much more clearly defined, and have shifted toward an examination of the ongoing interactions between infant and mother and other experiences. They no longer focus on a particular "trauma" during one or the other specific libidinal phase, but on the steps necessary for progressive maturation, on what encourages or hinders this process. The traditional psychoanalytic postulate that an unalterable personality structure would become predetermined through "fixation" or other vicissitudes of the instincts has been replaced by concepts of the innate neurophysiological structures being organized through the infant's early experiential transactions. Such early experiences bias his perceptions and action patterns so that he responds to subsequent situations, at least initially, in the light of these early experiences, which in turn are in a continuous reciprocal or circular interaction with earlier structures and later transformations. In a way these newer concepts give concrete content and meaning to many of the old expressions that are still widely used. To give a few examples: what has been called "fixation" can be redefined as an inadequate and deficient organization of a body function so that it remains vaguely defined and cannot be used effectively and appropriately. Deficits in necessary developmental experiences, unless corrected, will interfere with the next step. However, the far-reaching effects of early deficits do *not* need to be conceived of as "repetition compulsions" but rather as an inability to function appropriately when the necessary tools and inner guides are inadequately conceptualized and developed.

I find it difficult to compare my concepts to the one or other schools of psychoanalytic thought, except to say that most of the differences appear to be more theoretical constructs than based on factual events. Controversies between libidinal or interpersonal theories have no realistic basis, since biological development requires close and continuous interaction with another person. It is a mere abstraction which neglects the facts of human development to speak of "drives" without relation to the interpersonal environment, or of "interpersonal relations" without a biological body attached to them.

My emphasis on early feeding experiences as a pacesetter for infant-mother interaction does not imply an effort to revive the old psychoanalytic hypothesis that the gratification of oral drives foreshadows in a deterministic way later personality traits and emotional health or sickness. On the contrary, all modern evidence speaks against any concept that may still linger on of innate instincts, sex, hunger, or otherwise, which in a preformed way would carry their own messages to the conscious or unconscious mind. Such a view is incompatible with modern concepts of early development.

BIBLIOGRAPHY

1. Ainsworth, M. D. S., and Bell, S. M., Some contemporary patterns of mother-infant interaction in the feeding situation, pp. 133–170, in *Stimulation in Early Infancy*, Academic Press, New York, 1969.
2. Bruch, H., Conceptual confusion in eating disorders, J. Nerv. Ment. Dis., 133:46–54, 1961.
3. Bruch, H., Transformation of oral impulses in eating disorders: A conceptual approach, Psychiat. Quart., 35:458–481, 1961.
4. Bruch, H., Falsification of bodily needs and body concept in schizophrenia, Arch. Gen. Psychiat. (Chicago), 6:18–24, 1962.
5. Bruch, H., Hunger and instinct, J. Nerv. Ment. Dis., 149:91–114, 1969.
6. Bruch, H., Instinct and interpersonal experience, Comp. Psychiat., 11:495–506, 1970.
7. Cabanac, M., and Duclaux, R., Obesity: Absence of satiety aversion to sucrose, Science, 168:496–497, 1970.
8. Coddington, R. D., and Bruch, H., Gastric perceptivity in normal, obese and schizophrenic subjects, Psychosomatics, 11:571–579, 1970.
9. Hamburger, W. W., Emotional aspects of obesity, Med. Clin. N. Amer., 33:483–499, 1951.
10. Harlow, H. F., and Harlow, M., Learning to love, Amer. Sci., 54:244–272, 1966.
11. Hebb, D. O., *The Organization of Behavior*, Wiley, New York, 1949.
12. Henry, J., The naturalistic observation of the families of schizophrenic children, pp. 119–137, in *Recent Research Looking Toward Preventive Intervention*, R. H. Ojemann, ed., State University of Iowa, Iowa City, 1961.

13. Kron, R. E., The effect of arousal and of learning upon sucking behavior in the newborn, Recent Advances Biol. Psychiat., 10:302–313, 1968.

14. Langer, S. K., *Mind: An Essay on Human Feeling*, Johns Hopkins University Press, Baltimore, 1967.

15. Miller, R. E., Caul, W. F., and Mirsky, I. A., Communication of affects between feral and socially isolated monkeys, J. Personality Soc. Psychol., 7:231–239, 1967.

16. Miller, R. E., Mirsky, I. A., Caul, W. F., and Sakata, T., Hyperphagia and poly-dipsia in socially isolated rhesus monkeys, Science, 165:1027–1028, 1969.

17. Schachter, S., Obesity and eating, Science, 161:751–756, 1968.

18. Silverstone, J. T., and Russell, G. F. M., Gastric "hunger" contractions in anorexia nervosa, Brit. J. Psychiat., 113:257–263, 1967.

19. Stunkard, A., Obesity and the denial of hunger, Psychosom. Med., 21:281–290, 1959.

20. Stunkard, A., The relationship of gastric motility and hunger. A summary of the evidence, Psychosom. Med., 33:123–134, 1971.

21. Voss, W. R., Buss, D. H., and Carroll, L. W., A self-feeding device for infant baboon liquid diets, Lab. Anim. Sci., 21:901–903, 1971.

22. Wolff, P. H., The causes, controls and organization of behavior in the neonate, Psychol. Issues, 5:1–105, 1966.

5

Family Frame and Transactions

In the previous chapter I discussed how disturbances in hunger awareness develop out of inaccuracies in the reciprocal feedback patterns in the transactions between mother and child. This had been deduced from numerous observations and studies of the psychological processes in families which had raised a child in such a way that he had become conspicuously deviant in appearance and behavior, fat or cachectic, his abnormal size the result of abnormal eating habits and activity patterns. These individual observations revealed a common feature: the mothers superimposed on the child their own concept of his needs. This chapter will deal with the manifest behavior and overall functioning of these family groups.

Obesity

Early Observations and the Family Frame of Obese Children

The first observations were made 35 years ago, at first incidentally, then systematically, in a pediatric clinic for obese children in whom various aspects of disturbed behavior gradually became apparent, in particular marked inactivity and conspicuous overeating. These children were also extremely immature and clingingly dependent on their mothers, though they were advanced in physical and intellectual development. The manifestations of these qualities were not particularly dramatic until investigated in detail, but they occurred with great regularity. For example, an obese child would often sit in the only chair in the clinic office leaving his mother to stand. If the mothers were invited to sit down, they would insist that the child keep the chair. It was also commonly observed that many obese children, even those 10 years of age and older, were unable to dress themselves without their mother's assistance. The mother of one 14-year-old boy, as a matter of routine, would go down on her knees to help him take off his shoes. Many children stood like wooden puppets while their mothers put their clothes on them or took them off. When a question was directed toward the child, either the mother answered it for him or she would hardly let the child say a word without prompting or correcting him. The hovering, anxious attitude of the mothers interfered with the seemingly simple medical prescription of reducing the child's food intake and increasing his activity. This behavior could not possibly be explained by "glandular dysfunction" in the child, but suggested some disturbance in the family relationship and the way the child had been raised.

Inquiry into the children's living habits revealed that the inability to do things for themselves extended to practically every aspect of their daily life; they were equally unskilled and inactive in games, avoided athletics, and preferred sedentary activities. This reduced activity resulted in a diminished expenditure of energy and was thus important for the development and maintenance of obesity. Detailed inquiry into the background of this all-pervasive inactivity revealed it as related to deep-seated feelings of insecurity and fear of social contacts, and to severe disturbances in the parental attitude. Investigation of the food intake, which was often found to be grotesquely large, particularly during the phase of active weight increase, revealed also the importance of emotional factors which were closely related to the emotional climate of the families.

Occasionally, though rarely, situations were encountered where outer circumstances, not inner psychological problems, had led to overfeeding. As an example, I should like to report the observations on a boy who was nearly 100% overweight at the age of 2 and who completely outgrew his obesity. This child was born during the depression years, after his father had lost his job and his parents had taken a position as a "couple" in another household. The mother felt she had to keep the baby quiet and would feed him whenever he cried, much against her conviction that a child should not be stuffed with food. He became monstrously fat, weighing 42 lbs at one year. The father was so disgusted with his son's grotesque appearance that he wouldn't pay any attention to him. However, he was open to reassurance that this was not a glandular abnormality and as soon as the family had reestablished their own household, he took an active interest in the boy, played with him, and encouraged him in sports and other activities. The mother permitted him a free choice of food, neither restricting it nor prompting him to eat more than he took spontaneously. By the time this boy was of school age he was somewhat chubby, but active, friendly, and outgoing. At the age of 10, he was a good athlete, his weight was within normal range, and he had no problems at all about eating. He underwent normal puberty and was interested in dating girls. When last seen he was 18 years old, tall and slim. He had no memories of having been obese and was amused when he was shown old pictures of himself.

This example suggests that even severe early obesity can be corrected if it is done in a way that stimulates and encourages other activities, and that normal eating patterns can be acquired after infancy. It is of particular importance to point this out today because the recent discovery of increased cell count in the adipose tissue associated with early overfeeding has left the impression that a fat baby is automatically doomed to become a fat adult. This holds true only when the factors that make for overfeeding persist, when they are related to disturbed interpersonal processes, when motor activity, aggression, and spontaneity are inhibited, resulting in confusion in bodily and emotional awareness which then becomes integrated into the permanent patterns of maladaptation that are commonly associated with persistent obesity.

Signs of such disturbed relationships have been observed with great frequency. Psychiatric and psychoanalytic investigations in the 1930's focused exclusively on individual patients. The traumatic experiences that supposedly had caused the symptoms were reconstructed from the reports of their memories. Some direct observations on parents came from child guidance clinics where the focus was on certain features of maternal behavior, labeled as "overprotective," "rejecting," "ambivalent," etc., and these attitudes were considered the causal explanation of a child's difficulties. References to the fathers or to the interaction of the whole family were conspicuous by their absence.

In our family study, which was published in 1940 as "The Family Frame of Obese Children" systematic inquiry revealed as a common feature much marital discord with open fighting and mutual contempt and with marked differences in the temperament of the parents. There was a high incidence of obesity in parents, in particular in mothers, but the most severe cases of childhood obesity were observed in families where the parents were not obese (3).

Since this early report family studies have flourished, and with increasing understanding decided changes have occurred in the style, focus, and conceptual frame. I present here some of the earlier findings because they contain the descriptive features which the physician who sees only an occasional fat patient will observe. The aim of the early family study was to furnish a survey, to uncover possible similarities in the family frame of obese children, and to discuss the prevailing fundamental trends. Subsequent studies, in particular follow-up observations on the same children, revealed that this focus, the search for a uniform picture, was a false lead, that it beclouded the fact that there were different forms of obesity even in childhood.

In the early study, which emphasized easily definable features, small family size appeared to be a point of significance. The average obese family had 2.1 children, whereas families of cardiac patients, observed at the same time, had on the average 3.9 children. In an obesity study in Denmark, carried out during the 1950's, families with an obese child were also reported to be of small size (17). On Funen, an island known for its rich and lavish food, the average number of children in an obese family was 2.6 as compared to 3.4 in control families.

The position of the fat child in the family appeared also to be unusual.

Among the 225 obese children observed in New York from 1937 to 1940, 35% were only children, and 35% were the youngest, thus 70% of the obese children were rated as being in a special position. In the Funen study, 11 among the 40 obese children were the only child in their family, and 13 were the youngest; that means 60% were in this special position. In the control group there was just one only child and 8 who were the youngest, altogether 22.5%. A more recent sociological study in Germany showed that obese men were in the position of "only" child with a higher incidence than men in a control group (15).

Even at the time of the early study the position in the family was not conceived of as an explanation for the development of obesity. Its significance lay in providing the setting for the abnormal eating experiences which were related to disturbed interpersonal processes and which, in combination with inhibition of motor activity, aggression, and spontaneity, will result in confusion in bodily and emotional awareness and permanent patterns of maladaptation with severe and persistent obesity.

A composite picture was constructed from information obtained from diverse families. Though we know now that it is not applicable to all, it contains many features which are frequently observed in families of disturbed obese patients. Mothers who are insecure in their fundamental attitude toward a child tend to compensate for this by excessive feeding and overprotective measures; at times a father will play this role. Under such conditions food is endowed with an exaggerated emotional value, and serves as a substitute for love, security, and satisfaction. Muscular activity and social contacts, on the other hand, become associated with concepts of danger and separation, resulting not only in marked inactivity but also in poor social adjustment and emotional immaturity. The mothers were preoccupied with the physical safety of the children and instilled in them a hypochondriacal concern for their health. They rated other children as undesirable or dangerous playmates. An element of danger and threat clung to all activities that were not under mother's immediate supervision. Some mothers would go to fantastic lengths to keep control over their children.

The study was made during the depression years, from 1937 to 1940, and many families had undergone severe financial reverses. It was not uncommon that obesity in the child and in one or the other parent had developed after the economic collapse of the family. Life in a city like New York, which harbors many immigrants and newcomers, not only from foreign countries but also from rural areas or small communities, imposes conditions which are conducive to inactivity and overeating. There is also a great need to appease anxiety and tension, and food may gain inordinate importance. To many mothers the offering of food is their way of expressing their affection and devotion and of appeasing their anxiety and guilt about the child. The child seems to increase his demands as his needs for gratification and security in other areas remain unfulfilled. Although he may respond in many different ways to such contradictory handling, his developing obesity must be regarded as one form of such a response. It certainly will make a difference whether a mother offers food as a substitute for love and devotion which she cannot express in other ways, or whether she offers nothing; and also, whether the child is able to accept the food or refuses it, or develops feeding difficulties or other emotional problems which seem to flourish under similar environmental conditions.

The impression was that the fathers played a subordinate role in the family, though there were exceptions. Those with whom we had contact often gave the impression of being weak and unaggressive, and they were treated by their wives with contempt and reproach. Often they were held up to the children, particularly to the sons, as examples of something they should *not* be; the sons were expected to surpass their fathers and thus compensate their mothers for their husband's incompetence. In such an emotional climate, with the mother's domineering overinvolvement with the fat child, it is difficult, if not impossible, for a child to develop proper self-esteem and a feeling of inner emotional security.

I should like to illustrate some of the features in such an insecure family with the history of a little girl who had been overfed and infan-tilized to an extreme degree by her immature parents. They had grown up in an Italian neighborhood in New York City and had moved to another part of the city to be closer to the father's place of work. The mother was acutely unhappy, could not adjust to being separated from her family, and insisted on moving back to the old neighborhood.

The child was born 10 months after the wedding, when the mother was just 19 years old. The doctor in attendance supposedly remarked to the father that if a woman had such fine milk she should nurse the baby as long as there was a drop left. Consequently the little girl was allowed the breast whenever she wanted it and was nursed until she was 4 years old, and the girl herself became ashamed about anyone knowing that she still nursed. She was also given milk from a bottle and she was still receiving the bottle when she was first seen in the obesity clinic at age 5 years. In addition she had been fed unlimited amounts of any other food she wanted; since this was an Italian home macaroni and other starchy foods stood in the foreground. Though the parents lived close to both their families they took their child along when they went out and would not leave her in the care of anyone else. The girl was not allowed to play with other children because the parents did not want her exposed to the danger of infections.

Birth weight was reported as 7½ lbs but no later weights were remem-bered. Developmental landmarks had been normal with walking, talking, and toilet training at a fairly early age. When the girl was 2 years old a physician called attention to the heavy folds of fat over her abdomen but supposedly reassured the parents that she would outgrow the condition.

When she was seen in the obesity clinic at age 5 she was 46" tall and weighed 97 lbs (120% overweight). She was of such an enormous size that the question of precocious puberty was raised but there were no other signs. The parents had been advised that something needed to be done about the girl's weight to get her ready for school. The child clung closely to her mother but gave the impression of being intelligent, though exceedingly shy. There were no other children because both parents felt that even this one child was too much for them. The mother seemed to experience the child as something her husband had inflicted on her and conceived of her only as a burden, and did not express any joy or personal interest in the child.

An effort was made to stimulate some independence in the child and the parents were advised to send her to a nursery school. The father upheld the child when she did not want to go but after she had entered first grade, she attended school regularly and did fairly good work. Efforts to restrict her food intake were unsuccessful and the girl's weight rose to 108 lbs at age 6. The child did not resist having her food cut down but there was constant conflict between the parents because the father would not permit his daughter to be deprived of anything and insisted that she should get whatever she wanted or could possibly eat. The rate of gain slowed down somewhat after she had entered school where she could not eat continuously. It was not possible to affect a change in the parents' approach to the child or in their immature and selfish attitude toward each other. Both parents were slender and obesity was not a conspicuous feature in any other family member.

The early observations were made on a clinic population, chiefly of lower-class background where obesity occurs with greater frequency, even in children. Abnormal family attitudes were not always as crudely expressed as in this example, and fathers only rarely took such an active role in the care of a child. In private practice, dealing with patients from more successful economic backgrounds, disturbed patterns of family interaction may be less conspicuous; they are often camouflaged by outer conformity with middle-class standards. In these families the role of the father was less inconspicuous; yet lack of real closeness to the children, particularly to the obese child, was frequently observed. Obese adolescents will often complain that they felt they were just one of father's possessions; his interest was in how well they looked or how successful they were socially or in school, but not in how they felt or what they valued. Quite often, the children felt that the father's only interest was his business; if he showed emotions at all, it was that of exclusive devotion to the mother, and the child felt left out. Wherever detailed information was obtained the marital picture looked less rosy; there was less devotion and understanding between the parents than the children had assumed. Nevertheless, the role which the financially successful father played in relation to an obese child is different from that which had been observed in the clinic patients.

Financial success does not always mean more respect and admiration from a wife. The following observations were made during the analysis of a woman who was preoccupied with doing everything right and arranging everything in everybody's life in the best possible way. She was quite unaware of this drive to run everyone's life according to her own fantastic expectations. One source of continuous irritation and dissatisfaction to her was what she considered the inadequacies of her husband. He was highly successful in his work, had many cultural interests, and offered her a standard of living far superior to her own modest background. Nonetheless, she continuously complained about not having "the best" of everything, particularly for her children.

She dominated every detail of her children's lives. Her eternal concern was her oldest daughter, who was nervous and "too thin." This child tried hard to please her mother; at the same time she rebelled against her unreasonable demands for perfection. There were two younger girls who had a more robust physical make-up and who complied better with the mother's efforts to show that they received "the very best" in every respect. As a result, they both became overweight. This was a point of pride as long as they were small—"such sturdy and beautiful children"—but it aroused increasing concern as they grew older. The second girl became so obsessed with being too fat that she put herself on a diet when she was only 9 years old, and had no other interest except to lose weight. She complained: "All the time she says, 'Eat, eat, eat.' And now she is angry that I am too fat." When the youngest daughter, too, became fat, the mother was at last willing to consider that her "best" efforts might have been too much for her children.

Sometimes fathers take an acute, even grotesque, interest in the fatness of their children, as if nothing else mattered. I have been impressed by the fact that quite often these fathers are engaged in work that deals with women and their appearance. Three groups of fathers seem to consider fatness in a child, particularly in a daughter, as a personal insult: dress manufacturers, movie producers, and specialists in metabolic diseases. The daughters seem to be intensely influenced in a negative way by the father's anxiety about the obesity. Fathers with other professions are, of course, not exempt. Among the well-to-do and educated the concern about the obese state is much more frantic; fatness is rated as undesirable, if not outright disastrous, at a much earlier age and in milder degrees.

Debby's story, which will be offered in more detail in Chapter 9, may serve as an illustration of a father's morbid preoccupation with a daughter's obesity. She was the first child and the first grandchild in a large family, and there had never been a more beloved and better cared for little girl. Most devoted was her father, and all his suffering about her fatness was an expression of his boundless love and devotion. He was nervous and upset and so worried about her that he could not sleep, even threatened suicide, because he could not stand the shame and humiliation of having a fat daughter. He was the most successful son in a large family and he could not stand that they all pitied him for having a daughter who looked like a freak. That's why he brought her for treatment, so that she could be turned into a girl who would look and act as a young lady should. If psychiatry was needed, here he was and he could well afford it, but he wanted results. His daughter said much later, when she had become capable of expressing herself: "Father thinks that a personality change is something like a face-lifting. If you go to a doctor, then it is his job to change you into what he has ordered." The father was indignant at the mere notion that there might be something in the emotional climate of his home that had been damaging to his daughter. All he needed was a daughter who was slim.

The mother was an intelligent and pretty woman who felt, in retrospect, that maybe there had been too many people involved in raising Debby, that she had tried too hard to please them all. Maybe she had kept the little girl too close and had stuffed her with food. In the family's eyes Debby's fatness was an expression of her mother's failure. But she, the mother, had done all she knew and she was at her wit's end; nobody could do any more than she had done. She had made the girl's weight a full-time occupation, had taken her to many doctors, had followed advice she found in magazines or newspapers, had taken her to beauty parlors and other commercial institutions, all in an effort to make Debby lose weight.

The mother's reaction to the increasing obesity was genuine compassion; she wanted her daughter to look attractive and be happy. There was also growing resentment that she, the mother, was blamed for having produced such a fat daughter. In other ways she felt competent and capable but here she was completely helpless; she was desperate now, because whatever she tried to make Debby lose weight would make her eat more. Needless to say, Debby's self-concept was painfully low and she had a sense of absolute helplessness. "I could not imagine how I could ever have friends. I hated to look at myself. How could anybody like me or look at me and not be disgusted."

Modern Approaches to the Study of the Family

With increasing experience it became apparent that it was not the one or the other behavioristic feature or facet in the family constellation that accounted for healthy or abnormal development, but the dynamic interaction between all members of a family and the role they played in relation to each other. It had been recognized quite early that the obese child was "elected" to compensate parents for their own disappointments and frustrations, and this was observed both in clinic and private patients. There were many ways in which this was expressed. Quite often the child was looked upon as a precious possession, in need of the very best of care, but he was denied recognition of his own individuality. The sex of the boys had frequently been a disappointment to their mothers who had hoped for a girl who, they expected, "would stay close" to them. Dissatisfaction with the sex of a girl was also expressed, though less frequently.

It also became apparent that different forms of obesity, with different psychological constellations and transactions, needed to be differentiated. In *developmental obesity*, the disturbances resulting in abnormal eating behavior appear to be at the core and lead also to many other severe deviations in personality, with schizophrenia a not uncommon outcome. Understanding such generalized underlying patterns was even more necessary in anorexia nervosa, where in the primary form the surface picture is often that of a harmonious, well-functioning family.

There has been a rapid growth of family studies following World War II and one becomes impressed with something that looks like the mysterious working of a "Zeitgeist." Though many different groups worked independently, changes in focus and direction became apparent at about the same time. It seems that various investigators, after a certain period of time, suddenly and independently of each other, come to feel the need to reevaluate their approach and to reorganize their findings along new lines, formulating underlying unifying and synthesizing ideas. In spite of dissimilarities in the vocabulary and theoretical emphasis, there has emerged an encouraging convergence of ideas and points of view. It is no longer considered sufficient to give a family history in biographical or anecdotal details, as was done in the early part of the obesity study, but the essential aspects of the family transactions need to be formulated as generalized, even abstract concepts, which might then serve as a basis of comparison from family to family, and would also be applicable to different cultural and social settings. The development of hunger awareness out of the interactions with the mother, as described in the previous chapter, is an example of such a generalized formulation. Modern studies of the family have dealt with every conceivable aspect of family life, its inner functioning, the interacting roles of its various members, its social significance, and its relationship to various clinical conditions. It is now fashionable to speak of "systems" as expressing the multiple interactions in the family.

Decided changes have taken place in what is emphasized as significant in family studies, in clinical as well as in sociological and psychological research. In the earlier studies, during the 1940's and 1950's, the emphasis was on emotional aspects, on whether there was sufficient love and gratification of instinctual needs. Deprivation was conceived of as resulting from insufficient love and affection, with emphasis on isolated errors in a mother's attitude, or on emotional traumata. In recent studies the emphasis has shifted toward defining the forces which encourage or interfere with a child's growing into a distinct individual, with needs and impulses clearly differentiated from those of his parents, yet having acquired the necessary conceptual tools and ability to organize his behavior and reactions in such a way that he can face and adapt to the complexities of adult life. Instead of isolated behavior traits of one or the other parent, the multiple functions of the family have been clarified and defined, and emphasis has shifted to the way the different members interact. The importance of the repetitive patterns in basic learning experiences has been recognized. With clearer analysis of the prerequisites for competent and adaptable human development, the basic functions of the family (which have been taken for granted as inherent in the human state) could be described in detail (14). Increasingly, it was recognized that disturbances in family functions and structure resulted in deficits in a child's acquiring fundamental aspects of mental functioning. Deficiencies in the acquisition of the meaning of language, of need presentation, or of behavioral clues of others were recognized as the background and foundation of maladaptation later in life.

Family studies of schizoprhenia have been particularly informative in revealing many similarities to what has been observed in obesity as disturbances in the basic patterns of interaction and communication. According to Lidz (13), there is not one characteristic that would be found in all families that produce a schizophrenic offspring, except that all studied families were seriously disturbed. Common characteristics are the use of a child to complete the parents' life and to maintain the parents' marital relationship, failure of the parents to adhere to the respective gender-linked roles, and disruption of the boundaries between the generations. Often the parent of the same sex fails to provide the child with an acceptable model for identification. A large proportion of the difficulties seems to be related to, and is perhaps derived from, the parents' inability to establish boundaries between themselves and the child. They often limit the environment for the child and distort his perception of reality to maintain their own precarious equilibrium. The manifest relationships in such families may vary according to the degree of mental disturbance in either father or mother.

A mother interferes with a child's development of initiative and autonomy by solicitous overprotection, not permitting the development of ego boundaries between herself and the child. If the father is relatively more disturbed a child will be caught in the demand to complete the life of the parent of the opposite sex, and in bridging the schism between the parents, rather than investing his energies and attention in his own development. The communication within these families is grossly disturbed in content, in conflicting emotional messages, and in role allocation. To various degrees all these aspects can be readily recognized in the family interaction associated with *developmental obesity*.

Wynne and Singer (19) have pointed out the disturbed character of the parent's style of communication, which is amorphous or fragmented and interferes with maintaining focal attention. There are likely to be erratic shifts from closeness to distance, conveying a sense of meaningless, pointlessness, and emptiness. The child who grows up in such an environment, with elusive and perplexing communication from either parent, has difficulty in learning to focus attention on what is relevant. He can readily become hopeless and despairing about making sense out of things. In such a setting he will find it particularly difficult to satisfy his parents, and he may be torn in his efforts to fulfill their conflicting needs. All psychosis involves gross failures of ego functioning, that is, loss of the capacity to guide the self into the future. The essence of schizophrenia lies in the distortions of mentation that occur without degradation of intellectual potential. The nature of the essential thought disorder in schizophrenia has been variously defined as the loss of capacity to think abstractly, failure of categorizing or overinclusiveness, inability to exclude the irrelevant, etc. Much of what will be later described as characteristic of obese patients who became overtly schizophrenic, and also of many anorexics, appears to be closely related to this type of thought disorder.

In earlier studies the patient was conceived of as a victim, and much of his maldevelopment was thought to be due to the inner contradictions and inconsistencies under which he grew up; but he is also an active participant in this process, and in turn has an effect on the family. His symptoms alone provoke a response: the continuous stuffing in which an obese child indulges arouses hostility and condemnation, and there are few conditions that evoke such severe emotional reactions as voluntary food refusal by an anorexic.

Approaching the problem in this wider orientation permits us to recognize subtle patterns of disturbed interactions in various areas of family life. This approach is of particular importance for the understanding of severely disturbed patients whose parents report that their childhood had been free of disturbances, or even particularly satisfying and happy.

At times it is the memory of just one episode that has become part of the family saga that permits one to reconstruct the patterns of interaction. One was told by a highly successful professional woman who had been fat since infancy and who did not recall any time that she had not been fat. At age 14 she had weighed over 160 lbs and at no time in her adult life had her weight been below 185 lbs; her highest weight was 225 lbs. She had never felt the slightest concern or self-consciousness about her appearance, though her mother continuously criticized her for being so fat. At age 50 she and her husband shared a household with her mother, in whose apartment they lived.

She came for psychiatric treatment because recently she had begun to suffer from a diffuse sense of unhappiness, of loss, of loneliness, of not enjoying what she was doing. She had a general feeling that "I never got anything I wanted." Up to that time she had taken for granted, in spite of her varied experiences and widely recognized accomplishments, that what counted most in her life was to have her mother's approval. She had always felt that her mother was the most perfect human being, who was wonderfully attractive, happily married, a successful businesswoman, and the ruler of her home. Although it meant playing second fiddle, her father had accepted this and loved his wife deeply until the day he died, 6 years previously. For the first time she felt the need to get away from her mother's influence, and this coincided with her having suddenly become embarrassed about her weight. Up to then the weight was *her mother's shame,* and she had assumed the right to hound her daughter about it constantly. Even now the mother would make all the important decisions about the household and buy her daughter's clothes. Whenever this very accomplished woman would buy anything on her own her mother would criticize it severely. Lifelong experience had taught the daughter that it was easier to let mother direct her life than to oppose her and to do things according to her own tastes and needs.

An often-told story related to an episode in which the mother took great pride and which until that time had been to the patient a measure of her mother's perfection. One day, when she was taking the baby in her carriage to the park, the mother was approached by two elegant ladies who, mistaking her for a nurse, offered her twice her present salary to come to work for them because they had never seen a baby so exceptionally well cared for. The mother, of course, declined, but she was very pleased by this offer and never mentioned that the beautiful baby was her own child.

This story, which she had started to tell as one more illustration of her mother's superhuman perfection, suddenly brought home to the patient her mother's selfishness and her constant emphasis on her own goodness. She had accepted the praise for raising her child perfectly, not even acknowledging her own child and denying her the right to her own individual development. Seen from this angle this story and many other tales of her mother's superperfection helped her to recognize how she had been denied her own individuality and had been kept from leading a life of her own.

A literary description of the destructive interaction of a mother with her son, "Fat, bald and thirty-nine," is given by Carol Hill in her novel *Jeremiah 8:20* (9).

His mother's pink face lay flushed behind the glass of the car door. He stared at her a moment, under glass.

"Well, get in dear," she said, and Francis let his mouth move uncertainly into a crooked smile, then crooking up his hand pressed the fat wet palm of it over the glass covering her face, pink against pink, said, "Hi."

"You must be hungry," she said, "I brought you a piece of home-made cake," and with one hand steering she shoved a chocolate layer cake on a green paper plate, covered with wax paper, across the seat to Francis.

"I, I coulda waited until we got home," Francis said, uncomfortable at being baited.

"Well, yes," the high pitch came back, "I know you could have, I was just trying to be *nice,*" the high note pierced his ear.

"You don't have to eat it, dear," she said, staring straight ahead as Francis plunged into the cake, the crumbs spilling to his lap, "but be sure to wipe your hands. I don't want chocolate all over the seats."

And Francis felt again the old vortex rising, "Obey, don't obey, do, don't eat, not, spill not, mess not, wipe not, be not," and he sucked an extra long time on a chocolate crumb-encased finger.

This is a frightening account of the truly contradictory imperatives permeating the life in such a family and depriving a child of a sense of authentic individuality.

Anorexia Nervosa

Patterns of disturbed family interaction are less obvious in primary anorexia nervosa. This serious life-threatening illness develops in young-sters whose childhood, according to the parents' reports, has often been free of disturbances to an unusual degree. In atypical cases family disturbances are more on the surface, and quite often emotional problems have been recognized in the patient-to-be. A "morbid mental state" had been recognized as characteristic of anorexia nervosa since its description 100 years ago, but studies of the family background and pre-illness personality are rare and rather unsatisfactory. Lasègue (12) gave a sensitive description of the effect of the illness on family interaction, without reference to pre-illness factors. Crisp (5) reviewed the older literature and found little consistency in the studies of the family constellation. Most of the older reports dealt with the disturbed patterns after the condition had become manifest. As to predisposing childhood traits, the tendency has been to emphasize "oral" problems, food fads, or dyspeptic disturbances. A number of workers noted abnormal nutritional patterns during child-hood. Many patients-to-be had been "plump," while only a minority had been regarded as skinny.

Reports on the family background were equally contradictory. Some of the older authors speak of a family history of neurosis or psychosis, whereas others report absence of manifest psychiatric illness and failure to find significant psychological disturbances in the parents. There were a few reports of anorexia nervosa in a parent, and even more rarely in siblings.

Reports on family interrelationships showed little agreement between investigators concerning the nature of premorbid phenomena and influences. Crisp observed similar disagreements in the reports of the social background. Some found that these patients came from all social classes, others commented on the poor financial status of the families. Still other authors, Crisp among them, have been impressed by the high proportion of patients coming from prosperous and professional homes. The inconsistencies are probably related to the differences in diagnostic criteria; many of the reports were based on various forms of psychological weight loss and not on true anorexia nervosa. There is also great diversity in what is considered relevant information about the family background.

I should like to mention a few reports that focus on the pre-illness picture. Asperger (1) speaks of the mothers as unable to provide the necessary warmth and security because they themselves were neurotic. The fathers were described as soft, inactive, and unable to take a stand against their wives. To Asperger these traits are manifestations of a constitutional psychopathology which is handed down from mother to child, and does not indicate a psychological origin of the illness. Groen and Feldman-Toledano (8) felt these children suffered from "severe love deprivation," that the parents lived in loveless marriages that did not satisfy either of them, but they expected exemplary academic performance and correct behavior from the children. Blitzer and co-workers (2) observed a "family neurosis," expressed in the parents' abnormal attitudes and concepts about eating and food, and concern with weight.

In a recent Finnish study (16) the focus was on the mothers of 13 anorexia nervosa girls. Most had been more than 30 years old when the patient was born and patients were not first children. The mothers appeared inhibited in their sexual responses and dissatisfied in their marriages. They earned unusually high scores on intelligence tests, but their education, status, and work were often beneath their capacities. Six of the patients scored distinctly lower than their mothers, but were pressured into high performance. The authors felt that these women, frustrated in the use of their own intellectual abilities and gifts, had become resigned to their fate by the time the anorexic child was born, and had endowed this child with the task of compensating them for their own disappointment. They could only accept a passively receiving child, suffocating all tendencies to independence. Physical adolescence of the child aroused fear and panic in the mothers as an expression of independence they had not been able to prevent.

An interesting reconstruction of family interaction was presented by Duehrssen (6), based on observations made during psychotherapy with anorexic twins who suffered from different forms of anorexia. The parents were emphatic that the twins had been "perfectly normal—one heart and one soul." The father was extremely appearance-conscious and was actively involved with his twin daughters, encouraging and admiring the older and stronger for her athletic ability, and the younger for her academic brightness, her excellence in mathematics and in playing chess. He treated his wife and mother-in-law with condescension, relegating them to a servant role; their task was to provide "the best of the best" for the twins. At age 14 the older girl became depressed and then anorexic when a boyfriend with whom she had fallen in love paid attention to another girl. While the older twin was hospitalized the younger, who had always been smaller and the follower in relation to her dominant sister, developed true anorexia nervosa. Though the parents thwarted efforts to involve them directly in therapy, they did follow advice to encourage the separateness of the twins and this played a helpful role in their recovery.

There is a series of reports (4, 7) on identical twins discordant for anorexia nervosa, suggesting the importance of experiential rather than genetic and constitutional factors. Crisp (5) reported on two patients, unrelated to each other but brought up at different times in the same household by a married couple whose own marriage was unconsummated. The first patient had lived with the family for some time during World War II, during which time she became obese (the man was a biscuit manufacturer); subsequently she developed anorexia nervosa. The second anorexic patient was one of the children later adopted into this family, where both parents were preoccupied with diets.*

Own Observations

For presentation of my observations of 70 patients, I have subdivided the group into 51 patients with the primary syndrome (Chapter 14) and a smaller group of 19 exhibiting the atypical picture (Chapter 13). For completeness sake, I should like to give some of the descriptive figures on the families in Table 5-1. The families are of small size, which is more pronounced in the primary than in the atypical group. For all 70 cases there were only 7 instances (10%) of only children. This figure stands in contrast to the recent report by Kay and his co-workers (11) of an incidence of 50% of only children in a study of "hard fact" information for a multivariable analysis of the interrelated data. If there is a preponderance then it is the position of being first born; the first of two girls was the combination most often observed. Whatever the significance for the later development of anorexia nervosa, there is much more diversity than in childhood obesity, where the preponderance of only and youngest children is marked. In this group there are relatively few sons, something also observed by others who speak of the anorexic family as being woman-dominated, in contrast to the absence of daughters in the families of obese boys.

The age of the parents at the time of birth of the anorexics-to-be was rather high, a fact also commented on by other observers, but about half of the patients were first-born children. Ushakov's (18) patients, too, were the product of a first or second perfectly normal pregnancy, in contrast to

* From family therapy Selvini derived that certain common traits could be recognized in these families with apparent marital harmony. Both parents conceal their deep disillusionment with each other but view themselves as "giving" and "totally devoted" to the good of the family, particularly the patient. Secretly they carry on a sacrificial competition, each appearing to make the greater sacrifice. In subtle ways they transfer to the partner blame for anything that goes wrong, and responsibility for the action. Each desires the sympathy and support of the child, the later patient who, as the go-between of a couple, plays a part which is too difficult. All energies are directed toward satisfying competitive claims of the parents, and too little is left for investment in her own development. When the illness becomes manifest it is viewed as "something that has happened" from the outside, not as related to the parents' excessive and contradictory demands. Mara P. Selvini. *Anorexia Nervosa*, Chaucer Publ. Co., London, 1972.

TABLE 5–1

Families

	PRIMARY ANOREXIA NERVOSA		ATYPICAL ANOREXIA NERVOSA	
	FEMALE (N 45)	MALE (N 6)	FEMALE (N 15)	MALE (N 4)
Parents' age at birth of an anorexia nervosa child				
Father	36	31	34	32
Mother	30	27	27	26.5
Total number of children in families	128	16	48	15
Daughters	88*	6	38*	7
Sons	40	10*	10	8*
Average number of children	2.8	2.7	3.2	3.7
Position of Patient				
Only child	3	—	3	1
Oldest (11 no brothers)	23	2	6	1
Second	4	1	3	1
Later	4	1	1	—
Youngest	9	2	2	1
Twin (1 older brother each)	2	—	—	—
Social Class				
I	25	4	5	—
II	16	2	6	2
III	4	—	4	2

* including patient

the Finnish report that anorexic patients were born late in the marriage. The marriages appeared to be stable, at least in formalistic terms. In my series there were only two instances of separation or broken homes before the onset of the illness. Given the divorce rate in the United States this is an unusually low incidence. Most parents emphasized the stability, if not happiness, of their homes. Only intensive therapeutic work revealed the distortions and tensions underlying this facade of normality. Ushakov, reporting from Russia, observed that most of these adolescents came from prosperous families with a highly cultured background, good living conditions, and a quiet family environment. This stands in contrast to Kay's report on the frequency of broken homes and descriptively abnormal marriages.

The distribution of these families according to socioeconomic status appears to have some significance. Among the 51 families in the primary group, 29 were of upper-class standing, with at least 6 or 7 belonging to the class of the "super-rich." Eighteen were rated as middle-class and only 4 as of lower-class status. In the atypical group middle- and lower-class standing was more frequent. It appears possible that the success, achievement, and appearance orientation of these upwardly mobile families is in some way related to the driving search of these youngsters for something that earns them "respect." Ishikawa (10) reported from Japan that anorexia nervosa has been on the increase since the second World War. His patients came from so-called "modern" families, no longer traditionally Japanese, but not yet truly emancipated with a meaningful modern goal in life.

Reconstruction of the early development of the 51 patients with primary anorexia nervosa revealed, as a composite picture, that they had been well cared for children to whom many advantages and privileges of modern living had been offered. They had also been exposed to many stimulating influences in education, in the arts, in athletics, and the like. Yet on closer study, it was recognized that encouragement or reinforcement of self-expression had been deficient, and thus reliance on their own inner resources, ideas, or autonomous decisions had remained undeveloped. Pleasing compliance had become their way of life, and they had functioned with a facade of normality, which, however, when progressive development demanded more than conforming obedience turned into indiscriminate negativism, the most apparent psychological symptom after the illness had developed. No general picture can be given for the premorbid personalities in the atypical group.

The parents emphasized the normality of their family life, with repeated statements that "nothing was wrong," sometimes with frantic stress on "happiness," directly denying the desperate illness of one member. Often they emphasized the superiority of the now sick child over his siblings. The mothers had often been women of achievement, or career women frustrated in their aspirations who had been conscientious in their motherhood. They were subservient to their husbands in many details, and yet did not truly respect them. The fathers, despite social and financial success which was often considerable, felt in some sense "second best." They were enormously preoccupied with outer appearances in the physical sense of the word, admiring fitness and beauty, and expecting proper behavior and measurable achievements from their children. This description probably applies to many "success-oriented," upper-middle-class families. It is probable that these traits are more pronounced in the anorexia nervosa family, or that there is greater imperviousness to the child's authentic needs. The parents' denial of all difficulties in the present, except for their frantic concern with the weight loss, might suggest that earlier problems are also denied or not remembered. Usually there are school records of excellent academic performance and early popularity, which support the history of seemingly normal or superior functioning.

In a few instances information about a later anorexic patient has been available before the illness became manifest, indicating that the parents' concept of the child's satisfactory early development is not the result of falsification after the illness had developed, but that the child's over-conformity was perceived as ideal.

·   ·   ·

An example is a socially prominent upper-class family where there had been a consultation about an older daughter who was markedly obese at age 18 when the future anorexia patient was only 12 years old. The mother spoke in glowing terms about her youngest daughter, who in every respect was an ideal child. Her teachers would refer to her as the "best balanced" girl in school, and would rely on her warmth and friendliness when another child had difficulties in making friends. After the anorexia developed 4 years later, it could be recognized that the anxious and often punitive concern with the older sister's obesity had influenced the younger girl's thinking and self-concept, convincing her that being fat was the most shameful and deplorable condition. The rapid weight increase during puberty horrified her and she felt the only way of deserving respect was by being thin, and she went on a starvation regimen. This coincided with her beginning realization that life was not just filling the mold into which her parents had poured her, but that she needed to be "master of her fate."

In another family the mother of the later anorexic patient was in psychoanalytic treatment (with another analyst) because she felt dissatisfied in her marriage and suffered from recurrent depressions. She was of foreign (Scandinavian) background, from an educated upper-middle-class family who felt her husband's upper-class background was "superior" to her own. There was some discrepancy in social class but not nearly as much as the mother felt. This had led her to submit completely to her husband's "inner know-how." She was eternally preoccupied with trying to live up to his standards and pleasing him. It was rather extreme: he was never to be irritated, never to suffer an upset; his pleasure and satisfaction were supreme in the household. Increasingly the mother suffered from a sense of inadequacy. This growing dissatisfaction led her to seek psychoanalytic treatment.

The relationship to her daughter was the one great satisfaction of her life. The girl was 14 years old at that time and, according to the mother's description, had always been a happy child who had no problems and was perfectly content. Everything was done very systematically and the girl was "a good child" who did as she was told. Though there had been governesses the mother herself had supervised her upbringing, in particular the feeding, making sure that the girl always received the right food, tastefully and artistically presented, and there had never been any problem regarding eating. Mother just decided what it should be, and the child ate.

Shortly thereafter, after a brief period of plumpness, the daughter became anorexic. She presented a picture entirely different from her mother's. She remembered her childhood as a constant state of misery and frustration. She could never have what she wanted; everything always had to be *exactly* what mother had planned. She knew that her mother discussed with the pediatrician what she should eat to keep her from growing fat, and she had felt that every bite that went into her mouth was watched. Even when she got ice cream, or other "forbidden" food, it was never as much as she wanted, nor as gooey and rich as she craved.

Outstanding in this double report is the extremely opposite way things were experienced. All the daughter remembered was her constant state of misery and frustration, whereas the mother remembered her as a perfectly contented child who was happy and had no problems. The "problem" was that there was no real contact, that the mother was completely unaware of or unresponsive to what the child needed and asked for.

Though this lack of contact was most marked in the food area, where not the slightest deviation was allowed, there were other discrepancies. The mother spoke of the walks they took together as examples of how close they had always been, and of the happy times she had with her daughter. The daughter remembered how utterly miserable she was, not being able to keep up with mother's long stride. Mother would also talk to other people, and the child felt uncomfortable and miserable that she was talked about, but not listened to, or she felt completely left out. There were also walks with father on Sunday mornings; they, too, were remembered by the patient as torture. She was dressed up for this, but always in clothes which she felt were not comfortable and usually not warm enough, with emphasis on looking nice for father. To him the whole thing was very important: "Here I am, a father, taking his daughter for a walk," and he wanted to be proud of her.

When with puberty the girl grew plump it was a real disaster, and she went on a rigid reducing regimen, always hoping to come to the point, "When I don't need to eat at all." This was her only security against being fat. Her extreme fear of fatness was reinforced by the father's excessive concern with appearance. This was a wealthy home and there was always a lavish array of food. The father showed his superiority by eating very little and making snide remarks about people who did not control themselves but gorged themselves on all this good food. It was a mark of being something higher, to be on a diet in the face of plenty. When the girl began to fight her weight she tried to outdo her father in exercising aristocratic control. Being slim was what she felt she owed to him and their high social standing. Her whole life had been dominated by the question, "Can one ever satisfy father?" Though she did well in her studies she was haunted by the fear of being found out as "stupid" or "not working enough." After she had become anorexic she summarized her life experiences as, "I never deserved what they gave me." She felt she had proved in a great many ways that she was "worthless" and keeping her weight low was her only way of proving herself as "deserving" and having "dignity."

Even this brief sketch will have conveyed the egocentric atmosphere of the home, with the father using the child to bolster his pride and the mother her sense of rightness. In other families the disturbed patterns may be more subtle, even more camouflaged by conventional behavior. These distortions of the underlying transactional patterns are apt to be missed in simple inquiries which focus on readily describable abnormalities. They can be brought into the open by therapeutic work with the patients and their families, in particular through conjoint interviews. In an occasional instance conflicts and problems appear to be more obvious and may tempt one to blame them for the disorder. Sometimes such a direct relationship exists, but more often the basic symptoms, the disordered food regulation and the sense of inadequacy and ineffectiveness are related to persistent, though often subtle or seemingly insignificant, errors which have interfered with a child's developing autonomy or inner-directedness.

Bringing the underlying distortions into the open is of the utmost importance for effective therapeutic intervention. If the faulty patterns are recognized early and corrected, anorexia nervosa may be only a brief episode in the struggle for individuation. It has often been assumed that anorexia nervosa in prepuberty has a better prognosis than when it develops later in adolescence. In my experience this favorable course depends to a large extent on the way the families become involved in the treatment process. More commonly than in older patients parents of anorexic children are being included in therapy. If the abnormal patterns are effectively changed the anorexia may subside within a short time. If one's efforts in this direction are not successful, the course may be as serious and life threatening as in older individuals.

If the condition has existed for any length of time, the whole picture is overshadowed by the enormous conflicts and open fighting that develop from efforts to persuade or force the patient to eat. Whatever the earlier relationships, increasingly anger, frustration, retaliation, rage, and deception come to the fore. It would be misleading to explain anorexic development from this behavior, as has been done in many of the older reports. The significant underlying faulty attitudes and interactions can often be recognized only with improvement, when the frantic secondary reactions have subsided. One father whose son had become anorexic at age 12, in prepuberty, and whose illness had lasted more than 8 years and had resulted in bristling, hostile interaction, summarized it well during a final conference when the patient had recovered and "warmth" had come back into the family. He spoke of "overdoing things," of planning too much for the children and expecting too much in return. This had been expressed in the mother's overly rigid adherence to an already rigid pediatric program, in her being overly helpful in all areas of her son's development, planning and selecting every detail of what he should eat, wear, read, or do, and in the father's overly proud interest in his son's athletic achievement. Not one isolated act or attitude could have been called traumatic or abnormal; it was the aggregate of these influences that had resulted in the son's feeling that nothing he expressed was considered or important, that he did not even have ownership of his own body, that whatever he did was not for himself but for his parents' sake, though never sufficient to please them.

In these cases, the parents' conviction of their own correctness will blind them to all signals indicating the increasing doubts and frustrations from which their children suffer. With such failure in communication, even benevolent and appropriate parental actions are apt to be experienced by the child as over-control and as disregard or rejection of anything that comes from him.

BIBLIOGRAPHY

1. Asperger, H., Zur Problematik der Pubertaetsmagersucht, Schweiz. Med. Wschr., 92:66–68, 1963.
2. Blitzer, J. R., Rollins, N., and Blackwell, A., Children who starve themselves: Anorexia nervosa, Psychosom. Med., 23:368–383, 1961.
3. Bruch, H., and Touraine, G., Obesity in childhood, V: The family frame of obese children, Psychosom. Med., 2:141–206, 1940.
4. Bruch, H., The insignificant difference: Discordant incidence of anorexia nervosa in monozygotic twins, Amer. J. Psychiat., 126:123–128, 1969.
5. Crisp, A. H., Premorbid factors in adult disorders of weight, with particular reference to primary anorexia nervosa (weight phobia). A literature review, J. Psychosom. Res., 14:1–22, 1970.
6. Duehrssen, A., Zum Problem der psychogenen Esstoerung, Psyche, 4: 56–72, 1950.
7. Gifford, S., Murawski, B. J., and Pilot, M. L., Anorexia nervosa in one of identical twins, pp. 139–228, in *Anorexia Nervosa and Obesity*, C. V. Rowland, Jr., ed., International Psychiatry Clinics, 7, Little, Brown & Co., Boston, 1970.
8. Groen, J. J., Feldman-Toledano, Z., Educative treatment of patients and parents in anorexia nervosa, Brit. J. Psychiat., 112:671–681, 1966.
9. Hill, C., *Jeremiah* 8:20, Random House, New York, 1970.
10. Ishikawa, K., Ueber die Eltern von Anorexia-nervosa-Kranken, pp. 154–155, in *Anorexia Nervosa*, J.-E. Meyer and H. Feldmann, eds., Georg Thieme Verlag, Stuttgart, 1965.
11. Kay, D. W. K., Schapira, K., and Brandon, S., Early factors in anorexia nervosa compared with non-anorexic groups, J. Psychosom. Res., 11:133–139, 1967.
12. Lasègue, C., On hysterical anorexia, Med. Times & Gaz., 2:265–266; 367–369, 1873.
13. Lidz, T., Family settings that produce schizophrenic offspring, pp. 196–210, in *Problems of Psychosis*, International Colloquium on Psychosis, Excerpta Medica International Congress Series, No. 194, 1969.
14. Lidz, T., The family, Chapter 2, pp. 45–69, in *The Person, His Development throughout the Life Cycle*, Basic Books, Inc., New York, 1968.
15. Pflanz, M., Medizinisch-soziologische Aspekte der Fettsucht, Psyche, 16:579–591, 1963.
16. Taipale, V., Tuomi, O., and Aukee, M., Anorexia nervosa. An illness of two generations? Acta Paedopsychiat., 38:21–25, 1971.
17. Tolstrup, K., On psychogenic obesity in childhood, IV., Acta Paediat., 42:289–304, 1953.
18. Ushakov, G. K., Anorexia nervosa, pp. 274–289, in *Modern Perspectives in Adolescent Psychiatry*, J. G. Howells, ed., Oliver and Boyd, Edinburgh, 1971.
19. Wynne, L. C., and Singer, M. T., Thought disorder and the family relations of schizophrenics: II. Classification of forms of thinking, Arch. Gen. Psychiat., 9:199–206, 1963.

6

Body Image and
Self-Awareness

The expression "body image" is so widely used in the psychiatric evaluation of patients that it is surprising to note how vague the concept is. The need for the formulation of a "body schemata" was felt by neurologists who observed that patients with various lesions in the central nervous system experienced their body as markedly changed and distorted. Much experimental work with changing theoretical formulations has been carried out by neurologists and psychologists. This has been ably summarized by Fisher and Cleveland (6) and more recently by Shontz (18). Yet with all these efforts the concept of the body image has not yet been sufficiently developed, either theoretically or empirically, to enable one to measure it or its components with any degree of assurance.

In spite of these limitations it is a concept of definite clinical usefulness for summarizing the multitude of attitudes patients may experience and express about their body. It was Schilder who first extended the concept beyond what had been observed in neurological patients by including clinical psychiatric considerations (16). In *The Image and Appearance of the Human Body*, published in English in 1935 (17), he explored body-image phenomena in relation to normal and abnormal behavior. He spoke of body image as "the picture of our own body which we form in our mind, that is to say the way in which the body appears to ourselves." This is a plastic concept which is built from all sensory and psychic experiences and it is constantly integrated in the central nervous system. Underlying it is the concept of Gestalt, which sees life and personality as a whole.

Schilder conceived of the body image as something more than a postural model arising from the changing body movement and positions, but as representing an integrated pattern of all the immediate organic and psychic experiences. However, he emphasized the importance of motility, i.e., that we would not know much about our bodies unless we moved them. As a child moves around in his environment, sensations stemming from multiple perceptual and muscular feedback are integrated into a dynamically developing body image; thus motility plays an essential role, not only in defining the boundaries of the self, but in differentiating one's self from the total perceptual environment. The inactivity so characteristic of obese people thus appears to be related to their often disturbed body concept (12). Schilder emphasized also the continuous interaction of various factors, and felt that body image in some way preceded and determined the body structure. He felt it was an unsolved problem how the reflection in the psychic sphere was related to predisposition and constitutional elements and to life experiences.

A child's body perception is modified and gradually extended in the course of his growth so as to conform to the current body structure. At the same time his capacities for conceptualization and for experiencing and interpreting reality undergo great changes, as has been studied by Piaget (14). The child also absorbs the attitudes of others toward his body and its parts. He may develop a body concept that is pleasing and satisfying, or he may come to view his body and its parts as unpleasant, dirty, shameful, or disgusting (10). In earlier studies on body interest and hypochondriasis in children, Levy (11) had recognized that the attitude of parents was integrated into a child's body concept and that derogatory attitudes had a very strong effect. He gave the example of a fat girl whose mother always pointed out her obesity with disgust. This mother was quite hostile to the child and made that particular body configuration a mark of her disapproval.

Ideally there should be no discrepancy between the body structure, body image, and social acceptance. Obese people live under the pressure of derogatory social environment. Such a continuous insult to a person's physical personality may result in a cleavage between body structure and the desired and socially acceptable image. According to Schilder, psychosis may arise from such discrepancies.

Own Observations

My own observations were made over a period of 35 years on obese and anorexic patients, on severely disturbed as well as normally functioning individuals. I was greatly influenced by Schilder's work but gradually developed some independent formulations. In particular I came to the conclusion that correct or incorrect interpretation of enteroceptive stimuli and the sense of control over and ownership of the body needed to be included in the concept of body awareness or body identity. The study of obese and anorexic patients brought strikingly into the open the extent to which social attitudes toward the body, the concept of beauty in our society, and our preoccupation with appearance enter into the picture. The obsession of the Western world with slimness, the condemnation of any degree of overweight as undesirable and ugly, may well be considered a distortion of the social body concept, but it dominates present day living.

A young person whose constitutionally or experientially determined body structure does not conform to the socially acceptable image finds himself under enormous pressure and constant criticism. For an understanding of the disturbances of the body image of patients with a deviant body size, biological, psychic, and social forces must be conceived of as in constant interaction. The deviant body size itself is related to or even the result of disturbances in hunger awareness, or of other bodily sensations. Thus evaluation of enteroceptive awareness needs to be included in a study of the body image. Various terms have been used to indicate such inclusions: body concept, body identity, body percept, etc. This new concept includes the correctness or error in cognitive awareness of the bodily self, the accuracy in recognizing stimuli coming from without or within, the sense of control over one's own bodily functions, the affective reaction to the reality of the body configuration, and one's rating of the desirability of one's body by others. The range of attitudes expressed by patients talking about their concept and awareness of their body goes far beyond the earlier definition of body image. In evaluation of all of these experiences it is not always possible to make sharp distinctions.

Therapeutically it is important to help an individual come to a more realistic awareness of his functioning self, bodily or otherwise, and to integrate various experiences into a functioning whole with changing impulses, whereby it is important that he comes to experience them as being under his own control. The therapeutic encounter offers the chance of witnessing how a patient develops, how he gradually becomes freer in discussing his manifest concepts and feelings about his body, and how they are related to other aspects of his self-awareness. Gradually he comes to understand how the distortion of his structural as well as his functional body concept is closely interwoven with his experiences and interactions with significant people throughout his life.

Disturbances in Size Awareness

Best known among the disturbances in size awareness is the anorexic's denial, his vigorous defense of his emaciated body as not too thin but as just right, as normal. As a matter of fact, this complete denial of his starved appearance is pathognomic for true anorexia nervosa. Patients with severe weight loss for other reasons will not only readily admit that they are too thin, but often actively complain about the weight loss.

During the initial phase, when they reject anything coming from the outside, in particular all efforts to help them, this denial of thinness appears to be part of the general negativistic picture. However, even after a good therapeutic relationship has developed, when they appear to be actively interested in understanding the background of their condition, they will complain, with a certain bewilderment, that they cannot "see" how thin they are. A woman of 20, who seemed to be making good progress, admitted "I really cannot see how thin I am. I look into the mirror and still cannot see it; I know I am thin because when I feel myself I notice that there is nothing but bones."

Another girl of 19, also doing well in therapy, showed her physician two photographs taken on the beach, one when she was 15 years old and of normal weight, and the other when 17, with her weight down to 70 lbs. She asked him whether he could see a difference and admitted that she had trouble seeing a difference, though she knew there was one, and that she had been trying to correct this. When she looks at herself in a mirror then she sometimes can see that she is too skinny, "But I can't hold onto it." She may remember it for an hour but then begins to feel again that she is much larger. "I feel inwardly that I am larger than that—no matter what I tell myself. Even last summer I felt large, that was when I was at my lowest (67 lbs), but I felt I was very large." When first admitted to the hospital she felt that all the people around her were "too large," and even that the building was too large. She would look at herself in the mirror several times a day to help her maintain a realistic image, but each time it got larger. During a discussion her therapist used a comparison with a pumping mechanism, an analogy she eagerly took up. Regardless of what she saw in the mirror, there was this inner mechanism that kept on inflating her self-image. Only through repeated reality testing (looking into the mirror) could she "let the air go out again." A physician father described his daughter's attitude: "She appears to become profoundly depressed after a heavy meal and then feels as though she weighs 400 lbs. Conversely, when she is not eating and her weight is falling she appears in good spirits."

A realistic body-image concept is a precondition for recovery in anorexia nervosa. Many patients will gain weight for a variety of reasons but no real or lasting cure is achieved without correction of the body-image misperception. The resolution of the denial was studied through self-image confrontation in one case by Gottheil (8). After initial denial this patient began to see how thin she was, more strikingly on video tape than by looking into the mirror. After repeated self-confrontation it became more difficult for her to maintain the denial, and a change in her body image occurred so that thinness became ugly rather than comforting to her. The same observation is made with patients in long-term treatment without such direct confrontation with the video tape. Recovered patients invariably will express shocked amazement when they look at photographs from the time of their illness. When a new anorexic is admitted to the hospital they often will tell the personnel that it is useless to confront the new patient with her scrawny picture, or make her look at her ugly mirror image. Remembering how they felt, they will say "It's no use—she cannot 'see' how thin she is."

Fat people, in contrast, vary widely in the way they perceive themselves. It seems that people who become obese as adults rather than in early childhood have a more realistic perception than those who suffer from lifelong obesity. Misperception in childhood obesity extends even to the mother. More than one mother whose fat child is referred for treatment from the school will say with indignation, "They say he is too fat. He doesn't look that way to me." Here, too, little therapeutic progress can be made unless the abnormal appearance is perceived and acknowledged. I recall a 42-year-old man, highly successful in his career, who had been overweight since adolescence, who in spite of circulatory difficulties did not follow a diet, denying that there was anything wrong with his size. One day he reported that he had stood in front of the mirror, taking in all details of how fat he was, and that he finally acknowledged "All of this is me." Until then he had done what many fat people do, simply avoided looking into a mirror or being photographed. Characteristic is the often repeated cartoon of the fat lady looking into the mirror and seeing in it a slender, glamorous, beauty queen.

Misconceptions about size appear also as the opposite, an exaggerated interpretation of any curve and excess weight as grotesquely fat. This is the background of the patients who eventually become anorexic, but also of the much larger group whom I have called "thin fat people." One later anorexic girl described this process. She had experienced any bodily change during puberty with intense discomfort. She began to deny that she had breasts or rounded buttocks, and maintained these denials over the years, long before her anorexic syndrome started. In a way she had developed a negative phantom, not seeing and accepting her budding body.

Not infrequently patients who have been severely obese for a long time will not "see" themselves as thinner even after weight reduction of considerable proportion; they carry the image of their former size like a phantom with them. This phenomenon was studied at the Rockefeller Institute in a group of superobese patients following weight reduction. These patients expressed concern over the alteration of their body size and experienced something like increased permeability of ego boundaries (7). Their figure drawings following weight loss showed larger waist diameters, with the belt extending over the body line and body area. In spite of the weight loss they reported persistent feelings of largeness. Characteristic is the acute sense of amazement of formerly fat people when someone sits down next to them on a bus, or the surprise of formerly fat girls when they are looked at or whistled at with admiration, instead of being stared at as monstrosities.

Misjudgments may occur also in concepts of the body structure. A bright 14-year-old boy, extremely obese (225 lbs), was phobic and would not go out on the street alone. He spoke with much embarrassment about the reasons for his fears, particularly his fear of losing weight.

I really am afraid of any injury. I thought my body was like a thin layer of skin full of jelly. If you got hurt, the jelly would come out. I thought if you got hurt, *all* of it would come tumbling out—that there would be just a puddle of jelly or pea soup and a balloon of skin left around my bones. I did not really believe in what we learned in biology about bones and muscle. I thought it was only jelly hardened. I thought everything would just flow out—that I would become empty. I was so afraid of this emptiness; that was what led to the real stuffing.

He also had memories of having seen pictures of victims of concentration camps, which had filled him with real horror—that's what he would look like if he did not eat or if he got injured and the jelly ran out.

A student nurse who was hospitalized for an acute schizophrenic episode, and who had grown quite fat, was observed to eat ravenously whenever she had had an argument or felt threatened. Eventually she gave an explanation. She was afraid that the hostility of others and their angry words would rattle around inside her and keep on wounding her. By stuffing herself with food she would cover her sore inside, like with a poultice, and she would not feel the hurt so much. Similar distortions were reported by Petro about an 18-year-old anorexic girl (13). As she developed tender feelings toward the analyst, a desire came over her to sit snugly in his lap, to feel love and protective safety. She experienced it as a gradual shrinking of her body, turning into a baby, and being cuddled and held with infinite care. The patient's minute body softened up and finally merged with the analyst's body. On other occasions she would experience the analyst's body penetrating or engulfing or becoming one with her's in an indescribable way. This way her voidness was filled up, her separate existence ceased, and she was not able to feel who was in whom—and actually this distinction became meaningless.

I should like to add an artist's description of the fat person's misperception of herself. It is taken from *An American Home* by Helen Eustis (5).

There was Mrs. Harrington, a small boned woman who wore tiny high heeled shoes with platform soles to increase her height, and there was her maid, Pearl, a young woman with dark brown skin. She had a small pretty face, but she was obese to the point of deformity, and her features were nearly lost in the largeness of her cheeks and chins, just as her personality was nearly lost in the neuroses of her size and race. In a dim, mixed-up way, Pearl felt that inside her, underneath her layers of flesh and her dark skin, there lived a Mrs. Harrington, too, loving luxury, waiting to be born and enjoy the world, beautiful, slim, desirable and even white.

Misperception of Bodily Functions

The fat person's plaintive statement, "Everything I eat turns to fat," or its exaggeration, "I just have to look at chocolate cake and I gain 10 pounds," probably contains a kernel of truth; namely, that there are some metabolic disturbances facilitating fat deposition, but mainly it reflects his inability to judge correctly how much he eats. However much, there is always room for more. Others completely disassociate their size and what they eat. They act and talk as if they and their body were separate entities, and as if food they sneak (what they eat when nobody else watches) will not make them fat.

Conversely, the anorexic will complain of feeling "full" after a few bites of food, or even a few drops of fluid. I have the impression that this sense of fullness really is a phantom phenomenon, a projection of memories of formerly experienced sensations. An 18-year-old girl, intelligent and articulate, but obsessed with her size and with food, felt so little differentiated from others that she would assume the identity of whomever she was around and by watching others eat, in a way, "have people eat for her," and feel "full" after that, without having eaten at all. After having starved for some time, she reported, "I keep my mind eternally preoccupied with what size I am, always hoping it will become smaller. If I must eat—that takes too much mental energy to decide what, how much, and why must I. Every day I wake up in a prison, actually enjoying the confinement."

Another young anorexic patient "imitated eating—bite by bite—even the choice of food." She observed slim women or tall boys, not "voluptuous females" and would imitate what they ate. She is quite definite that she will *not eat* by self-choice.

A 29-year-old anorexic who had been sick for over 11 years and had several times been in critical condition, claimed that she had existed on fluids only for over six months, because food would make her "weak." She described the "weird ideas" she had in relation to food, "that it is the idea that solid food remains in the state I see it in after I eat it, and that it becomes part of me and thus has power over me." Even in talking about this she feels a sudden blankness, like from an electric shock, which she explains as "I suddenly saw an idea—my eating people in the same way as food."

Another frightening thought, "a depressed body thought," was:

How will I look if I eat? I always feel full right then—it is as if I have really eaten, not just thought about it. Then I see myself—all of me—or sometimes just the hands or feet, just the breast or just the stomach—grossly distorted into a balloon like protruding hideous things. It's not that I fear food as much as I fear the irrational feeling that somehow the food almost has the power over me that a person would—it is almost as if it (the food) could make me eat it.

Other functions, too, are misinterpreted by fat and thin people. I shall give a few examples of the distortions in the assessment of their strength. It had been recognized during the study of obese children that the accumulation of fat, the increased body size, was not just the passive sequel of a positive energy balance but that it expressed a child's inner picture of what he wanted to be. His great weight gave him a certain feeling of safety and strength. The heavy layers of fat act like a wall behind which the child

finds protection against a threatening outside world. Overt aggressive behavior is rare in obese children. Usually the eating itself seems to satisfy
their aggressive impulses, and their size is a way of self-assertion. Many
fat children have a dread of being small and skinny; although they are
unhappy about their large size, they find security in it. This was graphically expressed by a girl of 6 who had grown obese when she was 3 years
old, following a summer during which her high-strung and nervous mother
had cared for her in place of her placid nurse (3).

This shy and awkward child revealed her problems and conflicts in a
series of drawings. She was jealous of her younger sister, who was pretty
and well-liked and enjoyed playing with other children. She sensed her
mother's annoyance and disgust with her and was aware of her own
hostile impulses toward her mother. She expressed this in her drawing of
her mother when she said, "I make a ruffle around her dress, so she
trips—and shall I make a cage around her?"

The "cage" had been previously used to express her hostility to a
certain doctor whom she hated because he had "pricked" her. The drawings for this doctor and her mother were very similar in the symbolic use
of form and color. She had finished the doctor's picture by cross-hatching
the body, remarking, "I make a cage out of his dress and he will die."

She was very reluctant to draw a picture of herself. She would draw
pictures of a "fairy," emptier and cruder than her other drawings. When
asked to tell something about the fairy, she went into a singsong: "That's
a girl—any girl—5500 years old. She does not like herself. I don't like
myself. She is a fairy and she does not like to be a fairy. She wants to be a
real girl."

The theme of the "girl who does not like herself" was accompanied by
resigned remarks that there was nothing one could do to change her. She
tried repeatedly to draw a picture of a girl who could like herself. She
ended up by completely covering a picture that had been quite pleasing in
the beginning, with scribblings of different colored crayons, finishing with
a vigorous black scribble across the face. This was done with much display of emotion; "It's myself. I put every color in the box on it. I was not
good in school last year. I put black on her face, and now you can't see
her any more. *I hide her. She does not want to get hurt. We put her behind
a wall.* A black face, nobody likes her."

In discussing this picture she repeated: "I don't like myself," and explained, "because I am fat. I eat too much, my mother says." This was
followed by an enthusiastic description of all the things she likes to eat: "I
like spaghetti best. And do you know what else? I want them all in one
meal: spaghetti, hominy, rice, noodles, and grits."

Fear of losing weight, of becoming thin, is common in fat youngsters.
This fear is often shared by the mothers who in sly ways will refeed their
children after they have reduced. Sophisticated obese adults will rarely
express this explicitly, but do so rather indirectly by developing symptoms

of weakness and unbearable tension, or by getting depressed while on a reducing regimen.

Anorexia nervosa patients experience something like the exact opposite. A 17-year-old girl, who went on a diet and lost weight when she learned that her boyfriend at college was dating other girls, felt for the first time "that she was getting results." Gradually she developed the feeling that her body had magical qualities. "My body could do anything—it could walk forever and ever and not get tired. I separated my mind and my body. My mind was tricky but my body was honest. It knew exactly what to do and I knew exactly what I could do. I felt very powerful on account of my body—my only weakness was my mind." At that time she started *compulsive walking rituals*, would walk for many miles even though she was increasingly cachectic. She would walk whether it was hot or raining, or a thunderstorm threatened. She felt "I have will power to walk as far as I want anytime—no matter what the weather is." She felt the same about her weight, "This was something I could control. I still don't know what I look like or what size I am, but I know my body can take anything." She was condescending toward her physicians who were increasingly alarmed about her condition, for she knew that she was immortal.

A 16-year-old anorexic girl, when at her lowest weight, was afraid of being "strong." Her ideal was to be weak, ethereal, and thin so that she could accept everybody's help without feeling guilty. Her deepest desire was to be blind so that she could show how noble she was in the face of suffering, and then she would be respected by everyone for this nobility. There was no realistic awareness of what it would be like to be blind, of not being able to see. In spite of this desire she was extremely active and perfectionistic, and would not permit herself to go to sleep until she had done calisthenics to the point of her muscles hurting.

Another anorexic girl, from an upper-class background, felt being fat indicated that one was exploitative. "If you are thin they don't think that you are rich and that your life is too easy. Being fat is like the kings in the Middle Ages; they are just rich and powerful and do nothing and everybody works for them. Looking and being exhausted shows that one does a lot, and without that I feel so undeserving."

Changes in this functional awareness are necessary milestones on the road to recovery. To quote from a patient who was doing well, "I took a walk—not to wear myself out or to prove 'I could make it' but just to enjoy the bright blue sky and the pretty yellow flowers. I seemed to do it without this 'double track' thinking." Another girl reported with real joy, "Last night I ate a chocolate bar and I enjoyed it. I told the nurse what kind I wanted and when she brought it, that's what I ate. There was none of the old fear 'I shouldn't do it' or that I wouldn't be able to stop once I had eaten one."

A 19-year-old girl who had become severely anorexic when away at college, with her weight dropping from 110 lbs in September to 70 lbs in

January, made a serious suicidal attempt in February when her weight had risen to 75 lbs because she was afraid of getting "too fat" again. When there was further increase in weight she gave up all control as "useless," and in September her weight had risen to 140 lbs. Asked about this, she said, "It looks the same to me—I'm just fat." The only way she could imagine feeling proud again would be by being very slim, and she considered this a hopeless goal that she couldn't attain again.

Misperception of Sexual Role

It is generally assumed that obese people have difficulties with sex and that they are confused about their sexual role. Anorexia nervosa is conceived of by some as expressing a rejection of sex or of pregnancy. It is true that many obese people, particularly those who become psychiatric patients, express uneasiness about their sexual identity, but it is misleading to generalize from their problems to all obese people.

Among the many obese patients I have observed there was no instance of transsexualism, with the desire of changing his or her sex, nor delusional misconception of being a member of the other sex. There were a few instances of homosexuality or lesbianism, and one of transvestism. The incidence is not higher, maybe even lower, than among my nonobese patients. The great majority did not misperceive their anatomical structures, though anorexic girls tended to exclude awareness of curves and breasts from their body images. There was, however, marked confusion about the gender role. Rorschach records of obese children revealed, besides a preoccupation with the problem of "size," definite evidence of gender confusion, expressed by their tendency of interpreting symmetrical figures as "a man and a woman," or "a boy and a girl," a finding not observed in other patients (2). This type of interpretation was given more often by obese boys than girls.

Men who had been obese since childhood, or who had been obese children but had outgrown it, and who functioned adequately, often expressed doubts about their masculinity; they were convinced of not being right, of being too soft, not masculine enough. This was more marked when there had been breast development during adolescence, even though it had disappeared. Such men are exceedingly careful about maintaining their weight at a normal level, though one aspect of their feeling "not right" is the ease with which they tend to gain weight when they relent their vigilance.

From direct contact with mothers of fat children it was learned that many had openly expressed a wish for a girl child, and some had raised their sons as if they were daughters. Some mothers were able to follow advice to discontinue this and to permit their sons to be boys. The most seriously disturbed boy in this group had a mother who did not change in her attitude. He became openly psychotic in adolescence, pulled out his body hair in pubescence "in order not to be like an animal," began to bleach his hair, used cosmetics, and said in an artificially high-pitched voice that he wanted to be good and would not have any dealings with the dirty habits of other youngsters.

Many other obese adolescents will speak about not wanting to be like the rough boys. One spoke openly of his fear of growing up, of his fear of manhood, and he related this to his hatred for his father. "It is not that I want to be a woman—I don't want to be a man, the way my father is." He felt his father wanted him to be brave and to accomplish things, but since he felt his father wanted this for *his own* gratification, he would not do any of the things expected of a young man.

Men who become obese later in life seem to feel differently. Often they consider their girth a sign of their imposing power and virility. This was described as a cultural trait for German men, with upper-class men tending to be heavy as a sign of their status and power (15).

On the whole, obese girls and women are much more open and articulate in discussing their dissatisfaction with their sex or their concepts of what they would want to be. In psychoanalytic literature there are repeated references to the large body being equated with the phallus. Even during intensive analytic work, not one of my patients made such a statement spontaneously, though they would pick it up if it was suggested to them. Many obese girls and women openly expressed how, throughout their lives, they had felt they had been destined to be "more than a woman." Bigness means to be like father.

Consciously I fight being fat, but unconsciously I accept it. It has to do with the fact that father was fat. He eats all the things he is not supposed to eat, and he is big all over. Mother will put him on a diet which he follows for a few days and then he gives it up. As long as I remember he was big all over. He was quite slim when he was younger but when he became an important man he grew fat and has maintained his weight ever since. He has all the attributes of being busy and important—he could not be thin at the same time. I always felt just like him and I accepted it that it is the thing to be when one is so important. Mother was always so careful about what she ate. When she gained one or two pounds she would go on a diet. That proved to me "people with nothing else to do, they can keep on dieting." *I* had more important things to do, I am like my father. I always thought of mother as useless and unimportant.

This idea can be found in the thinking of many fat women, that only unimportant people can waste time and energy on dieting. "The littleness of it, so picayune. You have to be so careful—that is not living," or "I hate the small, chattering magpie kind of woman, so small—such small souls. When I am with skinny girls I feel like a mountain with lots of gnats around. They make sweetness and littleness important." Or, "Being a woman means doing things as a minor study. Being big is my real aspiration. That means not to be a woman but to be somewhat more than a man—a hero."

The openly expressed desire of such a woman was not to be a man, but, what the Greeks called the "third sex," to be both a woman *and* a man. Several had elaborate fantasies about their lives in both roles. One condition for this was *being big*, in spite of all the criticism and social ostracism their fatness implied. This is even more openly expressed by anorexic girls, whether they had been previously overweight or not. One girl with active fantasies about sex would stand in front of the mirror and she saw in the reflection not the scrawny creature she was at that time but the most attractive young woman, and in her mind's eye she experienced her viewing self, the body outside the mirror, as a young man who was going to seduce this girl. In a way she had established the absolute of independence, of needing nothing from the outside, of carrying out a love affair with herself.

Several of the anorexic girls had had active fantasies as children about being a boy—a young prince or pageboy. One carried on a continuous fantasy, silently entertaining herself at the dinner table where her parents and older sister were engaged in conversation, feeling that what she had to say was not important or would not be listened to. Puberty development put a shocking end to this self-image of being the long-legged prince who walked along with a striding gait. Even after she had become anorexic she could recapture this sense of being the prince by going on walks where she would take long striding steps.

Of particular interest are observations of patients who alternate between being fat and thin. A young divorced woman entered the psychiatric service after 3 months of compulsive eating during which she had gained 50 lbs, and had become completely incapacitated. Compulsive eating had been a problem for her for the previous eight years, but never to the same degree. She had been married at age 19, after a year and a half of college, and was divorced a few months later. She then went to live abroad where she stayed for some time. After her return she married again and this, too, ended in divorce. She began to eat almost without stopping, hoarded and hid food in her apartment, became untidy and seclusive, and appeared to be unable to care for herself. She was quite articulate, sometimes overly dramatic, in describing her experiences, and some of the alternatives she described were, I am sure, artificially constructed. She considered her fat self "unreal" and felt as soon as she had lost weight that she was cured, that she was "real" again. As this *real, thin self* she feels transparent, admired, acclaimed, active, capable of giving, well-groomed, interested in men, having many heterosexual experiences. But *when fat* she feels *unreal*, dirty, slovenly, a nothing, passive, always on the receiving end, gorging herself like in a stupor, only interested in women, even becoming involved in homosexual affairs. In working with her it became apparent that her inner perception was as confused during the thin, starving phase as during the slovenly, fat period. What was revealed was dissatisfaction with her sex, her size, her capacities, and her ability to relate to others.

Emotional, Affective, and Social Aspects

Body image disturbances are experienced also in the affective sphere; this is probably the aspect of which one is most aware, whether one is satisfied with or unhappy about one's body and appearance. I have tried, in the preceding discussion, to separate cognitive and perceptive awareness of one's body from the affective attitude, yet comments on the feeling tone invariably crept in. Similarly, it will not be possible to speak of one's emotional attitude toward his body without attention to the social value system. Our social climate praises slenderness to such an extent that it is astounding that not all fat people suffer from disgust and self-hatred for being fat. Many, in particular adolescents and those who have been fat since childhood, speak with real anguish about their terrible fate and their hatred for their ugly and loathsome bodies. There is a tendency to consider the social stigma, the feeling of being a member of a despised minority, as the main cause for the psychological problems and low self-esteem of the obese.

The experience of self-hatred and contempt for being fat is frequent enough, yet it appears to be not only determined by social attitudes; it is also closely interwoven with psychological and interpersonal experiences early in life. It is not surprising that a young man whose mother had said proudly "the family thinks the bigger he is the better he is" developed a basically self-accepting attitude, even though severely overweight since childhood. Entirely different is the self-image of a young girl who, under constant criticism, had become so discouraged that she had withdrawn from all activities and was so apathetic that she gave the impression of being stupid, if not feeble-minded. Speaking of her childhood she would say "as far back as I can remember I was too fat and my mother always harped on it. Everything was done to make me thinner; that was the only thing that mattered. That's why I hate myself and my body. Fat people just disgust me."

I have seen occasionally a fat adolescent in psychiatric consultation who could say with reassurance, "Yes, I know it is not fashionable but that's the way I'm built, and my mother can say what she wants. I have to go through life my own way." The great majority of obese youngsters who come to psychiatric attention express their dislike and disgust in many dramatic ways. If one would rely on first information only, one might be inclined to say that childhood and adolescent obesity invariably leads to hateful, negative appraisal of and disgust for one's own body, but with which one is deeply identified. In play sessions with children Homburger (Erikson) (9) observed that obese children constructed buildings which resembled the outline of their bodies, a finding not observed in any other group. Mixed with this expressed disgust is guilt for having only oneself to blame, and a sense of shame for being weak-willed. Some openly equate the guilt about overeating with guilt about masturbation. Being fat is a public display of their transgression, a demonstration of self-indulgence and lack of control and will power. Yet with extended contact (during therapy), the information often changes. Gradually it becomes apparent that dislike of fatness is only the surface response; it is a concrete symbol of everything one dislikes in oneself and of what one considers contemptible and bad. Many will state that their fatness is only what shows on the outside; their deeper shame is their conviction of being awkward and ugly on the inside.

Quite often an obese youngster will "advertise" his low self-esteem, his contempt for his ugly body, by the way he dresses and presents himself. Most of my observations were made before "hippie" dress had become the fashion. A boy of 14, who made it a point to look disheveled and neglected, explained: "You can tell me from my cover." Occasionally he would appear well-dressed and well-groomed, looking entirely different, not even as grossly obese as usual. This was on days when he planned to visit his wealthy grandfather. He feared that the doorman would not admit him in his disheveled garb. The 16-year-old daughter of a beautiful woman, repeatedly on the "best dressed" list, usually appeared in gray or brown sack-like dresses, bought at the cheapest stores. Even after she had lost weight, the color and fit of her dresses would announce her mood.

Anorexics, too, often express their body awareness through their clothing. Whether it is fashionable or not, they will hold their dresses in with tightly-drawn wide belts. The belt seems to serve as a control; as long as it can be closed at the same hole they feel reassured of not having gained an ounce. With all the denial of the scrawniness of their figures, many seem to dislike the skeleton-like look of their arms; summer or winter, they will wear long-sleeved dresses, covering their ugly-looking arms. As one expressed it, though she did not feel "too thin," she felt that her arms made her look like "a praying mantis."

In working with such people a much more complex attitude of their self-concept gradually evolves. Many speak quite openly of feeling like a dual person, a fat one and a thin one. "I seem to be two people; one wants to be thin, but the other *wants* to be fat." When asked about the personality of the fat and thin person, it turns out that many fat people conceive of the thin person as one who is doing everything that is expected of a young girl, who is conforming, studying, socially active, well-groomed, and well-dressed, but who deep down is a selfish and undesirable person who lacks inner qualities and values and who relies on looks, is ruthless, and babbles

socially, "having a line." In contrast, the fat girl, the one who procrasti-
nates with her studies, who is unhappy about moping around at home,
who is the constant butt of her parents' and friends' belittling remarks, is
deep down a worthwhile person, kind and considerate, honest in dealing
with people and truly valuing her friends. The deepest pain is felt because
the family and society at large praise and admire the thin one, regardless
of her selfish and ruthless traits, and devalue and despise the fat one with
the much more valuable human qualities.

A brilliant young college girl described her whole childhood as a time
of continuous humiliation. "I always felt I was dull and clumsy—even as
a child I was considered 'too big.' " She had become fat only after puberty
but the conviction of not being desirable, of not having "sex appeal," had
preceded the weight gain. "It was not the heaviness—there was something
about me, the bigness, the clumsiness." But with all her complaining,
there was also reluctantly admitted pride in being big. When she enrolled
in college, she was rather disappointed that nobody paid special attention
to her for being so big and heavy. Somehow the feeling of "specialness"
had been a comfort in this continuous shame and embarrassment about
her bodily existence.

One might say that anorexia nervosa by its very existence proves that
the hateful self-contempt is not really related to the excess weight, but to
some deep inner dissatisfaction. Not one of the anorexic patients whom I
have come to know over the years had set out to reach this state of pitiful
emaciation. All they had wanted to achieve was to feel better about themselves. Since they had felt that "being too fat" was the cause of their
despair, they were determined to correct it. Whatever weight they reached
in this struggle for self-respect and respect from others, it was "not right"
for giving them inner reassurance, and so the downhill course continued.
One girl had suffered all her life from the feeling of being "ugly," of not
being "a beauty." She was overweight and started a reducing program, at
first rather sensibly, reducing from 140 to 110 lbs between ages 13 and
16. But then, when things were still "not right," she went on a starvation
regimen, to a low of 67 lbs. She explained it as "about being fat I could do
something, but not about being ugly." She knew that her skeleton-like
appearance was hideous, if not from her own inspection then from the
reaction of others. Her argument was "What if my weight went back to
normal and I were still ugly, what would I do then?" At the same time she
knew that what was covered under the term "ugly" applied as much to
psychological attributes and to disappointment in her own achievements
and behavior as to the physical evidence.

Another anorexic girl said of herself, "I was trying to be what other
people thought I was. I am an unknown quantity—it all began with mother's obsession with social success."

A systematic study of obese people's emotional attitudes toward their
body was conducted by Stunkard and Mendelson (19) and Stunkard and
Burt (20). They found that almost half of the obese individuals who had

become obese before or at the time of puberty, but who were post-adolescent at the time of the study, had severely disturbed body-image concepts, along with greatly impaired interpersonal and heterosexual adjustment. In striking contrast not one of the patients who had become obese as adults had the same degree of disturbance in these areas. These findings are in agreement with my own observations that it is the distorting and undermining interpersonal experiences early in life that result in this self-concept of being monstrous and grotesque.

Ownership of the Body and Its Control

It was only through long-range therapeutic work that the meaning of the continuous complaint of "not being right" was gradually recognized through the discovery that these patients experienced their bodies as not being truly their own, as being under the influence of others. They felt they had no control over their bodies and its functions. It had always been known that fat people suffered from "lack of will power," and this term has often been used in a reproachful way. In the course of my studies it became clear that this lack of will power really represents one of the basic issues and is related to their inability to perceive their bodily needs. Fat people tend to talk about their bodies as external to themselves. They do not feel identified with this bothersome and ugly thing they are condemned to carry through life, and in which they feel confined or imprisoned. An English writer, Cyril Connolly, himself a fat man, expressed this graphically: "Imprisoned in every fat man a thin one is wildly signaling to be let out" (4). Another English writer, Kingsley Amis, paraphrased this: "Outside every fat man there is an even fatter man trying to close in" (1).

Anorexia nervosa patients will express this not being identified with their bodies even more definitely. I quote from the history of a 20-year-old woman who had become anorexic at age 15, reducing from 90 to 55 lbs. She made what looked like a spontaneous recovery but became depressed when she went to college at age 18. She also began to suffer from bouts of compulsive eating which terrified her because she was afraid of getting fat. Her weight fluctuated between 103 and 110 lbs, but from her continuous preoccupation with her weight one might have concluded that she was monstrously fat.

In the course of treatment she gradually recognized that her whole life had been an effort to fit into the idealized image her parents had planned for her, particularly her mother, whose own childhood had been deprived and who had wanted her daughter to have all the things she had missed. The dominant feeling at college, which led to the depressive withdrawal, was the question, "Do *I* have to go to college just because mother never went?" Toward the end of treatment she became concerned with the question of what had led to this particular illness. She had never thought of it in an active way, namely that she herself had stopped eating. She had always thought of it as an outside event, as "*It* happened to me." Once she had recognized the importance of this, she raised the question, "Do you think I was hurting my parents by not eating? Father is so overconcerned about anything that has to do with physical health. I realize now I was hurting them by not eating. The more they worried about it the more I was hurting them." It had never occurred to her that it was she and her body that were undergoing this ordeal of starvation.

A young fat girl from a similarly overprivileged background had one favorite daydream, namely that she would reduce to such an extent that she would look pitiful and her father would be worried and would plead with her to eat. There was a feeling of triumph that it would serve him right, "that will truly hurt him when I look miserable and scrawny and he cannot make me eat." Again there was no awareness that she and her body would be involved and suffer.

This was even more clearly expressed by a male anorexic who had been sick since age 12 and had successfully resisted all treatment efforts, weighing less than 50 lbs at age 18. Throughout this time all his struggles and fights had been directed against efforts to *make* him eat. He protested, "It's my life. If I don't want to eat why should my mother make a fuss over it." He had gradually developed a real fear of the scale. "I feel I get evaluated by it and then I am panicky. If I gain, *they* are so proud; and if I lose, my mother blows her head off. It is always somebody else's business."

In connection with a visit to his parents he used the expression "after all, I am their property." When this was singled out for discussion he at first wanted to dismiss it, and said that he had used the wrong expression. But then he took it up in detail, "Everything I have and own comes from them."

It was only after considerable therapeutic progress that he began to recognize his body and its functions as his own, and could let go of his long-standing symptoms. When he was transferred to an open ward he expressed the feeling: "I am free—*I own my body*—I am not supervised any more by nurses or by mother." His attitude toward his weight and what he ate underwent a complete change. "I have controlled myself so long, now I want to enjoy food." Or at another time, "Now if I lose weight it makes me feel sick that I am losing something that is *mine*." This young man, whose treatment will be discussed in Chapter 17, made a complete recovery.

Probably the most dramatic misperception of her body, and dissatisfaction and despair about it, was expressed by a young woman whose history was presented in Chapter 4. I shall repeat here a few sentences relevant for the development of her body image. As a child she had been under relentless pressure to fulfill her mother's image of what she should be. Unfortunately this image stood in contrast to the child's constitutional make-up. The mother had been in her late thirties when she became pregnant, at a time when she no longer expected a child. She had accepted that she would become a mother in the hope of having a child like her sister's plump and cuddly baby. Her newborn baby looked long and stringy and the pediatrician jokingly remarked, "Put some fat on those bones." The mother took this recommendation literally and a situation developed in which she shoveled food into the infant, who would reject it; she would shovel it back, forcing the child to swallow some more. Initially it looked as if the mother was winning this contest; the little girl grew fat but then was blamed for being clumsy and ugly.

This girl was unable to exercise any control over her eating; she was either monstrously fat or maintained her weight at an artificially low level. This she could accomplish only by forcing her parents never to have extra food in the home except what she needed to maintain this low weight. She reproached her parents for having created her as a monster; she now was waiting for them to change so that they could recreate her in a better image. She expressed in exaggerated degree the feeling of having no sense of ownership of her body or any effective self-awareness. She suffered from enormous self-hatred for being fat, though she could not "see" herself either as fat or as thin, and was completely unable to control her food intake or any other aspect of her life. She experienced herself as controlled from the outside, lacking initiative and autonomy, without a personality, the sad product of her parents' mistakes, "a nothing," and the despised body was, she felt, not really hers.

BIBLIOGRAPHY

1. Amis, K., *One Fat Englishman*, Harcourt, Brace & World, Inc., New York, 1963.
2. Bruch, H., Obesity in childhood and personality development, Amer. J. Orthopsychiat., 11:467–474, 1941.
3. Bruch, H., Food and emotional security, The Nervous Child, 3:165–173, 1944.
4. Connolly, C., *The Unquiet Grave*, Harper & Bros., New York, 1945.
5. Eustis, H., An American home, pp. 47–64, in *The Captains and the Kings Depart*, Harper & Bros., New York, 1949.
6. Fisher, S., and Cleveland, S. E., *Body Image and Personality*, Dover Publications, Inc., New York, 1968.
7. Glucksman, M. L., Hirsch, J., McCully, R. S., Barron, B. A., and Knittle, J. L., The response of obese patients to weight reduction, II. A quantitative evaluation of behavior, Psychosom. Med., 30:359–375, 1968.
8. Gottheil, E., Backup, C. E., and Cornelison, F. S., Denial and self-image confrontation in a case of anorexia nervosa, J. Nerv. Ment. Dis., 148:238–250, 1969.
9. Homburger (Erikson), E., Traumatische Konfigurationen im Spiel, Imago, 23:447–462, 1937.
10. Kolb, L. C., Disturbances of the body image, pp. 749–769, in *American Handbook of Psychiatry*, Vol. 1, S. Arieti, ed., Basic Books, Inc., New York, 1959.
11. Levy, D. M., Body interest in children and hypochondriasis, Amer. J. Psychiat., 12:295–311, 1932.
12. Nathan, S., and Pisula, D., Psychological observations of obese adolescents during starvation treatment, J. Amer. Acad. Child Psychiat., 9:722–740, 1970.

13. Petro, A., Body image and archaic thinking, Int. J. Psychoanal., 40:1–9, 1959.
14. Piaget, J., *The Construction of Reality in the Child*, Basic Books, Inc., New York, 1954.
15. Pflanz, M., Mediziniseh-soziologische Aspekte der Fettsucht, Psyche, 16:579–591, 1963.
16. Schilder, P., *Das Koerperschema: Ein Beitrag zur Lehre vom Bewusstsein des eigenen Koerpers*, Julius Springer, Berlin, 1923.
17. Schilder, P., *The Image and Appearance of the Human Body*, Psyche Monographs, 4, London, 1935.
18. Shontz, F. C., *Preceptual and Cognitive Aspects of Body Experience*, Academic Press, New York, 1969.
19. Stunkard, A., and Mendelson, M., Obesity and the body image: I. Characteristics of disturbances in the body image of some obese persons, Amer. J. Psychiat., 123:1296–1300, 1967.
20. Stunkard, A., and Burt, V., Obesity and the body image: II. Age at onset of disturbances in the body image, Amer. J. Psychiat., 123:1443–1447, 1967.

PART II

Obesity

7

Diversity of Clinical Pictures

Obesity has been called the number one health problem of the United States, or, in a more hostile vein, "a national scandal." Figures about its frequency range from 20% to 30% of the population, indicating that there are millions and millions of people who are overweight. The bias of the whole discussion implies that this is a deplorable state of affairs and the literature, medical as well as popular, abounds with generalized statements about the health hazards of being fat, its ugliness, its social handicaps, its psychological damage. Needless to say, terms like obesity, overweight, or overnutrition cover a variety of conditions; the large number of people suggests that any generalizations must be inaccurate and misleading. It is inconceivable that the excess weight in all these millions should have developed on the same basis, or would offer the same clinical or psychological picture.

Obesity As Deviation from Standard Weight

Looked at objectively, these millions of people have only one thing in common, namely, that their weight deviates, within an enormous range, from what has been proclaimed the standard or ideal weight. For marked obesity such a figure gives a rough estimate of the degree of excess weight which on inspection usually proves to be fat tissue. For the milder degrees of overweight, and this represents the great majority of people included in these statistics, the validity of the whole statistical concept has been challenged. Newer tables consider height and body build in addition to weight, but they are based on the implicit assumption that all body weight is equivalent and that "overweight" is a measure of relative fatness. In the lesser degrees of overweight it is quite arbitrary to decide from the weight deviation alone whether the excess weight is due to excess fat. It is now generally considered more accurate to estimate fatness by making a couple of judicious pinches of the skin folds than by merely comparing the weight of a moderately overweight person to the height-weight tables. Various refined methods have been developed for more accurate estimation of relative fatness. Another implied error rests in the assumption that the ratio between fat and other body tissues should be the same in all individuals.

For three-quarters of a century clinical medicine and research have accepted these so-called averages as representing the desirable normal weight for all adults. For some time Keys has raised doubts concerning the statistical validity of the whole campaign of the insurance companies against overweight, with its aim of preventing heart disease and other diseases which shorten life expectancy and are blamed on overweight (17). In spite of the large figures on which these arguments are based, Keys questions the justification of looking upon the 2% of overweight policy holders as representative of the very large number of overweight people in the whole population. He calculated that even after weight correction in all the people who are 20% or more above the statistical average, the death rate from heart disease would still be unusually high in American males. He also pointed out that it is potentially dangerous to enforce reducing in people with circulatory disorders. If they cannot maintain the lower weight the ensuing restoration of the previous weight places a damaging burden on the circulation.

During the last decade there have been increased objections against arbitrary standards which demand that everybody's weight should conform to that of 30-year-old Americans who have the longest life expectancy. In an international symposium on overnutrition held in Sweden in 1963, a good deal of the discussion focused on the question of "ideal weight" which obviously does not conform to body weight as it is actually observed (2). In a survey which included every member of the population in the south of Sweden, body weights were decidedly higher than these so-called norms. After 40 years of age, 70% of the female population was 10 kg "overweight," and 10% 30 kg or more, though upper-class women tended to weigh less and to show less variability in weight (1). There was nothing to indicate that these large numbers of "overweight" people suffered from the condition.

The participants of this symposium came from many different countries and represented different disciplines, ranging from basic science to animal nutrition. There was a convergence of opinion that many middle-aged people with a stable weight excess of 20 to 30 lbs who customarily were rated as "overweight" were probably normal for themselves; that this weight excess did not represent a health hazard, except in clearly defined abnormal conditions. There was also general agreement that "obesity" as a clinical condition represented not just an extreme on the normal distribution curve for weight but that it was a true disorder with metabolic and anatomic features of its own. The nearly automatic prescription of a reducing diet, or increased exercise, is often unable to overcome its irreversible features. Variations of weight within the range of the distribution curve due to various constitutional or nutritional factors also represent a much wider spectrum than the narrow standard figures indicate.

In spite of these cautious voices of people actively involved in nutritional research, the broad stream of discussions of obesity continues to label any deviation from the arbitrary standard as abnormal. The damage caused by this labeling technique is probably not as great as it might be because the majority of people falling in the range of statistical overweight just do not pay attention to it nor do they try to change it.

Even those overweight and obese people who come to the attention of physicians, nutritionists, or statisticians do not represent a uniform picture. Yet efforts at subdividing the various forms have thus far not been too successful. Each investigator analyzes his case material according to his line of interest and then generalizes from his findings as if they were applicable to all cases of obesity. I wish to state emphatically that this is a misleading procedure, that there is a need to evaluate the whole problem in terms of biological uniqueness and to group together only those who show comparable patterns of development and reaction.

Superobesity

The recently developed method of counting and measuring fat cells represents a step toward measuring biological differences. It permits us to differentiate between obesity due to overnutrition, which is characterized by large extended fat cells, and obesity based on fat tissues with a high adipose cell count. In such individuals, reducing empties the fat cells, so that on microscopic examination, the fat tissue resembles that of starving individuals. This was demonstrated by Hirsch on superobese patients who lost great amounts of weight on a restricted diet but whose fat layers still looked "too heavy." Microscopic examination revealed these tissues to contain numerous nuclei of fat cells, but very low fat content, indicating they were biologically in the state of starvation (14).

It was in these truly fat people, who are so large and heavy that they are outside all statistical considerations and in a class by themselves, that the extreme tenacity with which they clung to their weight was first acknowledged. Authors of the past reported on them with a certain awe. Wadd, in his collection of the most remarkable cases of corpulence that occurred in England, speaks with pride of Mr. Lambert of Leicester who weighed 52 stones and 11 pounds (739 lbs), as having no equal in "corporal greatness" (27).

Brillat-Savarin (3), the French gastronomist, describes in detail a fat man whom he met on his travels to the New World in 1795:

But the most extraordinary instance I have seen was an inhabitant of New York, whom many readers must have seen sitting in the Broadway on an enormous armchair with legs strong enough to bear a church. Edward was at least six feet four in height, and as his fat had swollen every part of him, he was over eight feet in girth. His fingers were like those of the Roman emperor who used his wife's bracelets for rings, his arms and thighs were cylindrical, as thick as a medium-sized ham, and his feet were like those of an elephant, covered with the overlapping flesh of his legs. The weight of fat had dragged down his lower eyelids; but what made him most hideous were three round chins of more than a foot hanging over his chest so that his face looked like the capital of a truncated pillar. He sat thus beside a window of a low room which opened onto the street, drinking from time to time a glass of ale, of which there was a huge pitcher always near him.

People with such extreme obesity are rare—so rare that they sometimes earn their living by exhibiting themselves as one of nature's curiosities. The discovery of a new fat man or woman is newsworthy.

Quite recently a 37-year-old man, who claims to have weighed as much as 1100 lbs, came to the attention of the Baylor College of Medicine (22). This man had been touring the country and exhibited himself as a warning against the dangers of "drugs," which he claimed had turned him into a compulsive eater. He had been in the Army at age 20, weighing 190 lbs. There was no history of obesity in his family, and he claimed he did not have an eating problem before he "freaked out" on drugs. After that, for the past 7 years, he had been hopelessly addicted to food, eating almost constantly, almost anything. When his weight reached 600 lbs he became unable to move and was bedridden. The weight increase continued and supposedly reached a high of 1100 lbs. At that time he contacted some entrepreneurs who arranged his new career as an exhibit. He lived in a specially built trailer, which also had room for his wife and 8-year-old son. Since he began his touring life, his food intake had been restricted to about 2000 calories per day, and he claimed to have lost 200 lbs in 6 months. His weight could be checked only indirectly, by weighing the trailer with him inside.

While on exhibit in Houston, he complained about abdominal and chest pains and feared a heart attack. Thus he came to the attention of the hospital. Whatever his accurate weight, he was so huge that no effort was made to move him out of his trailer and the necessary medical equipment was taken in. No evidence of heart disease was found; on the contrary, circulatory function was better than expected. He recovered within a few days and asked to be discharged from the hospital lot, before the physiological and particular psychological aspects of this extreme case of obesity could be studied in detail. The whole issue was beclouded by the publicity, and the physicians who were in touch with him did not feel that they got reliable information.

Such superobese people have found more clinical attention in recent years, since reducing by total starvation has become the vogue. Though they are capable of losing enormous amounts, they are apt to regain their weight, bringing their hypercellular adipose tissues back into metabolic balance. It seems that some of these superobese people accept themselves with more equanimity than the many people who struggle with minor weight deviations.

A 32-year-old woman, a nightclub singer, gave the impression of independence and strength. She had been fat since early childhood and gained progressively until her weight stabilized at 325 lbs. Her large size did not interfere with her career, nor with getting married three times, the first time when 17 years old. After she had two children she divorced her husband; she was then 22 years old. Shortly thereafter she remarried and had three more children; again the marital relationship deteriorated. Her third husband met her and fell in love with her even before she had obtained a divorce. She was reluctant to marry again, but finally consented. During the divorce proceedings her weight increased to 375 lbs and she developed circulatory and respiratory symptoms. For the first time she felt her sense of independence threatened. She entered a hospital for reducing, but only to her previous weight level. She had no desire to be slim; she was impressive through her size and her erect, proud posture.

Weight Stability and Instability

Even patients with much smaller weight excesses seem to cling to their "preferred weight" with great persistence (6). Having followed patients over many years I have come to doubt the validity of approaching the whole obesity problem with the assumption that a definite height-weight relationship and a definite fat-lean tissue proportion are "normal" for all people just because they are found in the majority. To superimpose a rigid and absolute concept of normality on all is not only useless but must be considered as potentially threatening and dangerous. A French clinician, Leray, has formulated his observations in a similar way, and expressed doubt about the statistical approach; he feels that one must instead approach heavy people in terms of their "physiological weight," which he defines as an individual's average weight which remains constant for many years and which is appropriate for him as long as he feels well and healthy (18).

It has long been known that there is a need to distinguish between two phases of obesity, an *active* or *dynamic* phase during which the weight increases progressively, and a *stationary* or *stable* form after a certain degree of fatness has been reached. The German language has two words for obesity: *Fettsucht,* implying a tendency, literally addiction, for progressive accumulation of fat tissue, and *Fettleibigkeit,* the state during which a stable, though high weight is maintained. The ongoing campaign against overweight is mainly directed at people who have attained this stable form of obesity, and who usually find it difficult to maintain their weight below the level at which it has come to rest.

By observing fat patients over many years I have come to the conclusion that the stability or instability of the weight curve over an extended period is a more accurate measure of the disorder than the degree of weight excess alone, and a fairly reliable guide for an appraisal of whether or not an overweight person is doing well. If the weight has been stable for a long period, and the individual has functioned adequately and with a sense of well-being, there is little to be gained by persuading such a person to reduce. With a valid motivation for reducing, be it of a personal, aesthetic, or psychological nature, or with a tangible medical indication, such as diabetes, cardiovascular disease, etc., the prospect for successful reducing is usually good. Without such motivation, it is nil.

As an example of stable stationary obesity I should like to quote from the record of a woman who was a patient at the Presbyterian Hospital in New York over a 40-year period. Her last medical examination when she was 63 years old was a checkup prior to minor surgery and her physician gave her a clean bill of health though her weight was 196 lbs. She had attended the clinic for the first time when 23 years old, shortly after she married and moved to New York. At that time she expressed concern about having gained 10 lbs during the preceding 6 months. She came from a poverty area and the gain may not have been more than her response to a more comfortable style of city living. This was the only time that she complained about her weight, which was 150 lbs. She came again to the clinic 5 years later with a broken finger, and her weight was 196 lbs but she did not complain about it. Over the years she attended the clinic with a variety of complaints: minor accidents, pains in her chest and joints, and persistent pains in her abdomen. A cholecystectomy was performed when she was 37 years old. Throughout the many contacts with the clinic numerous efforts were made to put her on a diet. One might literally say that for whatever ailed her she was sent to the nutrition clinic. Repeatedly she tried to follow the prescribed diet and lost as much as 10 or 20 lbs. Finally, when 40 years old, she made a definite declaration that she could not diet, that it made her feel nervous.

The record is an historical document insofar as it reflects the changing thinking and attitude toward obesity at a renowned medical center. Therapeutic enthusiasm alternated with expressions of disgust and the record contains statements such as "a hopeless situation," or "the patient is absolutely uncooperative, but will be given another chance." The final comment was: "This lady has managed to go through all our weight reducing programs—without effect." As far as is known, she has lived a satisfactory life and no one can say whether she would have been free of joint pains or moderately high blood pressure if she had kept her weight at a lower level. However, she felt disturbed when on a reducing regimen and she felt better and was more active when she kept her weight at her "preferred," admittedly overweight, level.

It is a matter of opinion whether or not to rate this woman's weight excess as "abnormal"; it was not, in her own judgment. Usually these debatable stable weight excesses are smaller, in the 20 to 30 lb range. I have known innumerable people, many in the professions, who felt they "weighed too much," and who in a burst of fashion consciousness would lose the extra pounds. Invariably they would regain them, not intentionally, and then would notice that they functioned more effectively at the higher weight.

In contrast there is no doubt whatsoever that something is drastically wrong with those who seem to be unable to stabilize at any weight. Most of my observations of such fluctuations have been made on adolescents and young adults. Their frantic efforts at reducing, self-imposed or medically prescribed and supervised, are an indication of severe maladjustment and this pattern may continue into adult life.

I give as an example the story of a 36-year-old man, weighing 255 lbs, who came for a psychiatric consultation when he finally realized that his frantic efforts of fighting his weight only increased his problems. For 20 years he had made many strenuous efforts at reducing; each one was followed by rapid weight increase; the amounts lost and regained which he could recall added up to nearly 1,000 lbs. He was the youngest child in a large family and had been fat, but nothing was done about it until he was 16 years old and weighed 265 lbs. At that time an older sister insisted on treatment for him and supervised his diet. He lost nearly 100 lbs during the next year and weighed 169 lbs when he graduated from high school. He considered this year "the golden age" of his life. But he could not maintain the lower weight; whenever he encountered difficulties in his jobs, suffered an accident, had conflicts in his family or marital difficulties, etc., he would gain enormous amounts of weight; his highest weight, at age 25, had been 270 lbs. Any decision to make a new start in life was associated with strenuous reducing at record speed; he would recite figures like having lost "50 lbs in as many days." If one plots the highs and lows of his weight on a curve it resembles that of septic fever, and reflects the many shifts in his efforts to find a better adjustment to life. He was haunted by the fear of failure, of not living up to expectation, and felt he was an object of ridicule. He sought psychiatric help when it had finally become clear to him that he could not solve his problems in life by manipulating his weight.

Even more drastic are the weight fluctuations of a 20-year-old college girl who had managed to lose and regain 530 lbs since her thirteenth birthday. She had been teased that she would become as big as a fat aunt, and went on a diet, reducing from 135 lbs to 110 lbs in little more than one month. She considered this her ideal weight and maintanied it for nearly 3 years. In preparing for college and an acting career, she felt she needed to be more glamorous and began a rigid reducing regimen. At 16½, her weight had dropped to 74 lbs and she stayed at this level for nearly 2 years. This makes her a fat patient who developed anorexia nervosa. The family life deteriorated to constant fighting about food and her parents were frantic in seeking help for her. Finally they found a physician who administered insulin injections. During episodes of mild insulin shock she refused to take sugar into her mouth, stating that she did not care whether she lived or died. But she began eating on the sly, sneaking to the refrigerator in the middle of the night and gorging herself. This she continued after the insulin was stopped. The eating sprees continued, with many ups and downs in her weight and she began vomiting after eating. She entered college at 18, weighing 110 lbs, hoping it would be easier to maintain her weight when living away from home. Instead she found she was unable to control her eating, to attend to her studies, or to hold a job. Her weight rose to 155 lbs and she became acutely depressed and suicidal. She was admitted to a psychiatric service where she was placed on a diet on which she lost 45 lbs in 3 months. After discharge there were frequent changes of psychiatrists until she finally stayed with one who was "eclectic" in his approach. He insisted that she should weigh exactly 110 lbs, and used various techniques—interpretations, hypnosis, amphetamines—to help her stay at her "ideal" weight. In spite of this, 6 months later her weight was back at 155 lbs; this was followed by a starvation period, with a drop to 105 lbs. After a disappointment with a boyfriend, she gained rapidly, to 140 lbs; again she went on a starvation regimen and her weight dropped to 110 lbs. She had become completely isolated, had lost touch with her former friends, was unable to hold a job, and just stayed at home eating; finally, embarrassed about the increasing weight, she did not go out at all. At age 20, when she was admitted for long-term therapy, her weight was 174 lbs.

It was felt that it was important for her to learn to establish controls over her own eating; it took some time before she believed that what she ate was truly left to her. During the first 6 weeks she lost 30 lbs, then went again on eating sprees and regained 20 lbs within 2 months. By that time she had established good therapeutic rapport and became interested in coming to an understanding of the relationship of her erratic eating behavior to her inner problems, upsetting life experiences, poor interpersonal relations, and deep conviction of her helplessness. She began to lose slowly and within a year her weight reached the desired level of 110 lbs, a weight she has since maintained. She had made considerable progress in understanding her psychological problems and no longer used food to camouflage them. She left the hospital at age 22 and resumed her college studies.

These examples illustrate the widely varying patterns of weight fluctuations in obesity. To draw a conclusion from just one weight is as inadequate as evaluating a febrile disease by taking the temperature just once. In evaluating weight disturbances many factors must be taken into account. We can speak of weight stability only when the stable weight is an expression of a more or less spontaneous regulation, without undue strain and continuous anxious concern about dieting. There are people who succeed in keeping their weight close to, or below, the so-called normal, but whose whole life is centered on maintaining this low weight. They will be discussed as "thin fat people"; their problems bear close resemblance to those encountered in anorexia nervosa.

Age at Onset of Obesity

Most people become obese as adults and the incidence of obesity increases with age. It is the middle-aged who make up the large numbers indicating its deplored prevalence. It depends on the attitude of an examiner whether this weight is described as ugly "middle-age spread" or accepted as part of advancing maturity. The old expression of "fat, fair, and forty" suggests that overweight has not always been considered the great disaster that it is regarded as in our time and age. Even today it is considered a more or less natural part of growing older that can be prevented only by constant vigilance and rigid control over one's eating. Though the number of obese patients is enormous, little is known about the great majority who seem to be indifferent to it, and who do not come for examination and study, even less for treatment. The outraged remark of the woman leaving her doctor's office: "Who does he think he is, putting me on a diet! I went to him just for a checkup," reflects the attitude of millions about whom the profession knows as much or as little as is expressed in popular prejudices. Even among those who come for treatment few cooperate to the extent of permitting us to learn more than their weight at one point in time and not what we need to know, namely their individual make-up, physiology, personality, and style of living.

Obesity is much more common in women than in men; but the incidence of heart disease which is assumed to be related to obesity is higher in men. It has always been known that there are marked differences in relative fatness between men and women. The old nursery rhyme tells us that little girls are made of sugar and spice; actually they are made of much more fat than little boys, who consist of more muscle and bone. This difference between the sexes persists throughout life and a slender-looking woman carries more fat tissue than an equally slender man. In spite of this, women have a longer life expectancy than men. If a woman would carry as little fat as a man, she would not be slim, but scrawny, and no longer beautiful—although fashion in recent years has declared skinniness to be beautiful and the "best dressed women" have all been emaciated.

The greater frequency of obesity in women has often been related to the sexual function. It is easy to demonstrate that obesity develops in a definite relationship to various phases of the sexual cycle, menarche, pregnancy, and particularly menopause. However, few if any systematic studies have been carried out. The assertions are often made on the basis of positive coincidence, which may or may not indicate a causal relationship.

It had been assumed for a long time that castration was followed by weight increase, but observations of patients who have undergone such an operation show that weight gain and subsequent adjustment depend on the previous pattern of adjustment and emotional maturity. Conversely, it has also been stated that weight gain would lead to sexual difficulties. Though individual cases in which this occurs stand out, there is no proof that this is a regular occurrence. Concurrent disturbances are often precipitated by the same noxious event, but do not cause each other. Menstrual irregularities are often taken as a criterion of sexual disturbances, yet it is well known that menstruation is a function that is highly sensitive to emotional upsets and drastic changes in nutrition. Some clinicians have blamed obesity for their patient's sterility while others have been impressed with the fertility of obese women.

Crisp, in England, made an attempt to compare some aspects of the sexual activity of 16 massively obese women (age range 16 to 21 years, with weight range 210 lbs to 325 lbs, average 250 lbs) with 16 nonobese patients with psychoneurotic illness (9). The obese patients tended to have menstruated earlier; a high degree of menstrual irregularity was reported after the onset of the obesity. He found there were no statistically significant differences between the obese and nonobese psychoneurotic subjects as to their heterosexual relationships and marital status, although there were more virgins among the obese group. The increase in weight to massive proportions had followed a crisis in their personal relationships in which their sexual activity had been involved and had evoked considerable guilt. In some the increase in weight to massive proportions had coincided with total cessation of sexual activities.

In my own experience the relationship between sexual function and obesity is usually much more complex than the initial information indicates (7). I recall a wealthy woman of 44, weighing 240 lbs, who stated that she had weighed 120 lbs when she married at age 22, and that her weight increase was due to her three pregnancies. She was depressed, not so much about her weight as about her husband's belittling remarks. She felt he was to blame for her obesity since, after all, he had made her pregnant. Exact information revealing an entirely different picture was obtained as therapy progressed. Though she had been slim at the time of her marriage, this had been achieved under her mother's pressure. She had been a heavy child and adolescent weighing 180 lbs, and had rebelled against her mother's efforts to make her reduce. Finally the mother won this fight and forced her daughter's weight down to the glamorous 120 lbs through strict dietary supervision. The young woman became pregnant soon after the wedding and it was easy for her to blame her increasing weight on the pregnancy. She had gained 10 lbs during each pregnancy, accounting for 30 lbs. The rest had been gained between and following the pregnancies; her youngest child was now 16 years old. Her attitude had remained embarrassingly identical to that of her teens; she blamed others and made her obesity somebody else's problem. This sophisticated, educated woman sounded like a resentful child when she described meals where her husband was "watching" whether or not she would take a rich dessert and thus "made her" take an extra-large helping.

In ordinary middle-age obesity it is generally assumed that the increase in weight takes place gradually, that it "creeps up" on an unsuspecting individual. In my own experience with this age group there has not been one instance in which obesity had developed in this gradual way. Whenever a detailed history was taken, weight increases were found to be related to certain events or changes in life patterns. This weight then became stable until some new event precipitated a new increase, such as incapacitating illness, surgery, or states of emotional dissatisfaction. The increase at any one time may not have been large, usually in the 5 to 10 lb range. But these episodic increases added up to "overweight." People who remain slim either do not gain in this way, or correct it immediately, some knowingly, others nearly automatically.

Many obese adults have been fat as children or adolescents. There appears to be general agreement that obesity with an onset early in life is much less accessible to therapy than that which develops later; it is also more often associated with serious personality problems. The conclusion has been drawn that obesity in childhood and adolescence always has a poor prognosis. It may appear that way if looked upon from the angle of those who remain obese in adult life. There are many overweight children who outgrow the condition; this will be discussed in detail in the following chapter.

Obesity in a young person appears much more abnormal or unnatural than in later life. Two paintings in the Prado by Juan Carreno (1614–1685) of an extremely fat 5-year-old girl are named simply "The Monster" (8). The lot of fat children, and even more of adolescents, is a sad one. Wherever they go they attract attention because they look ungainly, awkward, and slow. Their misshapen bodies and assumed sluggish behavior sets them apart as they stand in sharp contrast to the grace and liveliness of slim youngsters.

Gain in weight early in life is an integral part of growth and development. Even under normal conditions growth is a complex process influenced by many different factors; hence it is even more difficult than in adults to determine whether or not excess weight is normal or pathological at this age. An individualistic evaluation is essential to obtain a meaningful picture.

Pediatricians have been aware for a long time that simple height-weight

charts are not sufficient to evaluate the adequacy of a child's progress over
the years, and various grids have been developed which permit evaluation
of a child's growth in an integrated way, with consideration for his physique (body build), rate of growth, nutrition, and developmental achievement. It seems that each child travels in his own "channel" toward maturity, and that age of onset of pubescence is closely related to the rate of
growth throughout childhood. An early maturing child will be taller and
heavier during childhood. A mechanistic evaluation will brand such a
child as "overweight."

Etiological Factors

Modern scientific medicine aims at classifying clinical disorders according
to the underlying causes. The trends of current research in this direction
have been reviewed in Chapter 3. There is ample evidence that obesity
and the allied symptoms (overeating, inactivity, fat storage, and release of
fatty acids) are the outward manifestations of a variety of underlying
disturbances; this has been documented mainly through genetic breeding
and experimentation on animals. It has not been possible to delineate
clear-cut different pictures in human obesity. Instead, the regrettable tendency persists to apply bits and pieces of various research findings to all
cases of obesity, neglecting the very goal of research, which is to come to
a meaningful differentiation.

Clinical medicine has been, and continues to be, greatly influenced by
two contributions published at the turn of the century: Froehlich's report
(4, 12), in 1901, on a case of tumor of the hypophysis, and von Noorden's book, Die Fettsucht, published in 1900 (23). Froehlich's report
deals with observations on a 14-year-old boy who had developed severe
headaches, and subsequently complained about diminishing eyesight. He
suffered increasingly severe headaches, tired easily, and vomited, mostly
after meals. In spite of his complaints he gained weight excessively, and
pubertal development did not occur. Visual acuity diminished progressively until complete blindness in the left eye ensued; subsequently, vision
in the right eye also began to fail. Froehlich related the clinical findings to
a gradually expanding process localized at the base of the brain, in the
region of the optical schiasm. The importance of Froehlich's contribution
is that he recognized for the first time that adiposity and genital underde-
velopment could be used for the diagnosis and localization of a pathological intracranial process. He concluded that these disturbances pointed to
the hypophysis itself. Subsequent studies showed that lesions in the
hypothalamus alone resulted in obesity. Clinicians, however, clung to the
concept of a pituitary disturbance and the diagnosis of "Froehlich's Syndrome" was made on the basis of obesity alone, in the absence of hypo-

genitalism or other symptoms suggestive of a brain lesion. Fat patients, in particular fat children and adolescents, underwent extensive examinations to exclude the possibility of a brain tumor, or to define the exact nature of the pituitary or other endocrine disturbances. My own work was originally undertaken with this orientation but soon disclosed that observable facts did not fit this theory. In spite of the consistently negative evidence, clinicians were reluctant to abandon these concepts, and have not yet done so completely.

Von Noorden emphasized in his work the need for exact measurements, and felt that obesity was a disorder with a definable mechanism, therefore correctable. This stood in contrast to the time-honored assumption that obesity was due to innate and inherited factors, therefore more or less determined by fate. Von Noorden suggested a classification that still has followers. He differentiated between two main forms: obesity in the presence of normal metabolism, the *exogenous* type, resulting from a discrepancy between food intake and energy expenditure, or overeating and/or inactivity, and obesity on the basis of a pathologically diminished metabolism, the *endogenous* type. Von Noorden considered obesity of the endogenous type to be exceedingly rare. Nevertheless, the concept of endogenous obesity extended further and further, and became fused with the fast-spreading ideas of the endocrine origin of obesity. Von Noorden's ideas have been incorporated into medical thinking in such a matter-of-fact way that his name is no longer mentioned in connection with them, for instance the obvious physiological mechanism that obesity is always the outcome of a positive energy balance. Calorimetry at the turn of the century was still in its beginning and was such a cumbersome affair that one cannot miss the tone of justified pride when von Noorden quotes figures on 18 patients (his own and those of others) on whom measurement of oxygen consumption had been made. His work is rather simple in comparison with the elaborate modern measurements that deal with the same principles laid down by him.

Von Noorden tried to demonstrate that even small excesses in the food intake, or insignificant changes in living habits, would result in a steady increase in weight. The arithmetic of his examples is excellent. The same arguments and calculations are still being used by modern-day clinicians and nutritionists when they exhort the public to eat less and to increase energy expenditure by jogging and other activities. There is only one problem with this type of reasoning; there are so many people who appear unable to follow this simple, logical recommendation. Von Noorden pointed out that the imbalance between intake and output occurred only when the appetite did not regulate properly. Modern research has focused on the prerequisites for weight regulation or factors interfering with it.

Mayer suggested, on the basis of animal observations where such neat subdivisions are possible, that a differentiation be made between "metabolic" and "regulatory" obesity (21). Whether such distinctions are applicable to human obesity has not yet been established, but different types of obesity must be assumed to exist in view of the differences in the weight curve, eating and activity patterns, and behavior. It is to be expected that biochemical, neurovegativite, and other biological findings will eventually be isolated that correspond to various patterns of human obesity. For an understanding of the disturbance in integration, obesity must be looked upon as the manifestation of special adaptive patterns whereby physiological disturbances are intricately interwoven with a person's whole development and life experiences.

Psychological Factors

Study of the psychological problems in obesity has also suffered from the tendency toward unjustified generalizations. In recent years this has been mainly expressed in negative statements, such as that it is improper to assume that all obese persons are emotionally disturbed. However, I am not familiar with any psychiatric study that would make such a claim. Psychiatrists who work in this field usually restrict their statements to their actual observations. I quote from a paper that I wrote in 1957 which stated that the majority of obese people who are functioning well do not come to the attention of psychiatrists (5). For those who do:

The psychiatric problems of obese people are far from uniform. It is not possible to speak of the dynamics of one basic personality type as characteristic for all obese people. Obesity may be associated with every conceivable psychiatric disorder, with neurosis as well as psychosis. There are patients in whom hysterical features stand in the foreground, others who suffer from obsessive compulsive neurosis, character disorder or psychopathic personality. Both schizophrenia and manic-depressive psychosis may occur in obese patients. Furthermore, it is necessary to differentiate between those psychiatric aspects of the obesity problem that play a role in the *development* of obesity and those that are *created* by the obese state, in particular for people living in a culture that is hostile and derogatory toward even mild degrees of overweight; finally there are the conflicts *precipitated* by reducing. The picture is further complicated by the fact that in each phase physiologic and psychologic factors interact and influence each other (5).

Stunkard, in 1959, pointed out that it was not possible to define psychological characteristics of obese persons (25). He described a few subgroups of obesity according to certain eating patterns and disturbances in body image which were observed by him in about half of those who had been obese since childhood and whose obesity was closely linked to neurosis. He also analyzed eating patterns and described two as pathologic, the "Night Eating Syndrome" and the "Binge Eating Syndrome." The first is characterized by morning anorexia followed by evening hyperphagia and insomnia, and it is observed mostly in women. The syndrome seems to be precipitated by stressful life situations, and tends to occur daily until the stress is relieved. He describes the Binge Eating Syndrome as characterized by the sudden, compulsive ingestion of very large amounts of food in a very short time, usually with subsequent agitation and self-condemnation. It, too, represents a reaction to stress, but in contrast to the Night Eating Syndrome the bouts of overeating are usually not periodic but tend to be closely linked to specific precipitating circumstances.

Stunkard gives as incidence of the Night Eating Syndrome a figure of 10% and for the Binge Eating Syndrome less than 5% of obese persons. These figures illustrate how extraordinarily difficult it is to give definite figures about the incidence of any psychological problem. Among the many hundreds of patients whose psychological problems I observed in detail over a long period, I have found not more than two or three instances which would fit Stunkard's picture of the Night Eating Syndrome but innumerable Binge Eaters. I have seen quite a few teen-agers who would eat incessantly after coming home from school, waiting for the return of the rest of the family. But they lacked the other characteristics, the morning anorexia and insomnia. On the other hand, eating binges, uncontrolled eating in response to the slightest insult or disappointment, have occurred at some time or another in practically all of my fat patients. Quite often it was these uncontrollable eating bouts that had led to the psychiatric consultation.

In a discussion of emotional aspects of obesity, Hamburger reported four different types of hyperphagia (13). One group of his patients overate in response to emotional tensions which were essentially nonspecific, such as being lonely, anxious, or bored; another group reacted with overeating in chronic states of tension and frustration, using food as a substitute gratification in unpleasant or intolerable life situations that continued over a long period of time. In a third group overeating was a symptom of an underlying emotional illness, most frequently depression. In a fourth group the overeating took on the proportions of an addiction and was characterized by compulsive intensive craving for food that did not seem related to external life events or emotional upheavals.

In a group of obese and hyperobese lower-class women who were not seeking treatment for obesity, Holland and co-workers failed to observe gross psychiatric illness that differentiated them from nonobese women of the same social class (15). Severe psychopathologic signs were found in all groups, but nothing that distinguished the obese from the nonobese patients. The claim is made that since every third lower-class woman is significantly overweight, in this group obesity cannot be called abnormal. The logic of this argument escapes me. According to it if a ton of bricks drops on a dozen people and only one were injured, then this would be abnormal, but if half or all of them suffered injury, then they were "not abnormal." As in other social groups the lower-class patients must be evaluated in individualistic terms. Crisp and Stonehill, in extensive psychosomatic studies of obesity, observed that detectable "neuroticism," even severe depression, might not be recognized as long as the obese state is maintained (10). On the basis of my experience with clinic patients I have come to the conclusion that for many the obesity has an important positive function; it is a compensatory mechanism in a frustrating and stressful life. In others, however, it is associated with, and directly related to, severe personality and developmental disturbances. I have observed the most severe cases of mental disorder, intrinsically related to the weight disturbance, in lower-class patients. Follow-up studies of lower-class children, first observed 35 years ago, revealed significant differences in their psychological reactions, with widely different patterns of development. Stunkard reported that the patients with abnormal eating patterns usually had been obese before adolescence.

In my efforts to subdivide obese patients according to their psychological adaptation, I have evaluated for each patient the functional significance of the obesity in relation to his whole development, in particular in relation to his ability to adjust to life stress. With this approach I have found it possible to divide my observations into three main groups. There are many competent people who are heavy, probably in accordance with their constitutional make-up, whose weight excess is not related to abnormal psychological functioning. Stunkard observed that people in whom obesity developed after adolescence failed to show a distorted body image, in contrast to those who had become fat early in life (26). They may suffer from all kinds of psychiatric difficulties, which, however, are not directly related to their weight problem. In adolescence the excess weight may provoke humiliating criticism and social isolation, and thus reinforce or even precipitate mental disturbances. The weight excess of people with this type of obesity is usually moderate and fairly stable. They may be successful with a reducing regimen by watching their food intake carefully and keep their weight at a lower level. Others may gradually regain their previous weight, which they come to accept as their body build.

Patients in whom the obesity is related to psychological problems may be subdivided into two groups: those in whom obesity is intrinsically interwoven with the whole development, which is characterized by many other features of personality disturbance, *Developmental Obesity*; and those who become obese as a reaction to some traumatic event, *Reactive Obesity*.

Developmental obesity has its onset in childhood, although not all obese children suffer from it; in some being heavy is part of their constitutional make-up. However, in most obese children and many adults who have been obese since childhood, there is an intermingling of the constitutional factors with the severe emotional and personality disturbances of developmental obesity. The patterns of the disturbed family transactions and their relationship to disturbed hunger awareness have been discussed previously in Chapters 4 and 5. When these children reach adolescence their problems may offer many parallels and similarities to the premorbid personality problems of schizophrenics. The great variety of clinical pictures and problems associated with developmental obesity will be discussed in the following chapters.

Reactive Obesity

In this form of obesity, where weight gain follows some traumatic emotional experience, the importance of psychological factors was first recognized. Probably the oldest reference to such a psychologically determined form of obesity is Hume's Letter to a Physician (16), in which he describes his despondency:

. . . all my Ardor seem'd in a moment to be extinguisht, & I cou'd no longer raise my Mind to that pitch, which formerly gave me such excessive Pleasure." He gradually recovered his spirits but suddenly, when 20 years old, he grew obese. "For next Summer, about May 1731 there grew upon (me) a very ravenous Appetite. . . . This Appetite, however, had an Effect very unusual, which was to nourish me extremely; so that in 6 weeks time I passed from the one extreme to the other, & being before tall, lean, & rawbon'd became a sudden, the most sturdy robust, healthful-like Fellow you have seen, with a ruddy Complexion & a cheerful Countenance.

Hume remained fat and is always included in the list of Englishmen who achieved greatness in spite of being fat. An interesting comment on the change in cultural attitude toward obesity is his speaking with pleasure of this change, and of his friends congratulating him on his "recovery." In our time and age such a tolerant attitude toward obesity is difficult to imagine, and everybody would have been acutely concerned about his gaining too much weight.

In the medical literature the possibility of obesity being a symptom of nervous disturbance was discussed first in the French literature of the nineteenth century (19). The case of a father who began to put on weight immediately after the death of his son is reported as an example. He was embarrassed and could not understand how he could become fat in view of his grief and bereavement. Throughout his life he had never weighed more than 60 kg, but a few months after his son's death, in October, 1885, he weighed 82 kg, and the following January, 90 kg. He tried to exercise but without success. In May, 1886, his weight was 102 kg and in July 106 kg.

There are many references in the more recent literature of obesity developing after upsetting events and in periods of great emotional stress. Lichtwitz noted after the first World War that women who had lived for a long time in uncertainty or who were grieving over the loss of their beloved ones had a tendency to put on weight which could not be explained in a purely caloric way (20). He mentions the German vernacular word for this condition—*Kummerspeck* (fat of sorrow). After this, references to the relationship between "endocrine disturbances" (used as synonym for obesity) and emotional trauma become more numerous.

During the second World War, Dreyfus in France described a paradoxical form of obesity (11). He observed many instances of severe obesity, chiefly in young women who had been exposed to bombing or other hardships, and who also suffered from amenorrhea. The characteristic aspect of this type of obesity was the rapid development and spongy character of the fat tissue. Dreyfus assumed that acute traumatic experiences might influence the hypothalamic regulatory mechanisms, without bringing evidence in support of this. In my own observations, obesity develops not infrequently after the death of a family member, separation from home, when a love affair breaks up, or in other situations involving the fear of desertion and loneliness.

Reactive obesity is the form more commonly observed in adults. The obesity seems to develop in response to an emotional trauma, frequently to the death of someone close to the patient, or when the fear of death or injury is aroused. Overeating and obesity appear to serve the function of warding off anxiety or a depressive reaction. Though infrequent, this type of sudden increase in weight is also observed in children.

Bela came to the obesity clinic at age 10½ weighing 165 lbs, and was 62″ tall. She had always been a big child but only moderately overweight; suddenly she had gained nearly 40 lbs in less than a year. Menarche had occurred at her tenth birthday; once, while severely bleeding, she had stayed in bed for 10 days and had gained 10 lbs. Both sides of her family tended to be stout.

During the preceding year the whole family's attention had been completely focused on a severely ill older sister, the third among the 4 girls of the family. The sick girl was the only slim one and had been the mother's favorite. She had suffered from rheumatic fever since age 2, and had been doing well under continuous medical care. While preparing for the college boards she developed ankle edema. Though quite sick she insisted on taking the examinations. Her physician advised hospitalization, but the girl refused to be separated from her family who, in turn, felt it would "break her heart." The mother stated later, "It suited me so well. I did not want to send her to a hospital." The mother became depressed as there was no improvement, and the two older sisters took care of the sick girl, who died 6 months later. The whole family was broken up with grief and guilt for having postponed hospitalization. As the mother later explained: "During the time of illness she was neglected and I did not notice Bela. Suddenly she had gotten big and nobody had even known it."

In another instance a very bright 10-year-old boy suddenly gained 40 lbs during 6 months, following the death by accident of an older brother. His mother used the same expression as Bela's mother: "I did not even see him and suddenly he was fat." This mother recognized the need of help for herself. The older son had been her confidant and she admitted having felt closer to him than to her husband. After his death she became completely wrapped up in her grief, feeling guilty if she did not remember him every minute. The younger boy, though very bright, had always been treated like a baby, someone who could not be trusted. After the accident the mother lived in constant fear of losing him, too, and she would not permit him activities he had formerly enjoyed, or even let him continue his old friendships. It was in this setting that the sudden gain in weight occurred. As the mother faced her own problems she was able to let her son become more independent and thus capable of establishing control over his eating; he did outgrow his obesity.

Reactive obesity is the pattern of the more mature person, who has often been exposed to similar, though less intense, early psychological conditioning. Such people are often aware that they eat more when they feel worried or tense, and feel less effective and competent when they try to control their food intake. They are often referred to as compulsive eaters, and they are aware of the difference between real hunger and this neurotic need for food. They may use expressions like "I get 'mad' in my stomach," or "I get this gnawing feeling and nothing can change it but a luscious meal," or "It is my mouth that wants it; I know that I have had enough."

Quite often emotional problems are hidden under a complacent facade. These people do not get angry and thus contribute to the misconception that fat people are cheerful and good-natured. Instead of expressing anger, or even experiencing it, they become depressed and the overeating serves as a defense against deeper depression. It is in this group that the supportive and constructive value of overeating can be clearly recognized, in spite of the long-run detrimental effect of the obesity itself. Overeating may occur at times of such severe emotional stress that the question is not so much "Why overeating?" but "What would be the alternative?" All statistics agree that obese people have a higher morbidity and mortality rate for a whole string of diseases—with one exception: their suicide rate is significantly lower. In evaluating the life histories of such people I have often been impressed with the fact that the situations in reaction to which obesity developed were situations to which others might have reacted with despair. However much of a handicap obesity may become, as a defensive reaction it is less destructive than suicide or paralyzing deep depression.

It is my impression that many of the countless "uncooperative" fat people who are so discouraging to their physicians belong to this group. It has been recommended that one should convince such patients of the dangers of obesity by confronting them with the mortality figures of overweight people. This appears to me dangerous advice. Their control over underlying anxieties is so precarious that a scare approach might add to their difficulties, rendering them unable to maintain their fragile emotional balance and thus force them into more severe obesity or overt depression.

People who use food to combat anxiety and loneliness are apt to become depressed when dieting is enforced (24). Even without marked obesity, the secure knowledge that one's appetite and needs will be fulfilled is necessary for a sense of well-being. Mildly depressed patients are often concerned with the loss of satisfaction from ordinary activities. They often complain of having lost all interest, or of finding activities no longer worthwhile. The immediate enjoyment of food serves as reassurance that life still holds some satisfactions. People with this depressive mood are apt to eat between meals, often quite impulsively, as soon as the idea strikes them that something might be tasty or enjoyable.

A true loss of appetite will precipitate a deep depression. An intelligent, mildly overweight woman who was in analysis had always kept her weight under control by following various diets. She was in therapy because she suffered from repeated depressive episodes with fear of impoverishment, of complete desertion, and loneliness. While working through the genetic background of these experiences, with good clinical progress, she began a salt-free reducing diet with so little difficulty that it was not even mentioned in her analysis. It was one of the practical aspects of her life which she handled well. Then a mild respiratory infection changed the metabolic balance; hypochloremia developed and she completely lost her appetite, with definite revulsion against the very idea of eating. To this she reacted with a desperation bordering on panic, entirely different from anything she had ever experienced. She felt as if the last hope had gone out of her life, as if her old fear of remaining empty and unsatisfied had now become an unavoidable doom; that life no longer could offer any satisfaction, not even the primitive one of eating. The difference in feeling between these different depressive reactions was tremendous. The metabolically determined depression yielded to a diet high in salt; the neurotic depression lifted with continued analysis.

After World War II it was observed in innumerable instances that survivors of concentration camps who had been exposed to cruel starvation developed obesity with greater frequency than the general population. Obesity developed also in former prisoners of war who felt disappointed in their longing for love, happiness, and recognition, and who substituted overeating as the only source of satisfaction when they did not find fulfillment of their long-cherished desires and wishes.

Sometimes seemingly insoluble life situations, making for continued frustration, rage, and anxiety, provoke overeating. A woman of 25 who lived an unhappy and unappreciated life in a home that was dominated by a stepmother described her irrational use of food: "Sometimes I think I'm not hungry at all. It is that I am just unhappy in certain things—things I cannot get. Food is the easiest thing to get that makes me feel nice and comfortable. I try to reason with myself and tell myself that these problems cannot be solved by eating." She was one of the many fat people who succeeded in showing a fairly complacent attitude toward the world during the daytime. She was quite efficient in her work, although her severe obesity became increasingly a handicap. When she was alone at night, the tension and anxiety became unbearable. "I think then that I am ravenously hungry and I do my utmost not to eat. My body becomes stiff in my effort to control my hunger. If I want to have any rest at all, I've to get up and eat. Then I go to sleep like a newborn baby."

Patients with this type of eating pattern, to which Stunkard has given the label the Night Eating Syndrome, are unable to adhere to any dietary regimen as long as their problems and conflicts are unresolved, or as long as they remain in the anxiety- and rage-provoking environment. They can reduce without difficulty in a hospital but will regain as soon as they return to the old setting.

Increases in weight following operations or accidents are quite common; they lead to persistent obesity only under the special conditions with which we are here concerned. The following example illustrates a relationship between predisposing personality traits and the rapid development of obesity after a traumatic event. A 35-year-old man came for analytic treatment because he had difficulties in relation to women. He had been several times on the point of getting engaged; but each time he became panicky, broke off the relationship—and gained 40 or 50 lbs. When life looked safe again he would reduce and make another attempt at finding a wife. His weight oscillated between 200 and 260 lbs; he was so sure of these limits that he had two complete wardrobes.

He was the youngest boy, by many years, in a large family; a brother close to him in age had died at age 3 or 4, leaving him as the only recipient of care, concern, and restriction by a demanding, narrow-minded mother. As a child he was teased for being too much of a mama's boy, and he was given superior educational opportunities; as an adult, he was socially and financially the most successful member of his family.

He remembered having been a big and strong child, without being fat. He enjoyed vigorous games and had a reputation for being a champion swimmer. When he was 13 years old, he broke his leg during a summer vacation while playing "Follow the Leader." He had gotten caught by his own recklessness and felt guilty for having brought the accident on himself. He reproached himself for all the trouble and expense this caused his family. The fracture was slow in healing and necessitated several settings. A long period of invalidism ensued, although with an excellent outcome; he had no limp or any limitation of movement.

Although there were some gruesome memories about the accident, the surgical procedures, and the fear of being permanently crippled, more important were the memories of his pleasant reveries while he sat on the porch of the summer cottage with his leg in a cast, being taken care of in a most pleasant way. Mother had taken over again and there were many young girls who assisted her. His most vivid memories were of how all of them had brought him food, chiefly ice cream. The whole summer was an orgy of eating unlimited amounts of ice cream; even in retrospect a blissful expression would come to his face. He gained a tremendous amount of weight and from then on his weight remained above 200 lbs. As he grew successful he became quite a gourmet and entertained lavishly in his bachelor quarters; but nothing gave him quite the same sensuous satisfaction as ice cream. The women who had offered it so lavishly after the accident also retained the emotional characteristics of that period; they were needed and wanted as sweet companions, but were untouchable.

—The many events and stressful circumstances that play a role in provoking eating sprees or continued overeating need to be understood in the context of total life situations. The obesity of middle age often develops in response to psychological stress. The increases in weight are not as gradual and creeping as is commonly assumed. There may be sudden increases in weight in response to some distressing situation, followed by many vain efforts of losing it. The wife who nibbles and grows fat because she is worried about her straying husband may have lost him by being too demanding and dependent—rather than because of losing her figure. The mother who sits up all night and eats and eats waiting for her adolescent daughter to come home is apt to have conflicts about her daughter's growing independence, and may fear being useless and lonely.

Obesity which develops during or after pregnancy often belongs to this group. Sometimes gain in weight follows each pregnancy, sometimes only the birth of one particular child. Outstanding in the psychopathology are disappointment with the marriage, or unfulfilled, fantastic daydreams about what the child could do for the mother, or frank envy about the care which the child receives and resentment about the demands he makes.

— Much has been said and written about obesity indicating a desire for pregnancy, just as anorexia nervosa has been interpreted as expressing fear of pregnancy. To be sure, fat girls and women have pregnancy fantasies, but so have others. The big question is whether this is anything specific in obesity. The concept of oral impregnation seems to be a fairly universal childhood fantasy. But I have not found, in any specific way, that in the obese overeating was a fulfillment of pregnancy fantasies. The desire to have one's body changed, to achieve this magic through eating or refusing to eat, is quite common, both in men and women, but not the specific desire for pregnancy through eating.

What I have observed repeatedly in obesity is a definite rejection of pregnancy and of the mature maternal role, often with the outspoken desire that the woman herself wants to stay a child. When such women become pregnant, they may develop a terrific fear of being drained by the baby, and then stuff themselves in an effort to compensate for this. Some react to the delivery as if they were losing a part of themselves; they feel empty and make up for this by eating—with the feeling of never getting enough. This does not exclude the possibility that such women may make good, though usually overanxious, mothers by the mechanism of identifying with the infant and giving to the child the type of care they themselves would want. They literally live in and through their children—and it is not surprising that they raise them in such a way that the children, too, become fat.

Traditionally, the concept of a maternal woman is that of a plump and cheerful one. In our culture there is an overemphasis on the sexually attractive woman, who is conceived of as very slim, and a condemnation of the maternal type as being dowdy and even unfeminine. For some women this culturally induced dilemma between the two roles, motherhood and sexual attractiveness, may represent an insoluble problem. In despair those with the proper constitutional endowment may become really obese during and after pregnancy; or they may reject motherhood altogether, or become rejecting mothers.

Occasionally a father may become fat after the birth of a child; this occurs in extremely dependent men who, even before the baby is born, feel that they never received quite enough. They will resort to overeating to combat their anger and jealousy and to compensate themselves for what they feel they are missing.

An example is Mr. Smith, who was 32 years old when he applied for psychiatric treatment for his obesity, which he had tried to control without success. He was 5′9″ tall, weighed 250 lbs, and did not appear grossly unattractive. He smiled frequently in a boyish way, but occasionally there appeared a depressed expression on his rotund face. He had weighed 175 lbs when he entered college, which was appropriate for his height, and 220 lbs by the time he graduated. Before the board examinations he had reduced from 225 lbs to 185 lbs and was this weight when he married at age 24.

The first few years of marriage were harmonious and he maintained the lower weight, but then bitter quarreling developed because his wife insisted on becoming pregnant. He felt she was blackmailing him and by the time the baby was born his weight had risen to 250 lbs. From then on there was continuous marital tension and discord. He resented his wife's attention to the baby, feeling that she was neglectful of him. During the following years he made several attempts to reduce, each time after a fight with his wife. He finally bought a scale and matters improved. He discovered that with daily weighing, and his wife watching his weight, he was able to lose 2 or 3 lbs a week. However, as soon as she stopped watching, or he felt that she had stopped, he would cheat on his diet and his weight would increase; he would blame his wife for not having watched his weight, and a violent fight would ensue. Whenever the impulse struck him he would go to a restaurant for a meal, sometimes to two or three in a row. He explained that he needed to do this to relieve the tension about his marital problems. He described his wife as very fussy, compulsive, and rigid, and he reacted to her reproaches by becoming angry and eating more. He was still quite resentful about having a child, though he got along fairly well with his 4-year-old son, but only when he was alone with the boy. He would become acutely disturbed when his wife was present and the child showed his preference for the mother. There was also tension because they were continuously in debt. The amounts he spent on food and at times on alcohol were quite out of proportion for the family's budget.

I have emphasized the great diversity of clinical pictures that are covered by such global terms as "overweight" or "obesity." For a long time the mechanistic statistical approach has obscured the picture. It has labeled as abnormal many people whose individual body build falls outside the statistical average, or overlooked in others serious underlying problems that are not exposed by dry statistics. The preoccupation with so-called norms has led to a neglect of the variability of individual human beings. As long as we insist that being fat is ugly and undesirable and should not be permitted, we force a great many people to fight or to disregard the individual endowment of their own physique and to act as if this were not real. Gulliver in the land of the Lilliputians was suddenly very much outside the range of "average" size, but he himself had not become "abnormal." From the point of view of his size one might say that his environment had deteriorated, just as it has deteriorated in our culture for people of large body build. If he had tried to conform to the average and if it had been possible to shrink him to the size of a Lilliputian, he would not have been healthier. On the contrary, he would have been highly uncomfortable and quite "abnormal" in terms of his own biology. The differences in size and weight with which we are concerned are not as extreme as in Swift's satire; but they are just as real and often just as unalterable.

BIBLIOGRAPHY

1. Bjurulf, P., and Lindgren, G., A preliminary study on overweight in the south of Sweden, pp. 9–15, in *Occurrences, Causes, and Prevention of Overnutrition*, G. Blix, ed., Almqvist & Wiksells, Uppsala, Sweden, 1964.

2. Blix, G., ed., *Occurrences, Causes, and Prevention of Overnutrition*, Almqvist & Kiksells, Uppsala, 1964.
3. Brillat-Savarin, J. A., *The Physiology of Taste*, trans. R. E. Anderson, Chatto & Windus, London, 1889 (first French edition, 1825).
4. Bruch, H., The Froehlich syndrome, Amer. J. Dis. Child., 58:1282–1289, 1939.
5. Bruch, H., Psychiatric aspects of obesity, Metabolism, 6:461–465, 1957.
6. Bruch, H., The emotional significance of the preferred weight, Amer. J. Clin. Nutr., 5:192–196, 1957.
7. Bruch, H., Obesity and sex, Medical Aspects of Human Sexuality, 3:54–62, 1969.
8. Carreno, Juan (1614-1685), "The Monster," paintings #646 and #2800, Prado Museum, Madrid, Spain.
9. Crisp, A. H., The possible significance of some behavioral correlates of weight and carbohydrate intake, J. Psychosom. Res., 11:117–131, 1967.
10. Crisp, A. H., and Stonehill, E., Treatment of obesity with special reference to seven severely obese patients, J. Psychosom. Res., 14:327–345, 1970.
11. Dreyfus, G., L'obésité paradoxale: syndrome psychosomatique, Presse méd., 56: 107–111, 1948.
12. Froehlich, A., Ein Fall von Tumor der Hypophysis cerebri ohne Akromegalie, Wien. Klin. Wschr., 15:883–906, 1901; reprinted Res. Publ. Ass. Nerv. Ment. Dis., 20, 1940.
13. Hamburger, W. W., Emotional aspects of obesity, Med. Clin. N. Amer., 35:483–499, 1951.
14. Hirsch, J., and Gallian, E., Methods for determination of adipose cell size in man and animals, J. Lipid Res., 9:110–119, 1968.
15. Holland, J., Masling, J., and Copley, D., Mental illness in lower class normal, obese and hyperobese women, Psychosom. Med., 32:351–357, 1970.
16. Hume, D., A young philosopher analyzes his "Disease of the Learned," Letter to Dr. John Arbuthnot, pp. 360–366, in *An Enquiry Concerning Human Understanding, and Other Essays*, E. Mossner, ed., Washington Square Press, Inc., New York, 1963.
17. Keys, A., Obesity and heart disease, J. Chronic Dis., 1:456, 1955.
18. Leray, J., *Embonpoint et obésité, conceptions et thérapeutiques actuelles*, Masson et Cie, Paris, 1931.
19. Leven, G., *L'obésité et son traitement*, Baillière, Paris, 1905.
20. Lichtwitz, L., Ueber die Beziehung der Fettsucht zur Psyche und Nervensystem, Klin. Wschr., 2:1255–1256, 1923.
21. Mayer, J., Genetic, traumatic and environmental factors in the etiology of obesity, Physiol. Rev., 33:472–508, 1953.
22. 900 Sad Pounds, *The Houston Post*, Houston, Texas, December 30, 1971.
23. von Noorden, C., *Die Fettsucht*, Hoelder, Wien, 1900.
24. Stunkard, A. J., The "Dieting Depression." Incidence and clinical characteristics of untoward responses to weight reduction regimens, Amer. J. Med., 23:77–86, 1957.
25. Stunkard, A. J., Eating patterns and obesity, Psychiat. Quart., 33:284–292, 1959.
26. Stunkard, A. J., and Burt, V., Obesity and the body image: II. Age at onset of disturbances in the body image, Amer. J. Psychiat., 123:1443–1447, 1967.
27. Wadd, W., *Cursory Remarks on Corpulence*: or obesity considered as a disease: with a critical examination of ancient and modern opinions, relative to its causes and cure, 3rd edition, I. Callow, London, 1816.

8

Obesity in Childhood

Obesity in childhood, as in other age groups, is not a uniform condition. It may range from mild degrees of overweight during periods of temporary inactivity or overeating, to severe, grotesquely deforming weight excesses with poor functioning in all areas of living. It may develop gradually from infancy on in a baby who may or may not have had a high birth weight, or there may be a sudden increase in weight, as much as 40 or 50 lbs during a year, in a previously big but not overweight youngster. There may be extreme concern about even mild degrees of overweight, usually, though not exclusively, in upper-class families, or indifference or placid acceptance of enormous fat accumulation.

Medical evaluation of obesity in children has undergone the same changes in fashion and style that have characterized the study of obesity in general. During the 1930's when my own observations began, endocrine theories stood in the foreground and such a disorder was suspected in practically every fat child; the label "Froehlich's Syndrome" was freely distributed. Even today, many obese children, particularly those who have resisted dietary efforts, are being sent to an endocrinologist, although as far as I know evidence of endocrine pathology is as rare today as it was 30 years ago. Efforts have also been made to recognize disturbances in hypothalamic regulation or metabolic processes, but thus far with little, if any, confirming evidence.

Fat children have in common that their excessive nutrition interacts with the complex processes of growth which include dimensionl growth and differentiation. The first is commonly measured as the increase in weight and stature; the second can be assessed from structural progress in skeletal development as visualized in roentgenograms. During later childhood and the preadolescent period, the appearance of secondary sex characteristics indicates progressing biologic maturation.

The early observations were made in a pediatric clinic, from 1937 to 1940, on a large, unselected group of fat children who had come to the attention of various departments of the Columbia Presbyterian Medical Center for a variety of complaints. Only a fraction had come directly to the pediatric clinic for their obesity; none of them had been referred for behavior difficulties, though serious personality problems and emotional difficulties were recognized in many children and their families. The weight excess ranged from 20% to 120%, with few being less than 30% overweight and the majority more than 50%.

The outstanding somatic finding of the early study was that obese children were advanced in growth and biological development; they were unusually tall, showed accelerated skeletal maturation, and underwent puberty at a normal, or even early age (2, 5). These findings were not consistent with the then current explanations of obesity as due to hypothyroidism and hypopituitarism. Early maturation often results in a short growth period with the result that many, though not all, end up as rather short adults; this had been erroneously interpreted as a sign of growth disturbance.

It had been old pediatric knowledge that only tall children with a strong bone structure were predisposed to growing fat. There is a stimulating, quite modern-sounding booklet on children characterized by "fatness and colossal development," published by Jaeger in 1821 (12). This book has been previously reviewed, together with other early references (6). This once well-known fact had been completely overshadowed during the 1930's by the exclusive concern with endocrine disturbances and their supposedly retarding effect on growth and sexual maturation.

Though large size is characteristic for obese children, occasionally a short and small-boned individual will grow obese; commonly this is associated with rather severe emotional maldevelopment. Jean Stafford in her short story, "The Nemesis," describes a young girl who had been slender as a child but had grown fat as an adolescent (15).

Ramona Dunn was fat to the point of parody. Her obesity fitted her badly, like extra clothing put on in the wintertime, for her embedded bones were very small and she was very short, and she had a foolish gait, which, however, was swift, as if she were a mechanical doll whose engine raced. Her face was rather pretty, but its features were so small that it was all but lost in its billowing surroundings, and it was covered by a thin, fair skin.

Recent studies on the high count of adipose cells in obesity have brought additional evidence of physical factors that may predispose a youngster to excessive gain in weight. These predisposing factors may be genetically determined, but there is also evidence that excessive nutrition early in life may produce an unusually high fat cell count (10). There is at present a tendency to explain obesity in childhood, and later in life, as being the product of overnutrition during infancy, which would result in an excess number of fat cells and thus doom an individual to becoming fat. In my experience these predisposing factors result in obesity only through reinforcing interaction with environmental influences. In Chapter 5 the development of a boy was described who had been 100% overweight at age one, due to excessive feeding under external pressure, but who completely outgrew the obesity when permitted free development, with encouragement of physical activity and athletics.

Fat children, like all other children, grow up in families, and the other members can be observed in their interaction with each other and with the fat child. Sometimes they are helpful with his difficulties or, conversely, sometimes they create the conditions that lead to obesity by overanxious and hostile pressure thereby reinforcing the child's difficulties; such stresses may lead to further weight increase (Chapter 5).

The early studies were undertaken in the hope of recognizing common factors that would apply to all patients. Following these patients into adulthood revealed that this focus was a false lead; that searching for a uniform picture kept the issues vague and ill-defined instead of clarifying them. It was recognized that the various symptoms had different roots and individually different significance, and that obese children reacted in various ways to life stress and to treatment efforts. The patients were reexamined at various times, though with increasing attrition in the number who would respond to a letter or telephone call. Approximately 25% of the original group (113 boys and 112 girls) were seen in 1954 and 1955; a few were heard of as late as 1971.

Under the impact of the endocrine theories of the 1930's the importance of such "simple" factors as overeating or inactivity had been completely neglected. Both factors were evaluated in detail, and overeating as well as inactivity were reported in 70% to 80% of the cases, suggesting that both factors play a role (3, 4). Usually information on the child's inactivity was given freely and was complained of as laziness. On the other hand, overeating was often vigorously denied and it took some detective work, with visits to the home, to obtain an accurate picture. Characteristically, children who were rated as most inactive had also the highest food intake, and were most disturbed emotionally. Physical inactivity seems to indicate the more serious and persistent factor for the maintenance of obesity and abnormal personality development. Marked inactivity is usually associated with general immaturity and shows a high correlation with social isolation of a fat child, who was often described as oversensitive and sulky, or as bullying smaller children. Parents who were excessively apprehensive about the dangers of exercise and of the harmful influence of other children made great efforts to keep their child close to them, with marked, even paralyzing inactivity and social immaturity the result.

The extent of the inactivity suggested the possibility of some inherent defect or weakness. However, there were no indications of any delay in the early development of the locomotor function. No neurological abnormalities were found either. However, "lack of drive" was reported repeatedly in psychological evaluations. Many children who had been quite active when young had been kept away from all contact with other children and had been constantly impressed with the possible dangers of activities outside the home.

Though overeating is now generally recognized as important for the development of obesity, it is not easy to obtain correct information. It is also difficult to say how much a child overeats since even normal requirements show wide individual variations. The children were asked to keep a diary of their food intake; invariably they would lôse weight while recording what they really ate. It is an old quip that fat patients will lose weight if they eat what they say they eat. The most striking feature was one-sided preference for starchy foods, such as bread and spaghetti, and for sweets. Sometimes the food intake was no longer excessive when a child came for examination, particularly in older children who had made some effort to control their weight. Food intake varies with changing gain in weight. It is high during the *active phase* of progressive weight increase, and moderate in the state of *stationary obesity*.

Fat children often repeat their mother's assurances of getting fat on practically no food. Generally, however, the very change in alertness, when asked about their favorite dishes or the subject of food in general, reveals their exaggerated interest in and enjoyment of food. Some families have recognized this and describe it as "food is all he speaks and thinks of," or "her heart goes out for food." A marvelous description of this exclusive interest in food was given by Dickens in *The Pickwick Papers* in the character of Joe, the Fat Boy. Nothing but food seemed to interest him and he withdrew into a lethargic state when there was no food around. He was his master's despair, and the exclamation, "Damn that boy, he's gone to sleep again," is his leitmotiv. I quote from Dickens:

Sundry taps on his head with a stick and the fat boy, with some difficulty, roused from his lethargy. "Come, hand in the eatables!" (said Mr. W.).

There was something in the sound of the last word which aroused the unctuous boy. He jumped up; and the leaden eyes, which twinkled behind his mountainous cheeks, leered horribly upon the food as he unpacked it from the basket.

"Now make haste," said Mr. Wardle, for the fat boy was hanging fondly over a capon, which he seemed wholly unable to part with. The boy sighed deeply, and bestowing an ardent gaze upon its plumpness, unwillingly consigned it to his master.

During the 1930's and 1940's Joe's behavior was often cited as evidence of the sleepiness of the pituitary type of obesity. During the 1950's the eponym "Pickwickian Syndrome" was given to the clinical picture of extreme obesity associated with alveolar hypoventilation and hypoxic somnolence. Yet I doubt Joe suffered from it. I have never seen an organically determined somnolence in which one word had such a vitalizing influence.

The following case is an example of the "Pickwickian Syndrome" with the somewhat unexpected finding of a remarkable stoicism when this extremely fat girl was confronted with food deprivation and starvation. The medical observations were reported by Finkelstein and Avery (9). At 4½ years this little girl, Holly, was 41" tall, weighed 90 lbs (160% overweight) and had a bone age of 4 years with one 5 year center. She had been referred for hospitalization for evaluation of her extreme obesity, frequent attacks of dyspnea and orthopnea, so severe that she had to be propped up at night. She was extremely inactive and took several naps during the day. She was slow moving and fell asleep when stimuli were withdrawn. Respiration was rapid and noisy at rest; when asleep the lips and nails became cyanotic. Alveolar hypoventilation disappeared after a 48-hour fast, presumably from a decrease in gastric volume, and recurred on an ad libitum intake of 4,500 calories per day. Ventilation remained normal after a 10-lb weight loss had been achieved.

In addition to studies on ventilation and carbohydrate metabolism, a series of tests were carried out to assess the hypothalamic functions and the possibility of an intracranial tumor, including skull films, pneumo-encephalogram, electroencephalogram, temperature regulation (cold and heat stress), infection, pattern of basal temperature, and appetite control. The findings were all within normal range, speaking against a lesion in the hypothalamic centers. These examinations were carried out at the Johns Hopkins Hospital and I am indebted to Dr. John Money for the information.

When Holly was admitted to the pediatric service the mother told a dramatic story about toxemia of pregnancy and convulsions; later she said birth and delivery had been normal. The mother claimed that the child weighed 5 lbs, 2 oz at birth, lost some weight, and was so weak that she needed to be fed hourly. According to the report by the pediatrician, which was received only later, the child was never underweight, and the mother stuffed her with food in spite of all his advice to the contrary. The whole history the mother gave was characterized by contradictions and confabulations, which were not always immediately apparent. She claimed that the child weighed only 7 lbs at one year; at another time she said this was at age 6 months. Holly had developed asthmatic bronchitis for which she needed hospitalization. According to the mother, in the 2-week period after she had been put on Sobee, the weight doubled, rising from 7 to 15 lbs. From then on she kept gaining weight which the mother attributed to the child's constant looking for food and eating whatever she found, "lint off the floors, and cigarette butts and matches. At 3 years she learned how to operate a can opener and could open cans. She just kept gaining weight constantly." Weight at 2 years was 40 lbs. At first the mother denied that she had ever forced food on her child. Later she said she felt her child was "cute in her baby fat. I always felt that fat children were healthy. Now I know that 9 out of 10 fat children are healthy, but mine is not."

The mother gave the impression of an educated person, with a large vocabulary and often colorful and dramatic descriptions. She also gave detailed accounts of what other physicians had found and recommended; as it turned out these reports were often grossly exaggerated and distorted. She spoke for instance of a brain tumor that had been suspected.

When first admitted no attempt was made to restrict Holly's caloric intake, except for test situations. At first she searched eagerly for extra food and was often found in the kitchen looking for it. At no time did she eat inedible food, as her mother's account had indicated, and she had definite preferences and would spit out the peel of an apple, etc., in contrast to what one might have expected if she had a tumor of the brain. The searching stopped when she adjusted to the hospital situation and was told not to eat constantly. During a prolonged fast she asked for food once or twice during the first 24 hours, but seemed quite content afterward. Her respiration became less labored and her activity increased without her becoming cyanotic. She seemed more alert and interested in her surroundings. When after this deprivation she was allowed food ad libitum, regular meals plus access to fruit, cake, sandwiches, etc., she would eat huge quantities, up to 5000 calories, slowly but steadily in a very calm and methodical manner, until she became acutely uncomfortable, distended, cyanotic, and somnolent. She would sit holding her abdomen with one hand while stuffing herself with the other. This paradoxical feeding behavior was considered the most conspicuous abnormality, with complete disregard of her own signals of being sated or hungry, withstanding fasting without complaining or searching for food, but showing limitless hyperphagia when food was readily available. Her behavior reflects an extreme deficit in awareness of hunger and satiation, as was discussed in Chapter 4, and it appeared related to the extreme inconsistencies in the mother's attitude and behavior.

Holly stayed at a residential treatment center to be kept on a low caloric diet. There was a steady loss of weight, down to 62 lbs within 9 months. The respiratory symptoms and somnolence disappeared completely and Holly became much more active and alive. However, she did not maintain the weight loss. In 1971, when Holly was nearly 13 years old, she was 5' tall and weighed approximately 200 lbs. She had become diabetic and was on insulin. She still would "hook" food any way she could get it.

During the examination period the mother was seen for a few psychiatric consultations. Holly was the first child of young parents, both slim, who had married while the husband was in the armed services. After his discharge they considered divorce because they felt they were incompatible, but then "fate stepped in." The mother stated that she had married against her mother's opposition, and that her husband took her to live with his parents, and that they continued to live there. She resented this and perceived herself as some sort of Cinderella, forced to do all the hard housework. She had practically no contact with people outside her husband's family. His five doting older sisters lived in the same neighborhood. After a confrontation with her home-town pediatrician and her brother who had reported that she had crammed food down the baby's throat from the beginning, she made an effort to set the record straight. She wrote, "She was spanked and I felt guilty. I told her I was sorry and then would feed her to make up with her. Why did I tell you she could open a can? Did you ever say or think something so strong that it became the truth? I can't explain what I did. Telling a direct lie is not a habit. I don't do this—and why I did it this time, I'll never know."

Her psychiatrist felt that there was some suggestion of delusions, and doubted that her description of her baby as underweight was a conscious lie told to mislead the examiners. She certainly had acted as if she had perceived her girl as sickly and weak and as weighing too little when she was already much too obese. Feeding for this mother seemed to have been a way of showing love and expiation for her guilt, but also of showing hatred, for the fatness almost killed the child whose fateful arrival had kept a difficult marriage together. The mother was in psychiatric treatment for a while, with good improvement. In 1971 she reported that she had two more children, a boy and a girl, whom she had raised without this pathologic misuse of the feeding situation, and who were of normal weight.

This mother's misperception of her child's needs, and of her own behavior, illustrates in an exaggerated form how complex the factors are that lead to excessive feeding of a child, and also how they are related to psychological and interpersonal problems. This history is also an example of the failure of a superimposed reducing regimen, even of such length, effecting a change in the child's ability to control and regulate her own food intake.

There continues to be marked confusion and disagreement about the importance of emotional factors in childhood obesity, whether they contribute to its development, or whether the psychological problems are secondary to the social rejection obese youngsters encounter. In my experience these two aspects are closely intertwined. The full significance of the interaction of multiple factors was recognized through the long-range study of the former clinic patients.

In view of the incompleteness of the follow-up observations of these patients, no detailed figures for the relative frequency of the various patterns will be given; they probably would not be relevant for other groups since so many social and cultural factors enter into the total picture. The findings were analyzed according to the persistence or absence of overweight, and according to the overall social-psychological adjustment. Four possibilities exist for their combination, and all four were observed: namely, slenderness with good adjustment, continued overweight with good adjustment, slenderness with emotional maladjustment, and continued obesity with severe maladaptation. Information is probably least complete for those who did well and "outgrew" the condition. A larger proportion of those who had been rated as severely disturbed during childhood responded to the follow-up inquiry than of those who seemed to be doing well. Forty percent of the patients had serious adjustment difficulties on reexamination; all of them had been so identified during childhood.

About a third of the patients who were reexamined had done fairly well, though they might continue to be overweight. An example of a favorable outcome in a boy who had been a very obese infant was given in the chapter on family interaction. Several other boys who had become fat at a somewhat later age have done equally well. None of them had been socially withdrawn, though some had been quite inactive. They were able to correct their obese state, usually during adolescence, on their own initiative, or with support for their efforts at emancipation from an older brother or a friend. Several completed this process by enlisting in the armed forces, where they stayed for the required period, in contrast to those with severe personality difficulties, who, if they were inducted at all, were discharged after a short time. No fat girl from the clinic group reported this outcome of continued slimness and good adjustment, though several had extended periods of low weight during adolescence, with the lowest weight usually at the time of their wedding. On the other hand, continued slenderness was repeatedly observed in young private patients who obtained help, usually together with their parents, from psychotherapy.

A fairly large group consisted of patients with good social adjustment in spite of continued moderate obesity. I quote briefly from the history of a young man, 27 years old when last examined, who at age 7½ had been referred by the school as being too heavy. He was unusually tall, 52½", and weighed 97 lbs (+42%). The family's attitude was accepting and supportive: "The family thinks the bigger he is the better he is." He was now 6' tall, and weighed about 220 lbs. He considered this too heavy but had found out that he functioned better at this weight than at an artificially lower one. He was competent in his work, had been married for 5 years and had two children who were not too heavy. As an adolescent he had received some glandular injections and had undergone a reducing regimen, on the insistence of the family physician. Even in retrospect he spoke with bitterness about this period as the most miserable experience of his life.

A similar good adjustment was reported by Sophia who had come to the obesity clinic when she was 10 years old, 59½" tall and weighing 121 lbs (+36%). She was the younger of 2 children and had a good relationship with her older brother who had outgrown his childhood plumpness. There was cooperation with a reducing program, but in a relaxed way. Sophia was an excellent student and socially quite active, something encouraged by her mother. She became an effective secretary and has worked occasionally since her marriage at age 22. She was 27 years old and had a child of 3½, with whom she had never used sweets as a reward and whom she had kept away from starchy food. The child weighed less than the mother had weighed at the same time and showed no tendency toward gaining too much weight. Sophia was aware that she had a weight problem, without being frantic about it. She was very tall, 5'9½", and had tried to maintain her weight at around 160 lbs. Though she did not like being plump she did not feel that her weight had handicapped her life. She was a warm, cordial, and alive woman, well-groomed and tastefully dressed. She recalled with definite distaste her efforts at dieting when she was younger. "It was terrible as a child: you can't go out with the others; even when you work you cannot have lunch with them. The others eat what they want and you can't even look at it." Periodically she would go on a diet, but "one day you get tired of it and you are satisfied with the way you look." This young woman sounded like an ideal candidate for the current group reducing enterprises.

The common factor in the backgrounds of those who had done well was a warm and accepting attitude on the part of the parents, with support and encouragement, and absence of being persecuted for being fat. It appears to be important that the atmosphere of the home fosters growth toward independent maturity and does not hinder it. Characteristically the fat children who had done well did not cite their weight as a handicap in their life, and had gone ahead with their plans regardless of it. None of them was severely overweight; the excess was usually in the 20 to 30 lb range.

In contrast there were several who had been successful with keeping their weight under control, but who led lonely and isolated lives and complained bitterly about the injustices of life; among them they counted 'he need to watch their weight and to be careful about what they ate. An example is Faith, who had been rated as unusually successful with her reducing regimen. She had always been a plump child but had gained rapidly after age 7 which caused the parents to become alarmed and to bring her to the obesity clinic at age 10. During the next 3 years she grew from 56" to 64", had menarche at age 12, and her weight dropped from 141 lbs (+86%) to 128 lbs (+12%). This apparently excellent weight control was the result of her mother's rigid supervision; it did not express a better adjustment during adolescence. Faith was aware of her passive role: "When I'm unhappy I seem to lose all my will power"—and she was unhappy quite often. As an adult she remembered with bitterness the stress of being forced to diet. As long as she lived at home she maintained her weight at about 135 lbs. Then it went up slowly until it reached 190 lbs (height 5'5") when she was 26 years old, at what she described in a letter as "probably my most disturbed period." She had done well in a professional career and later married a man who was working in the same field. When last heard of she was 30 years old, quite happy in her marriage, and expecting her second child. Feeling more independent she felt she could now control her weight and had succeeded in stabilizing it at about 160 lbs.

The largest group seen during the follow-up study were patients who had done poorly weight-wise, and many of whom showed evidence of mental illness. In addition, examination of the clinic records showed that many of those who had not responded to the follow-up letters had been or were in state hospitals or had been in touch with social agencies for their difficulties. Not all patients with such poor outcomes had hospital records; many led restricted, lonely lives. An example is Vera's story. She had been seen in the obesity clinic when only 3 years old. Though small at birth she weighed 32 lbs at age 1, and 54 lbs at age 2. At 3 she was 41″ tall and weighed 69 lbs (+73%). She was seen again at age 5 with a weight of 91 lbs (+120%). There was no response to repeated follow-up letters, until her physician reported that her weight had been as high as 260 lbs at age 16, but now, at 18, reduced to 240 lbs. Though she had been a very good student and had graduated from high school, she was unable to keep jobs on account of her extreme obesity. She led a very restricted social life, had not been able to find partners at school dances, had no boyfriend, and was at times quite depressed.

I should like to give only one example of the many tragic situations in which the seriousness of the underlying problems was recognized early and psychiatric help was offered, but was rejected—with manifest mental illness later. John was only moderately obese when seen in the obesity clinic at age 6. He was 49½″ tall and weighed 68 lbs (+23%). He was a timid, whining, and listless boy, the only child of a mother who was acutely unhappy in her marriage to a much older man who took no interest in his son because the boy was something the mother had wanted, not he. The parents had been married 12 years before the mother conceived. She had been frantic about having a child, but had wanted a girl, because "a girl stays close to you." At no time was she reconciled to the sex of her child, and from the day of his birth on she found various things wrong with him physically. There were complaints about an enlarged thymus, or a heart murmur, or too much respiration, and finally his weight. She had never let the child out of her sight, and his going to school was a serious shock to her. As he grew older, the mother was as much concerned about his inactivity and clumsiness as about his extra weight. She belittled him for being slow, but did not encourage independence or activity. She absolutely rejected the advice to seek psychiatric help. Whenever she could afford it, she took her son to private physicians for endocrine injections. When puberty occurred at about 13 years, the boy's behavior became openly bizarre. He pulled out every hair on his body, spoke with a high-pitched voice, and bleached his hair and eyebrows. He explained it as the need to keep himself clean by correcting the dirty and animal aspects of his development. Now his mother, fearing that he might become a homosexual, was frantic in seeking psychiatric help for him. There were repeated psychiatric hospitalizations when he appeared disoriented and his delusions became too obvious. In between he stayed at home with his mother, who would strictly supervise his diet and every step he took. His weight would rise sharply whenever she relaxed her control. When last seen at age 27, he had no vocational training and was listless, depressed, and fat (220 lbs).

I should like to mention briefly two instances with indications of a serious emotional disturbance in childhood, both clinically and on psychological tests, where the parents accepted the recommendation for psychiatric help for themselves and their children. At that time it did not look as if much had been accomplished but the long-range effect appears rather remarkable.

David, now 38 years old, was severely obese when he came to the obesity clinic at age 3½. He was the third boy in a family with two older sons, 10 and 12 years his senior. The mother had always wanted a girl, and she had raised this child as if he were a daughter, having lost two girl babies who were stillborn. David had been a slender child until age 2; at this time his mother was pregnant again and lost another girl baby. He began to gain rapidly, developed fears, nail biting, and other neurotic symptoms. The mother was extremely concerned about his physique, focusing her anxiety on the adequacy of his genitals. She was aware that she worried excessively, and accepted the need for psychiatric help for herself. Though it was far from adequate, she was convinced that David needed to be more active and should associate with other children instead of staying with her all the time. When David was 14 years old his mother died, and he went to live with an older brother who supported him in his ambition to acquire a college education. When last heard of, in 1970, he was an associate professor in a mid-Western college and satisfied with his career.

When David was about 15 years old he had put himself on a diet and has kept his weight within normal range ever since. Puberty occurred early, but he was shy and inhibited in his relation to girls. While in college he sought psychiatric help and stayed in treatment until he felt secure in his overall adjustment. At 24 he married a young woman who herself had been plump as a child. In raising their 3 children they have succeeded in avoiding the errors of their own parents, with the result that the children are of normal weight and have normal eating habits.

The other young man, Leo, now 40 years old, was seen in the obesity clinic at age 5 years, weighing over 70 lbs (+55%). He appeared so inhibited, and his movements and speech were so slow, that some organic factor was suspected. However, neurological examination was normal, and he did well on verbal intelligence tests (I.Q. 134), less so on performance tests (I.Q. 112); the Goodenough Figure Drawings were so poorly done that they were not scorable. He was born a year after a first child had died, following a premature birth for which the mother blamed herself. She gave to her second child the name of the dead baby, and in talking about her son one gained the impression that she confused the dead and the living child. Concern about death determined her attitude toward health and safety, and she raised Leo with enormous restrictions. Her anxiety was so great that she accepted a few psychiatric interviews, and this resulted in her permitting Leo to go to camp when 11 years old.

In retrospect Leo considered the camp experience the most important event of his life. Miserable as he had been, he found out that he could survive without his mother. With the encouragement of his high school teachers he pursued an academic career and even had the courage to go to an out-of-town college. He became a mathematician, a field completely outside his mother's range of experience. He had remained severely obese and decided to reduce while in college. From then on he has maintained his weight within normal range. However, he must pay continuous attention to what he eats; the slightest relaxation is followed by weight increase. He married a woman sympathetic to his problems, who will prepare meals to meet his needs. They made it a point to permit their children to develop their own eating habits, in contrast to the way his mother tried to force food on her grandchildren, with the result that the children show no tendency toward overweight.

Though these patients had been seen in a pediatric clinic, little was done, except for some dietary prescriptions, to alter their or their family's way of life. Their clinical course represents the "natural history" of childhood obesity. Some had appeared to be great medical "successes" insofar as they lost considerable amounts of weight.

The largest amounts were lost by an Italian boy who weighed 265 lbs at age 11. He was cooperative with various diets and had no trouble losing prodigious amounts when under supervision. But he would invariably regain the weight when the controls were relaxed. The rate of gain appeared to be the same as if the interference with his weight had not taken place. He weighed over 450 lbs when he died of pneumonia, at age 24.

In this group it was recognized that weight reduction alone, without correction of the underlying problems, was a futile gesture; invariably the lost weight was regained as soon as the contact with the clinic was interrupted. Recommendations for psychiatric treatment appeared unacceptable to most parents to whom it was given.

Incomplete as this study is, as far as I know there is no other study where patients for whom detailed physiological, psychological, and sociocultural findings had been recorded during childhood were followed into adulthood. The general tendency is to observe and record only the changes in weight. Longitudinal studies, based on height-weight records of a school or clinic population, give only the statistical incidence of overweight later on, but fail to indicate factors determining differences in outcome (1, 8, 11).

In evaluating the long-term outcome no single factor could be identified that would have permitted a definite prediction of the long-range development. None of the then (1930 to 1940) current laboratory tests gave information that might have been of prognostic significance; nor do I know of any modern laboratory method that would permit a prediction of the long-range course. Recently there has been much emphasis on the significance of a high adipose cell count during infancy for later obesity. Based on my experience this results in lasting obesity only if other factors associated with overfeeding and inactivity persist.

Assessment of the problems within the family, of the emotional maturity of the child and of other behavioral aspects, appears to be of greater importance for a predictive appraisal than physical factors. Early onset and severe degrees of overweight commonly are signs of poor outcome, though there are exceptions. In this group approximately 30% had been fat since infancy, approximately 50% grew fat after entering school, and the remaining 20% during preadolescence. In a few instances some definite traumatic event, usually a death in the family, could be identified as having preceded a sudden gain in weight. None of these factors is predictive of the long-range outcome. This appears to be dependent mainly on the stability and warmth of the family or on the effectiveness of therapeutic intervention.

The described or observed food intake was found to be an unreliable guide for evaluating the long-range prognosis. Efforts at dieting may be harmful when a mother takes over and superimposes the reducing regimen, thereby further restricting a child's development. Inactivity is a more reliable index. Severe inactivity associated with social isolation or withdrawal foretells a poor outcome of severe progressive obesity and poor social adjustment, resulting not infrequently in manifest mental illness.

Quite early in the study it had been recognized that the various symptoms were closely related to family problems (Chapter 5). The significance of the disturbing factors has become clearer through the retrospective evaluation. It is not the one or the other aspect of the parents' behavior or of their background and sociocultural factors, nor the sibling position of the fat child, though there is a preponderance of only and youngest children. Of significance is the level of anxiety and discord that permeates these families, keeping the parents from permitting the child's development toward independence. Also significant is their overpowering and possessive clinging to the child. The underlying forces which interfere with a child's growing into a distinct individual with needs and impulses clearly differentiated from those of his parents could gradually be delineated

(Chapter 4). It was recognized that fat children who do not "outgrow" their childhood plumpness, neither physically nor psychologically, suffer from severe deficits in this process of self-differentiation which is associated with an inability to identify "hunger" and to differentiate it from other bodily and emotional states, leaving them helpless in their efforts to control their food intake, or to direct their lives.

Psychological tests have proven helpful in evaluating the degree to which a child has internalized the damaging influences. As a group obese children attained high I.Q.'s on verbal tests, but were rated lower on performance tests and were significantly low on the Draw-A-Person Test (7). By reevaluating the early findings it was found that marked discrepancies between the results on verbal and performance scales, and, even more clearly, poor performance on the Draw-A-Person Test, are signals of potential maldevelopment. Figure drawings appear to be closely related to a child's self-concept, and a severe disturbance in body image is predictive of a poor outcome. This poor self-concept becomes even more damaged when a fat child is exposed to continuous derogatory messages indicating that he is unsatisfactory or unacceptable the way he is.

The extent of the disturbances in total adjustment was also assessed by the Rorschach test, which, however, showed fewer similarities than had been expected. This suggested that in spite of the frequency of emotional disturbances in obese children, their nature varies in different individuals. These general observations are similar to those made by Ostergaard in Denmark, who observed that in spite of delay in attaining emotional adaptation and maturity corresponding to their age, fat children showed individual differences in their patterns of and capacity for adaptation (14). Not all children had difficulties in their social relations, indicating that the symptom of obesity in itself does not necessarily lead to isolation and social maladjustment. The majority of Ostergaard's group showed signs of difficulties in adapting themselves to others, but with great variability in individual behavior.

A direct measure of the parents' discontent is the amount of therapeutic efforts to which a fat child is being exposed. Characteristic for those who have done poorly, with schizophrenia a not uncommon outcome, is the parents' tendency to shop around for medical advice that will fulfill their own needs. Evaluation of the records reveals an embarrassing contrast: the more medical treatment, be it superimposed diets, repeated courses of endocrine treatment, or use of reducing drugs, the poorer the outcome. The determining factor appears to be the aggressive dissatisfaction of parents with their child, which finds an unfortunate collaboration by physicians, who, by believing in the magic of symptom relief, fail to deal with the underlying problems. During the 1950's I observed several cases of amphetamine addiction, based on medical prescription; this was long before the danger of "speed" had been generally recognized.

Reexamination of the clinic group after more than 30 years permitted the formulation of certain common psychological factors that are recognized as damaging, namely exploitation of a child as a compensation for disappointments and shortcomings in the parents' life. The same was observed in fat children seen in private practice; here, too, parents had looked upon the child as a personal possession, as something which proved something about themselves or reflected the parents' achievements. In spite of the overprivileged care these children had received, true regard for their individuality had been lacking. The role of the fathers in these families appears to be different. They are successful and frequently, though not always, have a more dominant position in the family; usually they take an active interest in the child. Sometimes this is of a supportive nature, more often it is highly critical—as if one of their possessions did not live up to expectations. Frequently the father's concern is with the physique and appearance of a child and may begin early in life when a son does not fulfill a father's dream by being a star athlete, or otherwise does not act the way the father wants him to act. It may become apparent only in adolescence when a fat daughter fails to become the beautiful showpiece of her father's success and social prominence.

In most instances the psychiatric disturbances in fat children seen in private practice are so severe that intensive psychotherapy is necessary. I shall give here briefly the history of a boy where redirection of the parents' concern permitted him a freer development. The parents requested a consultation for their 13½-year-old son, Stanley. They complained about his being too fat and not doing anything about it, though he was very intelligent and a good student. The father had tried to get his son interested in athletics since he was a small child and more forcefully after he entered school, fearing he might be "different" from other boys. The father himself was tall, slender, bronzed, and athletic looking, and had done better financially than anybody in his family. The mother had been affectionate and indulgent toward her son, with some awareness that he was too old to be so demonstrative. There was some concern about his jealousy toward a younger sister who was considered by both parents to be the "perfect child." Stanley was tall and heavyset, 20% overweight but not "fat." Puberty development was appropriate to age. He was suspicious and resentful about the consultation, but relaxed when he recognized that this was not another attempt to coerce him to reduce and to become an athlete. The therapeutic work was directed toward helping the father recognize that he could not force his image of success and perfection on his son. As the pressures diminished, Stanley became socially more outgoing and chose friends who shared his own literary inclinations. During his last year in high school Stanley himself felt that his excess weight was a hindrance and asked advice for a diet and followed through on it. When he graduated at age 17, he was tall, well developed, not too heavy, but not athletic looking either. Leaving for college was an escape from an overdemanding home. He has done well in his chosen profession and scarcely remembers his so-called obesity.

In this survey of the long-range development of obesity in childhood I have emphasized the importance of the parent-child interaction, in particular, the parent's role in encouraging or hindering a child's steps toward independence. This may have given the impression that I consider the fat child to be passive in this process. This he is not. However compliant the overt behavior, he is far from being passively molded, but is an active participant in this process. His very submissiveness, immaturity, and continued dependence on his parents are his ways of controlling and making demands on his environment. These "active" aspects of a fat child's way of life were more clearly recognized during intensive psychotherapy with fat adolescents.

The only fat children who "outgrow" their obesity are those who make the decision to reduce on their own initiative. Usually they are not too severely damaged in their self-concept; when recognizing the social handicap, they will respond with a decision to reduce, an effort in which they usually succeed, or they will accept the social attitude without too much self-recrimination. Others, with poor self-concept and without awareness of their inner resources, will react to the social rejection with shame, self-contempt, and helpless submission—and social withdrawal and increased obesity.

Gifted writers have recognized that social attitudes and a child's own achievement interact. In *The Story of Christina*, an unhappy fat girl runs away from her loveless home and joins the circus as the "fat lady" (13). Instead of being ridiculed she is now admired for her size and is treated as a respected friend by everybody. Much to her bewilderment, she no longer wants to eat as much as before and gradually loses weight, so much that she no longer can fill the role of the fat lady. There is a happy ending, of course, for the now slender and pretty young girl.

In a more recent book, *Pirate's Island* (16), the hero, Gordon Dobbs, grew up in a slum area as an overindulged and overweight child, the only son of a small, withdrawing pork butcher and a large, cosseting mother, who is constantly urging him to "keep his strength up" by overeating: "the sort of boy who was bound to be tormented in a tough council school." He has no friends but meets a waif, Sheila, an orphan who lives in a slum with a dejected aunt, and who escapes from the grimness of her life by living in a world of make-believe. She invites Gordon to go looking for pirate's treasures. Naturally, they unearth no treasures, but they do discover a plot to rob an old man of his life's savings. This provides Gordon with a chance to "find out if he has it in him to break out from the cocoon of overprotection, the boredom of a life bounded by comics and the radio and nibbles from the shop," by doing something hard and brave. When the opportunity comes, Gordon is no longer the greedy clod he used to be.

BIBLIOGRAPHY

1. Abraham, S., and Norsiek, N., Relationship of excess weight in children and adults, Public Health Rep., 75:263, 1960.
2. Bruch, H., Obesity in childhood, I. Physical growth and development of obese children, Amer. J. Dis. Child., 58:457–484, 1939.
3. Bruch, H., Obesity in childhood, III. Physiologic and psychologic aspects of the food intake of obese children, Amer. J. Dis. Child., 58:738–781, 1940.
4. Bruch, H., Obesity in childhood, IV. Energy expenditure of obese children, Amer. J. Dis. Child., 60:1082–1109, 1940.
5. Bruch, H., Obesity in relation to puberty, J. Pediat., 19:365–375, 1941.
6. Bruch, H., Physical growth and development in obesity, Chapter VI, pp. 106–128, in *The Importance of Overweight*, W. W. Norton & Co., New York, 1957.
7. Bruch, H., The mental development of obese children, Chapter IX, pp. 165–187, in *The Importance of Overweight*, W. W. Norton & Co., New York, 1957.
8. Eid, E. E., Follow-up study of physical growth of children who had excessive weight gain in first 6 months of life, Brit. Med. J., 2:74–76, 1970.
9. Finkelstein, J. W., and Avery, M. E., The Pickwickian Syndrome, studies on ventilation and carbohydrate metabolism: Case report of a child who recovered, Amer. J. Dis. Child., 106:251–257, 1963.
10. Hirsch, J., and Knittle, J. L., Cellularity of obese and nonobese human adipose tissue, Fed. Proc., 29:1516–1521, 1970.
11. Hubble, D., The underweight and the overweight child, Brit. Med. J., 1:1293–1295, 1965.
12. Jaeger, G. F., *Vergleichung einiger durch Fettigkeit oder kolossale Bildung ausgezeichneter Kinder und einiger Zwerge*, Metzler, Stuttgart, 1821.
13. Newell, H., *The Story of Christina*, Harper & Bros., New York, 1947.
14. Ostergaard, L., On psychogenic obesity in children, Acta paediat., 43:507–521, 1954.
15. Stafford, J., The echo and the nemesis, in *The Collected Stories of Jean Stafford*, Farrar, Straus and Giroux, New York, 1969.
16. Townsend, J. R., *Pirate's Island*, Lippincott, New York, 1968.

9

Obesity in Adolescence

There is probably no other age group as concerned and preoccupied with their physique and appearance as adolescents—before, and even more, after pubescence. They are forever worried about their size, whether they are too tall or too short, about the adequacy of their sexual development, about their hair and skin, and their attractiveness in general; but most of all they are preoccupied with their weight. Modern adolescents have it drummed into them, day in and day out, by well-meaning parents and physicians and most of all by the cosmetic advertising, that the only way to be respected and admired is to be thin. They are under severe pressure to reduce below what is biologically and psychologically comfortable. Their fear of being "too fat," or being rated as such, is an exaggeration of the weight consciousness of our whole society which condemns even mild degrees of overweight as ugly and undesirable and criticizes it as a sign of self-indulgence.

Adolescence is that period in man's life that bridges the gap between childhood and adult maturity. It is a time of rapid changes in physical size and bodily functions, in personality development and a person's role in society. The specific biologic event of the adolescent years is puberty, the maturing of the sex organs and the development of secondary sexual characteristics. It is this, and the need for integrating sexual adaptation, that is usually emphasized. Often it is not stressed enough that it is also the time when an individual attains his mature size and stature and a sense of personal identity. Under fortunate conditions the appearance and personality that develop are satisfying to the individual and publicly acceptable. Adolescence is also a time of decision-making about a career and social role that, hopefully, fit into the adolescent's self-concept and values, and encourage further growth and development.

Just as the attainment of personal and sexual identity does not take place automatically but requires positive integrating experiences, so is the development of a positive concept of one's bodily identity the outcome of many experiences and events. Human growth follows a specifically *human* pattern, rigid in its sequence but varying considerably from one individual to another in its intimate details. Growth curves based on average figures tend to conceal the magnitude of the events that take place in an individual child during adolescence. Puberty is related to other processes of growth. Stature growth precedes a gain in weight which also takes place before and at puberty. This gain in weight, the filling-out process, is greater in girls than in boys. Of the various factors involved in this complex process of growth, weight appears to be the one most determined by external conditions, and seemingly most under the influence of voluntary action, whereas height is more determined by genetic endowment, though it requires adequate nutrition for its full development.

It is not uncommon that during this period of exuberant growth some individuals become plump and deplore themselves as "too fat;" others become overly slim. Once growth and weight have stabilized, normal adolescents will correct their weight through adjustment of their diet, and most are successful with this, with or without medical help, and will remain slim. For the overly slender ones who may suffer from feeling puny and skinny, the filling-out process will take place somewhat later, usually without the need for medical intervention.

Large-scale statistics reflect the modern adolescent girls' concern with weight. Teen-agers today are taller and heavier than those of earlier generations. This applies for boys for the whole adolescent period. The average 15- to 16-year-old boy weighs approximately 10 lbs more and is approximately 1.6 inches taller than a teen-ager around 1900. For girls the increase in height is 0.4 inches, but weight, though higher during the early teen years, shows a decrease of 3.2 lbs for 17 to 19 year olds. These statistical figures indicate that most modern adolescent girls know how to control their weight, how to keep it below what previous generations considered attractive and desirable. This makes those who are unable to exercise such a steady control even more conspicuous, isolated, and despised.

Weight deviations in essentially healthy adolescents need to be differentiated from those in whom manipulation of the body size itself is a core problem in a rather serious maldevelopment of the total personality. There are those who are hopelessly and helplessly too fat and bemoan their fate. They use the obese state as an alibi for avoiding the normal activities of adolescence, and as an explanation for all their handicaps and difficulties. Yet they are unable to control their food intake or to increase their activities. They often arouse the contempt of their peers and are exposed to an endless stream of recommendations, pleadings, and threats from their elders.

Even for those who are "too heavy" there is a need to differentiate between different forms and degrees of overweight. It may be nothing more than a temporary imbalance during this period of most active growth; on the other hand it may be progressive obesity associated with severe emotional and personality disturbance. Sometimes a weight excess as low as 10% or 20%, or merely normal curvaceous development, will provoke enormous anxiety and overly rigid control of every bite of food. There are others who are grotesquely obese, having gained enormous amounts at the slightest disturbance and who suddenly embark on rigid diets to which they adhere as compulsively as they formerly indulged in eating binges. Such patients will show enormous weight fluctuations, seemingly unable to stabilize at any weight. In still others, the continuous social insult about their grotesque appearance and their inability to control their weight will lead to such discrepancies in their self-esteem and body image that psychotic behavior becomes manifest (Chapter 10).

Some obese adolescents have been fat children, and they continue to be overweight or gain even more at puberty. Others have been of normal weight until then, or may have even been tall and too slim. From following obese children into adulthood it was learned that an individual's experiences during adolescence are of utmost importance for the long-range development. Some seem to be able to grow into the excess weight, or even to lose it. Many do so on their own initiative, others with the help of an older sibling, friends, teacher, or some other support; rarely can a parent function in this role. A precondition for this is that the adolescents experience themselves as well-differentiated individuals, competent in their self-concept and sense of identity.

An example of such successful self-initiated dieting was reported in a women's magazine about 20 years ago. It concerned a 16-year-old boy who weighed 217 lbs and who had first learned about diets from the magazine. He is now a successful professional man, quite slim, and nothing in his appearance or behavior would suggest that he is a former fat boy. He himself is convinced that if he didn't pay attention to his diet, he would easily regain the weight. He was a high school student when he decided to lose weight because he did not want to look different from his friends. He approached the diet as one would a scientific problem. He began by writing down everything he ate and then proceeded to calculate his intake from a calorie book. With his physician's approval he began with a 1500 calorie diet, calculating meals to suit his taste; in counting the calories he included everything he ate, even chewing gum. He gradually lowered the calorie count so that in 5 weeks he had gone down to a diet of approximately 1000 calories, to which he stuck for over a year, losing nearly 70 lbs. He became aware of how much his former overeating had been "just a habit" and did not feel hungry while dieting. As he began to lose weight his mother and sister joined him in the diet; they had not been as heavy as he and they, too, lost the desired amounts. It is of interest that he, the *initiator*, maintained the weight loss, and eventually lost more, whereas his sister, the *follower*, gradually regained some of her weight.

In evaluating why this effort was so successful, the most important point is probably that he made the decision to diet through his own initiative, and that he approached it as an objective task which he handled in a systematic way, even keeping charts and records. He applied the same systematization to his school work, budgeting his time for work and other activities, and found that he did better work in school while losing weight. There are some other points that appear to be important. The overeating was not related to disturbances in the family relationships; the mother was a professional woman who had left the care of her children to a house-keeper who felt that it was easier to indulge them than to say no to their wishes. Most important is probably the fact that though he had been a fat boy he shared the interests of his slim friends, wanted to take part in their activities, and thus was well-motivated in his desire to lose weight.

As a contrast I should like to refer back to a history in Chapter 7, where the patient at age 16 had lost even more weight, but subsequently was unable to maintain the low weight. He had begun the diet because his sister took him in hand and supervised his diet, and there were serious family problems.

Those who are unable to obtain help, or who cannot make use of it even if it is available, have been disturbed in establishing their own iden-tity, in their ability to relate to others, and in developing a positive self-concept. The problems that face every adolescent appear overpowering to them. Commonly they will withdraw from social contacts, become increas-ingly inactive, seek comfort in food, and thus grow progressively fatter. Like other youngsters, the obese adolescent needs to emancipate himself and overcome his dependency on his parents. He must redirect his inter-est, affection, and loyalty toward friends of his own age. He must learn to recognize and pattern his sexual impulses in a way that permits gratifica-tion in a dependable form, compatible with his personal ideals and self-concept. Only through accomplishing these tasks can he find his adult identity and accept the role of an adult (1).

Those who have been obese as children or who have developed similar personality traits though they have not been fat before puberty face these tasks of adolescence with deficient tools and guideposts. The very circum-stances and experiences that made them fat children and had resulted in the deficiency in their sense of control and mastery will continue to handi-cap them in expanding their personal experiences, and will make them feel inadequate in facing these new problems. These mechanisms are in many ways self-perpetuating. Obese adolescents with serious adjustment prob-lems are often those in whom inactivity and overeating have been integral parts of their whole development. Often they are so blocked and inhibited that they cannot attain satisfaction and fail to develop their greater poten-tialities with increasing maturity.

Long-term intensive psychotherapy revealed that obese young people are defective in their awareness of being self-directed, separate individuals with the ability of identifying and controlling their body urges, and of defining their needs and presenting them in a way that they can find appropriate and satisfying responses. They suffer from a basic disturbance in the area of self-awareness, something they have in common with an-orexia nervosa patients. Manipulation of body size, resulting from manipu-lation of food intake, may serve as an overly rigid effort to establish a sense of effective identity, or it may express helpless ineffectiveness in this effort, in the face of biological needs and social demands. The abnormal body size is the outward manifestation of serious maladaptation in many different aspects of development. Patients often complain about feeling "empty," and behave as if their center of gravity were not within themselves but somewhere in the outside world, controlled by someone else. This disturbance in bodily awareness is associated with what has been called "weak ego boundaries," "disturbed body image," or "identity confusion." Physicians characteristically accuse such patients of having "no will power" because they are unable to follow a reducing regimen.

In the psychological study of adolescence, psychoanalytic theory has dominated the field to such an extent that many of its assumptions are repeated as if they were facts. There is a feeling that since we "know" the schedule of psychosexual development during childhood, we are prepared to see the various stages through which an individual supposedly has progressed as a child repeated and reenacted at puberty. These concepts of psychic determinism and repetition stand in contrast to modern dynamic concepts of growth and development. The organism has no time to waste on repetition, and the functional problems to be dealt with at each period are determined by the demands of the new situations and the organism's inherited or acquired ability to deal with them. As has been discussed before (Chapter 4), many potentially anorexic or obese children have been severely handicapped in the acquisition of such tools. To the extent that an individual is properly equipped, he will succeed in growing up healthy, with the feeling of being in charge of his life and of owning his own body. In contrast, obese adolescents with emotional problems suffer from a feeling of not being in control of their sensations or actions. They fail to achieve a sense of ownership of their own body. They lack discriminating awareness of the signals of bodily urges, and also the sense of emotional and interpersonal effectiveness. They suffer from a conviction that they are the misshapen product of somebody else's action and do not experience themselves as independent self-directed individuals, with initiative and autonomy.

The question of how ownership of the body develops has not been entirely overlooked in previous writings, but it has too often been dealt with in an overgeneralized fashion, with statements such as "until puberty the child's body is the mother's property." Such a statement contains a basic error: that of not differentiating between external events and *inner experience*. True, until adolescence it is part of a mother's function to provide and supervise her child's nutrition and hygienic care. But becoming aware of one's own sensations and needs, and learning to define and express them in a distinct way are part of a development that begins in earliest infancy and progresses throughout childhood. Self-awareness about functional separateness does not suddenly spring into existence during adolescence; although during adolescence there may be a daring testing out of the limits of one's strength and ability and a reckless struggle to have one's independence recognized in every area. Applied to food, eating what one wants is considered an adult privilege, and the adolescent, in his transition, is rudely outspoken about refusing or demanding certain foods. In spite of his extravagant food fads, the healthy adolescent seems to "know" and is sure of what and how much he wants to eat. His self-regulation is in harmony with his physiological requirements, though there may be a temporary imbalance.

This self-regulation appears grossly disturbed in obese adolescents, not on the basis of some organic defect, but on account of a learning deficit which has interfered with their developing awareness of and control over bodily sensations. The old reproach about obese people having "no will power" actually describes an important deficit in their functioning which is related, in part at least, to their inability to recognize and identify bodily needs. Not being clearly aware of their bodily sensations, they cannot exercise control over their functions.

Obesity in adolescence is considered a particularly difficult problem because its victims are attacked by a rejecting social attitude. Many have attempted to explain their severe psychological problems as having been caused by this rejection. There is no doubt that this plays a role; but its importance is related to an individual's vulnerability. Those with healthy self-esteem and a realistic outlook can face this unfriendly climate without withdrawing from life.

Amy's history may serve as an example. At 18 she was 5′5″ tall and weighed 170 lbs, but looked attractive, was well-groomed and well-dressed in clothes designed to flatter her figure. Her mother had arranged for a psychiatric consultation. A slim younger sister was in treatment at that time for serious emotional problems. This girl blamed her mother who she felt had been overcontrolling and overdemanding throughout her life.

Amy agreed that their mother was somewhat difficult; the consultation about her obesity was just one example of the mother's having to run everybody's life. But she had learned how to handle her mother; in addition, she always had had a supportive friend in her grandmother. She knew that her appearance was not fashionable, but she was not too concerned about it. She felt she had inherited her grandmother's make-up, her quiet and considerate temperament, and her short, stocky figure. The grandmother was quite an outstanding person, not only on account of her husband's wealth and prominent social position but in her own right, having stimulated and organized a number of well-known social projects. Amy was aware of the change in taste, that 50 years ago being plump was not the same handicap as it was now. Nevertheless, she had found that she functioned better, was more interested in what was going on in the world, did better in her studies, and, in particular, was socially more responsive when she was at what she felt was her natural weight. Under mother's pressure, she had repeatedly tried to reduce, and had sometimes even lost 10 or 20 lbs. However, she felt so tense and uneasy that she had come to the decision that to maintain her present weight was the wiser choice.

Amy was grateful for support of her view that her general functioning was more important than her appearance. About a year later she came to tell me about her engagement to an attractive young man with whom she had many interests in common. When she had raised the question that her weight might be socially embarrassing to him, he had replied that he was marrying *a person*, not *a figure*. Their marriage turned out well. There were two children, and Amy did not gain excess weight during or after her pregnancies. Ten years later her weight was exactly the same as it had been at age 18, too plump by contemporary fashionable standards but not interfering with her active and meaningful life.

Weight excess in adolescence is commonly blamed for interfering with sexual adjustment. Obviously, being fat is a serious handicap in being rated "attractive" in our weight-conscious society. But from my observations it is not the weight excess itself but the attitude toward it, or more correctly toward oneself, that interferes with any personal relationships, most of all in the sexual area.

Not uncommonly fat girls are provocatively unrestrained in their sexual behavior and become promiscuous. A 16-year-old girl from an upper-class home bragged about being the "biggest" whore in her school. She was proud that in spite of her size she could attract any boy she wanted. Not infrequently I have observed that youngsters who felt "unattractive" by being fat, after reducing will "substitute" sex for their former indulgence in eating. Others are more mature, in spite of the problems inherent in obesity, and make meaningful personal choices.

Gladys, age 17, the third among 6 children, mostly girls, had been markedly overweight since age 7. Gladys resembled her father, a huge man, outstanding in his career, who was never successful in his efforts to control his weight. The family was socially prominent and there was much pressure that Gladys should reduce. When 15 she had been discouraged about her weight and was sent to an out-of-town reducing hospital. In 6 months her weight dropped from 250 lbs to 180 lbs. On going home she was terribly disappointed that her family continued to pressure her to reduce more, that this was not slim enough.

The pressure increased when she met a young man who fell in love with her and spoke of marriage. Her parents were not pleased. With increased tension she gave up all efforts at dieting and her weight rose rapidly. Exactly one year after discharge she returned to the same medical center, now weighing 280 lbs, reluctant about the reducing regimen but determined to marry her young man. She was seen by a psychiatrist and came to recognize the rebellion and anger in her behavior. She also realized that her parents' concern about her desire to marry the first man who came along had some justification. She also had deep feelings of love and loyalty toward her boyfriend. By the time her weight was down to 230 lbs, her parents gave their consent to the marriage. Gladys felt no concern that her fatness might interfere with her sexual enjoyment; there was great desire and mutual attraction. A year later she reported a good marital adjustment, and also asked for advice about ambulatory reducing programs. This was the first time that she herself felt the need to bring her weight under control.

Both of these girls came from upper-class homes, illustrating that social class in itself does not preclude a fairly good adjustment even in severe adolescent obesity. Those with severe deficits in their self-concept and sense of competence suffer severely under the social disapproval, withdraw more and more behind the walls of their fatness, and literally stop living unless there is effective therapeutic intervention, with reference to weight as well as personality. Unfortunately it is in this group that negativistic refusal to cooperate often paralyzes all efforts.

An example is Myra who at age 20 had briefly been in psychiatric treatment. It was terminated, she said, because her father did not believe in psychiatry. She had made some progress toward a more independent life, had moved into an apartment of her own, and considered some technical training that would enable her to support herself. As soon as therapy was interrupted, she moved back into her parents' home, doing housework for her mother or babysitting for her sister or other unskilled work. At 20 she had weighed 270 lbs and "wanted" to slim down to 120 lbs, the weight of her sister. Under close medical supervision she had repeatedly lost 30 to 40 lbs but invariably regained the lost weight and more.

She asked for a consultation when she was 23 years old, weighing now more than 340 lbs. For several months she had attended Weight Watchers and had lost 30 lbs. Then she got tired of the routine and admonitions, and she discontinued it, just as she had terminated all other efforts before a decisive change had been effected. Now she was back to her former weight and she carried herself as an extremely heavy person. She complained that she felt helpless about her eating; she wanted a "change" but was sullenly angry at doctors and psychiatrists for not having helped her and for making her try to assume responsibility for herself. Myra had lost weight after an accident, when she could not move freely and her mother took care of the cooking and Myra did not have continuous free access to food. She knew that her present weight represented a health hazard; her blood pressure was high and her physician had predicted that her heart would give out.

Myra was the youngest in a professional family and had been considered normal as a child, bright and well-behaved. She had started gaining weight at menarche, when 12 years old, at about the same time her sister had begun to slim down. She did not appear unintelligent and had attended college on and off, but said, "I am not committed to any course of learning." She expressed the same attitude toward work and had done only the least difficult type of office work. Her previous psychiatrist felt that Myra's tendency to suspend reality to a rather striking degree had kept her "uninvolved" in therapy. Myra spoke of the previous efforts: "We had nothing to talk about," but then she expressed resentment that "He did not work a miracle; he did not give me will power." Her whole attitude reflected extreme passivity and reluctance to make any effort herself. During the consultation she claimed to be unable to answer the simplest questions about the past, "I can't picture myself at that age," or, "I can't remember anything about being in school." She became somewhat more lively when describing areas of agreement with her parents, for example, being critical of others, such as her brother's and sister's spouses, but also of society in general, "The Establishment," and "Washington." It appeared obvious that nothing constructive could be accomplished as long as she spent her days alone in either her parents' or her sister's home, in charge of the food supply. Efforts to involve her parents were sabotaged by her with the claim that they objected to psychiatry.

This course of events is unfortunately not uncommon and has given rise to the opinion that adolescent obesity has a poor outlook, and that psychotherapy is useless and ineffective. It is not, but it needs to be skillfully carried out over a long enough period. I should like to illustrate this with quotations from the histories of three young patients who had been considered hopeless failures when they were referred for psychiatric treatment in a spirit of desperation. Even under such conditions intensive therapy can lead to greater inner personal security and initiative which then permits a wider adaptive range, including the ability to handle the task of dieting. These three tremendously obese girls had several features in common: they were born during the early 1930's, they came from wealthy homes, and no effort had been spared to give them the best care and upbringing. They were in treatment during the late 1940's, maintained contact, and information about their subsequent development was obtained as late as 1971. In the expectation of finding some organic explanation for the obesity, they had undergone repeated extensive medical workups but no abnormalities were found. In all three repeated attempts had been made to enforce weight reduction, through hospitalizations or at commercial reducing establishments. Various weight losses had been achieved, even repeatedly, but each had immediately regained weight to her previous level or had even surpassed it. Three or four years had been spent in such efforts. When they were referred for psychoanalytic treatment at age 16, 17, and 18 years respectively, it was not only because the obesity appeared untractable, but because their total functioning had deteriorated, with depressive reactions and suicidal preoccupations, severe social isolation, and withdrawal from all activities except school. The length of psychiatric treatment had varied from 2 to 3 years. Details about the therapeutic approach which gradually evolved will be discussed in a later chapter. Information about their background and factors influencing their development was obtained during therapy and reveals the focus and emphasis of the therapeutic inquiry. The outcome in all three cases was better than one had dared to hope for at that time. All three got married, at ages 22, 24, and 29 respectively, and had children whom they were able to raise without creating weight problems for them. There were also marked differences which will be discussed under the following headings.

Weight History

Debby came for psychoanalytic treatment when she was 18 years old, 5' tall, weighing 180 lbs. She had slender bones and her fine features were nearly buried in fat. She was so inhibited and awkward that she gave the impression of being retarded in spite of normal intelligence. She was more passive and helpless than any other patient with whom I have worked psychoanalytically.

She had always been plump, which pleased her parents as long as she was young. She gained more rapidly after an operation at age 7, which the mother blamed on abrupt and cruel handling by the surgeon. Debby's weight became a terrible problem with the onset of puberty when she was suddenly declared "ungainly." From then on Debby's weight became a family obsession and she was dragged to numerous reducing doctors and commercial establishments. The harder the parents tried the more indifferent and withdrawn Debby became. On graduation from high school, at age 17½, she weighed 150 lbs. She joined a student group for a trip to Europe during which she gained between 20 and 30 lbs. The parents recalled with horror their shock when they saw Debby come down the gangplank looking, in their eyes, monstrously fat. Family life deteriorated to constant fighting about every bite Debby ate. A few months later she was referred for psychotherapy.

Kitty was depressed about her increasing weight when she was referred for psychiatric treatment at age 16½. She had always been a large (not fat) child, but had always been dissatisfied with her appearance, obsessed with the idea that there was something wrong with her body, that she was too big, awkward, ugly, or even misshapen. During one year there had been several deaths in the family, and she became preoccupied with the fear of dying. Thereafter, when 13 years old, she gained over 30 lbs, to about 165 lbs. From then on she and her family were preoccupied with her weight. When 14 she was sent to a commercial reducing salon where she lost 20 lbs. During the next year her weight stayed at around 140 lbs but she was extremely preoccupied with it. At age 15 she and a cousin went on a strict diet during the summer vacation and her weight dropped to 110 lbs. Though thin she continued to be frantically preoccupied with her weight. She looked so emaciated that her parents urged her to eat more, until one day she just couldn't stand the feeling of being always watched and decided not to pay any attention to what she ate. She had the feeling that she had lost all control over her eating and just gave up. As a result she gained rapidly. She also neglected her appearance and became more and more solitary. There were several attempts at reducing, all short-lived, twice with hospitalization which also included extensive laboratory studies. The second time she couldn't tolerate the idea of being locked up and left the hospital after one week. From then on there was a steady gain in weight and she had reached nearly 200 lbs when she was referred for psychiatric treatment.

She was depressed and expressed no interest other than enormous despair about her inability to control her weight. "If I could control my eating and be thin everything would be all right." She felt no need for psychiatric treatment, but kept her appointments regularly, in the spirit that if she didn't expect anything she wouldn't be disappointed if nothing were accomplished.

Tanya had been a rather poor eater and was very tall and skinny "like a beanstalk" until she was 12 years old, when she went to summer camp for the first time and discovered that eating could be used as a solace when she felt bored or lonely. In her wealthy home there had always been more than enough food, but eating more than what was absolutely necessary was just not done. There was another rule: whatever was on one's plate had to be finished—to the last morsel. Emancipation from home became for Tanya identical with the idea of "abundance," and she greedily ate foods that thus far had been doled out meagerly, such as cake and candy. She gained weight rapidly, reaching 190 lbs when she was 14 years old.

The next few years were spent in a continuous struggle with her weight. Tanya attended a boarding school where she was severely criticized for her eating. She might lose a few pounds but always regained it as soon as she escaped the strict supervision. One summer vacation was spent at one of the reducing salons. She accepted this in a spirit of defiance and resentment; she would "show them" that she could do it. She lost 30 lbs but considered this experience the most unhappy period of her life. She gained little or no satisfaction from being slim and regained the weight in brief time. She was seen in consultation when she was 15 years old, and came for psychoanalytic treatment when 17½, after graduation from high school. She was then 5'9" tall and weighed over 200 lbs. She had been a brilliant student with an enormous capacity for work, a driving compulsion to master any subject, "devouring" books and knowledge. Social relations, however, were poor and there were repeated fights about her attending the school dances which she refused to do. She suffered from great loneliness and periods of depression. She refused to be weighed and was so touchy about the whole issue that it was impossible to obtain exact information. The mere mention of food or weight would provoke deep resentment and depression. At graduation she was so depressed that she spent several weeks at a psychoanalytic hospital, where she was given a somber prognosis. She was considered "orally fixated" with a character structure built on this fixation. Her personality was considered compulsive in nature, including her eating. She expressed the idea that she felt that other people were just projections of herself, but she herself did not know who she was. It was felt that the "dissolution of her ego boundaries" was related to her "severe oral regression." However, her energy and superior intellect were rated as giving hope for successful therapy.

Family Constellation

A sketch of Debby's parents and their attitude was given in the chapter on family interaction (p. 72). Their enormous possessive involvement was as undisguised as in the most disturbed clinic patients. This was a family of immigrant background, with one decisive difference from the clinic group—the father was financially successful and therefore able to send his fat daughter to the best hospitals and reducing salons, to a progressive boarding school, and then for psychoanalytic treatment. Debby was the first child and grandchild in a closely knit large family and was excessively indulged by her parents and numerous relatives when small. There were 2 younger brothers and the parents took much more pride in them, and considered them superior to their fat daughter. During the early school years, it had been noted that Debby was exceedingly shy in making friends or in meeting other children. After puberty and after the persecution for her weight had begun, her shyness became so extreme that psychiatric treatment was arranged for. She never accepted the need for this and felt it was one more thing her parents did to make her "right." She then attended a progressive boarding school where the director and teachers took an active and outgoing interest in her, so that on their recommendation she accepted analytic treatment.

During the early part of treatment the sessions were taken up with monotonous complaints about her parents. There had been simply no contact between her and her family except in terms of her being fat and unattractive. What Debby experienced was, "My parents love or reject me according to whether I'm thin or fat. They do not like Me. When I gain weight they start hating me and then I hate myself, too. They have built their lives around my losing or gaining weight." Work with her parents, too, was a slow, uphill job. Although it had been discussed with them that they should stop their criticizing and insulting remarks, within a few months they took her again to a reducing doctor, which led to renewed fighting over Debby's eating. In spite of many conferences they never became convinced that their role was to permit Debby to develop some sense of control over her own life. Concern about her eating had been taken over by her parents so completely that Debby reacted in a childish, paradoxical way. When someone so much as mentioned that taking sugar with tea was fattening, she would take six teaspoonfuls; or when her father protested when she took a large second helping, she took three or four more. Debby presented herself as a passive victim, with endless complaints about her family and their interference.

The two other families were much more sophisticated and open-minded toward psychological problems. Kitty was the youngest daughter. For a long time she described her family and her relationship to every member as "wonderful." Gradually an enormous amount of resentment and frustrated rage came into the open. The parents, too, who in the beginning had described the home life as "very happy," began to speak of their disappointment and complained about Kitty's negativistic and inconsiderate behavior. Many years later she wrote that she had become interested in the Women's Liberation Movement because it expressed what she had felt throughout her childhood, that being a girl was a disadvantage, particularly when one's father expressed a derogatory attitude toward women.

The father was a successful banker and the family moved several times, each time to a more lavish home. Kitty felt that her father had been so preoccupied with his business that there was little time left for the family, except for checking up on how well everybody was doing. She remembered how much she had resented that he checked every day on her having practiced the piano, but later she was grateful for being an accomplished musician. The mother was slim, very well-dressed, with many social interests; she had had an artistic career. She could not give much information about Kitty's early life. Until age 5 or 6 she had been cared for by a reliable nurse. Kitty had two older brothers, college students, who in her view represented the "success" of the family. Actually the parents felt that Kitty was more gifted, original, and alert. Kitty had a good singing voice, enjoyed acting, and had always received a great deal of praise and admiration. Her having become obese had been a blow to all, because it dashed their hopes for an artistic career for Kitty.

Tanya was the younger of two daughters in an upper-class family who lived on a country estate. Her sister, 5 years older, went to boarding school when Tanya reached the age where they might have been companionable, and then married quite young. Thus Tanya grew up like an only child. She attended a school quite some distance from her home and rarely had companions during her free time, except for her parents, who, she felt, gave her a tremendous amount of love and admiration. This aroused in her a feeling of obligation, that it was her task to make up to them for their own frustration and disappointments. She felt she had let them down by growing fat. At the same time she was enraged about their continuous preoccupation with her weight. "Love consists of feeling so much for people that they tell you what is wrong with you. If I were as big as a barn, it is none of their business. Even now they just sit around 'controlling themselves,' *not* saying anything." Or she complained, "To mother it was more important what I looked like than what I was. What right does she have to demand that I should be thin—after all it is not her. She sits around staring at me as if I were a badly done wax work. She knows I have a lot of trouble, but she says, 'If you only had a less visible defect.'"

She felt her parents were deeply in love but that her father's habits and wishes dominated the home and that her mother went along with his rules of military punctuality and orderliness. As a child she longed to have a family that was "a unit and did things together" and she often wondered whether things would have been different if there had been brothers and sisters and she hadn't been the sole recipient of all this care and concern.

Feelings of not being in control extended to every aspect of her life. Though a brilliant student, she postponed going to college for awhile because she wanted to make her own decision, and not just go because it was expected. Her parents had been so concerned about doing right by her that she simply never could get the feeling that she was doing a thing because she wanted to do it.

I cannot do anything without doing what they want—I will never know what is ME without doing really something they object to. I do not want to do something drastic, but everything else they agree to. I should like to go to college because I *want to*, but the way they act I feel like *being sent*. They have given me so much leeway that they prevent me from "breaking out." There is this old awful burden of "being perfect." Everything I do appears so "reasonable"; they always agree with me, like humoring a child.

Instead of not having been loved enough, the way popular theories try to explain neurosis, she felt that she had been loved too much, that she had been the center of all her parents' attention and therefore she owed it to them to do something great and special. Her isolation and loneliness during childhood had deprived her of experiences that might have led to a correction of these unrealistic ideas of her tremendous responsibility. As a child she sometimes had the feeling of immense strength:

That I could do almost anything I set out to do. I wanted to be able to fly, also to be invisible; I would want " a wishing ring" and would use a definite ring for it. I did not just dream of a "glamorous life" but in all my daydreams something awful was going to happen, like being able to shoot and kill someone. I did not know how to end them, except by killing them off.

Psychological Tests

In spite of the great differences in family backgrounds, and also in their academic performances, which ranged from outstanding and brilliant in

Tanya to passing and uninspired in Debby, the psychological tests showed amazing similarities.

At age 16 Debby was so passive that on superficial contact she gave the impression of retardation, but she did well with verbal material, showing an I.Q. of 117, with her scores ranging from bright to superior. She scored much lower on the performance scale, with an I.Q. of 62 only. Her figure drawings brought out extreme rigidity, psychosexual infantilism, and confusion about body identity. At 18½ her achievements were similar, with an I.Q. of 122 on the verbal scale, with a good range of general knowledge and good ability for abstract thinking. But she scored only 87 on the performance scale, did very badly on the object assembly subtest, indicating a severe disturbance of her body image. The Draw-A-Person Test revealed her as exceedingly immature, self-absorbed, and narcissistic like a young child.

In Tanya psychological tests were done before she entered therapy at 17½. Her verbal I.Q. of 132 indicated a superior intelligence, but on the performance test she scored only 112. Her approach to situations was relatively scattered and unsystematic, with a tendency to overelaboration of acute observations and to draw conclusions that were too broad. It had been observed in the study of obese children that marked discrepancies between the verbal and performance scales suggested, as in nonobese individuals, underlying emotional and personality problems. This also holds true in adolescent obesity.

The Rorschach test showed great similarities also. It revealed for Kitty and Tanya superior intelligence with creative imagination and great potentialities, good intuition and sharp powers of observation, but with a tendency not to develop many ideas. Kitty appeared indecisive, fretting away her energies in aimless and often quite pointless irrelevancies. Tanya showed a tendency to live in her own vivid and absorbing fantasy world, without her sense of reality being disturbed. She appeared to be quite lonely, egocentric, preoccupied with herself and her problems, and not much aware of other people, though there were indications of extreme self-consciousness and the conviction of being regarded by others with disapproval. For all 3 the tests before treatment showed indications of severe anxiety and hostility, diffuse and all-embracing, but with no awareness of what they were anxious about. As treatment progressed, both the anxiety and hostility became more overt and focused. I quote from the report on Kitty, after 6 months:

Feeling hemmed in and tied down by her family's demands she appeared too insecure to assert herself directly but seemed to be engaged in a campaign of passive resistance. Feeling devitalized and drained she rejects everything, refusing to accept anything good that might come her way along with the bad, with a tendency of sabotaging her own potentialities. In the first record her hostility was directed to the whole world, 6 months later more towards her family, her father and men in general. She appears sure that people are looking down on her and she tries to protect herself against rejection by not getting involved. She appears decidedly uncertain and uneasy in her female role, and fear of men and sexuality color even her most casual heterosexual relations.

Initially Debby experienced conflicts not within herself but only between herself and the environment, and she projected blame onto others. She avoided sexually stimulating configurations of the Rorschach blots, indicating a marked sexual immaturity, and her capacity for fantasy dried up in the presence of sexually stimulating material. There appeared to be a good deal of anxiety but for the most part it was below the level of awareness. Love and aggression appeared closely intermingled, with ambivalence in all her interpersonal relationships. She was very demanding of others but too childlike to feel that any particular demands should be made on her. The psychologist considered the prognosis for psychotherapy rather guarded since her capacity for introspection and critical self-appraisal appeared quite limited. She was rated as too egocentric to be capable of any real rapport and without any real desire for growth and development.

Tanya's conception of her own identity was especially fluid; she saw herself as a "wanderer" or "artistic soul," but this image appeared to be part of a conscious attempt to rationalize her withdrawal tendency. She appeared to express a strong underlying tendency to reject the feminine role altogether, which seemed to tie in with her refusal to be what she was expected to be. She seemed to feel hopeless about ever having good relations with others, and the people of her imagination were more vivid than real people. She appeared confused in her self-feeling, not knowing who she was, or even what kind of a person she wanted to be. Although puzzled and disturbed by these contradictions, she appeared quite articulate and vocal about them.

After two years of treatment Kitty appeared considerably freer and more spontaneous. She appeared responsive to stimuli from the environment, less indecisive and now felt some trust in her good intuition; she felt less hemmed in and restrained. She seemed less hostile and revengeful toward her parents and showed some outgoing interest in the world, with less evidence of passive resistance. Since the others appeared less powerful and dangerous she seemed now more capable of living her own life. Her hostility had lessened with each test; she went from feeling menaced and threatened from every side to feeling this less generalized after 6 months, and was now less hostile but more forthright and healthily assertive. Frustration tolerance was still low and she tended to structure her environment so that she would not have to suffer. She appeared now more consciously aware of her sexual disturbance, still had difficulty in accepting the feminine role, and would prefer to think of herself as sexless. She appeared more spontaneous in all her relations, less withdrawn, and no longer in need of hiding herself from people.

On retesting after 2 years and with good clinical improvement, Debby's picture showed decided changes, with many of her problems having come into her awareness. She appeared now to be actively fighting against the lower status she envisioned femininity to have. Both the figure drawings and the Rorschach tests continued to show a severe degree of sexual ambivalence, amounting to actual confusion. Several responses indicated that she still felt helpless, trapped, held down by others, at the mercy of her parents, and that she was nothing but a bone of contention between them.

The tests revealed her as more aggressive, not so terrified at showing her feelings, but also as quite depressed. Whereas previously she lived almost entirely in fantasy with occasional outbursts of impulsivity, she was now not constantly acting something out. She no longer projected her deeply ambivalent feelings unto others, but was able to accept them as her own. Life to her was still extremely difficult, everything appearing like a gigantic task. But despite her insecurities there appeared to have been a rise in her self-esteem. In many ways the Rorschach at this time was more autistic, more bizarre, more deeply schizoid than earlier. However, the figure drawings, while still empty and inhuman, showed more maturity, at least some feeble attempt to differentiate between the sexes. She seemed to have gained considerable insight and was now striving toward further understanding. The summary of the previous report, "No real desire for growth and development" was no longer operative.

These excerpts from the psychological reports indicate the seriousness of the underlying personality disturbances, and also that real changes in self-concept and personal security take place during psychotherapy.

Daydreams Unlimited

His size is the visible expression of an obese youngster's attempt to escape from or compensate for the profound lack of self-confidence, the deep inner doubts, his fears of life and of rejection. It is the result of seeking comfort in food and avoiding all activities and social contacts. The size has a function of its own; in spite of all the bitter complaints and expressions of self-disgust and contempt, the large body conveys a feeling of strength and power. Behind their dull and complacent facade many young adolescents engage in daydreams of unlimited potential achievement. Usually the fulfillment depends on or will lead to their becoming thin. Like Falstaff, they are convinced, "If I do great, I grow less."

The discovery of this glorious fantasy life behind all the self-belittling and depressive ruminations was unexpected. It was even present in Debby with her enormous inner restrictions, though she was terribly reluctant to speak of her dreams. At a time when she was making just passing grades in junior college (she eventually dropped out) she wanted to become a physician. This was not the common transference phenomenon, but a dream of long standing—her way of outdoing and taking revenge on all the doctors she felt had tortured her.

Kitty had always been an excellent student, but several peculiarities became apparent during her early school years. When she did well in a subject and this was openly recognized, she would drop out of it for fear of not maintaining the same high standard. Once she refused to go back to a summer camp where she had won several prizes because she was sure she could not surpass this record the next year. Her great interest and talent was for acting, and she dreamed of a theatrical career, but felt discouraged that she might not accomplish this. Whenever she applied for a role she was told that she should lose weight first. She would make a strenuous effort and lose large amounts in a short time. Invariably she would gain it all back. Though slim she was offered only small roles, since she was still a beginner and was treated as such. She would be so outraged with these modest, realistic opportunities that she lost interest in acting— and in dieting. Angrily she protested, "I want real acting in a big hit on Broadway. Why should I try and try when nobody will promise that if I stay slim I'll be a star?"

Tanya hinted frequently at being engaged in rewarding and satisfying daydreams, without divulging their content. She might say, "There are so many of us," or, "Oh, we know how to amuse ourselves." During the second year of treatment she began to reveal some of her underlying preoccupations. She had been to see the play, *The Cocktail Party*, by Eliot, and was enraged that the psychiatrist in the play told people what to do, that he made "choices" for them. In her own life there had been a continuous conflict between "choice" and "duty." *Duty* was defined as something *one has to do* because it involves other people. *Choice* was what *one does for one's own sake alone*. Her continuous complaints about being "forced" to do things were revolts against this excessive sense of "duty," of feeling obligated to do things. (The differentiation between "choice" and "duty" seems to correspond to what I have called the difference between "self-initiated" and "superimposed" experiences.)

Returning from the theater she saw a beggar in the street and felt guilty because she walked by. Then it occurred to her that she would have felt just as guilty had she given him some money because, in a way, nothing would have been changed. She realized that this continued sense of guilt, this overwhelming feeling of what she ought to do, was an expression of the image she had of herself, namely, that she had gigantic power. It was her duty, more than anybody else's, to correct the ills of the world because she had this gigantic power. Her passivity led to a continuous sense of frustration, of not fulfilling her fate. She related this sense of her enormous responsibility to her childhood experiences.

Many obese children grow up with the feeling that they are expected to compensate their parents for their own frustrations and unfulfilled ambitions, and this results in a fantastic misinterpretation of their importance in the world. They live their lives in constant expectation of some very special achievement without which they feel they will be rated as failures. Though their restricted functioning in everyday situations will not reveal this, their evaluation of reality is gravely disturbed. Nothing they ever achieve comes up to the exaggerated expectation of what they feel they should do, or are expected to do. Not infrequently, fat adolescents with good intellectual gifts or artistic talents fail to fulfill the promise of their early achievements. They will give up in sullen despair when they are not recognized as "special," as first and best in everything, or when success does not come without effort. This type of self-sabotage, which turns every success into failure, may be part of other neuroses; it seems to occur with particular intensity in obese adolescents. The simple fact that success implies effort and work, something ordinary human beings have to expend, runs contrary to their concept of "specialness."

I should like to give an additional example of undisguised, unrealistic ambitions. Clark had been sickly as a child but had become quite stout after puberty. When he was 16½ years old he threatened to drop out of school. He had complained about being "bored" for the past year and about difficulties in concentration. His verbal I.Q. was 125, gifted enough to master the required work easily. His performance I.Q. was only 96. The projective tests revealed him as egocentric, impulsive, and demanding, with a labile and unstable personality structure, and a high degree of fear and anxiety.

On first contact he gave a number of rather stereotyped explanations for his dislike of school. Gradually, with much reluctance, he began to confess his nonrealistic aspirations. He was aware that what he wanted to do was impossible, but he lived in constant fear of failure, not being as good as he should be, that is, the best and smartest student in every subject. "What's the use of going to school and studying if you cannot be the best in everything?" This dream of being the best interfered with his doing any work at all. Whenever he sat down to do his homework, the questions flashed through his mind, "Even if I try hard, who guarantees that somebody else will not do better?" This idea paralyzed him and then he would eat whatever he could find. He wished that he were 6 years old again, starting first grade; he could then make only A's, and be the best student all through school; then he wouldn't need to worry.

Once the ice was broken, he gave a most amazing account of what he would have to do in order to find life worth living, and spoke by the hour about his dreams and fantasies. He had great ambitions; he wanted to do something so great, so helpful for mankind that his name would be remembered for 500 years. He knew about many great people of the past, but Galileo was his hero. Unless he could be sure that his name would be remembered for something spectacular, he felt, "What is the use of living? If you are not doing something great, if your name is not remembered, then I don't see why we should live at all. One day you will die, you will be buried—it would be much better not to have lived at all." To be known, to have a famous name, and to be remembered, that was what counted. If possible, he wanted to do something great. But he would not hesitate to commit a crime in order to get his name in the papers.

His second line of daydreams dealt with the perfect crime, how to outwit everybody, how to get away with it. If he could not be remembered for having done something great, then he wouldn't mind being remembered as the most vicious or the most conceited person, just as long as he were to become known. He knew that there were famous people who were also conceited, and he mentioned the composer Wagner. "I would be glad to be remembered if it were only for being conceited." At this point, I agreed that it was correct that Wagner had that reputation, "But that is not why he is remembered. In addition he was a superb musician; he is remembered for the music he created. He delivered the goods."

This comment touched him, because that was exactly the trouble; he was afraid that he could *not* deliver the goods, there was nothing which he felt sure that he could do really well. He needed to protect himself against this fear of not being good enough in anything, and tried to build himself up with all these glorious daydreams. Nothing but the extraordinary and spectacular could protect him against this basic fear of being nothing, or not feeling really alive, and not being acclaimed by others.

Mention was made of the fact that his great size fulfilled his desire to be outstanding and conspicuous. He hesitated—but then he admitted that he knew that his fatness was something special; it did set him apart. Although he said he hated it, there was a certain gratification in having his family continuously talk and worry about his enormous size. He knew he was ugly and awkward; yet he felt some gratification in being so large that he was outside the ordinary.

This pride in their size is expressed by many fat people, all the embarrassment and humiliation notwithstanding. Another boy, talking about his fantastic plans, added, "I am just not *big enough* for what I am cut out to do." Then, elaborating on the word big, he added, "I mean in my mind; just look at me—I certainly *look big* enough."

Course of Treatment and Outcome

During the early part of treatment Debby was so frightened, passive, and helpless that it was felt that the weight should be left strictly alone, though her awkward appearance was a decided handicap. An effort was made to work with the parents, to convince them that Debby needed to develop some inner independence. They had rated everything in her life according to whether it would make her fat or help her to lose weight. All kinds of activities were forced upon Debby in order to make her slimmer; that they might be fun never entered her mind and was considered frivolous by her parents. She expressed a desire for one thing only, namely, to learn how to cook. Both parents violently objected to this, because then she would spend time in the kitchen and she couldn't be trusted there. When she was finally permitted to go to a cooking school, it was like a revelation. Food became something objective, something that she could manipulate and submit to all kinds of processes and preparations, instead of being something to be devoured, or to be fought over when it was denied. With this more objective attitude toward food and eating she herself asked to be put on a diet, now that she felt she could control it. After much initial complaining, she settled down to the diet and lost over 50 lbs (from about 180 to about 125 lbs) during the next 6 months. The results were dramatic, not only because her appearance changed, but because she felt for the first time some independence from the bite-by-bite and step-by-step supervision, and also began to acknowledge her own role in creating many of her difficulties. She began to realize that she did not need to remain a helpless slave who either automatically obeyed, or indiscriminately resisted. She indulged less in daydreams of great achievements and became more realistic about plans for the future. But she was aware that her problems were not solved; whenever she became upset she still got the urge to eat.

As soon as she looked presentable her parents set out on a campaign to marry her off, pressed her to have dates and told her openly that they had taken care of her long enough, that it was time for her to find a husband. Efforts to discuss the dangers of this with her parents were met with complete lack of understanding. Treatment was terminated and the parents took Debby to another therapist who was supposed to encourage her to get married soon, and she did marry when she was 22 years old.

Many years later, when about 40 years old, she expressed regret for having interrupted treatment prematurely, saying that it had been a mistake to change analysts at that critical period. "It took me many years to come to this decision that you were acting correctly by protecting me— imagine someone with no sense of responsibility getting married, and no sense of what life is all about, including sex." However, the couple stayed together and both had been in therapy to achieve greater maturity. They had one child, now 8 years old, a bright and active boy, and Debby made sure he would not be fat by not overfeeding him or using food for reward. However, she herself had not been able to keep her weight under control, and continued to fluctuate. She went to Weight Watchers and lost 50 lbs, but then felt the supervision was childish and regained the lost weight when she discontinued.

Kitty's treatment was dominated by her declaration that nothing mattered but her weight and her complete inability to control it, and by her resistance for a long time against dealing with any psychological problems. She continued to gain and reached her highest weight, 225 lbs, when 17 years old. She refused to continue school and insisted on going to a commercial reducing establishment with rigid supervision. After she lost some weight she returned to her school and graduated with her class when 18½ years old. When she entered a local college, still living at home, her weight had dropped to 180 lbs. She did well during the first year of college and it appeared that she was ready to go to an out-of-town college.

While away at college she contacted a reducing doctor who gave her a prescription for amphetamines and she developed a severe amphetamine addiction while losing to the desired level of 130 lbs. She remained intensely preoccupied with every bite she ate and could not break away from the medication though she felt panicky about being controlled by a drug. She was convinced that her mind was not her own and became more and more erratic and increasingly disorganized in her work habits, losing the power of concentration. (Kitty is not the only patient in whom I observed the development of amphetamine addiction with a medical prescription, whose physician refused to discontinue it.) Finally, it became necessary for her to enter a private psychiatric hospital where the amphetamine habit was broken and where she continued her psychotherapy. She began to have meaningful relationships with men and married at age 29.

When last heard of she was 40 years old and had three children whom she described as "very attractive." She had maintained her own weight at about 140 lbs, never varying from a 5-lb span but not having made an attempt to lose more weight. She had maintained this stable weight by "keeping a careful eye on the scale." Her attitude toward her weight did not sound different from that of the average weight-conscious woman of her age who takes it for granted that one has to pay attention to the scale. Though not as self-confident and emotionally secure as she would like to be, she had handled the reality tasks of childbirth, raising children, maintaining a good marital relationship, and repeated moves to larger homes without undue tension or psychological symptoms, nor was there weight increase.

Treatment of Tanya was characterized by extreme negativism, suspicion, and aloofness. She would say that she liked or hated a person because the person represented somebody or some idea, not because she reacted to the real person—an isolation that made a therapeutic relationship exceedingly elusive. She strictly avoided accepting hostile or other feelings or behavior as "real": they were either fantasies or were directed at ideas and symbols and not at people. Progress in her concept of self-awareness and the reality of her experiences was extremely slow. The subject of her weight or dieting was strictly avoided since she did not acknowledge them as *her* problems. Though she had gained continuously during the preceding years there seemed to be no further increase in weight.

Her recognition of her drive for the extraordinary, which was discussed earlier in this chapter, was followed by a sense of great relief. She no longer felt that she was confronted with gigantic tasks which always remained undone, giving her a sense of being "too little." She could see a relationship between this deep sense of inadequacy and frustration, her uncontrolled eating, and her need to be so large. Following this she went on an unsupervised starvation diet during which her behavior became disorganized; this episode will be described in the following chapter. A year later, before a vacation trip which to her was a declaration of independence, she dieted under medical supervision and lost to about 160 lbs, a weight appropriate for her height and build. She was aware that she had a large frame and could not become small and ethereal looking.

During the second year of treatment she enrolled in college and again mastered the academic subjects with great success, though complaining that everything was forced upon her. She graduated at age 21 and worked in the literary field. She had become freer socially and was outgoing in meeting men; she got married at age 25. Fifteen years later she described her marriage as "not a bed of roses," but probably as good and stable as that of her friends from college days. Her three children were 9, 11, and 13 years old, tall and with no tendency to become fat. In her early thirties she felt the need for more challenging intellectual work, entered a professional school, and again did outstanding work. She has since held a responsible position where she does highly individual work reflecting her basic interests. During these years of decision-making she felt the need for additional psychotherapy. Her weight has stayed well-controlled and at age 40 she offered a striking, distinguished-looking appearance. She still felt occasionally, in "times of regression" (her term), an urge to eat sweets. She felt some sort of expert on being fat and was appalled by the amount of "garbage" that was written on the subject.

I have presented these three cases in some detail to convey the flavor of the complexities and problems of adolescent obesity. The current tendency is to explain all psychological difficulties as due to the sociocultural rejection. Neither in these cases, nor in any of the many others I have known, was this the dominant problem. The developmental deficits, the conviction of inner inadequacy, were the underlying factors which rendered these patients excessively vulnerable to real or dreaded rejection. As in these three girls, there are marked differences in the factors contributing to the serious disturbance in personality development. No general description can be given about the background features, except that they all used overeating and withdrawal from life in the face of overwhelming difficulties. The unfriendly social climate is only one of these difficulties, which a plump adolescent with a fairly healthy mental attitude can face with equanimity, and without becoming progressively fatter.

More damaging are the individual attacks under which such youngsters suffer. Often it is the parents who are vehement in demanding that an adolescent, in particular a daughter, should be slim, and they will conduct harsh campaigns against even mild degrees of plumpness. Invariably this is a sign of disturbed relationships within the family, and youngsters having grown up under the influence of such pervasive discontent are ill-prepared to meet the new demands of adolescence. Inability to control their weight is only one aspect of the underlying immaturity and incompetence.

Not uncommonly had physicians contributed to these difficulties. I mentioned before that frequently serious amphetamine addiction had developed from thoughtless prescriptions. I observed repeatedly that when one physician had outlined a reasonable treatment program, including correction of the severe emotional disturbances of the whole family, there was always another ready to promise a "get thin quickly" cure through a "special" diet, glandular injections, or reducing pills. The prevailing medical approach fails to take sufficient notice of the extraordinarily close interaction between physiological and psychological factors in obesity. This works a particular hardship for adolescents who want to do something about their condition but who become perplexed by contradictory advice, in particular by advice that contributes to the unbearable tension from which they suffer instead of helping them to achieve a more meaningful way of life.

BIBLIOGRAPHY

1. Lidz, T., Adolescence, Chapter 10, pp. 298–361, in *The Person*, Basic Books, Inc., New York, 1968.

10

Obesity and Schizophrenia

Athough the importance of psychological problems in the development of juvenile obesity has been stressed throughout my work, the discovery of a not infrequent and rather close association between obesity and schizophrenia was unexpected. It seemed at first to stand in contrast to the widely held view that schizophrenics are of slight, even puny, body build. Statistically, more schizophrenics are asthenic, thin, and tall, but that does not exclude the fact that obese individuals, too, may become schizophrenic. It is a further illustration of the need for an individualistic approach to complex clinical conditions.

There are great similarities in the professional approach to obesity and to schizophrenia. During the past century there has been a nearly continuous search for some causative organic factor for both conditions, and the concepts of heredity and constitution are often invoked as carriers of these organic abnormalities. In spite of the marked progress in genetics, which has brought clearer definition of the objectives of genetic investigations (namely to uncover disturbances in the informational code of the DNA molecule, or to correlate microcellular changes with certain constellations of clinical symptoms), the primary physiodynamic substrate of schizophrenia and obesity has yet to be specified (4). It probably never will be, because the diagnostic labels schizophrenia and obesity refer to a variety of conditions. Conclusions are based on statistical procedures that show that a person's risk of developing the condition is increased in the presence of the disorder in a parent or sibling. Among the case studies which will be presented in this chapter, obesity and schizophrenia, as well as other *overt* mental disease, are conspicuously rare in the antecedents of the patients.

Modern geneticists recognize that in such complex conditions as schizophrenia and obesity, genes determine only a norm of reaction. The actual expression of this depends on many prenatal, paranatal, and postnatal interactions. Subtle shifts in these etiological factors at various stages are conceived of as leading to divergent phenotypes, even in monozygotic twins. There is little doubt that in many instances genetic factors are involved; whether or not they lead to manifest illness, and what particular form this takes, seems to depend on the style and patterns of life experiences. Since these are the aspects that are clinically observable and, hopefully, amenable to change, the emphasis on experiential data appears at this time more revealing and rewarding and will be the focus of this chapter.

The trend in the medical and psychiatric literature, on the whole, has been in the opposite direction. It has disregarded or considered inconsequential the disturbances in personality integration, psychosocial competence, and symbolic functioning, however well they are documented, and focused on the organic pathogenic factors which, if recognized and corrected, would restore the patient to "normal." Isolated discoveries about abnormal functioning have been made, but most were soon recognized to be the consequence of the abnormal way of life associated with schizophrenia or obesity. In obesity in particular the tendency is to relegate disturbances in the psychosocial field to a secondary position, to consider them the consequence of being fat, denying the disturbing development influences that result in obesity and, under particularly unfavorable conditions, also in manifest schizophrenia.

Experiential Factors

Family studies have shown great similarities in the backgrounds and patterns of family interaction of patients who become obese, as well as schizophrenic. This was discussed in detail in Chapters 4 and 5. As basic questions were delineated, it could be recognized that the abnormal personality functioning was not the outcome of one traumatic event, as had been implied in older psychoanalytic theories, but had resulted from the fact that these patients as children had been deprived of experiences necessary for the development of appropriate guideposts for competent functioning, such as orienting themselves to their needs and feelings, and exhibiting behavior that would permit constructive integration. Inadequacies in positive parental reinforcement have been recognized as a common feature for schizophrenics and disturbed obese individuals (including many who do not become openly schizophrenic) and as leading to ego deficiencies. As a result patients have poorly organized inner tools and guides for self-directed action and self-regulation. This in turn results in a defect in self-identity, a diffusion of the boundaries of self and non-self, and a feeling of being influenced and directed from the outside. Specific for the development of obesity is the distortion of the eating function (Chapter 4). A fat person indiscriminately "feels hungry" whenever there is a disturbance in his interpersonal or intrapsychic equilibrium. Like the schizophrenic, the obese person has great difficulty in differentiating stimuli from within or without himself, and in distinguishing reality from fantasy, and in differentiating his own thoughts from those of others. In short, he is unsure where he leaves off and the other person or outer reality begins. Such absence of a firm sense of self-identity or ego boundary is also a basic disturbance in schizophrenia. It can be observed, in varying manifestations and with varying degrees of intensity, in individuals in whom disturbances in hunger awareness and self-initiated action have been a core problem throughout life, mainly those suffering from developmental obesity.

Obese youngsters and schizophrenics-to-be show many similarities in behavior and reaction throughout childhood and adolescence. Defects in adaptation can be recognized on many levels and are often expressed in overall immaturity. Difficulties in social relations are described by words like "withdrawn" or "seclusive." In obese youngsters these defects are usually "explained" as due to their being fat, and they are pressured into reducing in the hope of improving their social lives. This approach is not only futile, it may lead to a derogatory attitude toward their own bodies, which becomes the starting point of new problems. Frank psychosis may be precipitated through such discrepancies and inner conflicts.

Like the schizophrenic, the obese person has an exceedingly low frustration tolerance and will react with sullen withdrawal and undermining hostility to unexpected demands, and, unable to derive satisfaction or enjoyment from available opportunities, he will react with excessive suffering in the face of difficulties. Associated with this is a sense of helplessness, a conviction of inadequacy and inner ugliness. These derogatory and self-destructive attitudes are compensated for by flight into fantasies and daydreams. These daydreams of the obese, even of those who offer the facade of adequate functioning, are of an astounding grandiosity. They may deal with the transformation of their physical selves into glamorous-looking people, often with change of sex, with unlimited power over and admiration from everybody. Theirs is an all or nothing attitude toward life; when confronted with the fact that the unlimited knowledge or power is not obtainable or that there is no way of achieving their unrealistic goals, they are apt to give up in sullen despair. Most will resort to more avid overeating and grow still fatter, but some will suffer a schizophrenic break. A few may believe the cultural promise that slenderness will solve their difficulties in an exaggerated way, and pursue thinness relentlessly, causing a delusional disturbance in their body image and developing anorexia nervosa.

For many fat young people with dull, complacent surface behavior, the fulfillment of their daydreams of unlimited potential and unheard of achievements depends on their becoming thin. Their inability to follow a diet acts as a safeguard against putting these fantasies to the test of reality. Often they are convinced that no diet will work, and they will not even attempt to reduce. They dread the possibility of failure, and this possibility is great in view of the grandiosity of their expectations. They may become emotionally disturbed when pressured to go on a diet which is effective: now they must prove their specialness. There is no longer the face-saving device of blaming their difficulties on the ugly weight, and there is no longer the hope of being able to correct things by reducing. As long as they are fat, they feel they have it in their power, now or in the future, to set everything right by losing weight. By becoming thin, having made this choice, they face the bare facts of serious mental problems. The psychological problems come into full awareness after effective reducing. Until then, the large physical size had given at least a symbolic feeling of strength and permitted glorious daydreams. Now the sense of potential power and potential achievement is threatened.

When under too much pressure, whether from the outside or from their own efforts at emancipation, or with increasing awareness of and response to maturational demands, they appear to be no longer aware of the unrealistic quality of their magnificent daydreams and aspirations, and act and talk as if the dreams were realistic. It is sometimes impossible, even in cases that are studied in detail, to determine why in one situation the fantasies remain fantasies, clearly recognized as such and guarded as precious secrets, and why in other cases the border between daydreams and reality becomes vague and disappears. In talking about schizophrenia becoming manifest in some obese individuals, I have made this the dividing line: the ability to differentiate between reality and fantasy. The patients who become frankly psychotic begin to believe in or act on the false reality of their imaginary creations. Threatened in their deepest sense of personal and bodily identity, they relinquish their efforts to deal in realistic terms with a world in which they feel strange, unfamiliar, threatened, and helpless.

Developmental Obesity

Schizophrenic development may occur without a recognizable or definable outer stress other than the increasing demands of maturation itself. An example was offered in Chapter 8 in the history of a boy of lower-class background with serious psychological and social disorganization. There were several others who increasingly fell behind in their activities and achievement and who as adults led the indolent life of ambulatory schizophrenics.

Even in cultured and privileged homes, obesity in a child may foreshadow schizophrenic development that may become manifest during adolescence with or without recognizable precipitating events. This may occur when the inner struggles are more severe than usual, the interpersonal stresses more frustrating, or when the overweight is being fought with more harshness, arousing guilt, counter-aggression, and the collapse of all defenses.

Demands for superiority and perfection led to a schizophrenic disorganization in Flora when she was 16 years old. She came from a socially prominent and cultured home, and her mother had fought against Flora's being fat throughout her life. Now Flora defied her mother and ate whatever she could put her hands on; her weight had risen to more than 200 lbs. She became extremely careless in her appearance and began eating inedible material. She no longer attended school or maintained even the slightest social contact, but spent hours in what she called "trances," during which she was unable to differentiate between her fantasies and the realities of life. She dreamed of the prince who would come and release her from her ugliness; or of spending her time on a beautiful mountainside covered with bushes which produced the most delicious food, of which she could eat as much as she wanted without becoming fat, and without having the compulsive hateful feeling that she had when she ate sweets and other foods forbidden to her. Gradually, she imagined a whole secret world of her own, with language, laws, religion, and mores of her own creation.

As far back as she could remember, her mother had been "phobic" about her size and had tried to supervise every bite she ate. She had some vague memories that when she was little she was permitted to eat such "forbidden" things as chocolate pudding or cake. But she was sure that since age 6 or 7 these things had *never* been allowed, and throughout her life she had dreamed of feasting on them. When all food was locked away, with a lock even on the refrigerator, she began to eat staples—unprepared jello or uncooked cereals or spaghetti. She also would chew pieces of string and eat concert tickets and programs. Her behavior became so disturbed that hospitalization became necessary.

She was sufficiently in contact to give a picture of her family life. She felt that her mother's slimness and smartness were the result of eternal self-denial, and that her mother's fight against her weight was an effort to exercise complete control over her. Although the family had given her a great deal of cultural stimulation, Flora felt that they had not been really interested in her, only in her appearance and brilliance. The father had only two absorbing interests; his business, in which he was very successful, and a complete devotion to her mother. His concern about Flora's queer behavior was only an expression of his devotion to the mother who worried about it and, of course, anger that *his* daughter, one of his possessions, was not as perfect as he wanted her to be.

The relationship to the mother had been very close, but entirely in terms of the mother's wishes and needs. They had a great common interest, music. Flora had received a good musical education, but there was an exhausting struggle to make her conform to traditional standards. Her ambition was to compose unconventional works, so that she could express her own individuality. She wanted and needed accomplishment of her own, and despite the self-belittling terms in which she talked about herself, she was also convinced of her essential greatness, the ability to achieve something quite extraordinary that would be recognized by everybody. She felt her life would be wasted unless she accomplished something on the genius level.

At this stage in her development, she no longer cared about being fat. To be sure, she still dreamt of having the fatness taken away by the magic prince, but actually it would not help. It would not change the fact that she was inwardly mean and filthy. When she dropped some ashes on her dress during the interview, she became panicky: "That's me! I'm always filthy and I fill the chair and I flow over it. It's just my meanness coming out."

It seemed that when she could no longer hide behind her fatness as a cause of dissatisfaction and failure and became convinced that even reducing could not change her problem, reality checks broke down. The deep problems of the schizophrenic became manifest: the desperate search for her own identity, physical and psychological, for effective means of orienting herself about her own behavior and interaction with other people, and of facing the world with an adequate sense of mastery and self-respect.

Flora made an excellent recovery, not only by achieving control over her eating and other functions; she has made remarkable artistic contributions which have found wide recognition. At age 40 she is a beautiful woman who feels inwardly secure and satisfied, sharing her life and experiences with her husband and children.

Situational Stress As Precipitating Factor

Such a gradual transition to psychotic functioning is less common than precipitation through some stressful new life situation with unbearable tension and frustration. Quite often the onset of the psychosis is associated with uncontrolled eating and a rapid gain in weight.

Nellie, a student nurse, was referred to the psychiatric service after having spent some time in the infirmary. She had done quite well during her first year in nursing school but became apprehensive and fearful as the responsibilities increased. She had overwhelming urges to eat any food available, stuffing herself until she could eat no more. She could not explain these urges and was filled with shame and extreme guilt when she acted on them. She ate secretly and was fearful that someone would see her. If she resisted the urge to eat she became very apprehensive and tense, and could not remove the fixed idea of food from her mind. On evening duty she felt that she was not able to do her work properly; the responsibility made her apprehensive. She also felt uncomfortable and fearful about being alone on the ward and she suffered more and more from her obsessive thoughts about food. She ate constantly, interrupting her duties at frequent intervals to find food. Until now, in spite of occasional eating sprees, her weight had not varied to any great degree; now she gained rapidly, up to 180 lbs, and she became visibly depressed. She was admitted to the infirmary where her increasing indolence and depression became apparent. She began to speak of "a large, black, ugly mass in my chest" and said that *she had to eat* in order to prevent this bad thing from escaping. Because of the bizarre quality of her preoccupation and her increasing depression she was admitted to the psychiatric service. She remained preoccupied with this concept of the "black mass" or "black demon" which stood for all her frightening, hostile, and negative feelings. At times the black mass would grow to include the inside of her whole body. She felt that her good self was but a thin rim around this black, awful, ugly, and evil thing, and she feared that it would be discovered or escape when she was in contact with people.

Nellie was the older of two girls in a professional family. When she was 3 years old several events occurred that upset the family equilibrium. Her maternal grandfather died and the family moved into the home of the grandmother, who was a domineering woman; in addition, a sister was born. Nellie suffered from the conviction that her parents did not love her and she lived in constant fear of being abandoned. When she was 10 years old, Nellie was sent to a summer camp, but she was so obviously unhappy, crying continuously, that the mother felt obliged to retrieve her the next day. Nellie was aware that she did not love her parents either, that she actually hated them, but she had always felt obliged to keep these feelings under control.

As a child she had been quite obese, for which she was continuously criticized by her parents and grandmother. All the reproaches for her sloppiness and fatness fell on deaf ears until Nellie herself suddenly decided she wanted to be popular. She went on a diet and lost weight and was quite flirtatious during her high school years, had many dates though she never cared for any of the boys. She related the onset of her eating compulsion to her tenseness about sex. By watching her diet between eating sprees, she maintained her weight at a slender level. After graduation from high school she went on a trip to Europe, where she met a young man to whom she became engaged. He was in college on the West Coast and her contact with him was mainly by correspondence. As the wedding day approached, her apprehension and anxiety and the eating urges became uncontrollable. Her concept of sex was that it was bad and dirty; she felt that both her mother and grandmother had forced these ideas on her.

During treatment other disturbed concepts of her body came into the open. As "the hate was coming out," the big black mass was gradually replaced by a feeling of "emptiness." Whereas she had formerly eaten to control the black mass she now felt the need to fill in this "hole inside her," in particular when she had had a disagreement with others and she felt their bad thoughts and hate were rattling around in her. Feeling empty inside made her feel all alone and vulnerable, and bad feelings would hurt her. "If I am full—the food acts like a buffer" and she felt she could tolerate people better. This fear of not being liked and the feeling that other people were against her or would attack her, or that she might hurt them in return, had dominated her whole childhood.

Nellie stayed at the hospital for a year and a half. As she began to recognize the tensions and anxieties that had provoked the eating sprees, she gradually became able to handle situations more directly. Specifically she "learned" that sex was not "bad." She had rather primitive ideas of oral impregnation, that the mother swallowed something to produce a child who was born into the mother's stomach. Her weight fluctuated considerably during her hospitalization, between 130 lbs and 170 lbs. As her symptoms improved while she was still hospitalized, Nellie began working at a job where she did quite well. When her fiancé came East she spent weekends with him and gradually relaxed and became capable of greater intimacy; they married a few months later. Her relationship to her parents had improved considerably and she was now able to communicate with them. Her mother reported 5 years later that Nellie's marriage was going well, that she had a child and functioned well in her role as mother. She was slightly plump but no longer suffered from compulsive eating.

Another example of situational stress precipitating psychosis is Cecil, who had been obese most of his life, and who suffered an acute psychotic episode when he was 16 years old, shortly after entering a boarding school of his own choosing. At home there had been continuous conflicts about his insolent behavior and his greedy and unmannered eating. He himself felt he might do better at a boarding school than at home and also hoped that he might make new friends at a new school where no one remembered him as fat and awkward. Throughout his school years he had been quite lonely and friendless, though he was superficially friendly and outgoing.

Cecil was also attracted to the prospect of becoming a member of the football team. Though still obese, he had lost some weight during the previous summer and had developed better muscles. He was confident that his large size, which, until then, had been the source of his suffering, would now be an asset. The first day of practice was a terrible disappointment. The workout was hard and demanding, and there was no glory in it at all. He became very much afraid that he would be unable to stay on the team. He stumbled on the staircase and strained his ankle, and thus was dropped from the team. This was a great relief to him, but it also meant the end of his dreams of glory and special recognition.

The many rules and regulations at the school were disturbing to him. He had built up a case against his father for insisting on punctuality, cleanliness, and courtesy, and now he discovered, to his amazement, that the rules at home had been quite lax in comparison with the discipline at this liberal school. He came to see that what his father had demanded was no more than conformity to the ordinary rules of living. This insight, however, did not give him any relief, for it left him without justification for his hostile feelings and hatred. He was so preoccupied with this that he could not concentrate on his studies, and he became increasingly worried about failing. Then he began to worry about his mental state and became really panicky.

While he made some efforts to make friends and participate in certain group activities, he could not make real contact. There were a few boys who irritated him, and he tried to stay away from them. He withdrew more and more into a fantasy in which he was the leader of a group of boys who, as a kind of "people's court," controlled the student body. He was the "chief executioner" and dealt out the punishment. He loved the position of power, but he was afraid that he might abuse his power and that the others might take revenge. He thought continuously of new forms of punishment for boys who violated the commands of the people's court. It frightened him that he would like to kill someone and get away with it; but it also delighted him that he had this feeling of power over life and death. When recounting this, he felt unable to differentiate between fact and fantasy and would insist that he really had been the "head man"—the most respected boy in school. Actually he spent most of the time in the infirmary with vague complaints, chiefly headaches and abdominal pain. He became furious when it was suggested that his stomach pains might be related to his devouring enormous amounts of food, as a result of which his weight had risen to more than 280 lbs. He became more and more involved in his aggressive notions and one evening staggered to the house of the headmaster, asking permission to go home because he was in danger. He told a gruesome tale about a bloody fight between two other boys in which he had interfered to prevent them from killing each other. He was afraid that they would turn against him, and he no longer felt safe. The delusional nature of this request was recognized, and he was sent home. In discussing these events, he changed his story repeatedly, and it was not possible to determine whether there was a kernel of real events that had unleashed the stream of terrifying delusions.

Before the boarding school episode, Cecil had been in treatment for severe phobias. He had always had a strained relationship with his father. "My fear and dislike of father developed into a hatred of manhood." He had always been closer to his mother. She was much younger than his father and he felt she understood him better. He needed to be sure that mother was on his side and that she loved him. There were many things which he had done to please her or to be like her. When he realized this, he stopped it because he was afraid that people might think he was effeminate. Since he wanted to grow up and be a man, not something in between, he knew he had to learn masculine skills, and he began to take some interest in sports. He was proud of his developing muscles and at times he even enjoyed these new activities.

There had been a gradual improvement with treatment and he spent a successful summer in camp, where he lost weight without too much effort. At the end of the summer he was 6′2″ tall and weighed 220 lbs. Thus he appeared to be in fairly good shape for entering boarding school, but there he suffered the psychotic breakdown several months later.

Cecil required several years of treatment in a psychotherapeutic hospital in a different city. He was eventually able to pursue a professional career, but he did not return to his home. When last heard of at age 30, he was doing well, a big, good-looking man, not conspicuously heavy.

The association between stress and compulsive eating was even more dramatic in the case of a 22-year-old divorcee, Camille, whose complete social withdrawal and severe depression led to hospitalization. She had had eating binges off and on since she was about 13 years old. She would steal money for food and gorge herself on sweet things like pastries and candy. This was always done in secret, behind closed doors in her own bedroom or in the bathroom. The episode preceding hospital admission was the worst she ever had and she said that she had gained 50 lbs in 7 weeks. As soon as a decision about hospitalization had been reached, the frantic eating stopped; as a matter of fact she practically ate nothing. She was only moderately overweight when admitted; her weight had fluctuated in the past between 120 and 170 lbs.

To her the fight with the weight had been a losing battle, "You can never get rid of all of it." She aspired to the popular standard of beauty, namely, "emaciation," and she wanted to be empty on the inside, "dirt free," and had fantasies of being transparent. She loved the state of starvation. Though continuously preoccupied with her weight, at no time did she approach the low level observed in anorexia nervosa.

She had always felt uncertain and confused in her sense of personal identity—"My real self is not there,"—and in her sexual urges. When fat, she experienced everything as the opposite from when thin, but her doubts about the "real me" persisted. In her thinking, fat people were "slobs" and thin people were "beautiful." She tried to make herself beautiful by starving and by using amphetamines in large amounts. When she was dissatisfied with herself she would overeat in a self-punishing way to make herself ugly. She was extremely confused in her body-image concepts, both as to her size and sexual identity.

According to the mother's information about Camille's early childhood everything had been "absolutely perfect." The mother spoke also of her strong mother-love. "I look upon her as the *product of myself*, I live and breathe just for her." When Camille was 7 her father became an alcoholic and disappeared; the mother went back to full-time work; the child stayed with her grandmother after school. Her parents were divorced when Camille was 10 years old and her mother remarried two years later. Camille reacted with marked behavior changes, the most noticeable of which were eating binges which led to overweight which, in turn, became the focus of continuous fighting. She felt exceedingly resentful against her mother, who, she felt dominated every step of her life.

Going to college was for her the beginning of her fight for independence. She came first under the influence of some avant-garde intellectuals, who, she felt, "shaped me intellectually." She had relationships with men who were homosexuals, feeling that she should save them from their perversion. When 19 she married a man 10 years her senior with whom she had satisfactory sex before marriage, but not afterward. There were increasing arguments and at one time she made a suicide attempt. She also had a precipitous loss of weight. The following year she got a divorce and went abroad to study foreign languages and the theater and became involved in several homosexual affairs. After her return to the United States she married again; this marriage too went on the rocks, and following this second marital breakdown she withdrew into her eating compulsion. She also pursued an acting career and played in an off-Broadway show. The closing of the play coincided with her marriage breaking up, and she felt she had lost control completely and went on the most severe eating binge of her life. She explained later, "Eating is a friend," and that it helped to allay her anxiety. She felt like a picture puzzle coming apart.

One of the difficulties of therapeutic work with her was her rigid identification of being slim with being well. Gradually the treatment goal was achieved of her accepting herself and her constitutional make-up, so that she was able to integrate her image of her "I," "not-I," and her bodily self.

In contrast, in Wilma's case, the weight gain and concern about her thinking developed gradually while she was away in college and marriage plans to a fellow student broke down. She felt she was walking around in a fog and had other peculiar feelings which she could not explain. She also became worried about what she vaguely described as "coincidences," where she felt that what she had thought about a certain person had come true, and she felt she might have been instrumental in bringing these situations about. She kept to herself and ate compulsively and ravenously, and her weight increased to over 200 lbs. She felt her social withdrawal and her weight increase were correlated.

She responded well to psychotherapy, and felt that being in the hospital had given her a better perspective of life. She described herself saying,

Sometimes I feel like I was a mixture of many shadows; sort of not one person, but a lot of people's thoughts of me, like self-reflections of these things. And about these reflections, well, they are the ideas that different members of my family have of me; each one sees me in a different light and actually then I appear that way. I sort of change sometimes.

She had always tried to make adjustments to the surroundings, without finding herself. She began to feel:

I am going in one direction and not getting mixed up. There is more continuity and I know what I am doing and where, and I know what I want to do. Sometimes I watch myself and that's not good either. Sometimes it is like looking on somebody else, and that is a very uncomfortable business.

As the eating compulsion lessened she underwent a severe depression; following this she made a good recovery. Without a special diet she lost weight at a steady, reasonable rate. She decided to reenroll in college to develop her artistic talents. She also arranged to live in the dormitory to be more independent of her family without breaking off with them.

Reducing As Precipitating Factor

Reducing, when rigidly pursued or outwardly enforced, may precipitate a psychotic reaction. This is apt to happen in patients with precarious adjustment who attempt to solve all their problems by becoming slim. The importance of weight stability and adequate nutrition for the maintenance of mental health has found comparatively little recognition in the medical literature. During World War II, Keys and his co-workers made extensive observations on experimental starvation, including the psychological reactions (2). Severe deterioration of all functioning was common, with extreme narrowing of interests, irritability, and continuous preoccupation with food, even in those with the least psychological changes. These experiments were carried out on volunteers (conscientious objectors) who had been observed in a control period and rated as emotionally stable. Even in this carefully selected group there were a few who became so disturbed that the experiment had to be discontinued.

It is amazing how little attention has been paid to the psychological effects of the semistarvation regimen that is commonly imposed upon fat people. Traditionally physicians have shrugged off their patient's complaints as signs of weakness and poor motivation. Only recently have these complaints been seen as signals of biological distress which in individuals with emotional problems may threaten their precarious adaptive mechanisms. Federn, during psychoanalytic treatment of schizophrenics, observed that the psychosis was sometimes initiated and precipitated by intentional weight reduction (1). He felt that this manipulation of the weight was among the first symptoms of an oncoming psychosis. Kallmann concluded from his genetic studies that any factor which affected negatively the stability of body weight might reduce resistance to schizophrenic phenomena; he counted drastic diets among the damaging factors (3). In my observation it is not only the type or rigidity of the dieting, but the interpersonal turmoil that surrounds it, and the irrational goals and expectations that contribute to the schizophrenic disorganization.

This damaging effect of dieting without emotional readiness was observed in Tanya, whose history was offered in the previous chapter (p. 163). She began a starvation regimen during a brief interruption of therapy. She had made this decision in order to demonstrate to herself that she was now free of the obsession that she had to perform special tasks and achieve greatness. Although she had begun the diet "on her own," it soon became apparent that it was only a "partial" decision. The other part of her experienced it as a "command" and rebelled. She felt as if there had been a vote and that the "absent member" was now protesting.

When treatment was resumed, two weeks later, she was in a state of extreme tension. She still followed her self-imposed diet and was worried about not being able to break it even if she wanted to. She had an insane desire for all kinds of food, even those she ordinarily loathed, and the thought of food kept her awake. She felt tired and dizzy during the daytime, her knees felt weak and she felt she had to watch every step, in a physical sense as well as with regard to eating. "There is a feeling of walking right off the edge of something—a feeling of no volition." Temptation, as "an active thing," was around all the time. She consumed large quantities of tea, smoked constantly, tried escape by reading magazines, and talked to herself in an indulgent voice. At the same time she would tell herself to stay on the diet: "A command is a command—no matter where it comes from."

The result of this continuous struggle and tension was a complete deterioration of her daily activities. She was unable to do her work and "mastering" her studies had been one aspect of her special power. She withdrew from whatever friendships and social contacts she had gradually built up. When therapy was resumed and while reviewing what she had experienced she decided to discontinue the diet, convinced that the real danger was the danger of losing her hold on reality. She tried to explain her experience in an essay from which I quote:

How can I explain what a diet is, how can I explain any of it? They, they do not understand. How can I tell them, if I become as they are, then I will sacrifice myself to do so, and destroy what love I have for them. I must be so careful. The jealous God. I must watch where I walk, where I go, what I say, for I may destroy myself in this perilous transition from the worship of desire back to myself. The peace, the pleasing despair, the uncare.

If I build an altar to my deepest desire, what then is precious enough to be sacrificed thereon but the self-desiring? There is nothing too dark to be done in the soul. The shadows of reality are undone by the knowledge of the depths within, the deep rivers going back to the sea!

In the battle between myself and what I most wish, I have won the only victory. The desire must be sacrificed to the self.

After she discontinued the diet the panic and tension subsided within a few days and her weight quickly returned to its former level. There was no doubt in her or my mind that if she had persevered she would have suffered a breakdown.

Following this episode Tanya became more open in discussing her secret thoughts. She recognized that this effort at dieting had been an expression of her power drive; she wanted to prove to herself that she could reshape her body, no matter how hard it would be. Although she had always talked about her weight as the great cross that her mother had to bear, she now admitted that she herself was uneasy about it. "I still feel amazed about my weight. I do not feel as if it were my own, or my own self. How could one be 'one's self'? There is not one thing that I am sure is myself." Or, "When I put my name to a paper I always feel like laughing—that it refers to that so-called 'Me.' The TXY is obviously 'not me'—scarcely related to myself—my name is like a mistaken answer to an equation—as if 'the real me' had been given a job to materialize myself—but I did not do it right. I could never be what I have in mind."

She felt equally uncertain about other people, felt resigned that she never met the people she wanted to meet. She was particularly confused about the use of "power" as self-expression and in relation to others.

There were many episodes and misconceptions that needed to be worked through before she gained an appreciation of her own abilities, which were considerable, without the superimposed concepts of absolute power. A year later she decided to consult a physician for advice about a reasonable reducing regimen, not a crash diet as she had tried before. She had been too frightened by having been face-to-face with the "unhuman" part of herself.

In Wanda a frank psychosis broke out when reducing was rigidly enforced. She was 17 years old and had gained an enormous amount of weight at a boarding school where she had felt very lonely and unhappy. She had wanted to come home but had not been permitted to do so. Now the family decided on weight reduction and sent her, against her will, to one of the commercial institutions known in and around New York as "milk farms." It was mandatory that she be slim so that she would be a "success" at college. Wanda lost some weight but became tense, restless, and unable to sleep. She walked for hours by herself, grimaced, took on bizarre postures, twirled around, and was always mumbling to herself. The symptom that was the most upsetting to her parents was her habit of staring into the mirror for a long time, then giggling or bursting out in derisive laughter.

Her whole life had been an effort to fulfill what she felt her family expected of her, namely, to be perfect in every respect. In particular, she tried to live up to the high ideals of her older brother, to whom she was very devoted. In her strenuous effort to fulfill these ideals she became conspicuously overweight and that became the focus of all concern, since it spoiled the image of goodness and perfection. Several efforts at weight reducing were made, and when Wanda was 16 she had succeeded in forcing her weight down. The summer of this year was spent at the beach, and she was praised for her efforts at playing tennis all day and dating some boys. However, everybody came down upon her with scorn and fury because "she was going too far." This seemingly successful summer, during which she was beautiful and slim, ended with Wanda's becoming seriously depressed and resentful against her family.

A solution to the problems was sought by sending her to a boarding school, to which she agreed under pressure. There she gained an enormous amount of weight and at graduation everybody was shocked by her appearance. She had known about her brother's plan to get married; but it came as a great shock to her when the wedding date was set and she was told she would not be permitted to be a bridesmaid unless she was slim; then the acute disturbance became manifest. Wanda had always felt that her parents were too old and too preoccupied with their own health to ever really listen to her; only her brother had been interested in her development, and his influence had been paramount. Her goal and task in life was to live up to his expectations, and any criticism from him had a disastrous effect. When she heard of his wedding, she felt she was losing the only person who loved and admired her. Becoming slim assumed the terrifying connotation of preparing herself for a ceremony at which she was going to lose her brother.

Psychotherapy was directed toward helping Wanda develop sounder, more realistic and self-directed goals in life. She needed to learn that she could live her own life and not be her brother's admirer or imitator. She gradually worked her way out of the psychosis. She was able to give up the compulsive eating only after she had found a solid basis for her own life by making plans that she could carry through; she worked successfully in an artistic field. She was last heard of 10 years after the acute episode; she had maintained a stable weight, had been married for about 5 years, had two children, and was doing well in her marriage.

Even with medical supervision a psychosis may break out during a reducing regimen if the physician is not alert to the psychological implications. Eva was 30 years old and unmarried; her family considered her overweight the cause of her many adjustment problems, and there was much pressure to make her lose weight. A sympathetic physician encouraged her to adhere to a diet and gave her a great deal of praise and admiration for doing so well. She did lose 30 lbs in less than 6 months, "for his sake," as she later explained. To her, his encouraging attitude meant that he was romantically interested, and she in turn felt sexually attracted to him. She did not mention this to him, and the connection became clear only during psychotherapy, after the psychotic breakdown.

Eva came from a large Roman Catholic family and had always been considered a quiet and docile child, but undemonstrative. During adolescence she was conspicuously quiet, tidy in appearance, and did not show any interest in boys. She never had a close friend in whom she could confide. Her school work had been excellent, and she acceded to her parents' wishes and took a commercial course as being "more practical" than an artistic career. She did fairly well on her first job, but quit suddenly because she felt unnerved by its demands. She changed jobs several times after that, feeling increasingly unable to do any work, and a definite lack of direction became apparent. Several years earlier she had become seclusive because a family friend had propositioned her. She felt she had been sinful in arousing sexual desire in a man. The physician's admiration broke through the barrier of her repression; she became obsessed with ideas about sex, felt that men were staring at her and following her, and that her family did not protect her. The disturbance was so severe that she needed hospitalization, where she responded well to psychotherapy.

Sara, a 25-year-old married woman, came for intensive psychotherapy because of certain obsessive-compulsive symptoms which seemed to become more troublesome whenever she attempted to force her weight below a certain level—about 185 lbs. In the past she had had two psychotic episodes requiring hospitalization. Her psychiatric history was closely interwoven with enormous fluctuations in weight, the periods of acute psychotic disturbance coinciding with strenuous attempts at reducing. Sara had been a gifted child and did well in school, but she was shy and quite chubby and always felt she was an outsider. She was reasonably happy until she entered high school, where she definitely felt left out of social activities. During this miserable period she gained weight rapidly and became conspicuously obese, weighing more than 150 lbs at age 14. She went on a starvation diet and exercised compulsively, thus forcing her weight down to 90 lbs. At that point her parents became alarmed and arranged for psychiatric treatment. She gave up the compulsive reducing, and her weight went up to about 160 lbs; she maintained this weight during her high school years.

Sara went away to college, where she felt extremely lonely, and her weight rose to about 200 lbs. She became frantic about her appearance and began another starvation regimen, forcing her weight below 150 lbs. While on this diet, she became increasingly irritable and excited, then disoriented and delusional, so that hospitalization became necessary. She received insulin shock treatment, and was able to continue her college work. This time her weight rose to 235 lbs.

After a year, she made another effort at reducing, but again became acutely disturbed, with uncontrolled outbursts of hostility and aggression. The second hospitalization, during which she was treated with electro-shock and psychotherapy, extended over two years. After that she was able to finish her college course and then considered graduate work. She got married at age 24 and seemed to have made a fairly good adjustment. She came for intensive therapy in the hope of achieving a better under-standing of herself so that she would no longer need the excessive eating and large size to maintain herself, but could develop a more secure and stable self-concept and greater competence in her adjustment.

Alice, 22 years old, spoke in vivid terms about the manifold symbolic meanings of food and size during her recovery from a psychotic episode. She told about the beginning of her illness:

When I first knew I was crazy, and I knew it, I got so terribly sick I thought I would die and I was glad.
When I was 20, before I had this breakdown, I was nearly starving myself to death. I ate apples for two months and juice for three weeks, six glasses of fruit juice and black coffee ten times a day, that's all I took. I must have an iron constitution. My mother was at home and she did not think it would hurt me. I knew it would and I still don't know why I did not die. And then I ate all day long, anything and everything I could put my hands on. I decided to take days off from work and I would just eat, and I ate and I ate all day long.

Alice came from a socially prominent Southern family. She lived with her mother's family, and all relatives took an active interest in her, mainly critical, and decided what she should or should not do. At about 14 she began to gain weight, which was considered a disgrace. "They said I was like my daddy, trash, ignorant, stupid, dumb. They would not let me say a word. I also dislike fat people. I used to hate my father. My mother made me hate him and he was fat and I was afraid to be like him."

From age 14 on her life was a struggle with her weight. It fluctuated from 110 to 160 lbs or even more. She would keep on dieting even when she was quite thin, particularly when she was depressed and felt that she was inferior, then she began to overeat and could not stop. When she felt inferior about being fat she had to relieve her worry by eating more. "I am never really hungry, I really never have an appetite, but I have to eat. I get this craving for sweets. You feel as if you'd go mad if you don't get it. I would get up in the middle of the night to get some candy or ice cream or whatever I could find. I just had to get it." She felt her whole life had been an effort to get away from her family who had tried to make her feel inferior. Eating to her was one way of being big and independent, but then it got confused with the idea of having the family within her.

With me, when I gain weight, I feel like my people are in my head. When I lose weight then I seem to get rid of them. When I gain weight they come nearer; when I am thin they are far away. But when I think of them, then I have to eat and then they are near again. This aunt, the one who was so cruel and after me all the time, she is more in my mind than anybody.

This aunt had been particularly insistent on her being thin, and had been most abusive about her father. "The only things that count with her are physical beauty and money. She is one of these terribly domineering people and she is so cruel, so sadistic. When she came to see me I had a relapse. It seems that I dreamt once that I killed her. It was a terrible dream, like reality."

The whole period of her illness was characterized by acute weight fluctuation. During therapy it was gradually clarified that much of her eating and noneating had been an effort to come to terms with her family, efforts to be identical with them, deny their existence, or to kill herself. As she improved she felt she should try to stay thin so that she would make a good social impression. Since it was also something the family wanted, she hesitated because she did not yet trust herself to meet them without feeling that she was complying with their demands. "I don't really care whether I am heavy or thin, but I know I have to be thin—it is like an obsession, otherwise I get this terrible feeling of inferiority."

I have presented here a series of cases showing various forms of the interrelationships between weight fluctuation and schizophrenic development. They represent only a fraction of my observations of obese youngsters with schizophrenic disorganization. Most were so disturbed that they required psychiatric hospitalization of varying duration. They responded well to a treatment approach that focused on the underlying personality disturbances. Without effective psychotherapy they might relapse, even after physiological treatment methods bring about a remission.

In this series there is a conspicuous absence of schizophrenia and/or obesity in other family members. Since most of these patients were in intensive psychotherapy, information about other family members was quite detailed. It appears that some of the mothers owed their own slenderness to "eternal vigilance," which at the same time made them unusually harsh and punitive in dealing with their children's weight problems.

I have no way of estimating the relative frequency of this tragic course of events among obese adolescents. It is probably rare in statistical terms, but not unique, so that the possibility of a malignant development should be kept in mind when dealing with a young person who has unusual difficulties in following a reducing regimen, while at the same time violently complaining about his abnormal weight and feelings of social inferiority. Every one of these patients had been in treatment for obesity at one time or another. In some, behavior difficulties had been recognized, but the potential for schizophrenic development had usually been overlooked.

There is now increasing awareness of the possibility that the stress and dissatisfaction of dieting may trigger in some obese youngsters a latent schizophrenia. Quite a few years ago, a resident in psychiatry told me that he had heard my name in medical school and that I had been quoted as saying, "Inside every fat man is a skinny schizophrenic." Although the statement is a distortion of Connolly's aphorism, it does reflect the growing recognition of the fact that developmental obesity is not only a problem of weight and calories, but also an expression of serious personality disturbance. Tampering with the weight of an obese youngster with personality problems carries with it the danger of exposing the schizophrenic core of his development.

BIBLIOGRAPHY

1. Federn, P., Principles of psychotherapy in latent schizophrenia, Amer. J. Psychotherapy, 2:129–144, 1947.
2. Franklin, J. S., Schiele, B. C., Brozek, J., and Keys, A., Observations on human behavior in experimental semistarvation and rehabilitation, J. Clin. Psychol., 4:28–45, 1948.
3. Kallmann, F. J., *Heredity in Health and Mental Disorder*, W. W. Norton, New York, 1953.
4. Kallmann, F. J., and Rainer, J. D., The genetic approach to schizophrenia: Clinical, demographic, and family guidance problems, International Psychiatry Clinics, 1: 799–820, Little, Brown & Co., Boston, 1964.

11

Thin Fat People

Saul Bellow's brief sketch of Angela, Mr. Sammler's niece, could easily be applied to countless American women. Her appearance and behavior sound familiar to us, though it impressed her uncle as strange (1).

Angela was in her thirties now, independently wealthy, with ruddy skin, gold-whitish hair, big lips. She was afraid of obesity. She either fasted or ate like a stevedore. She trained in a fashionable gym. She wore the odd stylish things which Sammler noted with detached and purified dryness, as if from a different part of the universe. What were those, white-kid buskins? What were those tights—sheer, opaque? Where did they lead? That effect of the hair called frosting, that color under the lioness's muzzle, that swagger to enhance the natural power of the bust! Her plastic coat inspired by cubists or Mondrians, geometrical black and white forms; her trousers by Courrèges and Pucci.

In spite of her up-to-date, mod appearance and well-controlled figure, Angela was not happy. She was always getting involved in wild schemes to improve herself and the world, and she found solace in going to a psychiatrist. This, too, has a familiar ring. My own knowledge about the seemingly successful but desperate fight against obesity comes from many patients who came for psychiatric treatment for a variety of reasons, and who on first contact did not seem to be concerned with their weight at all.

Fat people are apt to blame all their difficulties on being fat and they hope for a new lease on life after they get thin. Many begin reducing confident of finding the pot of gold at the end of the rainbow. Few reach the goal; otherwise we would not be so concerned about fat people's inability to stick to a diet. But there are some who follow through, who can deny their desire for food and achieve the beautiful slim figure that is supposed to be the magic key to the doorway to success and happiness. And it may be that there are many for whom things work out this way; it so happens that I am not familiar with this course of events. People who are successful and stay reduced and are relaxed about it do not go to physicians with their weight problems; they certainly will not come to a psychiatrist.

From my observations there are three outcomes for people who reduce with the unrealistic goal of expecting a changed life before they have experienced the inner emotional changes which make these new adjustments possible. The great majority will try and try, will lose some weight and then, suddenly they will give up and regain and often overshoot their former weight. For others the stress of starving themselves, the loss of their size, the new real or imagined expectations may prove too much, and serious emotional disturbances, even frank psychotic behavior, may break through, as was discussed in the previous chapter.

There is a third group of people who succeed in becoming and staying thin, but whose conflicts are far from solved by having lost weight. On the contrary, their difficulties now have a chance to flourish, since the ugliness of being fat no longer prevents them from putting their unrealistic dreams to the test. Such people, though they no longer look obese, are far from cured; they still resemble fat people with all their unsolved problems, conflicts, and exaggerated expectations. Only they no longer *show* their fat. It is to this group that I wish to apply the term *Thin Fat People*, an expression I borrowed from Heckel, who stated in 1911 that we cannot consider a fat person cured, even though he has lost his weight, unless all the other functional symptoms have also disappeared (3). Loss of weight alone represents a pseudo-cure. The patient becomes "un obèse amaigri; mais il est toujours un obèse." The characteristics of a good cure, Heckel says, are that it should be lasting and that it should not make unreasonable demands on the patient.

Sometimes being slim is a professional necessity. I know a most attractive young girl who had made a place for herself as a model. She is pretty in a petite way, but by any standard of medical appraisal she is definitely undernourished, as is Twiggy, the most famous of the starved models. However, now that she is 19, it is doubtful whether she will be able to continue her career; whenever she applies for a job she is looked over and told that she must watch her figure, that she is getting too fat. She considers the great hazard of her profession the strain of constant fatigue. Only after we had discussed the details of her fatigue did she realize that most of it was due to being hungry all the time. She had observed that other young girls working as models frequently would faint and she was alarmed when she fainted for the first time, but then recognized it for what it was. In view of her enjoyment of the job, the good pay, and the sense of accomplishment she derived from being independent from her family she feels it worth the price, at least for a few more years.

A young woman with a magnificent voice noted a tumor, which turned out to be malignant, at exactly the time when she was first recognized nationwide as an artist. After the operation, she continued her career and achieved stardom, but was unhappy about her increasing weight. Though she "knew" better, she acted under the inner conviction that she *had to* eat to maintain her health, so that she would not suffer a recurrence. Once she felt "safe," more than five years after the operation, she decided to lose weight and consulted an experienced physician who supported her during an episode of resolute dieting. She brought her weight down to 10 lbs below her former weight and has maintained it at this low level for several years. She enjoys her youthful, slim figure and feels that all the personal and professional satisfaction she gains from it is well worth the sacrifice of being continuously food and weight conscious.

A friend of mine, psychologically gifted and probably more perceptive than most people, spoke about her own efforts to keep her weight under control, and what it meant to lose the extra 10 lbs that accumulated during a winter of sedentary habits and party-going. "I don't mind cutting out sweets or any one particular item. What I resent about dieting is that it makes one so terribly self-centered, so much aware of oneself and one's body, so preoccupied with things that apply to oneself only that there is scarcely any energy left to be really spontaneous, relaxed, and outgoing. It starts with thinking about what to eat and what not to eat, and gradually goes over to other fields, and it is this aspect that makes me resent dieting; it makes me less of a human being.

"Of course I don't want to look sloppy and fat and I want my husband and children to enjoy going out with me—but I sometimes wonder whether it is worth the strain and effort and whether I have the right to pay so much attention to my appearance at the price of being an unresponsive mother."

This woman had no tendency to obesity. The extra weight was not noticeable unless she drew attention to it. Her desire to stay slim and not to look dowdy is also that of a well-adjusted person, not of the fashion-plate compulsive type who wants to be thin for thinness' sake, as a matter of thoughtless conformity. But even for such a woman, pushing her weight below the level that is really comfortable for her involves a noticeable mental strain.

Problems become more severe for those who have a tendency to be obese, or who use overeating to ameliorate serious emotional tension. I am most familiar with this pseudo-thinness from my contact with the relatives of fat young people. Whenever one hears a thin, even scrawny-looking mother speak with particular vehemence and disgust about the fatness of her child it is not a far-fetched guess (and one easily confirmed) that this mother owes her fashionable figure to eternal vigilance and conscientious, semistarvation dieting. Fathers are not exempt from this rule. It seems to me that the hostile emotional overcharge is related to envy in the parent about the child's daring to satisfy his appetite and impulses. The parents' rage reveals their shame that the child's fatness exposes the despised family endowment. It is in families with this intense hostility about obesity that I have most often seen a malignant development of childhood obesity, with schizophrenic or anorexia nervosa as the final outcome.

Mrs. Jones is an example of such a mother. She is pretty and slim and considers it an insult and a disgrace for the whole family that her 12-year-old daughter is fat, moody, and unpopular. At first there was nothing to indicate that the mother herself has a weight problem—her weight has been stable for many years at 110 lbs. The first inkling of something wrong was the fact that all the complaints about her daughter's lack of attention and carelessness had to do with food. For example, one day while she was at the hairdresser's she sent her daughter to a certain delicatessen store for a sandwich, and the girl came back with a sandwich from another store which was not up to the mother's expectations. She made a terrible scene, shouting: "Do you expect me to eat *dirt*?" She takes pride in being so particular about food and will return a dish in a restaurant that is not absolutely perfect, though her husband and friends find her behavior embarrassing. Gradually she revealed that she had been quite plump before her marriage, that she had slimmed down for the wedding and has watched every bite she eats ever since. She is extraordinarily preoccupied with food, and has replaced the quantity she has sacrificed by the demand for superfine quality.

She is overly perfectionistic in her whole approach to her daughter, who complains: "Yes, I know, you love me a lot—you love me so much that you expect me to be perfect." In every respect this mother had tried to be perfect in her role, raising her child by the book, "Whatever was fashionable at that time." She was aware that her need to satisfy her own mother conflicted with her modern views and created confusion for the child. She felt her mother was lonely and unhappy, therefore she permitted her to overindulge the little girl, though the grandmother handled her quite differently from the mother. The girl was overly attached to the grandmother and reacted with real depression to her death. It was following this loss, when she was 5 years old, that the girl grew fat and became moody and withdrawn, and this provoked the mother's campaign to demand perfection.

Many women make a fetish of being thin and follow reducing diets without awareness of or regard for the fact that they can do so only at the price of continuous strain and tension and some degree of ill health. There are millions of young girls and women who starve themselves in order to look like these envied models for whom slimness is a well-paid professional pose. Ordinary young women do not get paid for being slim. When they become young mothers they will complain continuously about fatigue, about their children's problems, and about their own irritability.

Little attention has been paid to the fact that their attempt to fulfill fashion's demands to be skinny is directly related to these problems. Having grown up with the concept that thinness is identical with beauty and attractiveness and is desirable for its own sake, they have become used to living on a semistarvation diet, never eating more than their bony figures show. Never having permitted themselves to eat adequately, they are unaware of how much of their tension, bad disposition, irritability, and inability to pursue an educational or professional goal is the direct result of chronic undernutrition.

It is impossible to assess the cost in serenity, relaxation, and efficiency of this abnormal, overslim, fashionable appearance. It produces serious psychological tensions to feel compelled to be thinner than one's natural make-up and style of living demand. There is a great deal of talk about the weakness and self-indulgence of overweight people who eat "too much." Very little is said about the selfishness and self-indulgence involved in a life which makes one's appearance the center of all values, and subordinates all other considerations to it. I do not know how often people are aware of the emotional sacrifice of staying slim. An English writer, Clemence Dane, expressed it succinctly: "Staying slim is like being witty —it is beastly hard work."

Chronic malnutrition based on abnormal preoccupation with weight is common, but not readily recognized as abnormal because it appears under the guise of desirable slimness. These chronic reducers, the "thin fat people," are likely to escape correct diagnosis because our slimness-conscious culture will admire their starved appearance instead of offering them needed help. They come to medical attention only when the weight preoccupation interferes with their living, or when malnutrition gives rise to complaints of fatigue, listlessness, irritability, difficulties in concentration, or chronic depression. It has become customary to prescribe tranquilizers for them; three square meals a day would be a more logical treatment, but one that is equally unacceptable to physicians and patients who share the conviction that being slim is good and healthy in itself.

Frequently these people come to the attention of psychiatrists. Though successful in controlling their weight, they have remained unhappy and dissatisfied, and this theme, with endless variations, runs through their many complaints. Just as food never satisfied them, never gave them what they really wanted, so they are now dissatisfied with their new slim figure and disappointed in what it has achieved for them.

Toby, aged 18 years, became severely depressed during her senior year in high school. She had always felt that she was destined to lead a lonely life. She was convinced that no man would love her because she was a brilliant student and "too fat." Since the age of 15 she had been obsessed with dieting. She was tall (5'8") and her weight had never been excessive; 135 lbs had been the highest figure. At times she had forced it down to below 110 lbs. However, this did not relieve her problem; she was acutely unhappy and embarrassed by remarks about her being "too skinny." She also tried to be "like everybody else" by being less conscientious about her school work, but then was distressed when her grades dropped. She tried to participate in social activities and dated a young man who seemed to be in love with her. She had no real feeling for him and became alarmed when she gained some weight during this more relaxed period. Now she missed the remarks about how thin she looked. She became depressed and acutely suicidal, had to interrupt her schooling, and was referred for psychiatric treatment. The obsessive concern with her weight and figure was a camouflage for her deep-seated self-doubt and identify confusion.

Even without such acute disturbance, many are handicapped in their active participation in life. They seem to be successful in controlling their weight but in reality they are crippled in their whole adjustment because they often suffer from nutritional deficiencies and can maintain the low weight only at the sacrifice of mature development.

The case of Beryl is an example that successful reducing in itself does not solve personality problems. She came for psychoanalytic treatment when she was 20 and quite slim, but acutely dissatisfied and depressed. I had first met her when she was 16 and enormously fat. At that time she had succeeded in getting herself thrown out of a progressive boarding school, having deliberately behaved in a way that even the liberal policies of this school could not tolerate. Her attitude toward her fatness was also defiant. She was quite exhibitionistic and argued that she could be as free with her body and wear the same type of clothes as slim young girls.

Beryl was the youngest daughter of a couple who, after a stormy marriage, had finally separated and gotten a divorce. Her misbehavior at school had been an effort to force her mother to make a home for the children instead of sending them to boarding schools. When she came for treatment when she was 20 years old and in college, she had lost a considerable amount of weight and now spoke openly about her former attitude. Weight had been a problem since she had been about 10, and she had always been angry about being fat because it had meant "being inferior. I felt it was like a cross to bear. It is tough to be born that way. You either practically starve or you gain 10 lbs when you just look at sweet things. It is kind of a gyp, a lousy break to be born that way."

She was at her fattest when she was sent away from boarding school. She had never admitted the figure for her highest weight; it probably was in the neighborhood of 250 lbs. In the intervening years she had traveled a good deal, and by being careful about what she ate she had succeeded in holding her weight at about 170 lbs. She had spent one summer with her father who had formerly been so cruel about her being fat; she found that they had many interests in common, and that they were gifted in the same artistic field. For the first time she felt she was being valued by her father, and he convinced her that being slimmer would be a great asset for her. She went to a reducing establishment and forced her weight down to 135 lbs.

Although she now looked beautiful, she was not satisfied: "I want to be underweight so that I can stop worrying about what I eat. I still cannot eat sweets like ordinary people. The minute I eat sweets my system craves a lot. I have to do the one or the other, either diet—or go hog wild on sweets and all that stuff." She recalled the time she was at her fattest: "I really did not care about being fat then, but I did care about people infringing on my rights, on telling me what to do and what to eat all the time. I know what to eat and I know what is fattening, but I will not do it when they keep me on a diet." Her whole concept of childhood was that it was something that was inflicted on children. Being fat had been the worst and most painful experience of this state of helplessness.

Now that she was finally thin and glamorous, she expected that life would compensate her for her past suffering. Most of all she wanted admiration; she did not just want to be liked as an intelligent and pretty young girl, but she wanted special admiration for the fact that she had done it herself, and that she had sacrificed to be beautiful. She also wanted praise, admiration, and spectacular recognition for her intelligence and artistic talents, although she had done nothing to develop them.

At the same time she was disgusted with the overemphasis on looks. "All they care about is looks. I want them to like *me*. I felt lousy the way I looked when I was fat, but then they put *all* the emphasis on looks. Now I have got looks and I know I am right, but I hate people who make comments about it. That shows they don't like *me* for what I am." Yet if a young man did not make a great fuss about her good looks, or did not admire her in an articulate way, she was quite angry.

She developed an exaggerated interest in clothes, showing that she was far from content with her appearance. "I am never satisfied with the way I look. I always keep changing things around me, everything. I change my dress as often as four times a day, and even then I don't like the way I look. I would like to have a different color hair. A girl should not be as tall as I am. I disapprove of everything about myself. Just everything about me is wrong." Or,

When I see a dress in a window, or see another girl has something, I just cannot stand it not to have it. I feel I have to grab it, and I don't care about anything else. I have to buy it. It makes me feel so good, it makes me feel secure, standing there and looking at them—there they are! You can't think about clothes and eating together. If I get clothes, I don't care about eating. They just don't go together. I want my clothes to be special, but I also want to have what other people have. I just want everything. I want the best and the most, and I just love to see a sparkling arrangement of clothes.

One kind of hunger (for clothes and glamour) takes the place of the other hunger (for food). I never understood how women could keep so thin, just having coffee for breakfast. I always thought they were bitchy women and everybody hated them, but now I want to look glamorous the way they do.

But her desire for food was not gone. She heard about someone who was dying of a chronic disease, and she tried to imagine how she would feel if she had only a short time to live. She had a vision of herself lying in bed and indulging herself. "Then I would do nothing but read and I could eat all the things I am not allowed to eat now—chocolate, cake, and ice cream, and everything as much as I wanted. I just would stay in bed and eat and read. Of course, I would get fat, but I would not mind it. If I was going to die anyhow, at least I could eat, and eat, without worry."

With her craving for attention and admiration her relationships to other people, particularly to young men, were quite unsatisfactory. She always felt that *they* had not lived up to *her* expectations. She was very slow in recognizing how this self-centered need to have *her* wishes fulfilled interfered with all her relationships, even with her long-standing friendships with some girls. This became clear to her when one day she visited her best girl friend who had just gotten a new spring and summer wardrobe. "I envy her because I know that I will never get anywhere near that number. I will get some clothes before I go on vacation, but I'm sure it will never be that number. I am not jealous of Mary in other ways, I wouldn't like to have her parents or even her life particularly, but I want to have her *things*."

Later at night she could not sleep and she had the impulse to sneak over to her friend's house and steal her clothes, or cut them to pieces so that she would not have them either. She recognized this as vengeful and childish, but also admitted that she was envious of friends who were gifted the way she was gifted. Clarification of the neurotic attitude expressed in this demanding and grasping envy was an important aspect of her treatment, and it was a significant step toward a more mature concept of herself when she began to recognize this.

Quite often continuous preoccupation with weight is recognized only during therapy, without the outer appearance suggesting it. A 35-year-old married woman came for psychoanalytic treatment because she had marital problems and suffered from recurrent depressions and severe anxiety attacks. She was good-looking and well-dressed, and it was obvious that she paid a great deal of attention to her appearance. Her only sister was a well-known dress designer with whom she felt in continuous competition. She had never been fat but was phobic about the possibility of gaining weight. She had a good figure, but when she was depressed she would gain rapidly, as much as 10 lbs in a week or two. "During times like that, I eat and eat, though I don't even enjoy it—all kinds of things I don't care for, like bread. Then I feel sick, really nauseated, when I look into the mirror." Since she was young, her concept of beauty was looking like a serpent, long and slim, without any curves; once she had a dress of shimmering silk in which she felt like a serpent. "Sometimes I have the strength to be cautious. Then I can become slim: that shows I am *strong*. I am so pleased then if anyone remarks on how pretty I look. I never know what happens when I suddenly cut loose again; just anything may happen and I have to run into the kitchen and eat."

When she feels fat all over, bursting out of her beautiful clothes, she feels thoroughly ashamed of herself and will decide to diet. The dieting usually starts with a big job of housecleaning. She herself will do the work and feels she does it much better than any cleaning woman would do it; the last thing to be cleaned is the bathroom. Then she takes a bath so that she herself is completely clean and after that the diet begins with 3 days of complete fasting. After having been so hungry it is easier to stick to a diet; even a plate of salad is enough. She feels much better when dieting; at least in the beginning.

Such episodes are preceded by letting everything get very dirty; only when things are really run down can she do something about it, be it dirt or fat. However thoroughly she cleans, she never has the feeling of being as clean as she should be, nor does she ever feel she is as well-dressed and slim as she would like to appear. When she feels "empty" while fasting, she feels slim even before she has lost weight. She is continuously preoccupied with the impression she makes, but has a compulsion to confess "bad things" about herself. Even as a child, when anybody mentioned something positive about her, she would feel terribly embarrassed. "They say it only to make me feel better." She always felt that she suffered in comparison with other children, and thought she looked "horrible," and "fat" was the word for it. Looking at childhood pictures now, she is amazed how pretty she was, not fat at all. When her breasts developed she felt like the fat lady in the circus, and when she sees pictures of a really fat woman, she has the dreadful feeling, "That's what I look like."

The outstanding emotional tone of her childhood memories is the feeling of envy, that others got more, were loved more, got a better education. As a second daughter she felt at a disadvantage, not getting enough education, not even getting new clothes. Most of all she envied boys because much more was done for them. Being fat reminds her of being feminine; she resents it and becomes depressed and starts an eating binge. She always felt cheated and left out, but most things were outside the reach of her power and she could not alter them but had to suffer in silence. The one great advantage about being fat is that one can do something about it; she can achieve beauty if only she wants to. That's why she gets so exalted if she starves and loses some weight fast; it proves that she has the power to change herself.

Her weight fluctuated between 120 and 130 lbs. When she reached the upper point she would begin her cleaning and fasting rituals. It is possible that without this regimen she might have become quite heavy. Though she had never accumulated the extra weight, she was as preoccupied with her figure and every bite she ate, as if she actually were big and fat.

Not infrequently parents, and also physicians and psychiatrists, reinforce a fat person's unrealistic expectation about what he should weigh. Ingrid, aged 20 years, was referred for consultation by her psychiatrist, who mentioned in the referring letter how "stunning" she had looked when she had brought her weight down to a very low level. She had been successful with reducing while in therapy, but then had suddenly relapsed and was now heavier than at any time before.

Ingrid was the youngest child in a wealthy, achievement- and appearance-conscious family; her mother and older sister were small-boned, slim, and well-dressed. In contrast, Ingrid had been a fat baby and by the time she was a toddler her mother insisted that the pediatrician do something about her weight. He put her on a diet and gave her appetite depressants. Ingrid remained large and heavy as a child, but was continuously pressured to be slimmer; several times she was hospitalized to force her weight down. Like her older siblings she did well in school, but at 10 or 11 she had refused to work at all, feeling unable to endure the competition. From then on there were repeated efforts to get her into psychiatric treatment, but she refused to cooperate with any plan.

With adolescence Ingrid became severely preoccupied with her weight. She began to demand that her mother keep no extra food in the house. Gorging herself alternated with bouts of faddish and unrealistic dieting, all to no purpose. She retained good social relations with both boys and girls, but there was no dating. When 16 or 17 she became involved with a group of hippies and drug addicts. After a brief period of feeling "accepted" she became frightened about their activities. At this point she asked for psychiatric help. She formed a good relationship with her therapist and quite early in therapy said that she had put herself on a diet, that she had heard people ate as a substitute for love; she felt she was loved and therefore did not need to stuff herself. Whatever the dynamics, at the end of about the first year of treatment she had lost 90 lbs, down from nearly 225 to 135 lbs, and she was beautifully slim. This first weight loss was a relatively slow accomplishment and it was felt at the time to be related to her firm and positive relationship to her therapist. However, in reevaluating this period it appeared that even this first reducing was associated with rather faddish diets and excessive use of amphetamine pills. But Ingrid was still not satisfied at reaching this weight and from then on there were many ups and downs. She would gain as much as 30 or 40 lbs in a few weeks but then immediately reduce again. The last impetus for losing was a stay at a famous seaside resort by the whole family. Ingrid wanted to look attractive in a bikini bathing suit and lost about 30 lbs in a very short time, and lost some more while at the resort. When she returned home she was at her lowest weight, nearly 120 lbs. She looked strikingly beautiful and people stared at her on the street. She also received boundless praise from her parents and from her therapist who noted, however, that during this period of forced thinness she was tense and anxious, almost manic. During her hippie period, she had dropped out of school; now she decided to take courses for a high school diploma, and also began ballet dancing and yoga exercises. Suddenly she had many dates, something virtually nonexistent before.

Ingrid maintained her low weight for a few months, but then launched herself upon the most compulsive eating binge of her whole life. Jealousy seemed to be related to the eating problem. Her older sister expected her first child and even before the baby was born Ingrid resented that it might receive more attention than she. She would eat constantly, day and night, and during frequent nocturnal icebox raids would eat absolutely everything edible in the house, so that there was nothing left for anyone else. She would eat to the point of being sick, and when she could no longer eat would throw the remaining food down the incinerator.

Ingrid continued in therapy but now was angry at her therapist for not having cured her. She appeared frightened and severely depressed by the sudden awareness that she did not want to be thin, though consciously she insisted that she wanted to lose weight. There was rapid increase in weight and by the time she came for consultation she looked as though she weighed more than 200 lbs; she absolutely refused to go near a scale. However, she did not look as monstrous and grotesque as her parents' and therapist's description had suggested. Ingrid was tall and broadly built; she looked massive and too heavy for her frame, but her high weight was not as abnormal as the weight she demanded. She had said that she could not possibly be happy unless she could force her weight down to 115 lbs and keep it at that figure. She reminded me of Binswanger's patient, Ellen West, who complained: "Fate wanted me to be heavy and strong, but I want to be thin and delicate" (2).

In reviewing her life story and her previous treatment experiences, Ingrid felt she had always been under mother's domination, overcontrolled and forced to do things; her only way of asserting herself was saying No. During the consultation she was quite responsive and we focused on the deficits in her concepts of control, psychologically and biologically, and on the futility of trying to achieve a better self-concept through the manipulation of her weight. She had proven to herself repeatedly that she could reduce but the effort and tension made it impossible to maintain the weight loss. The same applied to her other efforts to achieve something worthwhile.

Progress in long-standing, fluctuating adolescent obesity cannot be measured in terms of weight, but only in terms of overall competence. Better weight regulation becomes possible as a result of better adjustment; it is not a precondition for it. Ingrid absolutely rejected a treatment approach in which weight was not the first consideration. But with such a phobic compulsive preoccupation with weight, the first treatment goal must be correction of the unrealistic expectation. Weight regulation must be seen as a positive achievement after other aspects of coping have been mastered.

To weigh less than is comfortable is an all-American preoccupation. The young, the college crowd, have revived the Roman custom of regurgitation after indulging in large meals. This method has become commonplace. When I first heard about it more than 20 years ago, it was considered unconventional, to say the least. Gloria had been introduced to the method during her second year in college, after she had gained excessively during her first year. To her this seemed the perfect solution to her problem and she brought her weight down from 180 to 115 lbs. When Gloria came for treatment five years after she had begun this routine, her weight was approximately 125 lbs and she was panicky for fear she would grow fat again. Actually she was quite slim, and her preoccupation about fatness was quite unrealistic. She had tried to prove to herself that she had a perfect figure by applying for work as a model; when she was accepted she felt reassured and immediately dropped the plan.

Although Gloria had thus succeeded in creating a perfect figure, her adjustment to life had not only not improved, it had deteriorated to a race between overeating and maintaining the perfect figure. This was the important point: it was proof of her power to defy nature. If she could eat as much as she wanted and still stay thin, then she was doing something nobody else could get away with. She took her weight every morning and when she had gained she would become depressed, unable to do what she had planned for the day, because "her power was slipping." This preoccupation with maintaining the perfect weight was part of her approach to life; she needed to be continuously reassured of "complete perfection in every respect."

Going to college had meant leaving home for the first time. Gloria became preoccupied with the idea of being prominent and popular, and worked hard, "like a politician," during the first month to be well-liked and known by everybody and was chosen president of her dormitory. Once she had accomplished this, her interest in other girls and all activities lagged. She became quite depressed but hid it from everybody in order not to spoil the image of perfection. She overate and gained a considerable amount of weight; from then on fatness became the big obstacle standing in the way of her accomplishing anything. She changed to another college nearer her home; "There too, I majored in being different. If I could not be the best in my work, then I had to be unique in other ways. I just cannot help it, I have this compulsion to be special, and I'll do anything to accomplish it." It was during the second year in college that she was introduced to the "method."

Instead of using it to compensate for an occasional large meal, Gloria made it a routine. She had to eat increasingly larger amounts because it became harder to bring the food up. She gorged herself until her stomach bulged, then she emptied herself and felt relieved. The whole procedure took approximately 2 hours. She would eat one or more large meals in a restaurant, then have 6 or 8 hamburgers, approximately a quart of ice cream, pounds of chocolate and candy, several quarts of milk, and even then she might find that it was not enough and eat a whole pie or cake in addition. These eating spells took up so much of her time that she could not finish college. She tried several times to work, even for a few hours a day, but was unable to stick to any job.

Nevertheless, she felt a certain triumph in having achieved her goal. She felt reassured about her attractiveness because young men flocked around her, although her need to feel superior and acceptable was not sufficiently appeased by this. She wanted to excel in other respects too; she wanted to do something really big that would make a real impression, something like saving the world and doing good for all oppressed people, or saving and elevating individuals she had met in the course of her many activities. These efforts got her involved in many embarrassing situations. Whenever reassurance about her being superior and perfect was not forthcoming, she would go on an eating spree, as many as three or four on some days. The slightest disregard for her feelings, an unplanned evening, or the fear of not living up to somebody's expectations was enough to provoke this urgent need to eat.

Gloria had recognized the neurotic character of her many activities, and had made several attempts at psychotherapy. Yet each time treatment was terminated for various reasons after 4 to 6 months. In the course of her work with me it became apparent that she had used her previous therapists as tools to help her accomplish the godlike perfection which she felt was the true goal of her life. Whenever she felt that the therapist was not helping her enough, she would find a plausible reason for breaking off treatment. It was only after this delusional goal had been clarified that a valid treatment relationship could be established.

Even then it took long and painstaking work to help her develop a realistic self-concept. The eating binges gradually diminished in number and lost their specific meaning. Treatment came to an end after she had done well in an interesting job for over a year; she was capable of relationships other than ones that involved her being the goddess adored by slaves. The eating compulsion had diminished considerably, also. Gloria has been married now for over 15 years to a man who is aware of her old problems and difficulties, and the symptoms have gradually disappeared. She has two children who have not developed any weight or eating problems. She has also been able to put her outgoing interest in others to constructive use in a realistic way.

·   ·   ·

Though the psychiatric exploration reveals severe underlying psycho-pathology and an unrealistic approach to life, these women impress the casual observer and their friends and acquaintances as enviably slim, attractive, and interesting. In contrast to the patients described in the previous chapters they continue to function in a socially acceptable man-ner, though under severe tension and strain, and far below the level of their potential abilities. They also differ from those in whom the wish to be thinner and the refusal of food results in anorexia nervosa, which will be discussed in the following chapters. The difference is one of degree, in-sofar as the anorexia nervosa patient continues on the downhill course and aims at a body weight far below normal. There is also a difference in kind: in anorexia nervosa a true misperception of reality takes place; though rational in many respects, the distortions concerning weight and food and the reasons why they must deny themselves are truly delusional. Anorexia nervosa is a rare disease; one may think of it as the end stage of the unrealistic preoccupation with weight and size. Just as only a few of the numerous shy and withdrawn obese adolescents develop into full blown schizophrenics, so only a few of the countless thin fat people will progress to the malignant state of anorexia nervosa.

It is not always a clear-cut decision whether to assign the diagnosis thin fat or anorexia nervosa to a patient. Pamela, whose mother had developed a severe depression at her birth and had taken no interest in her upbringing, grew up as her older sister's shadow. "I let her speak for me." She measured herself only in terms of her sister's achievements, and the sister had been a brilliant student. When she was 14 she felt she could no longer keep up the competition. Finally, she refused to go to school. She spent one year moping around the house and had some private in-struction. She ate excessively and her weight went up to 165 lbs. When 16 she was sent to a small boarding school which she hated, "I felt like my inside was torn apart, bit by bit. My eating habit blew up—I was really hooked on stuffing my face and I vomited just by bending over." Pamela finally ran away from this school and did not go back to school at all. In spite of her high intelligence and giftedness in artistic fields, at age 22 she had had no vocational training. The idea of competing, of having to face a test, threw her into a panic. Though it is far below her capacities, she supported herself through menial work, choosing nighttime or very early morning hours.

Pamela filled her days with eating binges and throwing up, and by the time I saw her in consultation she had maintained this routine for over 6 years. Her weight had dropped when she was in boarding school and after she ran away, but not to the level of emaciation observed in anorexia nervosa; she had maintained it at or around 100 lbs. She agreed that this was too thin, but she said she would not want to weigh more because then she would be worried about getting too fat. Pamela also knew that the continuous vomiting played havoc with her electrolytes, that her twitching and muscle cramps were related to this. She willingly took medication to compensate for it. She thus differed from patients with true anorexia nervosa, particularly in not being delusional about her body and its functions, but resembled them insofar as she became increasingly isolated, not participating in any social activities.

The observations reported here run counter to the whole campaign against overweight which, in fact, says exactly the opposite: that reducing is necessary to improve one's physical health, social position, and emotional outlook. These arguments are used daily to convince fat people that they should reduce. It seems to me necessary to point out that a mechanical approach to overweight carries grave mental health hazards. The road of propagating scientific standards of nutrition is littered with landmarks of overly zealous errors and failures. It is my impression that the over-eager propaganda about reducing diets, even though obesity is an abnormal state of nutrition, overlooks a basic human problem, the need for satisfaction of vital needs. "The best women are rich and thin" may be a good slogan for the jet set; it is a potentially dangerous ideal for the ordinary overweight person.

BIBLIOGRAPHY

1. Bellow, S., *Mr. Sammler's Planet*, The Viking Press, New York, 1969.
2. Binswanger, L., Der Fall Ellen West, Schweiz. Arch. Neurol. Psychiat., 54:69–117, 1944.
3. Heckel, F., *Les grandes et petites obésités*, Mason et Cie, Paris, 1911.

PART III

Anorexia Nervosa

12

History of the Concept of Anorexia Nervosa

Anorexia nervosa became a clinical entity with the independent reports by Gull (10) in England and Lasègue (14) in France, just 100 years ago, although occasional references to self-inflicted starvation were discovered in earlier literature. In spite of its rarity and short history there exists an amazingly large amount of literature on it. I shall not attempt to be complete in my historical review but shall refer only to a few authors who reflect varying efforts to understand this enigmatic condition. The genuine picture is so dramatic and unmistakable that it is puzzling that increasing observations, instead of leading to a clearer description, have resulted in the picture becoming blurred and poorly defined.

Richard Morton whose *Phthisiologia: or a Treatise of Consumption* (17) was published in London in 1689, is credited with the earliest report in the medical literature. He calls the condition "A Nervous Consumption." I quote from him because his description and crisp images evoke immediately the most dramatic aspects of the condition. He gives the history of Mr. Duke's daughter in St. Mary Axe who became ill in July, 1684, in her eighteenth year, and the son of the Reverend Minister Mr. Steele, in his sixteenth year, whose history will be presented later (Chapter 15). The young woman is described in vivid terms:

In the month of July she fell into a total suppression of her Monthly Courses from a multitude of Cares and Passions of her Mind, but without any Symptom of the Green-Sickness following upon it. From which time her Appetite began to abate, and her Digestion to be bad; her flesh also began to be flaccid and loose, and her looks pale . . . she was wont by her studying at Night, and continual pouring upon Books, to expose herself both Day and Night to the injuries of the Air . . . I do not remember that I did ever in all my practice see one, that was conversant with the Living so much wasted with the greatest degree of a Consumption (like a Skeleton only clad with Skin) yet there was no Fever, but on the contrary a coldness of the whole Body . . . only her

Appetite was diminished, and her Digestion uneasie, with Fainting Fits, which did frequently return upon her.

Like a modern anorexic she rejected the medication he offered and died 3 months later, following a fainting fit.

Thus the first effort at differential diagnosis was directed toward distinguishing anorexia nervosa from tuberculosis. Even today every young person who suddenly wastes away undergoes extensive medical examinations to exclude tuberculosis or other systemic disorders. Boss (2) speaks of a peculiar relationship between anorexia nervosa and tuberculosis, namely that of mutual exclusion. Several of his patients, while severely cachectic, were exposed to tuberculosis and remained free of it, while other people in the same environment became infected. He mentions severely cachectic nurses who cared for tubercular patients and who remained somatically well during the period of self-starvation, but developed tuberculosis after their weight increased. Conversely, he observed that young girls who had become slightly obese while undergoing a rest cure for tuberculosis later went on starvation regimens because they felt repelled by their bodies. Dally (6) reported that five of his 140 patients developed tuberculosis, late in the course of the disease, several after they had regained weight. Boss raises the question whether one might expect an increase in anorexia nervosa when treatment of tuberculosis becomes more successful, as if an individual trying to achieve emaciation would pursue this goal by different means.

The medical literature of the eighteenth and nineteenth centuries contains occasional references to states of self-inflicted emaciation, and they have been ennumerated in several recent monographs (6, 22, 25). I shall refer here to a case which, as far as I know, has not been revived elsewhere. Its particular point of interest is that this girl was reported on by Worthington, in a book on obesity (29) published after Gull and Lasègue had published their observations.

A 15-year-old girl, the daughter of a physician, was described in 1868 as being short and having a "jolie" figure, but looking with envy upon her slim friends and complaining about her "exaggerated embonpoint." A year later, in 1869, her weight had increased and had become embarrassing. Later in the year, she was scarcely recognizable. She, who 8 months previously had been so fat, was now quite frail, her breasts had nearly disappeared and her stomach no longer protruded. Her cheeks, previously so bright and fresh, were now in deep folds and had lost their color. There was an atmosphere of sickness about the girl as if she had acquired a fatal illness. During the previous 7 months the girl, with the aid of her mother, had been on a diet of "nothing but roast beef and water." This had been kept a secret from the father who at first approved the weight loss, but in April 1870, became concerned about his daughter's illness. With a stay in the country and long walks in the fresh air, her strength came back a little but the poor complexion with deep folds and wrinkles in her face persisted. In February 1874 she seemed to be in good health and was happy that she had remained thin; as soon as an inkling of fat reappeared she began her roast meat diet again.

Since the reports by Gull and Lasègue, the picture has remained alive in clinical thinking and has become the object of systematic studies. Gull coined the term *Anorexia Nervosa* and it is by this name that it is referred to in the English-speaking countries, Germany, and Russia; Lasègue called it *Anorexie Hystérique,* a term later replaced by *Anorexie Mentale,* the term in use in France and Italy. In the German-speaking countries the condition is also called *Pubertaetsmagersucht.* Many other names have been applied to this condition, and many cases have been published in the psychiatric, gynecological, and endocrine literature without special reference to anorexia nervosa.

From the onset a certain atmosphere of controversy attached itself to the discussions. Lasègue (14) in 1873 reported on 8 patients suffering from what he called anorexie hystérique, with severe emaciation and food refusal, though without absolute fasting. He differentiated this anorexia from that observed in depression. The loss of appetite showed different facets in different patients, with repugnance for all food in some, and aversion only to certain foods in others. The typical picture was observed in young girls between 15 and 20 years, with the onset related to some emotional upset, something the patient would be inclined to conceal. He considered the starting symptoms some hysterical disturbance in the digestive tract, such as vomiting, gastric pains, hematemesis, etc. For this reason he decided to call the condition "anorexie," and not "hysterical emaciation."

Gull's first report was published in 1874 (10), but it is almost obligatory, to ensure him priority, to add that he had referred to the condition in 1868 as "hysteric apepsia," and had presented his series of cases with detailed descriptions in a lecture in 1873. He published an additional report in 1888 (11). He observed anorexia nervosa usually in young females. According to Gull the outstanding symptoms were emaciation associated with amenorrhea, constipation, loss of appetite, slow pulse and respiration, and absence of somatic pathology. He commented on the restless activity, "It seemed hardly possible that a body so wasted could undergo the exercise which seemed so agreeable," and "Miss K. R., age 14 . . . persisted in walking through the streets to my house, though an object of remarks to the passerby. . . . It is curious to note, as I did in my first paper, the persistent wish to be on the move, though the emaciation was so great and the nutritive functions at an extreme ebb." He attributed the want of appetite to "a morbid mental state. . . . I believe, therefore, that its origin is central and not peripheral. That mental states may destroy appetite is notorious, and it will be admitted that young women at the ages named are specially obnoxious to mental perversity."

As I mentioned before, from the beginning there were marked differences of opinions concerning the disorder's proper definition and etiology. Gull's emphasis on the "central origin" expressed his contrasting view to Lasègue's concept of a "peripheral" disturbance. Lasègue was also impressed by the patient's contentment, "That she was not ill pleased by her condition" and that a propensity for activity persisted in spite of the abstinence from food. Lasègue gives vivid description of the interaction between the patient and her family, how her position of being "a patient" shifted to that of a "capricious child," and how the girl's condition and her refusal to eat gradually became the sole topic of conversation and preoccupation of the whole family.

The contradiction and confusion in the literature that has accumulated during these 100 years is considerable. Some of this may well be related to the tendency to explain all cases through the same mechanisms, the unwillingness to concede that the same surface picture, namely emaciation due to noneating, may be a manifestation of different underlying factors. Gull explicitly stated after his attention had been directed to Lasègue's simultaneous report, "It is plain that Dr. Lasègue and I have the same maladie in mind, though the forms of our illustration are different." It is conceivable that they, too, saw different forms of what looked like the same disorder. Though it is difficult for us today to grasp what was meant by "disturbed nerve force" (Gull), or "hysterical affliction" (Lasègue), which at that time was conceived of as a constitutional hereditary disorder, their descriptions suggest the possibility that at least some of their patients suffered from different forms of the condition. The "sameness" rested in the somatic picture, with severe weight loss, amenorrhea, constipation, etc. If Gull stressed the remarkable hyperactivity, and Lasègue focused on the pains in the patient's stomach, then it is possible that the key patients, on whom the clinical descriptions are based, differed in this respect, though Lasègue, too, observed that some of his patients were remarkably active. There were several attempts, to which Dally (6) has drawn attention, to subdivide the picture according to different symptom combinations.

The whole issue became even more confused when Simmonds (23), a pathologist, reported finding destructive lesions in the pituitary gland of an emaciated woman who had died following pregnancy and delivery. Until then it had been generally accepted that psychological factors were the cause of anorexia nervosa. Following Simmonds' publication, in 1914, the whole approach changed and any case of malnutrition was attributed to some endocrine disturbance, resulting in increasing vagueness concerning what was included in the anorexia nervosa concept.

It was only during the 1930's that persistent efforts were made to distinguish a psychological anorexia nervosa syndrome from the so-called Simmonds disease. There was acknowledgment that anorexia nervosa was brought about by psychological factors, but they were considered "fundamentally alike clinically," with the patients suffering from "concealed conflicts." Concepts of the endocrine origin of anorexia nervosa persisted longer in Europe than in the United States. This orientation has not necessarily interfered with a careful psychiatric study. To give some examples: Meng's (15) original and insightful observations were published in 1944, in a book entitled *Psyche und Hormon*, which indicated that he took the pituitary origin of the cachexia for granted. Binswanger (1), too, speculated in 1944, in "Der Fall Ellen West," about whether the tragic outcome might have been averted with more advanced endocrinological knowledge. Quite recently Ushakov (26), after a brilliant psychological reconstruction of the illness, suggested a second causal mechanism, a constitutional neuroendocrine deficiency, with hypophyseal failure as its main feature. In support of this assumption he quotes a paper of von Bergmann and Berlin on "hypophyseal insufficiency" published in 1934.

Once it had been reestablished that anorexia nervosa was a disease of psychological origin, publications with this orientation appeared in a steady stream without diminishing the confusion. There are many reasons for this. Anorexia nervosa is not a static condition, but its very existence constantly provokes new problems, and patients come to our attention at various stages of their illness. The state of starvation itself is associated with marked psychological changes which are often denied or camouflaged by rationalized explanations. The patterns of interaction in a family undergo marked changes, with progressively rising anxiety and concern, but also rising annoyance and resentment. In addition, the social isolation deprives them of the new and broadening life experiences so necessary for and characteristic of the adolescent years. The ambition to "explain" such a complex picture with one psychodynamic formulation has resulted in imposing stereotyped explanations on a condition that defies such a simplistic approach.

At first there were generalized statements which were soon followed by detailed psychoanalytic case studies. Some of the "key" publications, illustrating the evolution of the concept, were selected in a monograph by Kaufman and Heiman (12). Though the book was published in 1964, its most recent paper was originally published in 1943; that means the work of the past 30 years is not included. I shall focus here mainly on publications from 1930 to the present. Two main trends can be recognized: *first*, those dealing mainly with the chief symptom, the "oral" component of the disturbance and its symbolic significance; and *second*, those concerned with the personality of the patients and their whole life style, with emphasis on disturbances in ego functions and interpersonal relations.

Symptomatic Approach

This section will deal chiefly with psychoanalytic studies which have flourished since 1930. By making the disturbed eating the focus these observations often include psychogenic vomiting and other forms of neurotic eating disturbances. Basically they all rest on Freud's assumption that impairment in the nutritional instinct was related to the organism's failure to master sexual excitation. This one-sided emphasis on the "oral" significance and its relation to sexuality has contributed to the confusion with which we are today confronted and led to the neglect of other important aspects.

One of the first reports of the psychoanalytic treatment of a patient with anorexia nervosa was presented by Maria Oberholzer in 1929 before the Swiss Psychoanalytic Society (20). It concerned a 13-year-old girl whose weight had dropped to 33 kg, who refused to eat because she had become disgusted with food. She claimed to have lost her hunger sensation and she vomited so severely that a pylorospasm was suspected. The analysis revealed intense father-fixation and the desire for a child from the father; this was looked upon as the psychic motivation for the vomiting. The intense food refusal, however, was interpreted as relating to the wish for a penis, something not observed in ordinary neurotic vomiting. The anorexia picture was thus viewed as having developed out of the conflicts between the desire to be like a man and the desire for a child from the father. The case was presented 6 years after what was considered successful treatment, with the diagnosis of hysteria, though the possibility of a schizoid picture was raised in the discussion.

Other classical psychoanalysts viewed the problem similarly, as symbolically expressing an internalized sexual conflict. Efforts were directed toward becoming more and more specific about the nature of this conflict. The high point of this approach is a paper published in 1940 by Waller, Kaufman, and Deutsch (27), that:

psychological factors have a certain specific constellation centering around the symbolization of pregnancy fantasies involving the gastrointestinal tract. . . . The syndrome involves not a physiological system but rather a functionally coordinated unit subjectively important to the patient. . . . The wish to be impregnated through the mouth, which results at times in compulsive eating, and at other times, in guilt and consequent rejection of food, the constipation symbolizing the child in the abdomen and the amenorrhea as direct psychological repercussion of pregnancy fantasies. This amenorrhea may also be part of the direct denial of genital sexuality.

The authors noted that the eating disturbances were related to conflicts with the family, and that the syndrome was precipitated by the need of adjustment to adulthood, with anorexic patients regressing to an infantile level instead.

The concept that anorexia nervosa was an expression of repudiation of sexuality, specifically of "oral impregnation" fantasies, dominated clinical thinking to such an extent that even a sophisticated author with independent observations, not having found this constellation, would add, "While similar associations in my patients might have been traced to deeply repressed fantasies of impregnation by father's incorporated phallus, it must be stated that further material explicitly relevant to this complex did not appear in the analysis." Even today, "oral impregnation" is the one psychodynamic issue most consistently looked for. This type of thinking worked also in reverse; if fear of impregnation could be elicited from a patient, even mild degrees of weight loss or neurotic vomiting were diagnosed as representing anorexia nervosa, though the clinical picture was quite unspecific.

Modern psychoanalytic thinking has turned away from this merely symbolic, and often rather analogistic, etiological approach and focuses now on the nature of the parent-child relationship from its beginning. Meyer and Weinroth (16) pointed out that the onset at the time of puberty had given rise to an erroneous evaluation of oedipal conflicts in the genesis of anorexia nervosa. The development of a symptom or syndrome in terms of a set of critical experiences, as in the competitiveness of oedipal strivings, needs to be connected with the effects of earlier, pre-oedipal experiences. The nursing experience often appears to be a nexus of trauma, confusion, rejection, and frustration, a precursor of subsequent open conflicts. Nemiah (18) demonstrated that the expected outcome of a mother's overprotective attitude, namely excessive dependency, unquestioning obedience, and a wilted kind of passivity, materializes early in many anorexic patients. Increasingly the emphasis has been on factors that served to precondition the eating experience in the future anorexic—who finally comes to relate to the environment exclusively in terms of undereating or overeating.

With this increasing emphasis on early development, and on behavior and attitudes not directly related to food, recent psychoanalytic studies are approaching the views that had been expressed by others since the early 1930's. There are, of course, still reports in the old orientation. Thomae's monograph (25), published in 1961, is based on the psychoanalytic study of 30 patients who had come from all parts of Germany to the psychosomatic clinic at the University of Heidelberg. His book is written in the classic psychoanalytic tradition and gives the impression of belonging to a bygone era of medical and psychoanalytic thinking. In spite of excellent and detailed clinical observations, he gives his theoretical conclusions as a priori statements and overgeneralized formulations. He interprets anorexia nervosa by stating, "obviously it is a drive disturbance," or "we can say definitely that oral ambivalence underlies the whole symptomatology." In a later publication he and his workers described atypical cases, characterized by onset late in adolescence or early adulthood, in whom asthenic, hypochondriacal, hysterical, or obsessional features could be recognized (9).

Life Style Orientation

A few analysts during the 1930's recognized that the one-sided focus on the eating function, the "oral" component, failed to deal with the underlying disturbances in the total personality. When they made their observations, the concept that anorexia nervosa was endocrine in origin was taken for granted and psychoanalytic thinking, too, was much more concretely biological. Under this orientation, there is no contradiction between an endocrine and psychological approach.

Meng (15) felt that the regression in anorexia nervosa surpassed what was observed in neurosis and compared it to the regression in psychosis. However, he felt that a psychosis in the ordinary sense did not exist, and he proposed the term "organ psychosis" because these patients regressed much more deeply in a much more instinctual way than neurotics. He was aware that the term "organ psychosis" contained a certain paradox, and it has not been accepted by other psychiatrists. However, his observations and deductions appear to be in excellent agreement with some of the recent developments in anorexia research. Meng focused on a deformation in the ego structure. In neurosis the ego is involved only in a secondary and quantitative way, adapting itself to the symptoms without changing the essential aspects of its functions, even though many are outside of its awareness. Symptoms are an expression of inner conflicts, but the ego is essentially normal. In psychosis, however, it is the ego that is diseased in its primary structure, even though external factors may play a role in the development of the disorder. He views the changes in the ego as the essence of the illness, if only in its lowered resistance against being used. Meng compared his observations to those made by Federn (8) in his studies of schizophrenics (which were quite new at that time) and referred specifically to the complaints of schizophrenics about depersonalization and their inability to recognize true feelings, noting that anorexics suffered from similar difficulties.

Meng's observations have found very little attention in the American literature, except by Eissler (7) who, in 1943, referred to Meng's concept of "deformation of the ego," and applied it to the experiences of his own patient with anorexia nervosa, who complained that "her mind was in the mind of other people," a concept which was not delusional in character though it is difficult to visualize. The ego being in another person is contradictory to fundamental psychic experiences. In anorexia nervosa the ego feels weak and stunted. Eissler, too, felt this mechanism had evolved out of the past physiological and psychological patterns of interaction between mother and child. This attitude toward the mother is different from the dependency on the mother so frequently encountered in neurosis which, however, does not result in this permanent "deformation of the ego."

In 1938, Nicolle (19) reported important observations in which she differentiated between anorexia nervosa and symptomatic food refusal in hysteria. Nicolle considered true anorexia nervosa as a serious mental disorder, often a prepsychotic state, which needed to be differentiated from hysteria to permit a relevant treatment approach. She compared two patients who were in treatment at the same time, one with anorexia nervosa and the other with hysteria.

The hysteric makes a parade of her inability to eat and undoubtedly eats when it suits her; the anorexic tries to dissimilate the fact that she does not eat. The hysteric desires to elicit sympathy. This is far from the anorexic, but she may enjoy in some less direct way her ability to tease and deceive those about her. I should say that the purpose of the anorexic to starve herself is of fundamental importance.

She drew attention to the potentially schizophrenic aspects of anorexia nervosa and compared the affective state with that described in the early diagnosis of schizophrenia with both exhibiting shallowness and the cooling off of all feelings.

This paper is included in Kaufman and Heiman's monograph (12). In keeping with their own theoretical orientation they cite Brown's discussion "as the best commentary" on her paper. Brown says, "Her explanation is superficial and inadequate, as it does not recognize the active repudiation of sexuality which is going on in these cases and which I should like to stress. At the deeper and more primitive level of the mind where this occurs the ingestion of food symbolizes impregnation and obesity in pregnancy." It is regrettable that this paper has not been given the attention it deserves. In spite of an outdated endocrine bias, its psychiatric thinking is closer to present-day observation than any other paper in the monograph.

Despite the fact that Binswanger (1) does not report "The Case of Ellen West" as an example of anorexia nervosa, it represents a sensitive and detailed account of the inner experiences of a patient suffering from it. His reports, published in 1944 and 1945, refer to a patient observed 30 years earlier, when she had already been sick for over 13 years. This woman had great artistic abilities, wrote poetry, and kept a diary before and after she became sick. Binswanger reconstructed her psychological development from his contact with her, her previous medical history, and chiefly from her extensive writings.

Regrettably little is reported about her background, except that she had been educated in Europe and was the daughter of wealthy Jewish parents to whom she remained closely attached and who maintained control over her. Twice her father interfered when she became engaged, and when she finally married, at age 28, it was to a cousin.

At 16 she was in love with a young man for the first time and she began to act in a more feminine way than before, but continued to wish to be a boy, wanting "to be a soldier and to die joyously with a sword in my hand." Even before her illness she wrote of wanting to attain immortal fame, so that for centuries afterward her name would still be on the lips of humanity. "Only then will I not have lived in vain!"

After graduating from high school, during a period of traveling, she noted that she could not be away from her parents, although she had many friends. In her nineteenth year, after she had become engaged and broken off because her father wished it, she noticed the beginning of a *new anxiety, namely the fear of becoming fat*. She developed an enormous appetite and grew so heavy that her friends would tease her. Immediately thereafter she began to castigate herself, denying herself sweets and other fattening foods, omitting supper altogether, and going on long, exhausting walks. When, at age 21, she returned home, her family was horrified at her miserable appearance and depressed mood. She was only worried about getting too fat and continued her endless walks. She suffered from feelings of worthlessness and a pervasive anxiety. She was disgusted with herself and desired to be recreated in a better form or to die young. Her life became a continuous struggle with her weight; she stopped eating as soon as there was some increase. Simultaneous with this fear of becoming fat, her desire for food increased. She could not eat in the presence of other people, only when alone. The persisting conflict between the dread of overweight and greed for food overshadowed her whole life. Food she believed not fattening, she would eat with greed and in a great hurry.

Her diary has recurrent passages like, "the most horrible thing about my life is that it is filled with continuous fear. Fear of eating, but also fear of hunger, and fear of fear itself. Only death can liberate me from this dread." Or, "since I am doing everything from the point of view of whether it makes me thin or fat, all things lose their real value. The same with work. I was looking for other purposes in order to distract myself; to distract myself from my hunger and greed." At another time she writes, "I do not think that the fear of becoming fat is the real obsession, but the *continuous desire for food*. The desire, the greed for eating, must be the primary cause. The fear of becoming fat acts like a brake. I see in this 'Fresslust,' the real obsession. It has fallen over me like a beast and I am helpless against it. It persecutes me continuously and drives me to despair." For a while she was in psychoanalytic treatment, which proved disappointing. "The desire to stay *thin* remains unchanged in my thinking. . . . This compulsion (to think about food) has become the curse of my life, it follows me when I am awake and when I am asleep; it stands next to me like an evil spirit and I feel as if I could never escape from it."

Throughout the years of her illness, she continued to walk excessively. At one time she took large amounts of thyroid tablets and developed hyperthyroidism. Six weeks of bed rest was prescribed, and she gained weight rapidly, up to 160 lbs. She became depressed, but continued her long walks and worked actively on several social projects. At age 28, she married her cousin. Her weight at that time was 145 lbs and on her honeymoon she began to diet, saying that she hated her body. At age 31, there was a rapid decline in her vitality; she looked old and haggard. She continued her excessive walking, increased the amount of laxatives she took, and ate even less. She confessed to her husband, with elementary violence, that her whole life was dominated by the need to stay thin; that every action was done from this point of view. It was a fixed idea that had a terrible power over her. She tried to drown it through work but the concern always broke through. Calorie counting and collecting recipes were her great preoccupation. She would fill every free minute by copying recipes or tasty dishes, thinking the people around her should eat the rich food she denied to herself. The craving for and the compulsive thinking about food were associated with feelings of severe depression. At this point she was hospitalized. Increasingly suicidal thoughts appear in her writings, particularly when she must reproach herself for having lied, such as telling her physician that she no longer took laxative tablets though she continued to do so.

She had vivid dreams, always of hunger or death; she would see the most beautiful dishes in front of her, experience the most terrible hunger, but was not permitted to eat. She dreamed, "War had started and I was ordered to go to the front. I said goodbye to everybody in the joyful expectation that I should die very soon. I look forward to it so that towards the end I can eat everything, even a big piece of Mokkatorte." Suicidal thoughts increased.

If there were only a medication, or some food that could be given in the most concentrated form, that would permit one to stay thin, then I would enjoy being alive. All I want is to become thinner and thinner, but I don't want to pay attention to it continuously, and I do not want to miss anything. It is this eternal tension between wanting to be thin and not to give up eating that is so exhausting. In all other points I am reasonable, but I know on this point I am crazy. I am really ruining myself in this endless struggle against my nature. Fate wanted me to be heavy and strong, but I want to be thin and delicate.

She was discharged from the sanitarium at the request of her family. On the third day after she returned home she appeared like a changed person, unusually quiet and relaxed; for the first time in 13 years she ate ordinary meals, even sweets, and enjoyed a walk with her husband. All the depression and heaviness seemed to have fallen away from her. In the evening of this festive day she took a lethal dose of poison. In death, "She looked the way she had not looked in life, serene, happy, and peaceful."

I have cited only a few of the endlessly repeated statements of wanting to stay thin and the eternal preoccupation with food, including the desire to enjoy it before death. The similarity to the thinking and preoccupation of other anorexia nervosa patients is startling.

Of particular interest are her comments not related to her weight and food. In all these struggles she experienced herself as completely passive, a helpless spectator who just watched scenes in which hostile forces were destroying each other, with a feeling that there was nothing she could do about it. "I seem to be fighting against sinister powers that are stronger than I, but I cannot get hold of them or reach them." These images beautifully express what I consider an essential aspect of anorexia nervosa and to which I have referred as an "all-pervasive sense of ineffectiveness."

There are also many references to extreme isolation and loneliness, a feeling of being excluded from all real life. "I am completely isolated, I sit like in a glass sphere. I see other people through a glass wall, their voices penetrate to me. I long for being in real contact with them. I try but they don't hear me."

I have heard many of my anorexic patients use similar words and images to express their sense of utter unrelatedness. Will (28) reported on a young schizophrenic woman who as an adolescent had suffered from severe and persistent decline in weight, and who felt "hopeless," "empty," and "hollow." She was exceedingly aloof toward his efforts to establish therapeutic rapport. "My first steps often seemed to be misdirected or ill-timed. One day as I sat in silence Catherine suddenly turned and struck me. I held her arms and she wept, saying: 'I haven't been able to hear you. You have been staying behind that wall of glass. It had to get broken somehow.'"

Though preoccupation with food and weight dominates the picture, it has been my experience that the essential underlying disturbances in anorexia nervosa are related to patients' defective self-awareness and their disturbed interpersonal experiences. Only by focusing on these deficits are we able to be therapeutically effective with these desperately ill patients.

Recent Contributions

A comparison of the two preceding sections might have left the reader with the impression that entirely different illnesses were discussed. Earlier authors neglected to separate different types of anorexia nervosa, or rejected the possibility when the idea was expressed. There has been a definite change since 1960, and there is now an increasing convergence of opinion about the need to differentiate between various subtypes. Reports in the past were usually based on a few patients only. Authors would draw generalized conclusions from their limited experience and apply their observations to all cases of weight loss. They would attack other findings as incorrect, as exemplified by the fate of Nicolle's paper.

In the recent past, several reports have appeared based on larger numbers of cases, with the emphasis on the need to subdivide the condition. King (13), reporting on 21 patients from Australia, observed distinct variants. He identified 12 patients for whom abstinence from food was a "positive pleasure" and a primary gain, and 9 in whom abstinence from food was secondary to phobic dread, delusions, or depressions. This latter group failed to show clusters of common traits or symptoms, whereas members of the first group showed many features in common. These included upbringing by a dominant and restrictive mother and a passive father, high intelligence, childhood traits of athleticism, dyspepsia, petty stealing, post-pubertal disgust with sexual thoughts and development, absence of even minor sexual activity, post-pubertal dependence on the mother, irritability, lack of humor, paranoid sensitivity, withdrawal, and marked obsessionality. King concluded that primary anorexia nervosa was a specific syndrome, while the secondary picture might occur in various psychiatric states. He considered anorexia nervosa an obscure organic disease, but felt that psychological factors played an essential role and the disease became manifest only in the presence of disturbed parent-child interaction.

In 1969 Dally (6) reviewed the course of illness of 140 female patients in whom the diagnosis of anorexia nervosa had been made. The population consisted of 42 former patients seen at a general teaching hospital in England between 1940 and 1957 and 98 patients treated since 1957. Dally subdivided anorexia nervosa into an "obsessional" and a "hysterical" group, but since these terms were not "strictly accurate" he called them group O (74 patients, 53%), and group H (30 patients, 21%). In addition there was a group with mixed etiology, group M (36 patients, 26%), representing a secondary form of the illness. In group O the outstanding feature was the refusal to eat because of fear of possible weight gain or loss of self-control. These patients were interested in cooking and liked to feed others, but they resorted to many subterfuges to avoid eating; later on they tended to overeat and to become obese. They induced vomiting after eating and increased their activities voluntarily. Patients in group H were not hungry, had no appetite, and showed no tendency to overeating. They avoided eating because of gastrointestinal discomfort. Vomiting was unusual and their increase in activity was involuntary. Patients in group M had no hunger or appetite, refused to eat because of abdominal fullness or nausea at the sight of food, had involuntary vomiting, decreased their activity because of lack of energy, and were usually depressed.

Ushakov (26), reporting from Moscow on 65 patients, considers anorexia nervosa a separate nosological entity that needs to be differentiated from unspecific cases of food refusal in various psychiatric conditions. His lively, detailed characterization of his patients could be applied to my own. Leading in the psychopathology is the *desire to be slim*, which he conceives of as the expression of a *supervalent thought*, which grows into an all-important nucleus, "which focuses a mighty power on a single point." Patients are often extremely conscientious children of high intelligence, with excellent achievements in school and great persistence in any set task. The manifest symptoms include hyperactivity which in the beginning has the appearance of purposefulness, but all are symptoms dominated by the need to be thin and the fear of gaining weight. Ushakov considers that there is a deficiency in the process of personality development, i.e., a psychogenic mechanism, and notes that this is one of the causes which operates in the presence of a constitutional neuro-endocrine deficiency.

Even more dynamic and issue-oriented is Selvini's approach (22). Her monograph is based on the treatment observations of 26 patients, including 3 males. To her the central phenomenon is the need to exercise control over the body, which is experienced as threatening and indestructible. It "must not be brutally destroyed, but must merely be held in check." There is no true absence of appetite, and hunger persists in the starving patient until the terminal phase. What these patients exhibit is "anorexic behavior"; they act *as if* they were without appetite. Food is actually very important for them, frequently the most important thing. These seemingly detached and apathetic patients are excited by casual conversation about food, as long as it is not their food that is mentioned. This is also revealed by their making cooking for others a hobby, their knowledge of recipes and delicatessen shops, compulsive reading of menus, etc.

Selvini considers the diagnosis of anorexia nervosa "a highly clinical operation," implying a psychiatric analysis of the patient's experiences and behavior. Since anorexia nervosa patients are reserved, evasive, and not always truthful, the correct diagnosis requires experience and knowledge of the syndrome by the examiner. The combination of "conscious and stubborn determination to emaciate herself despite the presence of an intense interest in food" distinguishes anorexia nervosa from other forms of psychological malnutrition and weight loss.

My own experience has independently led to similar formulations, that a primary form of anorexia nervosa, with relentless pursuit of thinness as the driving motivation, must be differentiated from unspecific atypical pictures (3). This will be discussed in detail in the subsequent chapters.

In 1970 Theander (24) reported on 94 female patients who had been observed at a university medical center in the south of Sweden between 1930 and 1960. Most of these patients were reexamined by the author; he excluded patients who did not fulfill definite criteria for a positive diagnosis. This important study covers the total population of a section of the country, and includes patients seen on the medical and gynecological services, not only in the psychiatric department. Theander defined primary anorexia nervosa, from which the majority of his patients suffered, by using the psychiatric criteria for which Selvini had suggested "anorexic behavior" and Bruch, "a relentless pursuit of thinness." He found these criteria useful to distinguish genuine anorexia nervosa from atypical cases and from other forms of malnutrition that in the past had erroneously been included under this diagnosis.

Other authors, too, such as Russell (21) and Crisp (4, 5) in England, who have made important contributions to the psychobiology of anorexia nervosa, consider it a distinct disease entity, with Crisp defining it as "almost invariably a state of weight phobia," and Russell as "a morbid fear of being fat."

I have quoted only a few of the authors who in recent years reexamined the concept of anorexia nervosa. Independently they arrived at comparable formulations, that one-sided preoccupation with the eating function, the "oral component," deals with only one aspect of the problem, or only with one category of patients, and leaves other equally important features unexamined. There is agreement among these various workers that there is a genuine syndrome, precipitated by "fear of fatness," which is related to preexisting underlying disturbances. The marked similarities, independently arrived at, speak in support of the validity and usefulness of this approach.

BIBLIOGRAPHY

1. Binswanger, L., Der Fall Ellen West., Schweiz. Arch. Neurol. Psychiat., 53:255–277, 1944; 54:69–117, 1944; 55:16–40, 1945.
2. Boss, M., Einfuehrung in die Psychosomatische Medizin, Huber, Bern, 1954.
3. Bruch, H., The psychiatric differential diagnosis of anorexia nervosa, pp. 70–87, in Anorexia Nervosa, J.-E. Meyer and H. Feldmann, eds., Georg Thieme Verlag, Stuttgart, 1965.
4. Crisp, A. H., Some aspects of the evolution, presentation and follow-up of anorexia nervosa, Proc. Roy. Soc. Med., 58:814–820, 1965.
5. Crisp, A. H., Premorbid factors in adult disorders of weight, with particular reference to primary anorexia nervosa (weight phobia). A literature review, J. Psychosom. Res., 14:1–22, 1970.
6. Dally, P., Anorexia Nervosa, Grune and Stratton, New York, 1969.
7. Eissler, K. R., Some psychiatric aspects of anorexia nervosa, demonstrated by a case report, Psychoanal. Rev., 30:121–145, 1943.
8. Federn, P., The analysis of psychosis: On technique, Int. J. Psychoanal., 15:209–214, 1934.
9. Fleck, L., Lange, J., and Thomae, H., Verschiedene Typen von Anorexia nervosa und ihre psychoanalytische Behandlung, pp. 87–95, in Anorexia Nervosa, J.-E. Meyer and H. Feldmann, eds., Georg Thieme Verlag, Stuttgart, 1965.
10. Gull, W. W., Anorexia Nervosa, Trans. Clini. Soc. (London), 7:22–28, 1874.
11. Gull, W. W., Anorexia Nervosa, Lancet, 1:516–517, 1888.
12. Kaufman, R. M., and Heiman, M., eds., Evolution of Psychosomatic Concepts. Anorexia Nervosa: A Paradigm, International University Press, New York, 1964.
13. King, A., Primary and secondary anorexia nervosa syndromes, Brit. J. Psychiat., 109:470–479, 1963.
14. Lasègue, C., On hysterical anorexia, Med. Times & Gaz., 2:265–266; 367–369, 1873.
15. Meng, H., Psyche und Hormon, Hans Huber, Bern, 1944.
16. Meyer, B. C., and Weinroth, L. A., Observations on psychological aspects of anorexia nervosa, Psychosom. Med., 19:389–398, 1957.
17. Morton, R., Phthisiologica: or a Treatise of Consumptions, London, 1689.
18. Nemiah, J. C., Anorexia nervosa—a clinical psychiatric study, Medicine, 29:225–268, 1950.
19. Nicolle, G., Prepsychotic anorexia, Proc. Roy. Soc. Med., 3:1–15, 1938.
20. Oberholzer, M., Aus der Analyse eines dreizehnjaehrigen Maedchens, Schweiz. Arch. Neurol. Psychiat., 26:287–292, 1930.
21. Russell, G. F. M., Anorexia nervosa: Its identity as an illness and its treatment, Chapter 6, in Modern Trends in Psychological Medicine, J. H. Price, ed., Butterworths, Great Britain, 1970.
22. Selvini, M. P., L'Anoressia Mentale, Feltrinelli, Milano, 1963; Chaucer Publ. Co., London, 1972.

23. Simmonds, M., Ueber embolische Prozesse in der Hypophysis, Arch. Path. Anat., 217:226, 1914.
24. Theander, S., *Anorexia Nervosa. A Psychiatric Investigation of 94 Female Patients*, Acta Psychiat. Scand., suppl. 214, Munsgaard, Copenhagen, 1970.
25. Thomae, H., *Anorexia Nervosa*, Huber-Klett, Bern-Stuttgart, 1961; International University Press, New York, 1967.
26. Ushakov, G. K., Anorexia Nervosa, pp. 274–289, in *Modern Perspectives in Adolescent Psychiatry*, J. G. Howells, ed., Oliver & Boyd, Edinburgh, 1971.
27. Waller, J. V., Kaufman, R. M., and Deutsch, F., Anorexia nervosa: A psychosomatic entity, Psychosom. Med., 2:3–16, 1940.
28. Will, O. A., Jr., Human relatedness and the schizophrenic reaction, Psychiatry, 22:205–223, 1959.
29. Worthington, L. S., *De l'Obésité: Etiologie, Thérapeutique et Hygiène*, Martinet, Paris, 1877.

13

Psychogenic Malnutrition and Atypical Anorexia Nervosa

In the previous chapter I have reviewed various efforts at defining anorexia nervosa in meaningful terms and have tried to come to an understanding of the underlying psychodynamic factors. There are many contributions which seem to aim at the exact opposite, applying the term to every case of malnutrition with psychological problems. Many authors have drawn attention to this as creating confusion and as interfering with the understanding of the condition. Clauser found it difficult to draw conclusions from the data compiled from the literature because the clinical material was so heterogeneous, ranging from mild uncomplicated cases of weight loss to severe psychiatric disorders associated with cachexia (4). He also commented on the fact that the patients often had not been observed by the authors themselves; instead, information had been culled from hospital records which had accumulated over an extended period of time, where somebody with unknown experience had diagnosed some weight loss as anorexia nervosa. From my own evaluation of certain long-range surveys, I have drawn the same conclusion. More often than not, the original diagnosis had been made by a house officer without him or his supervisor ever having seen a patient with true anorexia nervosa. Often it looks as if the experience of the authors of such reports, who draw their authority from the large number of patients or the renown of the medical center at which the observations were made, is also limited and not based on actual observations of their own. Notable exceptions are the recent surveys by Dally and Theander (5, 8).

The monograph by Bliss and Branch, which was published in 1960 with the title *Anorexia Nervosa* (2), is a prime example of considering any weight loss for psychological reasons as meriting the diagnosis anorexia nervosa. The authors give a stimulating review of the early cases, and they note that with increasing reports, the syndrome to which Gull had given the name "anorexia nervosa" had become blurred and poorly defined. They themselves, "having failed to find in the literature a neat solution for differentiating anorexia nervosa from other forms of undernutrition," decided to accept, admittedly arbitrarily, a loss of 25 lbs or more as a suitable figure for defining the condition, if the drop in weight was attributable to psychological causes. Some of their patients were referred by outside physicians, a few were discovered on the medical wards, but most were patients on the psychiatric wards, *who were there usually for reasons other than malnutrition.* This approach with its vague and colorless definition amounts to abolishing the whole concept. It also implies abandoning efforts at using the tools of psychiatry for defining the condition.

Their report of 22 cases, 19 females and 3 males, illustrates how broad and unspecific their definition is. Their descriptions are sufficiently detailed for the reader to gain a picture and to form, in many instances, an independent opinion of each case. To anyone at all familiar with anorexia nervosa, this group of patients must appear as most unusual representatives. Ages range from 15 to 56 years. Only one patient is below 20, and in one other the illness had developed at puberty. Nearly half of their group is over 30 years old, with 3 patients over 40, and 3 more than 50 years. Whatever is disputed about anorexia nervosa, there is agreement that it is an illness of adolescence and young adulthood. It is doubtful whether this assortment of patients suffering from a wide variety of psychiatric conditions, middle-aged depression, schizophrenia, life-long neurasthenia, hysteria, etc., and who have nothing in common except that they have lost some weight, would have inspired Sir William Gull, or anyone else, to recognize a special clinical syndrome.

On the basis of what Bliss and Branch offer as case material one can only agree with their conclusion that it is "puzzling that the state of nervous malnutrition which could convincingly have been classified as a symptom of mental illness akin to insomnia, anxiety, or an obsession, should ever have been designated a medical syndrome. Even more arresting is its longevity in medical literature and the persistent attention accorded to it." As a monograph on malnutrition in various psychiatric conditions, this book is a valuable clinical contribution precisely because it brings into sharp focus that not every patient with severe weight loss suffers from anorexia nervosa. The title of the book is confusing because it is obviously a report of what is *not* anorexia nervosa.

Patients with unspecific psychogenic malnutrition come to the attention of every psychiatrist, certainly to one whose interest in nutritional disturbances is known. I shall present in this chapter two groups of patients with psychologically determined weight loss. The first is an *unspecific* one in whom the weight loss is incidental to defined psychiatric or somatic illness. The other group is comprised of patients who on first impression resemble true anorexia nervosa but who are rated as *atypical* because the motivational and dynamic focus differs from what is observed in the genuine picture; the patients included in this group differ greatly in their dynamic constellations.

Psychogenic Malnutrition

I shall give here a few brief sketches of patients in whom the possibility of anorexia nervosa had been considered but was rejected. In Chapter 3, I described the case of a 20-year-old girl who suffered from a neurological disorder and had lost an enormous amount of weight, going from 397 lbs at age 17 to 108 lbs at age 20. She appeared as unconcerned about this severe weight loss as about her neurological condition and former obesity. She spoke of "no interest in eating" as distinct from the hunger and appetite that she had formerly experienced. The question of anorexia nervosa had been raised by the neurologist, but was answered in the negative. There was neither the morbid interest in food nor active rejection of it, nor concern with weight or a relentless pursuit of thinness.

Weight loss for psychological reasons covers a wide range. I shall give here a few brief vignettes of patients suffering from a variety of psychiatric or somatic disorders, ranging from chronic schizophrenic reaction, acute catatonic schizophrenia, mental retardation and schizophrenic disorganization, depression with severe social pathology, to various undiagnosed organic disorders.

Chronic Schizophrenic Reaction

In the case of a 45-year-old woman of lower-class background the question of anorexia nervosa beginning in middle age was raised and answered in the negative. Her weight had declined during the preceding year from 130 lbs to 70 lbs; she became unable to take care of her home and children and appeared confused. In the past she had reacted with depressive withdrawal to whatever difficulties she had encountered. The first time occurred when she was 20 years old, after an austistic love affair, when she heard that her "lover," whom she had met once 3 years earlier, had married. Sometimes disinterest in food was part of the depression which was then accompanied by severe weight loss. She did not marry until she was 34 years old and whenever she was worried about the stability of her marriage she would decompensate, with or without weight loss. The diagnosis was that of a chronic schizophrenic reaction, with marginal adjustment throughout life.

Acute Catatonic Schizophrenia

A 20-year-old Jewish man, of high intelligence, interrupted his college studies because he could not concentrate and was bizarre in his behavior. He returned to his parents' home "for a rest." His behavior appeared inconspicuous, although he was very quiet, until, trying to make a perfect shot on the golf course, he had a sudden vision of Christ. He became even more withdrawn and was anxiously preoccupied with the question of being worthy and clean. Though he had no concern about eating as such, he considered food "dirty," refused to eat, and lost over 30 lbs. On admission to the hospital he looked emaciated, and was in a wheelchair because he held himself so rigid that he could not walk. There was no debate about the diagnosis of schizophrenia, catatonic type; the noneating was incidental to this.

Mental Retardation and Schizophrenic Disorganization

A 13-year-old boy was seen in consultation because of the question of possible anorexia nervosa. He was the first child of young middle-class parents who had never accepted the fact that he was retarded, though this had been diagnosed quite early on the basis of his slow development. When the public school advised entering him in a school for the retarded, they placed him in a parochial school, where he could not take part in the program and had no rapport with other children. The mother was very persistent in "teaching" the boy. The parents acknowledged for the first time that something was wrong when their son lost weight by cutting down on his food. He had always been undersized for his age; suddenly he became concerned about not "wanting to get too big." Then he began worrying that his father would not eat enough, or that his mother might eat more than his father and thus become the bigger of the two. The anxiety about his father's eating increased to the point of his crying when the father would not eat more than the mother. He developed other fears, had episodes of irrelevant laughter, and became concerned with ventilators, fearing that small men might be sucked in. This poorly endowed child of whom too much had been expected appeared on the point of schizophrenic disorganization.

Depression with Severe Social Pathology

In the case of a 34-year-old Negro woman, severe economic and social problems combined with depression in producing a picture that superficially resembled anorexia nervosa. She was admitted to the medical service with anemia and cachexia, weighing only 65 lbs. This severe malnutrition had developed over a period of 5 years, after her marriage had broken up. She lived in the same household with her invalid mother and a psychotic sister. She had married 10 years earlier and her husband went overseas for 3 years of military service; he left her 2 years after his return. There was much tension between the patient and her sister. She was frequently upset, felt esophageal constriction, could not eat, and would vomit if she did. She became increasingly depressed and ate less and less without paying attention to her progressive weight loss. When she came to the hospital she was strikingly small, emaciated, and pitiful looking. She was suspicious, guarded, withdrawn, and severely depressed, expressing suicidal ideas, but she responded well to psychiatric attention, antidepressant drugs, nursing care, and adequate nutrition.

Depression with Form Fruste of Anorexia Nervosa

The preoccupation with food and exercise of this woman of 29 years suggested the possibility of anorexia nervosa. She had been married for 6 years and had been obsessed with the fear of injuring her little girl who was born a year after the marriage. She read extensively on the Battered Child Syndrome, visualizing how her child would look if she were injured. To compensate for these thoughts she insisted on feeding her child well, even forcing food on her. She herself became preoccupied with her weight and eating after a miscarriage when she lost some weight, going from 125 lbs to 118 lbs. Suddenly she felt it was very important to maintain this lower weight, and she became very "logical" about what she ate, absolutely refusing a bite beyond what she had calculated as permissible; she lost her sexual appetite but never her appetite for food. Her weight dropped to 97 lbs and stayed at this level for a year. She often felt acutely hungry and was upset about her suffering. She would force food on her child, and felt it was an insult that her child voluntarily refused to eat while she herself was starving.

When they moved to a different city she found that she could no longer maintain her rigid food control and would indulge in sprees of overeating to the point of feeling nauseous, though she was never able to throw up. Such binges were followed by a day or two of starvation; she was puzzled about this fear of fatness since no one in her family had ever been heavy. The fear of fatness overcame her only when she was in the grip of an eating binge. Her weight had gradually returned to 120 lbs, which she did not consider too heavy. One might call this a case of form fruste of anorexia nervosa which failed in protecting her against pervasive anxieties and severe depression with several suicide attempts.

Esophageal Stenosis with Family Psychopathology

Manifest family pathology pointed to a psychological reason for the weight loss of a 7-year-old girl who was removed by her father from her mother's care because he felt his wife was mistreating the child. He also had noted that his plump little girl had become thin and wan, and vomited frequently. The vomiting persisted while the girl stayed with an aunt who gave her loving care. She was admitted to a pediatric service, weighing only 42 lbs, having been quite plump, nearly 80 lbs, the previous year. Extensive examinations, including roentgenograms of the G.I. tract, failed to reveal an organic cause for the weight loss. Anorexia nervosa was suspected. Detailed psychiatric evaluation of her history and her eating habits revealed that she was actively interested in food but would spit out what she had eaten after a short interval. This suggested that there might be a mechanical obstacle interfering with her ability to swallow. Esopheograms were done and revealed an extensive stenosis.

Hunger Strike

The noneating of this 39-year-old woman, with a weight loss from 140 lbs to 82 lbs within 4 months, was officially considered a "hunger strike," a label she herself rejected. She had been arrested a year earlier for having been associated with a robbery for political reasons, and had received a long sentence. While awaiting the result of an appeal, she made every effort to stay in good health, supplemented the prison fare with high protein food, and kept strictly to an exercise program of walking. She was mentally active and worked on a political treatise.

After more than a year in jail a number of changes occurred. She had hallucinations, completely lost her appetite, then lost the will to live and decided to commit suicide by not taking any liquids. After 2 or 3 days she developed renal colic which led to transfer to the prison ward of a general hospital; her weight had already dropped to 120 lbs. Intravenous fluids were given as an emergency treatment. After 10 days she was switched to tube feeding, which she administered herself. In spite of regular tube feedings she lost weight progressively to a low of 82 lbs at the end of 4 months. She refused any food by mouth, and also refused to talk so that "nothing crossed her lips"; nor would she "take anything in from the outside" and did not read; she also refused to wash or bathe.

Throughout this time she had episodes of visual hallucinations, "representations of freedom," vivid images of beautiful landscapes, or of walking in the woods or floating in water. After several months she had also auditory hallucinations, hearing several different voices, some unpleasant and threatening. Increasingly these voices commanded her to commit suicide. This was at the time when her appeal had been rejected. One day she made several suicidal attempts, hanging herself from the bars of the bed, running her head against the wall, and finally trying to escape in the hope of being shot. She was so weak that the nurses and guard had no difficulty carrying her back to her bed. She underwent something like a religious conversion and she no longer felt that violence was the way to achieve social change. She gave up her refusal to eat or to speak. At first she forced herself to take food by mouth. As she began to gain weight her appetite returned and 6 weeks later her weight was 116 lbs.

She was cooperative in several interviews that focused on her reaction to food deprivation and bodily changes. She said she had not felt anything like hunger or appetite during this whole episode. She also had not been preoccupied with food, not even in her dreams or hallucinations. In spite of her suicidal thoughts she had become increasingly alarmed about the deterioration of her body and the sense of extreme weakness. She was not concerned about gaining weight, or about gaining too much, since she had always watched her weight. She was seen 4 months later in the penitentiary and her weight had returned to the old level of 140 lbs. She watched her diet as before, and exercised to prevent further increase. She spoke of the period of weight loss as entirely due to lack of interest in food, and repeated that there had been no preoccupation with food during the period of starvation. Though convinced that she had been given an unjust sentence, she was remarkably calm when discussing her problems and the chances of another appeal.

These examples will suffice to illustrate the manifold circumstances under which weight loss for psychological reasons may occur. Cases of this type have found their way into the anorexia nervosa literature only to becloud the issue.

Anorexia Nervosa

Description of Own Group

The 70 patients (60 females and 10 males) on which this report is based were seen over a period of nearly 30 years, from 1942 to 1971. All patients were referred for psychiatric or psychoanalytic consultation and treatment; some were in-patients on a psychiatric service. This implies that this is a selected group, representing the more difficult cases, including many in whom previous treatment efforts, usually with hospitalization, had been unsuccessful. Of the 70 patients, 44 were seen in private practice; 10 were in intensive psychotherapy or psychoanalytic treatment, and 34 were seen in consultation.

The next largest group are 22 patients hospitalized at the New York State Psychiatric Institute. Fifteen of them were in long-term therapy under my supervision, usually for 2 years but extending to 5 years in one case. The 7 others were either seen in consultation only, with someone else supervising the treatment process, or they stayed for a short period only. In addition there were 3 hospitalized patients in Houston whose long-term therapy I supervised and one ambulatory patient.

With increasing experience I found it necessary to reevaluate the theoretical concepts underlying the various psychodynamic explanations. I saw my first anorexia patient in 1942, when I was a resident at the Phipps Psychiatric Clinic of the Johns Hopkins Hospital in Baltimore. I approached her, and the few others I saw during the next 10 years, with the classic psychoanalytic orientation, expecting to find conflicts over "oral impregnation" as the key problem. Gradually the need to differentiate between different types of anorexia nervosa was recognized. The dramatic differences forced themselves into the open when patients Eric and Nathan (Chapter 15) were observed on the same service at the same time. Subsequently each case was diagnosed as either *atypical* or *primary anorexia nervosa*, the definition of which will be developed later (3). Among the 10 male patients, 6 were diagnosed as having the primary syndrome, and 4 as atypical; they will be discussed separately in Chapter 15. Among the 60 females there were 45 instances of primary anorexia nervosa, to be described in Chapter 14, and 15 atypical ones who will be described in this chapter.

The seriousness of the illness and the difficulties in treatment are of the same order of magnitude in those with the primary and those with atypical symptomatology (although 4 of the 5 who died belonged to the primary group). The duration of the illness seems to be approximately the same, with similar treatment difficulties, namely poor cooperation, impulsive breaking-off, and frequent changes of physicians and hospitals. In each group of female patients there were 2 who had been in treatment for more than 10 years, with 16 years as the longest treatment period in a woman in the atypical group. Only 8 patients were seen during the first year of illness and most of them were young, 10 to 12 years old at the time of onset. One 14-year-old boy with the primary picture died in the fourth month of his illness.

The long duration of the illness must be considered in the diagnostic evaluation because there are few conditions in which the illness itself produces so many changes, in the somatic and psychological picture as well as in the patterns of interaction within the family.

Even the accuracy of simple information about "hard facts" is affected by the passage of time. Though great efforts were made to be precise, the records did not always contain clear-cut information about as simple a fact as the "weight at onset." Sometimes the highest weight of a patient was recorded, which may or may not have been identical with the weight when the illness began. In some it was discovered in the course of therapy that before the anorexic picture developed the patient had been overweight and had maintained her weight at a reduced level over several years before the pathologic self-starvation began.

I offer some descriptive figures in Table 13–1 to give a general picture of the magnitude of the deviation. The average weight for the female patients at the time of onset was 121 lbs and 124 lbs, respectively, with a range from 70 lbs to 170 lbs in the primary, and from 95 lbs to 160 lbs in the atypical group. The lower weights in the primary group reflect the fact that it includes the younger patients. The same holds true for the male patients in the primary group, all of whom were still in prepuberty when the anorexic picture developed.

The table does not reflect the marked differences in the height of these patients. If anorexia develops in prepuberty or in early adolescence the patients are apt to be short, something the girls value but which in the long run is deeply deplored by male patients. A few patients had reached their full height when they became anorexic, (one woman of 20 was 5′9″) and a weight loss of 60 or 70 lbs may be relatively the same as 25 or 30 lbs in a young, short individual. In spite of these restrictions the weight loss in pounds and in percentage loss is rather similar for all 4 groups.

TABLE 13–1

Anorexia Nervosa

N 70

(60 females; 10 males)

	WEIGHT (IN POUNDS)			
	PRIMARY		ATYPICAL	
	FEMALE N 44*	MALE N 6	FEMALE N 15	MALE N 4
High				
Average	121	105	124	131
Range	(70–170)	(91–115)	(95–160)	(91–158)
Low				
Average	75	70	76	90
Range	(45–103)	(57–86)	(56–90)	(60–118)
Loss				
Average	45.5	35	48	41
Range	(21–77)	(29–42)	(30–85)	(31–53)
% loss	36.5	33.5	38	30
	(21–53)	(25–38)	(26–54)	(25–34)

	AGE (IN YEARS)			
	PRIMARY		ATYPICAL	
	FEMALE N 45	MALE N 6	FEMALE N 15	MALE N 4
Onset				
Average	15.9	12.5	20.3	24.5
Range	(10–26)	(12–13)	(13–28)	(13–27)
	N 39†	N 6†	N 15	N 4†
Menarche				
Average	12.6	——	12.4	(mature)
Range	(10–16)	——	(10–15)	3

* One patient not included.
† 6 female and 7 male patients were prepubertal.

Not included in the table and calculations is a 13-year-old girl who did not lose any weight but in whom the diagnosis of primary anorexia appeared indicated on the basis of the psychological constellation. She had noted at the time of her annual checkup that she had gained 12 lbs during the preceding year, in contrast to the 5 lbs she had gained in previous years. She became alarmed that this was "too much," was afraid of "eating like a pig" and of becoming "too fat." She lost a few pounds during the next few weeks, and then made every effort to maintain her weight at the same level, namely 82 lbs, for several years.

The age of onset was not always easy to establish. Atypical patients become anorexic at a later age, with an average age of 20.3 for the females and 24.5 for the males. However there is no definite cutoff point and several young patients exhibited the atypical picture. The average figure given for age of onset for females in the primary group is probably too high (15.9 years with a range from 10 to 26 years). In 3 married women with a reported onset at age 25 or 26 years there was justified suspicion of an earlier episode, for which the information was vague and inaccurate; therefore the reported age was included in the calculation. No difference was observed in the age of menarche. The oldest age for continuous menstruation was age 16 in the primary group. Most cases still in prepuberty (6 females, 6 males) were in the primary group; only one atypical boy had not undergone pubertal development.

Atypical Anorexia Nervosa

Patients with atypical anorexia nervosa and those with the genuine syndrome look deceptively alike, particularly after the condition has existed for some time. In most instances there is a recognizable time of onset of the weight loss, and concern with the eating difficulties and progressive emaciation stand in the foreground of the picture. In contrast to the genuine syndrome, where relentless pursuit of thinness and denial of even advanced cachexia as being "too thin" are key symptoms, atypical patients will complain about the weight loss, do not want to stay thin, or value it only secondarily, as a means of coercing others. Early in the picture the differential diagnosis is usually easy. Inability to eat, due to various symbolic misinterpretations of the eating function, is the leading symptom in the atypical group. Often there is the desire to stay sick in order to remain in the dependent role, in contrast to the struggle for an independent identity in the primary group.

As time goes on some of these differences may become blurred. When the condition has existed for some time patients may be reluctant to give exact information or take delight in confusing "the experts," and patients with genuine anorexia will deny their "denial of thinness." I have observed this repeatedly when patients after many years of illness finally consent to one more consultation. They will describe in a submissive, pious-sounding voice how guilty they feel for having caused their family so much unhappiness. They say they know they are too thin and they want to regain their strength so that they can lead a normal life. They will promise that they will cooperate with whatever is necessary for them to get well. Within a few days, in particular if they gain a few pounds, the whole tone will change; they are concerned about weighing "too much," want to have a voice in what the physician prescribes, and state outright: "I am happy looking like a skeleton." A few patients with long-standing disease were shifted from one group to another when more detailed and exact information became available. Assignment to the *atypical* group is

TABLE 13-2
Atypical Anorexia Nervosa

NO. NAME	SUB-GROUP	AGE AT MENARCHE	ONSET YEAR	ONSET AGE	WEIGHT HIGH	WEIGHT LOW	WEIGHT LOSS	WEIGHT %	CONSULTATION YEAR	CONSULTATION YEARS AFTER ONSET	LAST INFORMATION	YEARS AFTER ONSET OF ATYPICAL ANOREXIA NERVOSA
1. Selma	S	14	1939	19	120	80	40	30	1945	6	1954 m*	15
2. Vicki	H	14	1934	18	118	74	44	37	1948 m*	14 (relapse)	1948 m*	14
3. Flora	S	15	1953 m*	24	120	56	64	53	1953	½	1963 m*	10
4. Zelda	S	11	1955	18	123	65	58	48	1956	1	1962	7
5. Lee	S	12	1958	20	125	80	45	37	1959	1	1961	3
6. Nancy	H	n.i.†	1959	.28	120	74	46	38	1960	1	1961	2
7. Netty	S	12	1956	25	130	90	40	30	1961	5	1961	5
8. Frances	H	13	1957	14	124	87	37	30	1961	4	1963	6
9. Fanny	H	11	1960	13	115	85	30	26	1962	2	1962	2
10. Kate	H	13	1961	18	103	73	30	30	1962	1	1963	2
11. Opal	H	10	1958 m*	28	160	75	85	54	1963	5	1964 m*	6
12. Rena	S	12	1963 m*	25	140	84	56	40	1964	1	1969 m*	6
13. Dale	H	n.i.†	1966	20	160	85	75	44	1968	2	1971	5
14. Margo	H	n.i.†	1962 m*	20	95	65	30	32	1968	6	1969 m*	7
15. Lynn	D	12	1969	14	110	68	42	38	1970	1	1971	2
Average				20.3	124	76	48	38				
Range				(13–28)	(95–160)	(56–90)	(30–85)	(26–54)				

* m = married.
† n.i. = no information.
S = schizophrenic, H = hysteria, D = depression.

based on the *absence* of the *characteristic features* of the primary syndrome, namely, pursuit of thinness in the struggle for an independent identity, delusional denial of thinness, preoccupation with food, hyperactivity, and striving for perfection.

Among the 60 female patients with the diagnosis of anorexia nervosa, there were 15 (25%) who were diagnosed as exhibiting an atypical picture. The outstanding figures for the 15 atypical female patients are given in Table 13–2, arranged according to the year when they came to my attention. There are few if any differences in the descriptive data between the atypical and genuine group. The weight loss is of the same order of magnitude, 48 lbs on the average, with a range from 30 to 85 lbs, or an average loss of 38%, with a range from 26% to 54%. Age of onset in the atypical group is slightly higher, with more patients married at that time, though a few atypical patients were quite young. Amenorrhea was not present with the same regularity as in the genuine group. Both groups proved equally resistant to treatment efforts. Though the term "atypical" indicates absence of regularly recurring symptoms, certain subgroups can be recognized and I shall present my observations accordingly.

Neurotic and Hysterical Symptomatology

I shall discuss this group of patients first because they are the largest subgroup, including six with marked hysterical symptomatology and two with pronounced neurasthenic behavior. Under the influence of psychoanalytic teaching the prevalent idea has been that anorexia in girls around puberty expressed their aversion to sexuality. In 1940 Waller and his coworkers refined the concept by focusing on a specific constellation, namely the relationship of eating to the symbolization of pregnancy fantasies (9). This theory of the fear of oral impregnation was considered the cornerstone in the psychodynamics of anorexia nervosa. I approached my first anorexia patients under this orientation, and was puzzled that I observed this morbid preoccupation with sex and pregnancy only in exceptional cases. Subsequently I have come to rate patients with this preoccupation as *atypical*. In this group one will find true anorexia (that means loss of appetite as the leading complaint), though refusal to eat may also occur for fear of abdominal pain or of vomiting. Usually the loss of weight is complained of, though some may value it secondarily. Most of these patients complain of their weakness and lead the life of invalids. In some cases there is a certain blending with the problems encountered in true anorexia nervosa, because "control" is an issue for them; however this is not an effort to establish a sense of their own identity but a way of coercing others, to force them into permitting continued dependent behavior. In my presentation I have arranged the cases according to the dominance of hysterical symptomatology.

In her parents' opinion, Fanny (No. 9)* had been the "ideal" child in contrast to her older sister who, though more beautiful, had been "a disappointment" because she had wanted to go her own way. Fanny, on the other hand, had always been close to her parents and had given them the satisfaction of being "a great performer." The mother was very reluctant to give detailed information but her face lit up, radiating with pride and glory, when describing the applause and praise Fanny would receive for performing, something she had done for family gatherings since age 2. This is the point on which both parents agree, that they were proud of this daughter for being a "complete exhibitionist." Offstage she had always been quiet and somewhat shy. Though a good student she had never been popular with other children, which pleased her parents because it meant that she gave and received all affection at home. Fanny had grown and developed well, with menarche at age 11.

Following mumps at 13½ there was a complete change in her behavior. She complained of abdominal pains, suffered from muscle spasms, and lost her appetite. Her weight dropped from 112 lbs to 85 lbs and her menses stopped. After about 6 months Fanny felt too weak to attend school and didn't want any of her school friends to visit her, "How can I see people when I am in pain." She also refused a home teacher, saying that she couldn't concentrate when in such continuous pain. She complained about stiffness in her legs, walked very little, and her posture changed. When she was seen at age 15½ she offered the picture that has been described as camptocormia. The mother had noticed that when she entered her room unexpectedly Fanny might stand straight, even be dancing, but would bend over immediately when she saw her mother and complain about pain. The father felt that the relationship to the mother was too close; "The way I see you, she sings for you, you look into her eyes, she sways and sings and the pain goes away." He had felt for some time that the mother "kept it going" and compared their home to a hothouse in which weeds were growing; but in the next breath, he said he would "fight" any implication that family problems had to do with the illness.

There had been repeated hospitalizations to find the cause for her constant abdominal pain. Pancreatitis was suspected at one time but then was ruled out. Each hospitalization was terminated because the family felt frustrated in their quest for an organic explanation, and the doctors spoke of disturbing emotional factors instead. They found every physician and every psychiatrist unsatisfactory. They reported that a psychologist who had done extensive tests had found "nothing wrong." Actually the report indicated severe disturbances with the diagnosis of "narcissistic character neurosis with depressive and projective features, and marked hypochondriacal trends."

A promising therapeutic contact with visible improvement was interrupted by the parents because they felt that Fanny told things "as she saw

* (No. 9) refers to Table 13–2. All other names and numbers in this chapter also refer to Table 13–2.

them," and that she was "incorrect." In contrast to the parents' warning that she would not cooperate with a woman doctor, Fanny was rather eager to talk about her problems and went about it in a systematic way. At first she wanted to establish whether her symptoms were organic or psychological, and soon decided herself on their psychological nature because she noticed that the pain got worse when she felt emotionally upset. Then she attacked the problems in her family. While she had been sick at home she had been close witness to her sister's manipulation of two boyfriends. She condemned the sister for having involved mother in lying about whom she dated, and for not living up to Fanny's high moral standards. Then the mother became the object of her attack for being a hypocrite in relation to the sister's fiancé and the father's family. More and more she focused on the fact that what mother said and what she really felt did not coincide. In a joint session she was quite direct in accusing the mother, "Tell the truth—that isn't what you said at home," or asking directly, "Isn't that why you took me to the doctor—to find out what the trouble is?" Finally she talked about her father walking around in his undershorts, not concerned about exposing himself, and, with much hesitation and guilt, about his petting her, putting his hands into her shorts or touching her breasts. At first she was hesitant, but then quite definite, that this had preceded her illness. When she pulled away from him or complained to her mother she was reprimanded, "Don't be so cold; be affectionate toward your father." When this was discussed as unsuitable behavior toward an adolescent girl the mother was indignant, saying that it was all "innocent," and he was as much entitled to getting "father's love" from his daughter as she was getting "mother's love" from her. The father not only objected but became openly threatening; his behavior was not seductive, that it was just how it looked to Fanny; he didn't mean it this way, and neither he nor his wife felt this had anything to do with Fanny's illness. There were stereotyped protestations that all this could not possibly have anything to do with Fanny's illness, that she was just exaggerating, and that the therapist made her condition worse by believing her.

Thereafter Fanny became overcautious and felt she no longer could talk about her family. Her father criticized her for being sick and accused the therapist of "having a dirty mind." She reported the following dream: "I wanted to wear my hair long but mother persuaded me that it should be short. When I looked into the mirror I agreed with mother, that short was more becoming, but I woke up with a dreadful feeling, that this was a great tragedy." She hesitated to tell this dream; she had told it to her mother who felt it was too trivial and that she shouldn't tell it. She was relieved when the therapist agreed with her feeling about the dream, that it was a tragedy, regardless of whether the issue was big or small, that mother superimposed her opinion. Following this session the father canceled further treatment, as it was not dealing with the real problems of his daughter's illness.

The clinical diagnostic impression was that of conversion hysteria. However, the psychological tests had suggested "narcissistic character neurosis." This was in agreement with the pattern of family interaction, the style of communication between husband and wife, and of each parent with Fanny, which had many features of what has been described by Wynne and his co-workers as characteristic of families of schizophrenics (6). Three joint family conferences were recorded and their analysis revealed as the most consistent feature a nearly systematic denial or destruction of meaning.

The diagnostic problems in the next case also illustrate the difficulties of trying to classify anorexia nervosa according to the traditional psychiatric nomenclature. In both the primary and the atypical group, the clinical diagnosis in the beginning tends to be psychoneurosis, with a schizophrenic picture developing later on.

At age 14, Frances (No. 8), weighing 124 lbs, and a friend decided to go on a diet. The friend soon stopped it but Frances continued to a low of 87 lbs. Menarche had occurred at age 13, an event which disgusted her. In spite of the weight loss she did not become amenorrheic, although her menses were irregular. One motive for her wanting to lose weight was that she wanted to be thinner than her younger sister who was slender, and with whom she had always been in jealous competition. She would take all kinds of medication to make herself vomit or to have her appetite taken away so that she wouldn't eat.

Frances felt that her symptoms also had some relationship to the birth of a child to a favorite aunt. She reacted to this event with disgust and horror, and when holding the child in her arms felt like wanting to dash it to the ground. More severe symptoms developed when a girl friend of hers was discovered to be illegitimately pregnant. Frances was terrified and disgusted at the thought that her friend had had sexual relations. She often spoke with disgust of the idea of sexual intercourse and she said she hated her parents because they had performed this act in conceiving her, and she wished she had not been born.

At age 15, triggered by the disappointment of not receiving an academic prize, she became aphonic and would speak only in a whisper. The whispering continued until age 18 when she was admitted to the Psychiatric Institute. Once, while whispering, "I can't talk; I can't; I can't," a nurse stated emphatically, "Yes, you can!" to which she replied with a loud shout, "No, I can't." She then spoke, for a few days only, with a normal voice, which she disliked because, she felt, she sounded like her mother. She whispered continuously about her fears, fear of eating, fear of giving up the whispering, and fear of getting well.

Frances was the oldest of 6 children, with two brothers and three sisters, the oldest of whom was the object of lifelong jealousy and resentment. She spoke openly of her anger and envy toward her sister who was slim and sickly. Frances had always used complaints about pain and illness to stay in the center of attention. During the 4 years of her illness there had been continuous efforts at treatment on an out-patient basis, as well as repeated admissions to state hospitals, where at one time she received 20 electroshock treatments and at another time drug therapy. Efforts were also made to use hypnosis and amytal interviews. There was temporary improvement, with Frances showing an amazing ability to produce new symptoms.

At one time, at her own insistence, she went to live with her maternal grandmother some distance away. This "change of scene" did not result in improvement, and she began to limp and was admitted to an orthopedic hospital. There were no organic findings but on discharge she was on crutches, because her limp had become so disabling. While living with the grandmother she complained of severe abdominal pains, and a kidney stone was suspected. What was found was that she had inserted a pencil into her bladder, which was removed through a superpubic incision. This incident was accompanied by active sexual and aggressive fantasies.

With this long 4-year history of invalidism the situation at home had become impossible. Frances had a violent temper and kept the entire house in a state of continuous turmoil and excitement; she refused to eat, had vomiting spells, remained up all night, and refused to let her younger sister practice the piano. Even though she had once been an excellent student she had dropped out of school and had also given up her ambition of a musical career. Finally arrangements were made for long-term psychiatric hospitalization.

On admission she appeared depressed, tense, self-centered, and self-absorbed, although she was generally well-behaved, cooperative, and compliant. She was greatly preoccupied with sex and had many sexual daydreams whenever she felt unhappy or deprived of something. "I think about being sick when I feel deprived. In my daydreams the doctors always examine my genitals and I feel again as if I were getting something that had been taken away. I always receive more attention than the other patients, and this makes me satisfied because I feel spiteful towards them. In my dreams I never get well."

She blamed her mother for her problems, saying that she had refused to answer her questions about sex and childbirth, saying "It is not nice to talk about it," but then mother herself indulged in sex and had so many children. She considered herself a "hypocrite"; though religious, she would think of God in hateful terms, that He allowed such horrible things as sex to go on, particularly for the way He had arranged for people to be born. She had enormous anxieties about her abdomen, afraid it might bulge. She also wished she were completely flat-chested. She had daydreams of plunging a knife into the abdomen of a pregnant woman and pulling the baby out.

Alternating with this vision of herself as the eternal invalid child who would get attention for being sick, she had had periods of being the perfect child, excelling intellectually and artistically. In her damaged self-image there were only two alternatives: to be a sick, crippled, and helpless child extorting irate attention from her parents, or to be an overcontrolled good girl who completely denied her genuine feelings and worked hard to fulfill the ambitions of her father.

The diagnostic impression was that of schizophrenia, in spite of the prominent hysterical features. Schizophrenia was suggested by the degree of her personal confusion, the almost constant state of anxiety and anger, the multitude of often changing, neurotic symptoms with obsessive, phobic and hysterical features, and evidence of reality distortion, including probably auditory hallucinations.

This patient remained in the hospital for 2 years, and the treatment was a combination of medication, in particular Thorazine, occupational therapy, school attendance, use of the hospital milieu, and intensive psychotherapy. The intrinsic difficulty was that this patient had, throughout her life, used illness to maintain her position in the family and had felt "the need to be sick." Initially there was rapid improvement and the more visible symptoms dropped out. However, psychotherapeutic progress was retarded by many relapses into various symptomatic behavior whenever upsetting topics were touched on. Frances made significant strides toward maturity and self-reliance, and was free of symptoms during lengthy visits to her home. She felt more ready than ever to attempt to live there and left in the hope that she would function more maturely.

A clinician who had seen only these two girls would undoubtedly have concluded that the anorexic picture developed when confronted with sexual issues. But it would have been an error to generalize from these two instances to all cases. These are the only two girls out of 70 cases with this degree of sexual preoccupation. There are a few others in whom hysterical mechanisms play a role, though involvement with the reproductive function does not appear to be a central issue. More often a coercive factor stands in the foreground—the need to be sick and thereby get attention.

The remaining six patients in this group were considerably older when they became anorexic. Kate (No. 10) was 19 years old when she lost 30 lbs during her first term in college. When she was 14 years old her mother underwent life-threatening surgery. From then on Kate had been unable to eat, "unless she could observe the exact amount mother ate," without anybody noticing it. At college she lost weight rapidly because "I did not know what mother ate." Subsequently many other phobic symptoms became manifest.

Dale (No. 13), a 20-year-old college student, became infatuated with her family physician who had suggested and then supervised a reducing regimen. She reduced from 160 to 110 lbs, was praised for it, and then discharged. When she consulted the physician again, he reassured her about her weight and she felt rejected. Then she became afraid to eat, and her weight dropped to 85 lbs. Later, when in psychiatric treatment, she repeated the pattern of immediate infatuation, going to great lengths to force her attention on her therapist and his family. There was great preoccupation with being "in control," not as a step toward independence but in an effort to coerce her physicians into permitting clinging dependent behavior.

Margo (No. 14) and Opal (No. 11) were 26 and 32 years old respectively. They were competent in their professional fields and both were married. Both used weight loss, even to dangerously low levels, to attract attention or force issues in relation to their husbands. The noneating and weight loss were merely accidental symptoms in life patterns pervaded by hysterical reactions; they were valued for their coercive effects.

Two other patients, Nancy (No. 6) and Vickie (No. 2), were 29 and 32 years old when they were admitted with severe weight loss. Nancy, after witnessing her sister-in-law's miscarriage, was frightened by the amount of blood and became obsessed with the smell of it. First she could not eat meat because it smelled of blood; then all food smelled of it. After losing 20 lbs she felt so weak that she took to a wheelchair, and with further loss she demanded bed care. In Vickie's case it was fear of intense abdominal pain, "like a tight band around my waist," that kept her from eating.

Schizoid Reaction

The patients in this group are more disturbed in their sense of reality and misinterpret the whole eating function. They often have delusional fear of vomiting or refuse food because they feel unworthy. Characteristically they are apathetic and indolent, and show no signs of hyperactivity or perfectionistic strivings. They are usually indifferent toward their emaciation and none expresses pride in it.

A vivid description of a schizophrenic's fear of eating is given in the *Autobiography of a Schizophrenic Girl* (7).

I was, however, eating little; the System's orders forbade me to eat. . . . Nor could I truly say I wasn't hungry; on the contrary, I was starved, but the System would not allow me to satisfy the hunger. . . . I had a dreadful fear of my hands and the conviction that I would be changed into a famished cat, prowling in cemeteries, forced to devour the remains of decomposing cadavers. . . . Mocking voices sneered at me, "Ah, ah, wretched creature, eat, eat, only eat, do eat." They kept urging me to eat, knowing it was forbidden and that I would be severely punished if I acceded to their promptings.

The patients included in this section appear less overtly schizophrenic, but their fear of eating for irrational reasons seems to be just as terrifying. Selma (No. 1) was referred for therapy when she was 25 years old because she was confused, chronically depressed, and unable to make a career decision. Five years earlier, in 1939, while a refugee in France, she had suffered an episode which had been diagnosed as anorexia nervosa and which was so severe that she was permitted to enter a nursing home while her parents were put into an internment camp. She had previously been a student nurse but it was noted that she was unusually untidy and she was rated unsuitable. She refused to eat because she was "not worthy," having failed in her effort "to serve people." A physician took her to live in his own home but she would not eat because "I do not deserve it." She did not want to stay in the house but wanted to crawl into the doghouse out of a sense of humility and unworthiness. Finally she was placed in a nursing home where she received Metrazol shock treatment and made a recovery. At 25, she was tall and gaunt looking, and was delusionally preoccupied with her appearance.

Similarly, Nettie (No. 7) refused to eat because she felt unworthy, when at age 25 she was in love with a man who did not care for her. She had been exceptionally effective as a secretary, but was always very stubborn and rather quiet. Gradually she withdrew from all activities, with progressive weight loss. There were repeated admissions to psychiatric hospitals where she responded to electroshock treatment which increased appetite; but each time she gradually would lose the weight she had gained. At age 30 she led the indolent life of a schizophrenic.

Zelda (No. 4) was hospitalized at age 18 because she was continuously preoccupied with food, had peculiar scruples about religion and sin, and felt paralyzed in doing anything. She had been quite popular in high school and was class president, but she was continuously preoccupied with the fear of losing her friends. She began to have peculiar thoughts about food and her digestion. She also felt that what she ate would affect others; if she did not eat, others would not eat. Increasingly she became preoccupied with her sins and fear of punishment. It was her parish priest who referred her for psychiatric treatment. On admission she was quite depressed and suspicious. She lost some more weight but then accepted nourishment and her weight went up. She was readmitted when she was 25 years old, having become increasingly obsessed with delusions about her digestion. Five years earlier she had been obsessed with germs, fire, electricity, and mortal sin, now she was concerned with the influence of thoughts on her digestion. She had maintained her weight at around 100 lbs, but it had dropped to 82 lbs during the 6 months preceding readmission.

Flora (No. 3) was 19 when she was caught in a subway train which had broken down between two stations. She felt nauseated and was afraid she might vomit. From then on she avoided eating for fear of vomiting; at first only when she was about to go out; then she developed fear of traveling and of eating in general. At that time she was in conflict with her parents about wanting to marry a young man of whom they disapproved. She did marry him at age 21, weighing approximately 100 lbs. Following the birth of a child, two years later, she became increasingly withdrawn, would not go out on the street, felt unable to do the housework and just sat around wanting to be left alone. She ate less and less and became eccentric about saving money and food and would react with jealous anger when her husband ate. Her weight dropped progressively, to a low of 56 lbs. She appeared apathetic and was underactive, and Simmonds disease was suspected but ruled out by extensive laboratory examinations. When hospitalized she responded well to special nursing and feeding of very small portions of high caloric food which she ate readily.

Rena (No. 12) came for treatment when 26 years old. She had suffered a severe loss of weight since the birth of her only child, a 4-year-old girl. She was of foreign background and had met her husband on an American Army base. She had married against her parents' wishes. It was not clear whether the weight loss began immediately after the birth of her child, or after she had taken the child to her home country to show her mother. The weight loss was progressive, from 140 lbs (5'8") to a low of 84 lbs over a 3-year period. Though she acknowledged she was "too thin" she was rigidly determined that her weight should not exceed 90 lbs. This was to her the only way to be sure not to become pregnant again. Actually the chance of it was nil because since her visit home she did not even want her husband to touch her, though she emphasized that they were deeply in love. There were increasing paranoic features, with concern about secret messages she received from her mother. She consulted a gynecologist who introduced an intrauterine device without any effect on her attitude. Nine years after the birth of her only child she still focused on fear of pregnancy as the reason for staying thin.

Lee (No. 5) was a 21-year-old college student when one of her professors noted a change in her behavior, peculiarities in her style of writing, increasing inattention, and advised her to see a psychiatrist. Instead she just stayed home, ate less and less, and finally did not leave her bed. Her mother had died when she was quite young, and she had moved from one foster home to another. Now she lived with her father but felt uncomfortable with him. She complained that he had not "welcomed her properly" when she came back from a summer vacation. When she came to the hospital she had lost 45 lbs, looked emaciated, and was weak. There was nothing conspicuous about her attitude toward eating and she regained weight steadily, back to the previous level of 125 lbs. She also responded well to psychotherapy and was able to free herself of her hateful dependence on her father.

I have given a brief sketch of each patient to illustrate the wide variety of precipitating events and personality features. If there is anything the patients have in common it is a severe sense of inadequacy and discontent with their lives. Eating difficulties develop when reality demands become overpowering and their fragile sense of self is further undermined.

Adolescent Depression

Depressive feelings are common in anorexia nervosa, particularly if the condition has existed for a long time. There was only one patient where indications of a serious depression went back to early childhood. Anthony recently described adolescent depression as evolving out of the development phases of childhood, rather than those of adolescence itself, although they may be overlapping (1). He described how well-defined clinical depression may develop in those who enter the adolescent stage already sensitized to depressive reaction. One of his patients, oversensitive to fear of rejection, separation, and loss of love, suffered a severe weight loss, from 123 lbs to 55 lbs, in association with a depression. Similarly, the patient, whose history follows, had experienced repeated separations and had felt unable to live up to what was expected of her. The anorexic episode represented a short interlude in this depressive reaction, and had the earmarks of being an attempt at making herself feel better.

Lynn was 14 years old when she suffered a severe weight loss (from 110 lbs to 68 lbs) for which she was hospitalized. She seemed to make a recovery but was readmitted following a suicide attempt. She struck a cheerful note and only gradually admitted to having been severely depressed for the past several years, unable to cope with angry and jealous feelings. She was the first of 3 daughters, born two years apart, to achievement-oriented and psychology-conscious parents. This family was plagued by illnesses of unusual nature, requiring repeated hospitalizations, each of them having at one time or another a life-threatening disease. Lynn responded to the repeated hospitalizations of her parents, which occurred from her early life on, by becoming quiet and withdrawn, and to some extent imitated their symptoms. When her father had an operation on his vocal cords and had to be "mute" for six weeks, Lynn, too, stopped talking, and when her mother became concerned about going blind, on account of a premature cataract, Lynn developed blurred vision. When she was 8 both parents developed serious, potentially fatal diseases, requiring repeated hospitalizations. Though the children were told about the parents' will and to whom they would go in case of their death, there was an atmosphere of secrecy about all this illness.

Despite all this Lynn did quite well in school and was popular in a superficial way. She would spend much time daydreaming on how to escape responsibilities. Menarche occurred at $12\frac{1}{2}$ and she would become depressed with every period. When Lynn was 13 years old her mother nearly died from a hemorrhage following a biopsy. After this it became apparent that Lynn had become "indifferent," would often cry and feel guilty because she did not love her parents. She felt progressively uneasy and worried about their possible death.

This family had been unusually diet conscious, but no one ever seemed to lose weight. When Lynn was 14 years old she noticed suddenly that she was developing a pot belly, "almost like I was pregnant." Her weight was 110 lbs at that time, appropriate for her height, but she decided to lose weight. She was exhilarated when she lost 5 lbs during the first month and decided to continue. She became more and more isolated and also had trouble sleeping. Although the family argued with her, she stuck to her restricted diet and 6 months later her weight was down to 68 lbs. At that time she was hospitalized, and met some other patients with anorexia nervosa. Within 3 months she regained her appetite and her weight rose to 88 lbs. She was discharged and returned to her school, but did not enjoy life and felt increasingly "pressured." Now instead of starving she gorged herself, "enjoying the sensation of food going down my throat." One day, after stuffing herself with food, she took pills from her mother's cabinet in a suicide attempt. After readmission to the hospital there were several stormy family sessions where Lynn displayed hostile emotions toward both parents for the first time in her life. She expressed despair about "not being in touch with her feelings." She had always known that there was something wrong, because she could not let herself go and never had gotten angry.

A depressive tone is frequently encountered in anorexic nervosa. In Lynn's case hints of depressive reaction can be traced to episodes early in her life that appear to be related to the repeated experiences of separation. Depression and social withdrawal had preceded the onset of anorexic behavior. During the anorexic phase she was compulsively preoccupied with being thin but gave this up soon after hospitalization. Missing are defiant pride in being thin (so characteristic of primary anorexia nervosa) and hyperactivity and perfectionism. Her good school performance was an effort to please her parents, not an urgent desire for her own accomplishment.

BIBLIOGRAPHY

1. Anthony, E. J., Two contrasting types of adolescent depression and their treatment, J. Amer. Psychoanal. Ass., 18:841–859, 1970.
2. Bliss, E. L., and Branch, C. H. H., *Anorexia Nervosa—Its History, Psychology, and Biology*, Paul B. Hoeber, Inc., New York, 1960.
3. Bruch, H., Anorexia nervosa and its differential diagnosis, J. Nerv. Ment. Dis., 141: 555–566, 1966.
4. Clauser, G., Das Anorexia-nervosa-Problem unter besonderer Beruecksichtigung der Pubertaetsmagersucht und ihrer klinischen Bedeutung, Ergebn. inn. Med. Kinderheilk., 21:97–164, 1964.
5. Dally, P., *Anorexia Nervosa*, Grune and Stratton, New York, 1969.
6. Schaffer, L., Wynne, L. C., Day, J., Ryckoff, I. M., and Halperin, A., On the nature and sources of the psychiatrists' experience with the family of the schizophrenic, Psychiatry, 25:32–45, 1962.

7. Sechehaye, M., *Autobiography of a Schizophrenic Girl*, Grune and Stratton, New York, 1951.
8. Theander, S., *Anorexia Nervosa. A Psychiatric Investigation of 94 Female Patients*, Acta Psychiat. Scand., suppl. 214, Munsgaard, Copenhagen, 1970.
9. Waller, J. V., Kaufman, R., and Deutsch, F., Anorexia nervosa: A psychosomatic entity, Psychosom. Med., 2:3–16, 1940.

14

Primary Anorexia Nervosa

In his essays on *Spain*, Kazantzakis reports his encounter with a young Spaniard (12).

> "That's Manola," my Spanish friend laughed as he told me. "All day long he lies there stretched out in the sun. He doesn't want to work, even if it means he has to die of hunger."
>
> I went up to him.
>
> "Ah, Manola," I called to him. "They tell me you're hungry. Why don't you get up and work? Aren't you ashamed of yourself?"
>
> Manola stirred sluggishly, then raised his hand with kinglike grandeur: "En la hambre mando yo," he answered me. "In hunger I am King!"
>
> As though hunger were some boundless kingdom, and so long as Manola remained hungry, he kept the scepter of his kingdom in his own hands.

This line, "In hunger I am King," expresses the essence of the inner problem in genuine anorexia nervosa. Like Manola, the anorexics struggle against feeling enslaved, exploited, and not being permitted to lead a life of their own. They would rather starve than continue a life of accommodation. In this blind search for a sense of identity and selfhood they will not accept anything that their parents, or the world around them, has to offer. Just as Manola's hunger failed to solve the social and economic problems of his country, so will the anorexic fail to achieve his goal of becoming a respected member of his group, capable of mature interdependent relationships, through his angry isolation and food refusal.

This view of anorexia nervosa as a desperate struggle for a self-respecting identity developed gradually from contact with many patients. It was formulated through the effort to identify the psychological issues and adaptive patterns at the crucial period in an anorexic's life when the refusal to eat began. While reevaluating the traditional theoretical concepts and psychodynamic explanations I compared details of my own observations with reports in the psychoanalytic and psychosomatic literature and could confirm every interpretation, though they were often contradictory, that had been considered as of specific psychodynamic significance by various writers. Gradually I recognized that the multiple psychological data and clinical symptoms needed to be understood on a level different from the traditional motivational conflicts, namely as manifestations of disturbances in the perceptual and conceptual field, and that there was need to differentiate between different forms of anorexia nervosa (3, 4).

Defining the underlying basic disturbances in psychiatric terms, with focus on the core dynamic issues, revealed that the noneating and associated weight loss were late features, secondary to underlying personality disturbances. Most patients had functioned so smoothly as children that no attention was paid to their problems and they were seen only after the secondary symptoms, the severe emaciation, had developed. Traditionally, the order has been reversed: anorexia nervosa is defined in somatic terms, as emaciation due to abstinence from food, amenorrhea, constipation, etc., and whatever psychiatric problems a particular patient exhibits is then considered "characteristic" for anorexia nervosa. For a dynamic understanding it is essential to isolate the focal points of disturbed patterns of functioning, to recognize the crucial problems, and to assess the patient's tools for dealing with them. Such an evaluation implies a clearcut distinction between the dynamic issues of the developmental impasse which had resulted in anorexia nervosa, and the secondary, even tertiary problems, symptoms, and complications that develop in its wake.

Most patients who came to my attention had been sick for a considerable period of time. It is necessary to reconstruct the behavior and problems of the patient and the patterns of family interaction and concern *before* the illness became manifest. This was done with the aid of the reports from previous physicians, psychiatrists, hospitals, schools and summer camps, and through the results of former psychological tests. Most of all, we worked with the families and the ongoing patterns of interaction gave clues to the developmental deficits.

Through these elaborate reevaluations it became apparent that *two* distinct types needed to be separated. In the larger group, which I shall refer to as *genuine* or *primary anorexia nervosa*, the main issue is a struggle for control, for a sense of identity, competence, and effectiveness. Many of these youngsters had struggled for years to make themselves over, and to be "perfect" in the eyes of others. Concern with thinness and food refusal are late steps in this maldevelopment. In the *atypical* group, no general picture can be drawn, as was discussed in Chapter 13. The concern is with the distorted experiences of the eating function itself; the loss of weight is incidental to this. These patients will continue to be confused with true anorexia nervosa because the severe emaciation and the superimposed conflicts and concerns make them look deceptively alike by the time they come to psychiatric attention.

In contrast to the various problems encountered in the atypical group the true syndrome is amazingly uniform. Three areas of disordered psychological functions can be recognized. The *first* outstanding symptom is a *disturbance of delusional proportions in the body image and body con-*

cept. Cachexia may occur to the same pitiful degree in other patients. Of pathognomic significance for true anorexia nervosa is the absence of concern, the vigor and stubbornness with which the often gruesome emaciation is defended as normal and right, and as the only possible security against the dreaded fate of being fat. The true anorexic is identified with his skeleton-like appearance, denies its abnormality, and actively maintains it, in contrast to the atypical anorexic who deplores the weight loss but feels helpless to change it.

As was discussed in the chapter on Body Image, recognition of this disturbance is important for differential diagnosis and for appraising treatment progress. Anorexic patients may gain weight for many reasons, or they may seem to make progress in psychotherapy. Without a corrective change in their body concept, improvement is apt to be only temporary.

The *second* outstanding characteristic is a *disturbance in the accuracy of the perception or cognitive interpretation* of stimuli arising in the body, with failure to recognize signs of nutritional need as the most pronounced deficiency. The disturbance is more akin to inability to recognize hunger than to a mere loss of appetite. The developmental background of this disturbance has been discussed in the chapter on Hunger Awareness.

Anorexic patients are apt to be defensive and uncommunicative on this topic, and it is difficult to give an exact delineation of this conceptual disturbance, because evidence for it depends on self-reporting. Awareness of hunger and appetite in the ordinary sense seems to be absent, and a patient's sullen statement, "I do not need to eat," probably expresses what he feels and experiences most of the time. Usually there is denial and nonrecognition of hunger pains, even in the presence of stomach contractions. On the other hand, there are endless complaints about acute discomfort and fullness after the intake of even small amounts of food.

There has been endless discussion in the literature about whether these patients are truly "anorexic," meaning without desire for food, or whether they "repress" their hunger sensation or obstinately fail to act on it, though they may be tormented by their need and haunted by the thought of food. The crux of the matter is that very little is known about hunger and hunger awareness and about how normal people know why they eat what they eat. I have learned to listen and to accept as literal what such patients say about their bodily sensations. Detailed information may not be forthcoming until considerable therapeutic progress has been made when there is greater trust in the therapist, and also when the patient has become capable of identifying bodily sensations more distinctly. Frequently, the first discovery may not be in the nutritional area but in some other sensory perception. Patients will describe in retrospect how confused they had been about this disturbance in the awareness of their bodily sensations.

The outstanding clinical symptom is the curtailment of the caloric intake. However, much more is involved. There is not only a rigid restriction of the amount of food, but the whole eating pattern is disorganized—food preferences, tastes, eating habits, and manners. Details of bizarre and outlandish practices will be discussed in the cases of a few patients. In the analysis of various facets, those relating to the organistic disorganization must be differentiated from the secondary interpersonal and social reactions, such as the pretense of eating a meal, provocative lying, secrecy, stealing, and hiding of food.

The nutritional disorganization has two phases, absence or denial of desire for food and uncontrollable impulses to gorge oneself, usually without awareness of hunger, and often followed by self-induced vomiting. Patients identify with the noneating phase, defending it as a realistic expression of their physiological need. In contrast, they experience overeating as a submission to some compulsion to do something they do *not* want to do and they are terrified by the loss of control during such eating binges. Patients express this as "I do not dare to eat. If I take just one bite I am afraid that I will not be able to stop." This occurred in about 25% of the cases with primary anorexia nervosa. No patient in the atypical group reported such episodes of bulimia.

In advanced stages of emaciation true loss of appetite may result from the severe nutritional deficiency, similar to the complete lack of interest in food in the late stages of starvation during a famine. This indifference to food must be differentiated from the spirited way in which the anorexic defends her noneating before the stage of extreme marasmus has been reached.

In the battle against fatness and in an effort to remove unwanted food from the body, many patients resort to self-induced vomiting, enemas, the excessive use of laxatives, or of diuretics which may result in serious disturbances in the electrolyte balance. Although the urgent need for keeping the body weight low is given as the motive, other aspects must be considered—namely, that here, too, disturbances in the cognitive awareness of bodily sensations play a role.

Another characteristic manifestation of falsified awareness of a bodily state is *hyperactivity* and *denial of fatigue*, which impressed the early writers but which has scarcely been mentioned in the recent psychoanalytic reports. It has often been claimed that the actual amount of exercise may not be great but only seems remarkable in view of the severe undernutrition. Through pedometric measurements Stunkard and his co-workers could demonstrate that anorexic patients were indeed hyperactive, walking an average of 6.8 miles per day despite their emaciation, while women of normal weight walked an average of 4.0 miles (2). Patients who continue in school will spend long hours on their homework, intent on having perfect grades.

Drive for activity continues until the emaciation is far advanced. The subjective feeling of not being tired and of wanting to do things stands in marked contrast to the lassitude, fatigue, and avoidance of any effort that is symptomatic for undernutrition in chronic food deprivation, and is regularly complained of by patients in the atypical group. This paradoxical sense of alertness must also be considered an expression of conceptual and perceptual disturbances in body awareness.

One might also consider the failure of sexual functioning and the absence of sexual feelings as falling within this area of perceptual and conceptual deficiency. Such disturbances precede the starvation phase and often continue after nutritional restitution. While still menstruating many had no cramps or other warning symptom of the approaching periods, which usually were irregular. They were often embarrassed by unexpected bleeding—one more reason for their often expressed disgust with this function.

Other bodily sensations are also not correctly recognized or responded to. I have been impressed with how often these skinny girls seem to be completely indifferent to changes in temperature. They might come to the office without coat or stockings in the midst of winter, blue with cold but denying feeling cold. We have become so habituated to give motivational interpretation to behavior of this type that it is often referred to as "self punishment." What has been overlooked is the fact that such patients experience their bodily sensations in a way that is bewildering and foreign to them, something they will not or cannot describe unless specifically encouraged. There are also marked deficiencies in identifying emotional states. The limited range of these patient's descriptions of anxiety and other feelings and emotional responses, and the fact that even severe depressive reactions remain masked for a long time, can be discussed from this point of view. When Eric (Chapter 15), aged 20, started to work he was asked about his experiences after his first day on the job. He gave many vivid details, in particular how he had managed the lunch period. When asked whether he had been anxious he denied this vigorously, but then added: "Why is my face so red and why are my hands so wet?" He seemed unable to identify the feelings associated with the physiological correlates of anxiety.

The *third* outstanding feature is a *paralyzing sense of ineffectiveness*, which pervades all thinking and activities of anorexic patients. They experience themselves as acting only *in response* to demands coming from other people in situations, and not as doing things because *they want to*. While the first two features are readily recognized, the third defect is camouflaged by the enormous negativism and stubborn defiance with which these patients operate, and which makes personal contact so difficult. The indiscriminate nature of rejection reveals it as a desperate cover-up for an undifferentiated sense of helplessness, a generalized parallel to the fear of eating one bite lest control be lost completely.

The paramount importance of this third characteristic was recognized in the course of extended psychotherapy. Once defined, it could be readily identified early in treatment. If the therapist communicates his awareness of the patient's sense of helplessness without insult to the patient's fragile self-esteem, meaningful therapeutic involvement becomes possible, avoiding the exhausting power struggle or futile efforts at persuasion that so often characterize treatment of these patients (Chapter 17).

The discovery of this deep-seated sense of ineffectiveness was surprising and seemed to stand in contrast to the vigorous behavior of these patients and the reports of normal early development which, according to initial reports of the parents, appeared to have been free of difficulties and problems to an unusual degree. The patients were described as having been outstandingly good and quiet children, obedient, clean, eager to please, helpful at home, precociously dependable, and excelling in school work. They were the pride and joy of their parents and great things were expected of them. The need for self-reliant independence, which confronts every adolescent, seemed to cause an insoluble conflict, after a childhood of robot-like obedience. They lack awareness of their own resources and do not rely on their feelings, thoughts, and bodily sensations. This deficit in initiative and autonomy that underlies the obstinate facade will be recognized readily if looked for. It has always been puzzling that this serious illness is usually precipitated by commonplace events or trivial remarks. Once this lack of autonomy has been defined, detailed histories will reveal subtle earlier indications of the deficits in autonomy and in initiative. The characteristic patterns of family interactions that result in such a lack of autonomy, have been described in Chapters 4 and 5; individual vignettes will be added in this chapter.

Precipitating Events

The group of primary anorexia nervosa is comprised of 45 girls and young women who have become sick between the ages of 10 and 26 years; they will be discussed here (see Table 14–1). The 6 male patients with primary anorexia nervosa will be described in the following chapter. Most gave a fairly definite time of onset and also recalled the event that had made them feel "too fat," and convinced them of the urgent need to lose weight. This decision did not initially appear to be different from that of countless adolescents who watch their weight in our slimness-conscious society. The question which arises is, are there symptoms that should help one to recognize the dieting youngster who is potentially in danger of progressing to this severe state? Little is known about this; by the time these youngsters come to psychiatric attention a severe weight loss has occurred and the illness has persisted for at least 6 months and usually longer, often for many years.

Most of these diets are started without medical supervision and physicians, too, do not see such youngsters until a good deal of weight has been lost. The exceptional patient who consults a doctor will stick religiously to the diet, but eating less than what has been prescribed. The

TABLE 14-1

Primary Anorexia Nervosa in Forty-five Female Patients

NO.	NAME	AGE AT MENARCHE	ONSET		WEIGHT		LOSS		CONSULTATION		LAST INFORMATION		YEARS AFTER ONSET OF PRIMARY ANOREXIA NERVOSA
			YEAR	AGE	HIGH	LOW	LBS	%	YEAR	YEARS AFTER ONSET			
1.	Fay	13	1942	19	140	83	57	40	1943	1	1946	Psychiatric hospital	4
2.	Rhea	10.6	1942	12	125	75	50	40	1943	1	1945	Psychiatric agency	3
x3.	Beth	12	1948	14	120	80	40	33	1949	1	1952	Restricted	4
x4.	Nora	14	1949	16	140	72	68	48	1954	5	1954	Died (after pregnancy)	5
5.	Elva	14	1954	19	175	98	77	44	1956	2	1962	Accidental death	8
6.	Neva	No	1950	11	110	68	42	38	1956	6		n. i.*	6
7.	Edna	12	1956	13½	118	73	45	38	1957	1	1971	Recovered	16
x8.	Toni	13	1954	16	135	74	61	46	1958	4	1971	Recovered	17
9.	Cynthia	13	1952	14	95	55	40	42	1958	6	1971	Recovered, m*, twins	19
x10.	Gail	12	1953	14	140	96	76	45	1960	7	1970	Obese	17
11.	Marcia	10	1959	11½	103	61	42	41	1960	1½	1962	State hospital	3
x12.	Celia	15	1959	19	120	95	25	21	1960	1	1970	Recovered	11
x13.	Sharon	14	1961	16	138	103	35	21	1961	½	1970	Restricted	9
14.	Sheila	12	1959	17	115	85	30	26	1961	2		n. i.*	2
15.	Mary	12	1960	14½	125	77	48	38	1961	1	1971	Recovered	11
x16.	Rachel	14½	1958	14½	112	64	48	43	1961	3	1963	Psychiatric hospital	5
17.	Kay	12	1960	18	112	70	42	37	1961	1		n. i.*	1
18.	Emma	12	1952	15	120	90	30	25	1962	9	1962	Not recovered	10
x19.	Christine	13	1962	18	120	74	46	39	1963	1½	1970	Recovered, m*	8
20.	Cindy	12	1962	15	130	88	42	35	1963	1½		n.i.*	1½
21.	Donna	12	1960	15	145	90	55	38	1963	2½	1964	Restricted	4
x22.	Fern	12	1962	14	108	80	28	25	1963	1	1971	Recovered, m*	9
23.	Sherry	14	1951	14	n.i.							1966 Restricted	14
			1962	25 m*	130	90	40	30	1963	1			

TABLE XIV—continued

Primary Anorexia Nervosa in Forty-five Female Patients

NO.	NAME	AGE AT MENARCHE	ONSET		WEIGHT		LOSS		CONSULTATION		LAST INFORMATION		YEARS AFTER ONSET OF PRIMARY ANOREXIA NERVOSA
			YEAR	AGE	HIGH	LOW	LBS	%	YEAR	YEARS AFTER ONSET			
24.	Hazel	13	1958	15	n.i.	65	30	31	1963	1	1971	Restricted	13
x25.	Naomi (twin)	15	1954	18	95	90	25	21	1963	9	1970	Recovered, m*	16
x26.	Dora	No	1960	11	115	45	50	50	1964	4	1964	Died	4
27.	Yvette	No	1963	12	117	77	40	34	1964	4	1970	Recovered, m*	7
28.	Elsa	10	1964	10	96	58	38	40	1964	½	1965	Anorexic	1
29.	Doris	13	1963	22	128	74	54	42	1964	1	1968	Restricted	5
x30.	Karla	14	1963	15	115	75	40	35	1964	1	1968	Restricted	5
x31.	Karen	16	1963	16	116	74	42	36	1965	1	1971	Restricted	8
x32.	Karol	11	1961	17½	120	65	55	46	1966	5	1967	Restricted	6
x33.	Felice (twin)	13	1956	18	115	65	50	43	1967	11	1971	Recovered, m*	15
34.	Betsy	n.i.*	1962	25 m*	100	65	35	35	1967	5	n.i.*	Restricted	5
35.	Toby	12	1965	15	140	107	33	23	1968	3	1970	Restricted, m*	5
x36.	Thelma	12	1967	14	110	57	53	48	1968	½	1970	Died	3
37.	Barbara	12	1965	18	160	90	70	44	1969	4	1970	Schizophrenic anorexic	5
x38.	Claire	No	1968	12½	84	82	—	—	1969	1½	1971	Recovered	3
39.	Juanita	No	1969	12	98	71	27	27	1969	½	1971	Recovered	2
40.	Freda	14	1960	18	n.i.	76	42	33	1970	3	1971	Recovered	11
41.	Olga	No	1969	26 m*	118	49	21	30	1970	½	1971	Anorexic	2
42.	Virginia	12	1970	12	70	82	83	40	1970	½	1971	Recovered	1
43.	Delores	15	1966	12½	135	58	67	53	1970	4	1971	In treatment	5
44.	Norma	13	1969	18	118	70	48	40	1970	1	1971	Anorexic	2
x45.	Mona	13	1966	17	125	67	58	46	1971	5	1971	Anorexic	5

* m = married.   n.i. = no information.   x = Patient is referred to in Chapter 14.

grim determination with which they pursue the task sets them apart from the ordinary plump adolescent on a diet. The potentially anorexic will insist that they do not need to eat, that they are not hungry. They consider not wanting to eat normal and fight to maintain it. In contrast, the ordinary dieter is aware that he makes a sacrifice, and he tolerates the hardship and suffering only by exercising his will power. Most people who become anorexic and lose weight will go to a doctor to find out what is wrong. Loss of appetite is considered abnormal and reason for concern. In contrast to the truism, "One has to eat to live," the anorexic declares, "I do not need to eat and why should I eat if I don't want to?"

Probably the most important signal of something wrong is that dieting which is explicitly undertaken with the intent of becoming more attractive and more respected does not lead to better relationships as the weight drops, but results in increasing social withdrawal and often extreme isolation. Conversely, if the weight is regained and there is no improvement in social relations, it is apt to be a false cure. The anorexics' very appearance announces their loneliness. Giacometti's strange, emaciated sculptured figures are invariably interpreted as expressing remoteness and isolation.

Since anorexic patients uniformly say they restricted their food because they were "too fat," it has often been assumed that anorexia nervosa is preceded by obesity. This holds true only for a fraction of them. Among these 45 patients there were 6 whose weight was 140 lbs or above at the time of onset; the highest weight was 170 lbs for a 19-year-old girl who was 5'9" tall. This is far below the weights observed in the patients described in the chapter on adolescent obesity (Chapter 9). About a third were slightly plump. The lowest weight at onset was 70 lbs in a 12-year-old girl who was only 4'5" tall but who looked quite plump having received cortisone for uveitis and iritis. In most the weight was quite normal for the filling out phase of adolesecnce. It, however, drew comments about their having curves or being chunky. Quite a few were on the thin side when they began this crazy dieting, but they felt they weighed "too much," or that they were gaining too rapidly.

Frequently the onset of this drastic dieting occurred when confronted with new experiences such as going to camp or entering a new school or going to college. In this new situation they felt embarrassed about being "chubby," or not athletic enough or otherwise at a disadvantage, and they were afraid of not being able to make new friends. Some were downright unhappy and depressed without the familiar supports; others disliked the new food, etc., and the first loss of weight might have been accidental. When they got praise and admiration for this, they began to enjoy being slimmer and then decided to continue to lose weight to earn even more respect, or to be on the safe side. In others the decision to reduce is attributed to some derogatory comment about their figure, not different from the teasing other adolescents undergo during this phase of rapid development. It is only during intensive psychotherapy that the manifold meanings of this fear of being "too fat" become clarified, when the relationship to underlying personality problems is understood, with excessive vulnerability to any criticism that makes them experience teasing comments as an insult to their self-esteem, as proving that they do not deserve respect.

I shall give a few examples to illustrate that this seemingly sudden dieting is not quite as sudden or as simple a reaction as the first information would suggest. In Chapter 5 I briefly mentioned Sharon (No. 13)* whose attitude toward fatness had been determined by the fact that she had an overweight older sister. She was 16½ years of age when she began to reduce and very soon developed a regimen of rigid food refusal alternating with eating binges and vomiting. Sharon had been considered happy and well-adjusted and it came as an utter surprise to her family that she should have difficulties since she had always been considered the "best balanced" child and "all around" girl.

Sharon had spent the preceding year abroad at a boarding school. The food there was much more starchy than in her home and it was not surprising that she gained some weight. She came back resolved to lose this excess weight, but instead she found herself eating too much, and her weight rose to about 138 lbs. The determination to do something about her weight was precipitated by the shock of seeing a snapshot of herself in slacks, taken from behind, while she was bending over. This convinced her that she looked despicable. She decided to cut her eating down to a minimum but was troubled and upset over her inability to stick to a diet, and even more, by finding herself eating so much that afterward she felt heavy, bloated, uncomfortable after an eating binge, and "became sick." She was as tormented by the need to eat as by the fear of getting fat.

As she talked about her problems it became apparent that the concern with weight had not begun suddenly. She had been preoccupied with the fear of eating too much and becoming fat since she was 10 years old. Since the whole household was diet conscious, it was fairly easy to be careful about what she ate. This preoccupation became excessive during the year at the boarding school where the food was poor by her standards. She also noticed that her manners were changing. Even in retrospect she spoke with real self-hatred for having grabbed food and having revealed herself as greedy. When beef was served she was at first modest, with the result that she got only a very small piece. Gradually she got into the habit, like the others, of reaching for the largest piece. But she felt she was violating her standards and she talked about this as something dreadful which had lowered her self-esteem. When on her return she gained weight instead of losing she reacted with depression and decided to diet. She felt she could not possibly be fat because nobody would respect her, and she could not exist without respect from people. At first she felt she

---

* Sharon (No. 13) refers to Table 14–1. All other names and numbers in this chapter also refer to Table 14–1.

got a lot of respect for losing weight, which she missed after her weight had stabilized.

Karol (No. 32) was 23 years old when she came for treatment, having been sick for nearly 6 years. It had begun when she was a freshman in college, 17½ years old, and she "lost her appetite after the flu." This was the official version to which her parents still clung, that she had never recovered from the flu. Karol herself admitted that she never had the flu, that she had taken to her bed out of despair for having "failed." Fear of failure had troubled her in high school; she was bright but socially never did quite as well as her parents expected. She had belonged to several clubs and had held many offices, but had never been president. Going to college also became a series of failures. She had hoped that going away from home, being on her own, would help her become free from her mother's domination which her friends had told her was abnormal but which she could not shake off. She applied to one of the smaller women's colleges, but was not admitted, and she was forced to go to the state university, which was so close to her home that her mother continuously "dropped in." She also did not get into the sorority of her first choice and would not join another one which she considered inferior. But the great shattering disappointment was in relation to her studies. She had played the violin since she had been quite young, and had spent many hours practicing, often under her mother's supervision. She enjoyed playing for herself, had never wanted to perform for others, but she felt she owed it to her mother to become a concert artist. When she played before the committee on music education she was terribly disappointed; she was not admitted to advanced standing, as she, her mother, and music teacher had felt she deserved. The crowning blow, however, was that her mother had attended the audition, and that there was no way of hiding this supreme failure from her.

Her weight at that time was 120 lbs, which was rather slim for her height of 5'6". She had felt uncomfortable about this weight as being "too much" because she felt she should not weigh more than her mother who was petite and weighed only 115 lbs. It also happened that her roommate at that time had decided to lose weight and began by skipping lunch. She joined her in this, and far outdid her in losing weight; a few weeks later she had lost so much weight that her health became a matter of concern and her "failure" in music was forgotten.

Two patients, Naomi (No. 25) and Felice (No. 33), were identical twins who became anorexic after entering college, when their co-twins, who in each instance had been the dominant, the leader twin, established their independence and separateness (5). In both instances, monozygoty had been established at birth. Though most developmental landmarks had been very close, the patients-to-be had been smaller and somewhat more difficult to raise. Both had accepted the dominance of the "executive" twin without question or complaint. Naomi even stressed that she had always felt fortunate for having "an agent" who was doing things for her and was facing difficult problems. In both instances the parents had stressed the twinship, had objected to advice to separate the children, seeing them so much as a unit that the mothers at times did not remember to which twin to attribute certain events or clever sayings. When the question of college came up, the leader twin chose the college of her choice; the patient-to-be, the follower, not having a specific preference, ended up in the same college, even in the same dormitory. The illness became manifest when the leader twin was swept up in college activities and openly enjoyed the new independence, feeling distinct and separate, fulfilling her resolve of being an individual, no longer "a twin." The patients, having been perfectly contented in their twinship, were the first time confronted with the problems of an independent existence for which their role of follower had left them completely unprepared.

A detailed review will reveal in other cases, too, that the urgent need to lose weight is a cover-up symptom, expressing an underlying fear of being despised or disregarded, or of not getting or not even deserving respect. Desperate about their inability to solve their problems, the patients begin to worry about their weight and get a sense of accomplishment from manipulating their body.

Pre-Illness Personality

As puzzling as the seeming triviality of the precipitating events are the nearly uniform reports of special goodness and great achievements of these youngsters before they became anorexic. There were only very few exceptions where behavior difficulties had been in the open. One example was Gail (No. 10) whose history was presented in Chapter 4. Some parents had recognized that their daughters had been trying too hard, or had been too sensitive, or had been doing too much for others. Sometimes the parents disagreed in their retrospective evaluation. Claire (No. 38) was a 12½-year-old girl who declared that a weight gain of 12 lbs in one year was "too much" and who kept her weight low until she was 16. Claire's mother described her as having been a "tortured child," and "hard to reach," whereas the father felt she had been a warm and responsive girl, intelligent, interested in the same things as he was. In contrast, Thelma's (No. 36) mother had noticed "nothing wrong," not even that the dieting of her daughter at age 14 was excessive, but the father had recognized the underlying tension and self-doubt. In most instances the parents agreed that this had been their perfect child—and they maintain this view in spite of the increasing difficulties.

The progress of Karen's (No. 31) therapy was hampered by the father's continuous declarations that there was nothing wrong, that she did not need treatment; all she needed was to be told to eat more. Her mother, too, doubted that "it could be serious." Karen, her youngest daughter, had been the one she had not felt the need to worry about, in contrast to her older daughters who had been pregnant when they got married. After each visit with the parents, Karen would regress, would refuse food altogether, and would resort to her stereotyped complaints about her worthlessness and emptiness.

In the atypical group, early behavior difficulties and conflicts in the family are much more in the open (Chapter 13). Among the 15 patients in that group there were 5 broken homes due to death or illness of one parent. In contrast, in the primary group, the families appear to be stable, and the parents show outgoing concern for their children. It is only in therapeutic contact that the subtle disturbances are revealed, as was discussed in Chapter 5. The parents' failure to see a child's distress, and their persistent perception of her in unrealistic terms, according to the image they carry in their own mind, are the very factors that have interfered with the child's developing a realistic self-concept and reliable self-esteem—and will make treatment impossible if uncorrected.

Sharon's (No. 13) mother spoke repeatedly of her disbelief that her well-balanced daughter should have been so troubled and under such strain; she had always been such a gay, warm, and kind child, had been well liked in her class, and her fellow students and teachers had thought of her as "wonderful." Sharon agreed that she had always been popular, frequently elected to class offices, a trusted student, surrounded by many friends, and she would befriend girls who were "on the outside." She admitted that this special position had created much strain, but that she *needed* to be recognized because otherwise she was worried about not feeling fully accepted. It gave her great satisfaction to help outsiders, and thus be reassured about her own position. She felt threatened when a girl she had befriended suddenly preferred other girls as her friends. This was a bitter disappointment and she felt rejected.

She was disturbed about her French being only fair, and plans were made for her to go abroad. This was a blemish on her outstanding record and made her academic standing "unbalanced." While abroad she spent every day in anguish that she was not learning enough, that she was falling behind in other subjects, that she still would be "unbalanced" when she returned to her old school. She needed her high class standing, not only for her own peace of mind, but also as an obligation she owed her parents, who, she feared, would be disappointed if she were not quite so popular and superior. Life at home had also been much more complex than the early reports had suggested. She had always been so overly cooperative, even docile and subservient, that it would have been difficult for her parents to recognize any discontent, even if they had suspected that all was not well. When 6 years old she had discovered a box of toys which she recognized as her intended Christmas present. It was something that she definitely did *not* want, but she concealed this, and instead, dropped several hints that she hoped for this type of gift. Even now she would feel guilty and selfish if she were to express a wish; she always tried to guess what her parents wanted to do for her. The same applied to her dresses, which her mother selected, and she had never objected to mother's choice. While in treatment she finally began to assert her own taste and she had her first serious clash with her mother about a dress she had chosen—it was a painful defeat that she suffered.

It was very difficult for Sharon to admit that there had been difficulties in her relationship with her parents, in particular, with her mother. In a common conference the mother stressed that there had *never* been a problem, that Sharon never needed to be reminded, that she had been a perfect child who always did the right thing. The parents find it difficult to recognize that such overconformity reflects a serious problem, namely a child's self-doubt about her ability to stand up for herself, or of even having the right to assert herself. In Sharon's philosophy "Fate" directed everybody's life and all she had to do was to fulfill it. She had considered herself fortunate that she had such good parents who had prepared such a desirable Fate for her. It was an upsetting discovery that she had to lead her own life, that she had a say in what was happening, and that her life depended upon her own decisions and actions. She dated the real onset of her illness to a class in literature, at least 2 or 3 years before the onset of her dieting, where she had suddenly felt uncertain about herself, not knowing how to be "the captain of my soul" and "the master of my fate." Until then she had taken it for granted that she, Sharon, should live up to the role her mother had assigned to her, which was to be "just right," "perfectly balanced," and an "all-around girl." As a child she had been considered helpful and kind because she liked to "volunteer" her help; but she remembered that if her mother requested her to do something she would feel unhappy about it, or even say, "No." When in therapy she expressed some criticism of her mother, she felt guilty for not behaving properly, but increasingly she complained that she felt "intruded upon" by her.

Another example of enormous discrepancy between parents' concept of their daughter and her actual experiences is the case of Christine (No. 19), who became anorexic at age 18 while at college. She came for a psychiatric consultation only 1½ years later. Her parents still did not believe that there could possibly be any psychological problems because Christine had been normal and happy to an unusual degree. She was the oldest of 4 children, had been very helpful with the younger ones, and had been the object of much praise and admiration. She had been a straight A student, had participated in sports and social activities, and had been popular. It came as a shocking surprise that she had done not as well on the college entrance examinations as everybody had expected. After entering college she concentrated on her studies to the exclusion of all social activities. When her grades were "not A" she worked even harder. There was some loss of weight during the first term, from 120 to about 100 lbs, which aroused concern but not enough for her parents to give in to her expressed desire not to return to college. Her weight loss continued and when it had dropped to 74 lbs and she became depressed, the college insisted on treatment.

The first psychiatric consultation was arranged for only after her behavior had begun to interfere with the functioning of the family. After having refused to eat for about a year, she began to suffer from eating binges and was terrified by them. She found out that *she* did not want to eat when *she forced her brother and sisters to eat* instead. This created terrible scenes at home; she would not let the younger children go to school until they had finished everything she had prepared. A plan for psychiatric treatment was outlined, but was unacceptable to the parents. Christine did not come into treatment until 3 years later and it was then gradually recognized that her life had not been as idyllic as her parents had described.

She had been born during the war when her father was overseas. An often-repeated anecdote was about how surprised her father had been when meeting his little 4-year-old daughter. Pictures sent to him overseas had depicted her as a blonde curly-haired child; when her father met her she was a brunette with straight hair. To Christine this story was the symbol of her having been a disappointment to her father, not worthy of his love, and she dedicated her life to protecting him from any further disappointments. She described in many details the agony of living a life of perfection, never being able to do what she wanted to do or felt like doing, always under the compulsion to do what she felt was expected of her.

The nonperfect score on the college board was the first crack in this facade. Problems multiplied rapidly. She could not make up her mind about a long-range professional goal and the frantic search for perfect grades was in preparation for the eventual choice, to be prepared for everything, when she finally *knew* what to choose. Her request not to go back to college was the first admission of being unable to continue a life entirely directed toward pleasing her parents, without a purpose and goal of her own. She continued to perform with the old perfectionism, but felt life had lost its meaning. The weight loss had been at first incidental to her excessive concentration on her studies. Now it became a goal in itself. Not to eat, not to look like her mother, became a step toward self-assertion, the expression of not being completely compliant, of refusing to do what her parents expected. It was also a concrete way of making them "see" that she could no longer fulfill their ambitions. Throughout her life they had been blind to her unexpressed emotional needs, and then they had been deaf to her expressed plea to be relieved from going back to college.

Eating Behavior: Hunger and Appetite

The target symptom in anorexia nervosa is failure to eat sufficiently. As was discussed in Chapter 4, confusion in hunger awareness and in the recognition of the signs of nutritional need is part of the essential underlying aspects of the disturbance. Efforts have been made to differentiate different forms of anorexia nervosa according to differences in the experiences of hunger and appetite, i.e., by Dally (8). I have not been able to recognize differences in the presence or absence of hunger or appetite in patients with primary anorexia nervosa, though they differ in the urgency of their efforts to control their eating. They are reluctant to talk about this topic when asked directly, particularly in the beginning of their illness. There is only the sullenly repeated statement, "I do not need to eat," or defiant denial of feeling hungry. If they begin to talk about this it becomes apparent that they experience sensations relating to the need for food quite differently in different settings and at different periods of their illness. When mistrusting the therapist, they will violently deny any hunger sensations, but after an atmosphere of trust and confidence has developed they might reveal as a closely guarded secret the torture of their self-starvation. Contact over an extended period reveals how bewildered and confused they are about their body sensations.

It is exceedingly rare to get information about these contradictory and changing sensations during the early part of the illness. A 14-year-old boy, Elliot (Chapter 15), kept a diary when first hospitalized, 3 months after the onset. His diary alternates between complaints and worries about his condition, desire for help, and a desire to be punished. "I still want an ulcer to punish myself, and eat only cream of wheat. A blindness or deafness, I even thought of cutting myself like the other girl (on the psychiatric service), or falling badly. I am wasting so much time."

Then he writes, "I would like to eat very much, yet I also feel that food is a thing of the past now, something to look at and admire. To save and put on a shelf where it looks nice. It seems so valuable that I don't even dare to touch it." Or, "I still don't see why I should eat. I don't want an appetite when I get home and I think I can control this. I just want to be left alone to starve my own way. I don't know why I feel food is not necessary."

"I think I will fast today because I didn't talk to you yesterday and it is Friday the 13th. I want to see if I have the will power to fast again; I don't think I have it anymore."

In most instances the food restriction at first does not look different from ordinary dieting, with the exclusion of all "fattening" foods. The characteristic diet of an anorexic is relatively high in proteins. In this respect they differ from other starving people nutritionally, who invariably subsist with practically no protein. It seems probable that the startling and persistent alertness is in part at least related to this relatively high-grade nutrition. The rare anorexic on low protein intake will feel fatigued and also suffers from edema, hypovitaminosis, and other signs of nutritional deficiency that are conspicuously absent in most. Dora (No. 26), one of the girls who died, had eaten mainly celery sticks, supplemented by large amounts of chewing gum, during the last year of her life, and had vigorously objected to more nourishing food. Mona (No. 45), who suffered from edema and fatigue after 6 years, had begun with a protein-rich diet but then eliminated one item after another, meat, eggs, cheese, because they "set too heavy" in her stomach, and she now took only cereal, rice, and other soft food.

Most, however, stick to the protein diet, becoming more and more specialized in what they permit themselves to eat. Beth (No. 3), who felt at the age of 14 that she was gaining "too much," made a real study of nutrition and decided on two chicken livers as an adequate daily ration. Rachel (No. 16) chose one lamb chop, late at night, in addition to a few ounces of buttermilk during the day, as what she permitted herself to eat. Most become more and more obsessed with excluding carbohydrates, or will wipe every bite of meat on blotting paper to remove the last trace of fat or gravy. The intent to cut down on food as far as possible was graphically described by Eric when he was asked about his breakfast: "Of course, I ate my Cheerio." Invariably they will eat more and more slowly, taking an hour or longer to finish a meal, however small, particularly when they are supervised. This leads to exhausting struggles and exasperating impatience on the part of people trying to help them.

Dawdling over food and continuous thinking about it are nothing specific for anorexia nervosa; it is commonly observed during starvation. In an experimental study of semistarvation, carried out in Minnesota during World War II, a group of normal young men were given a reduced diet, planned to simulate in quality and quantity the severe food shortages in Western and Central Europe (9). In this diet items like milk and meat were served only in token amounts. The men would "toy" with their food and made what under normal conditions would be considered weird and distasteful concoctions, with marked increase in the use of spices and salt. There was no diminution in the desire for food as the starvation progressed, but some of the men would dawdle for almost two hours over a meal which previously they would have consumed in a matter of minutes. Richter reported on his own observations on a drastically restricted fare, made while in prison for several months (15). Only a few of the prisoners were able to eat the limited meals in a normal way. Most developed methods to stretch the tiny amount over long periods, one using an hour and a half to two hours to eat one slice of bread, and eating was treated with great secrecy. The prisoners spoke continuously about food, recipes, and favorite dishes and indulged in fantasies of what they would eat when free. The same was observed in the Minnesota experiment and has also been reported by survivors of concentration and internment camps—

that food was the dominant topic of all conversation and thinking.

Much of what is reported in the literature as specific for anorexia nervosa, and what has been called "anorexic behavior," such as obsessive, ruminative preoccupation with food, narcissistic self-absorption, infantile regression, etc., is identical with what has been described in externally induced starvation. The telling difference is, of course, that under enforced starvation food is not available, and that the victim will eat whatever he can find. In contrast, the anorexic is starving, in whatever distorted form this is experienced, in the midst of plenty and lives under the paradox of internal inhibitions forcing him *not* to satisfy his needs, even to reject food that is constantly offered, urged, and forced on him. This gives to his preoccupation with food the peculiar bizarreness and frenzy. Rather absurd situations develop when they try to force feed others. Fern (No. 22), 14 years of age, would begin cooking and baking after she came home from school and refused to go to bed until her parents had eaten every morsel of her rich cakes and desserts. Dora (No. 26) was obsessed with the fear that her brother was starving and always carried cake and candy for him, with the result that he grew quite obese.

Manipulation of food intake is only a means to an end, the relentless pursuit of thinness. Though eternally preoccupied with food, the majority accomplish not eating by rigid control, though they live in constant fear of not being able to maintain the control. Others, after a time, begin to indulge in enormous eating binges, alternating them with days of fasting. Christine (No. 19) was an example of this type. She would compensate for the extra food by skipping several meals and by becoming more frantic in forcing food on others. A few will surrender to the impulse to gorge themselves and then grow fat. Sometimes it looks as if the weight regulating function has "gone wild." Toni (No. 8) has been briefly referred to in Chapter 7. She had been slightly plump at age 13, and from then on dieted. For about two years, from age 16 to 18, she maintained her weight at 74 lbs, and it climbed to 174 lbs at age 20. While hospitalized she went through two episodes of nearly complete starvation, with rapid loss in weight, and one episode of uncontrollable gorging with even more rapid gain in weight. Not once did she identify sensations as hunger or satiation, though she was eternally preoccupied with food and with the question of whether to eat or not to eat. Others will follow these eating binges with self-induced vomiting. Among the 45 female anorexics there were at least 10 in whom overeating with subsequent vomiting played a significant role; in 6 of them it dominated the picture and had developed quite early. In one case, Nora's (No. 4) throwing up to prevent obesity had preceded the anorexia nervosa.

Selvini has suggested subdividing patients suffering from primary anorexia nervosa according to differences in their eating behavior and attitude (17). By evaluating the Rorschach records of her patients for communication defects and deviances, according to the method described by Wynne and Singer (18), she observed differences in the style of thinking in patients with different eating behavior. She found more signs of disorganized thinking in those patients who had eating binges and vomiting, or who were otherwise frantically preoccupied with the fear of losing control. She also found that patients with this fragmented type of thinking had a poorer prognosis than those who maintained stable control. Using the same scoring technique, I was unable to establish such differences, neither on Rorschach evaluation nor clinically. Three girls (Nos. 4, 26, 36) died; in one, vomiting had been a conspicuous feature over many years, and the fatal outcome was attributed to irreversible damages due to disturbances in the electrolyte balance (6). The two other girls had been rigid in their food restriction and had never vomited, the type Selvini calls "stable anorexics." One died directly of starvation and the other of starvation and circulatory failure.

It may be accidental, but patients with eating binges and vomiting seem to come more often for intensive psychotherapy and to persist in it. The families appear to be much more involved and are more alarmed by this absurd behavior of gorging and vomiting than by the quiet, steady refusal to eat.

Celia (No. 12) had begun her noneating regimen during her second year in college, when her boyfriend commented that she weighed nearly as much as he. He was of slight build weighing only 130 lbs and was sensitive about this, feeling that his manliness was at stake. He expressed the desire that she lose a few pounds and she went on a diet in an effort to please him. However she resented that he had "fixed" their relationship at a certain weight. When she first talked about this she said "I completely lost my appetite"; later she added that she had been continuously preoccupied with food but denied it to herself. There was a sense of glory and pride in the self-denial and in feeling hungry. As she began to lose weight she experienced a great sense of strength and independence. Though she had begun to lose weight to please her boyfriend it became now her own project. She lost over 25 lbs. Being skinny made her feel better and she defended it as the right weight for herself.

She was admitted for long-term treatment 1½ years later, after several efforts on the outside and two or three brief hospital admissions elsewhere. She felt that her efforts at independence had been frustrated, that she now was being forced to be dependent again. "Dependent on society, on a hospital, on a doctor and on other people and patients. It follows that if much of my independent defenses are broken then the one involving food should be too. Hence, I have become very dependent on food also." She began to have eating binges, eating out of a sense of panic, or out of emptiness; she denied that they ever occurred out of feelings of hunger. "I don't eat when I feel an inner strength derived from being independent, but when this independence is destroyed my defenses against eating also are." Sometimes she would throw up after such eating binges, usually she refused meals for several days. Though she never had been heavy, she was preoccupied with the fear of getting fat and fear of being rejected. Paradoxically, she also felt that food gave her a sense of security. "I feel always more secure when I have eaten a lot, when I have a full stomach. It is just as I would be gratified from getting attention, socializing successfully. Quantity is an important element; the more I can get into my stomach the safer I feel. When my stomach is empty I often feel anxious and panicky. . . . I associate power and strength with what I eat, as if there was danger in not eating."

But when she ate she felt exceedingly guilty, full of self-contempt and disrespect for herself which contributed to her sense of worthlessness, "because food has become my only source of satisfaction; because I can't control my eating or my feelings; because my illness represents the ultimate of failure to cope with life." Following eating binges she would bang her head against the wall, or punch her lips to the point of bleeding. She also became very depressed, and there were several suicide attempts. A definite relationship between suicidal impulses and eating binges was observed. When she could control her eating and would lose weight, she felt strong and cheerful. When she gave in to the urge for food she became depressed and suicidal. Not eating gave her a feeling of superiority and she had dreams and fantasies of "subjugating" others by forcing them to eat. When not eating she felt more peaceful, uninvolved, and distant from her family. When she ate, she felt she had betrayed herself. She wanted to avoid being plump, which to her meant being feminine. The many episodes of compulsive eating were not due to hunger but to what she called "an unknown need—a feeling of being empty and panicky." She used eating as punishment, as "hurt" to herself, but suicide attempts occurred only when she had been unable to control her eating.

She also connected her eating impulses with the need for sex. She would gorge herself, often on ice cream, "like a baby," with a feeling of oral greediness and desire which she compared to masturbation. When she first met her boyfriend she had normal enjoyment of sex but when she stopped eating she stopped having sexual feelings and sex was no longer part of the relationship. For quite some time after her weight had increased her sexual feelings did not revive. She clung to her boyfriend and at the same time resented his close attention. She began to yearn for a feeling of independence, for mastery over her loneliness and sense of alienation.

In the various efforts to understand anorexia nervosa it has been referred to as "suicide in refracted doses." Though anorexic patients may die from their condition it is not death they are after but the urgent need to be in control of their own lives and have a sense of identity. It is only in the despair of being too weak, of not being able to achieve their goal of self-determination, that suicidal despair appears. This was most apparent in Celia's case, but was expressed by many others. Theander (19) found in his large series that 3 patients had committed suicide. There were marked differences from one patient to another and they represented atypical forms of the syndrome. The clinical symptoms had diminished considerably at the time of the suicide; one patient had been severely overweight. A recent report (2) mentions one suicide which occurred after the patient had gained a considerable amount of weight with a behavior therapy regimen. Five weeks after discharge from the hospital, and before a planned psychotherapeutic program had been instituted, she immolated herself after an argument with her mother and actively resisted attempts to treat her burns.

When Karol's (No. 32) weight had dropped to a dangerous level, she was admitted to a psychiatric service. She was outraged about being treated like a mental patient and was particularly upset about another young girl who had made a serious suicide attempt. She felt insulted that she was compared to someone who had done something as incomprehensible as trying to kill herself.

It will be noted that all these explanations of eating and noneating are related to problems in the interpersonal field and to doubts about personal adequacy and self-respect. This was expressed by Sharon (No. 13) who developed episodes of eating binges and vomiting quite early. At first she denied that there was anything wrong and insisted that she had a feeling of "accomplishment" by eating as much as she wanted and still staying slim. She loved certain foods; as a matter of fact, she loved them so much that she was afraid of eating too much and not being able to stop. She had trained herself to "enjoy" the feeling of hunger, just as she had trained herself to like "awful" food. After she had been sick for quite some time she was greatly upset by the idea that she no longer could "enjoy" hunger but suffered from it. She declared at first that there was nothing wrong with eating binges, that she could stop them any time she wanted to; but then she became more and more bewildered over her eating behavior. The need to eat in the early morning was interpreted as "my stomach wants it," but later in the day urges to eat overcame her when there was rising tension between herself and her mother. The force that made her eat was experienced as something outside of herself; she compared her helplessness vis-à-vis this compelling force to the way inmates in a concentration camp would surrender to brutal guards. She differentiated between what *she* wanted and her automaton-like behavior as if she were a compulsively driven robot.

Her eating binges were directly related to feeling upset in relation to others, be it an argument with her parents, her sense of loneliness, or the lacking feeling of intimacy in any relationship. She recognized that her preoccupation with weight was abnormal, but all her life experiences were tied together by the idea that one can be respected only by being thin. Now that she was thin, she discovered this was not so, but the fear of being too fat persisted just the same. There was no longer the feeling of accomplishment, and the eating binges were now quite outside her control, just as she could not judge realistically how much school work she needed to do when the fear of not being perfect dominated her behavior. She had always enjoyed learning and was a relaxed student at school; but when she sat down to do her homework an abnormal tension overcame her and made her study until the middle of the night.

The ritualistic aspect of her eating behavior became gradually clearer; it was the compulsion that she had to get rid of the food as a punishment for having eaten at all that harassed her life. She was aware that much more was involved than ordinary distress about not being slim because she was obviously too slim, but there was real guilt that she had done something that she should not have done. What she was afraid of is something she called "emptiness." If she ate "too much" she would not rest until she had a chance to vomit. There might even be a delay of two or three hours and she knew that by that time the first food had been digested, but she could not rest until she went through the whole act. There was a peculiar double reaction. She got an uncontrollable urge to eat when she felt lonely, and she was panicky at the idea of utter desolation without rapport with anyone. But she also became upset when visiting with friends because she would not have the time or opportunity to get rid of food in case she ate too much.

Increasingly there have been arguments with her mother about the type of food she uses for the eating binges. Instead of buying bulk ice cream she insists on having icicles with a particular cover and crunchiness, which cost more than ordinary ice cream. Although this is a wealthy home, this wasteful procedure provokes many angry reproaches. One reason for her increasing anguish about her eating binges is the fact that they have made her dishonest. She had always taken pride in having high moral standards and having been meticulously truthful, in particular about money. Now she takes money out of her mother's purse in order to buy food or charges this extra food against her mother's expressed wishes not to do so. She never touches a penny of her father's money, even if she sees it lying on the dresser.

The tendency to steal has been observed in many patients with anorexia nervosa. King (14) reported it as part of the pre-illness picture. Thomae (20) linked kleptomania to hyperactivity and considered them both to be related to the nutritional drive as "the desire for reaching out." My observations are quite different. In no case was stealing reported before the illness had developed, nor was it related to hyperactivity. Stealing of food or of money is closely associated with a sense of failure, of having given in and of not being in control. I have observed it mainly in patients who indulge in eating binges, though others who strictly starve themselves may occasionally steal some candy or take other ready-to-eat food. This action was always associated with much anguish and shame.

Ushakov's observations (21) appear to be very similar to my own. He describes these adolescents as "meticulous to the point where their punctiliousness became ludicrous; their high principles were excessive for their ages; they had an unequivocal honesty and an exaggerated sense of duty." He considers the deviousness and dishonesty that later develop to be part of the personality changes of the illness.

Bilz (1) offers an interesting interpretation of the eating behavior, namely, as a throwback to a more primitive, vagabond type of feeding, a flight from the feudal organization of the family table; these patients live on secret snacks, obtaining their food here and there, even sometimes resorting to stealing. He interprets this as a reaction to a narcissistic insult, of a girl condemning herself to the desert of starvation, with regression in her feeding behavior.

These examples and references will suffice to demonstrate that the abnormal eating behavior in anorexia nervosa cannot be summarized as indicating presence or absence of hunger and appetite. It is a symptom that on detailed inquiry reveals a multitude of meanings, closely related to the inner confusion and conflicts from which these patients suffer. I gave details for a few patients only. They could be endlessly enlarged by citing amazingly similar experiences and expressions of all the others.

Hyperactivity and Overachievement

As startling as the gruesome appearance in anorexia nervosa are the hyperactivity and drive for achievement which persist in spite of severe emaciation. Hyperactivity is rarely complained of, or even mentioned, by the patients or the parents; but it will be found with great regularity if looked for. Detailed questioning usually reveals that the hyperactivity developed before the noneating phase. It may take on many different forms. Sometimes an existing interest in athletics and sports becomes intensified. Others engage in activities that seem to be aimless, such as walking for miles, chinning and bending exercises, refusing to sit down, or literally running around in circles. Others roam around at night, too restless to sleep, or they will do housework, cooking, and cleaning by the hour. The patients themselves do not feel that they are exercising too much, and parents do not notice it or are not alarmed about excessive activities; therefore they deny hyperactivity. Uniformly one will learn that these girls had done exceptionally well in their school work, bent on having perfect grades, but that they were also popular, socially active, and excelled in athletics.

There is usually less objection to the overactivity though occasionally the restless running around is more provocative to parents than the silent refusal to eat. Karol (No. 32) had returned to her home when her weight loss at college had become severe. She developed a routine of "march-

ing." This family lived in a Southern town, and their lavish home
a slight knoll. After she had eaten, even the smallest amount, and a
there had been tension or disagreement with her parents, she would w
up and down the driveway, to the point of exhaustion. This to her fathe
was a most shameful demonstration that there was something wrong in
his home. Karol continued her "marching" throughout her illness, walking 6 to 10 times around large city blocks when living away from home,
always expressing fear of not burning enough calories.

During treatment she began to experience some changes in herself and
reported.

> For the first time yesterday, I felt hungry. I acknowledged it for the first time
> and I also allowed myself to feel tired. I did not feel like losing control—I was
> not driving myself as much. I was able to eat and not to feel guilty. But I was
> frustrated to feel tired—it was something new to me. I always run around at
> high speed but this time I was tired. At home I was roaming around all night
> until I was completely exhausted; you can do it only so long. I did it on
> purpose and maliciously—I didn't permit myself to rest.

Sharon (No. 13) had always received a good deal of praise for being
an accomplished athlete, excelling particularly in group sports. She was
often the captain of her team. From what was first reported there was
nothing unusual in Sharon's continuing to participate in sports. Rather
accidentally it was learned that her activities had now an entirely different
flavor. While on a weekend visit with a friend's family she felt rather
awkward about sharing a room with her friend, though she had done so in
the past. Now she mentioned for the first time that, however late it was,
she *had* to do her calisthenics and exercises, to the point that her muscles
would hurt; without this she couldn't go to sleep. She added that she had
also gotten into the habit of going to school early in the morning, to
spend one hour in the gym for bar exercises. In other cases, too, exercise
and activity that had formerly been part of socializing became lonely
pursuits.

Many parents mention that these starving youngsters spend hours on
their homework, and often will not permit themselves to eat a bite until
they have completed everything to perfection. Frequently the striving for
perfection results in all kinds of additional habits.

Rachel (No. 16), the older of two girls in a professional family, had been
a "very easy child" to raise in the description of her parents. They also
said she was "a real perfectionist—wanting to prove herself all the time."
When 12 years of age she went to a summer camp which she did not like
and she wanted to come home, but her parents persuaded her to stay and
so she stayed "because she never fought back." At camp she felt that her
weight of 112 lbs was too heavy, and she began dieting, maintaining her
weight at about 105 lbs through the next 2 years. Pubertal development
started early but menarche did not occur until she was 14½ years old.
Her reaction to this was to stop eating and her weight dropped rapidly. In
spite of her very restricted diet she continued to grow, and when she was

ₙ at age 17½ she was 5'7" tall and weighed 66 lbs.
to attend school and to do excellent work. She had
former friends and went alone on long bicycle rides.
ₙgy, saving her parents any "unnecessary" expendi-
picking up pieces of paper, and walked around the
, doing her studies with the smallest light possible.
anything "unnecessary," would not watch televi-
ₙould turn off the car radio when driving with her father. This
stinginess extended to her personal care; she would take a shower only
once a week and was even stingy with toilet paper. Her father described
his daughter as suffering from a "denial complex—she denies herself
food, clothing, light, information—she denies herself life."

Stinginess, often to extremes, is not an uncommon symptom, with patients refusing to have more than one dress or one change of under-
clothes, or anything else that might indicate that they were "dependent"
on their parents, or the world at large. These symptoms, like hyperactivity, may precede the manifest anorexic picture.

In Karla (No. 30) excessive striving developed in her struggle to overcome a severe physical handicap. She had always been a pleasant and
outgoing girl, socially active, well coordinated, athletic, and also an excellent student. At the age of 12 a brain tumor was discovered and surgery
for this left her with a paralysis of the left side and some visual problems.
To help her recover good functioning she spent some time at a rehabilitation center where she was exposed to a program of patterning, creeping,
and push-ups. This she pursued with enormous energy and she succeeded
in establishing sufficient control to get herself into an upright position and
to learn some kind of walking. She was disappointed that perfect functioning had not been restored, something she felt had been the implied
promise and reward for all her efforts.

She went back to school on a part-time basis and felt upset about being
a year behind her former friends. Then she was invited to a swimming
party which turned into a traumatic experience where she felt completely
left out since she could not take part in the roughhousing, though she was
a good swimmer. After that she rejected every suggestion which involved
her with other young people and began to diet, reducing from 115 lbs to
75 lbs, rationalizing it as necessary for her condition, saying that it would
be easier for her to regain control if she were not fat. She continued
swimming but as a grim task, doing as many as 30 laps in the pool, and
keeping herself completely isolated. Her interests focused on how to avoid
gaining weight and how to achieve control over her crippled body.

Hyperactivity and striving for perfect achievement as essential aspects
of the anorexia nervosa picture have been comparatively neglected in the
literature, particularly in psychoanalytic writings. Thomae (20) includes
hyperactivity in his discussion, but having defined anorexia nervosa as "a

drive disturbance" he includes every symptom under this heading, and considers hyperactivity as derived from the nutritional drive. He described the lifelong interest in athletics of one young girl as an "Amazon-like attitude," and explained it as expressing her fear of becoming pregnant without offering any factual information to support this farfetched claim. As the illness progresses patients commonly rationalize hyperactivity as helping them stay slim; and undoubtedly it is often used in this way. Yet drive for achievement (and not always in a calorie-consuming form) often precedes the whole syndrome. The noneating and the fear of being fat are resorted to after previous efforts at establishing a sense of "being in control" have failed. This need becomes urgent when the severe deficiency in autonomy comes into the patient's awareness as a sense of ineffectiveness when they are faced with changing demands during the crisis of puberty or early adulthood.

Sexual Adjustment and Problems

Since puberty is the characteristic time of onset it has been generally assumed that anorexia nervosa is in some way related to sexual problems. Anorexia may become manifest a few years earlier or at the time of a developmental crisis in young adulthood. Amenorrhea is a characteristic feature; as a matter of fact it has been considered so essential that some felt that its absence precluded the diagnosis. With modern emphasis on psychodynamic issues, amenorrhea can no longer be considered a precondition, although it is usually present.

Among the 45 female patients there were 6 who were still in prepuberty; all 6 male patients were in prepuberty. Amenorrhea was observed in all of the remaining 39 cases. Spontaneous menstruation usually occurs after the condition has existed for several years, sometimes in relation to some event with recognizable psychodynamic significance, in others without this. In recent years the picture has become somewhat beclouded because many receive endocrine preparations to induce periodic bleedings, though some resist carrying out the prescribed program.

Crisp (7) observed that the later anorexic girl is heavier at birth than her sisters and tends to have an early menarche. He feels that this premature demand for sexual adjustment, in combination with an immature personality, precipitates the illness. My own observations do not bear this out. Menarche had occurred at a normal age in the 39 patients in the primary group—12.6 years with a range from 10 to 16 years. Early menarche was a rare exception. In two instances of monozygotic twins, discordant for anorexia nervosa, the later anorexic twin had been smaller at birth, and menarche had occurred later than in the healthy twin (5).

Although regularly occurring, amenorrhea is not specific for primary anorexia nervosa. The menstrual cycle is a function easily affected by emotional disturbances. Amenorrhea is commonly observed in women under severe stress and strain and does not automatically suggest sexual maladjustment. Under wartime conditions, in concentration and internment camps, incidence of amenorrhea was high and occurred long before serious loss of weight. On the other hand, secondary amenorrhea occurring without such drastic conditions seems indeed to be associated with a state of psychological immaturity in general, most evidenced in the attitude toward sex (13). It is not surprising that many cases of anorexia nervosa, or of anorexia-like states, have been included in reports on secondary amenorrhea.

Under the influence of psychoanalytic teaching the rejection of food was equated with the rejection of and disgust with sex. The explanation of the syndrome was reduced to one complex which was considered to be specific, namely, a defense against unconscious fear of impregnation (22). This type of sexual anxiety may play a role in certain cases of atypical anorexia nervosa (Chapter 13), but in primary anorexia nervosa it is rarely encountered and it is the manifestation of immaturity and other developmental disturbances, not the cause of them. Selvini (17) has come to the same conclusion; she found impregnation fantasies only rarely, and observed when such fantasies were uncovered that the fear of pregnancy was not related to true sexual fears, but was rather a sexual symbol of a more primitive experience, namely the fear of being invaded by the object.

It is difficult, if not impossible, to evaluate reports about such unconscious fantasies. In their basic personality structure these patients are deficient in experiencing themselves as being self-directed and having an identity of their own. Hence in therapy, when not rigidly negativistic, they will be chameleon-like in their capacity to pick up cues from the therapist and will relate to him what he expects to hear, or even regurgitate ideas which he might have suggested through his questions. Anorexia nervosa patients invariably complained about feeling "full" after eating even a small amount. If the therapist is convinced that this is the symbolic expression of an imagined pregnancy then it does not take much inventiveness for a patient to answer sooner or later to his persistent questioning that this fullness feels like having a baby in her stomach. Hospitalized patients often repeat what they have learned from other anorexic patients as interesting psychodynamics.

My cautionary remarks about "explaining" anorexia nervosa as "caused" by certain unconscious fantasies do not imply, of course, that these patients' attitudes toward sex and adulthood are not seriously disturbed. Under the fragile facade of normality, their whole development has been so distorted that it would be inconceivable if they functioned normally in this area. Characteristically they are confused about their bodily sensations and feel unable to control their bodily functions. To them the changes of pubescence, the increase in size, shape, and weight, menstruation with its bleeding, and new and disturbing sexual impulses, all represent a dangerous challenge for which they are unprepared, threatening what little control they had. The frantic preoccupation with weight is an attempt to counteract this fear of losing control; rigid dieting is the dimension through which they try to accomplish this.

Failure to deal with puberty and the experience of sexuality in an age-appropriate way finds expression in many different forms. Many show it as a complete lack of interest. Sexual curiosity or exploration and dating are issues that do not concern them, and they put up a rigid fence against becoming concerned. As the illness persists there is increasing isolation, including a general withdrawal from their friends who are developing new interests. Many had been compensating during childhood for the lacking sense of mastery by engaging in masculine pursuits or by fantasies of being a boy. Only rarely is this associated with an acknowledged or recognizable desire to become a man; being like a boy is equivalent to wishing to be effective. Pubescence puts an end to such dreams—and what develops now is a general retreat from adulthood and its demands. In some there is an exaggerated display of femininity, acting the role of the cute little girl who will be admired and approved, particularly by father, who, they always feel, pays attention only to something he can exhibit with pride.

Anorexics' resistance against learning about sex was documented through a series of psychological tests by Hiltmann (11). She considered the possibility that the psychosexual vulnerability was in a way related to errors or deficits in the cognitive assumptions with which the ordinary adolescent approaches the problems of maturity. Though they rated in overall intellectual performance and academic achievement as high as a control group, an analysis of the content of subquestions revealed that anorexic girls were deficient in defining the concept of "marriage registrar," and of "egg and semen," failing to give common definitions. This may be related to deficiencies in early learning or to a more or less intentional repression of earlier knowledge. The findings are consistent with an assumption that throughout childhood there had been some inadequacy in integrating new information, that these girls are unable to assimilate certain thoughts and objective information in a realistic way and that the subsequent emotional-social disabilities are related to disturbances in perceptual and conceptual integration.

One girl, Claire (No. 38), spoke spontaneously about being afraid of becoming pregnant—not from eating, but from "picking up germs" in a bathroom used by boys. Until age 7 Claire had been an only child; then a sister was born and 2 years later a brother. She showed no particular reaction, neither a mothering interest in the younger children nor open jealousy. Later she was outspoken in expressing her envy about their being small, that they could stay at home whereas she would be pushed out into the world as soon as she was grown. She had been a "very good child" with excellent table manners, careful about her appearance and grooming, and an honor student. She became visibly unhappy while at summer camp at age 11, where, she reported much later, on a trail ride she had the peculiar feeling that God wanted her to be a missionary, though she felt she did not want to be one. From then on she became concerned with religion, sin, and cleanliness. She began to feel less comfortable in school, wanted to be only with students whom she knew well, and over-reacted to any form of teasing. After school she would spend hours in the bathtub to get rid of "the germs" and then would scrub the bathtub to protect the younger children from these germs. It was in connection with this that she spoke of her fear of becoming pregnant.

At the time of her annual checkup she noted that she had gained 12 lbs during the preceding year and she became alarmed that if she kept on gaining like this it would be "too much." Her weight was 84 lbs and she wanted to bring it down to 77 lbs—in harmony with her former gain of 5 lbs per year—but reached only 82 lbs. She maintained this level and was visibly thin when she was seen in consultation a year later. Her expressed fear was that of becoming an adult, and she used dieting like a magic charm that would keep her body from changing. She clung to the rigid weight for nearly 2 years though she continued to grow and had menarche at age 14½.

Anxiety about sex was only one aspect of her fears; the more disturbing fear was that of losing the support of her parents. She was quite aware of her hostile feelings against her mother and of her envy toward the younger children. She felt she *had to* become a missionary to atone for these evil thoughts and feelings. At 16 she weighed 95 lbs and was much more relaxed in relation to her family and schoolmates. One day she confessed to her therapist that "the worst has come to pass. It is terrible that I don't think it is terrible to think about it"—namely about sex and boys.

Karol (No. 32) had been anxious about and preoccupied with sex as far back as she could remember. As a child she was severely constipated and was given many enemas, which she considered horrible, but her mother gave them to her in spite of her objections. Her mother also insisted on repeated rectal examinations by the pediatrician, which was to Karol a humiliating experience. "She told me that they did this to you when you went into the hospital to have a baby, and I have always been frightened at the idea of having children." From the time Karol was 15 there had been enormous emphasis on dating; she felt her parents forced her to date, whether she wanted to or not and that they did not care with whom she went out as long as she did go out. Quite often her mother chose her boyfriends for her and told her to be "free." Karol, on the contrary, felt proud about being puritanical and never permitting anybody to come close or to touch her. "I act as if I were a glass person—'don't touch me'—as if I would break." When her father approached her she pulled away and he reacted with great hurt. It was the same with the boyfriends whom her mother selected. "I was always frightened about sex—when double dating I was panic stricken when a boy kissed me." This pattern of being pushed into dating went on through her whole adolescence and continued after the anorexia developed.

However, the development of anorexia was not related to any upsetting event while dating, where she behaved as before, but to the failure of her efforts to prove herself. Her anxiety about her body and sex were fused.

It is as if I had to punish my body. I hate and detest it. If I let it be normal for a few days then I have to deprive it again. I feel caught in my body—as long as I can keep it under rigid control it can't betray me. It could make me vulnerable and I have to keep it thin. I am really afraid of sex; and I am terribly afraid of childbirth. I want to have children but I am afraid of getting fat.

When it was noted that she looked better, she was terribly upset that it was so obvious. "I did not feel any satisfaction, all I felt was 'I am getting fatter.'" The feeling of being a horrible person, "a nothing," persisted.

I am like a blown up balloon, with hot air on the inside and just some skin on the outside. I am like the frosting on a cake with no cake inside. I have denied myself so much that I didn't even notice thirst and hunger. Everywhere I left destruction—I did some horrible damage to myself and to my life. . . . I have denied my body, I have pretended it did not exist, it was not worth anything. I did let it disintegrate as if "myself" and "it" were different—like two separate people. "I" was in my body—but severed from "it"—I did not want what it stood for—to live like a mature woman. It had been a good body—but it was too much for me to handle and the safest thing was to "forget about it." I felt very attached to my mother and if I left my own body I would become part of mother's body. Mother was set on making me her doll to play with—I never felt I was my own self. I was just a play thing.

The most pressing problem was that now her mother wanted her to get married, and she felt guilty that she was not giving mother what she wanted. All her life she had wanted mother's complete attention, wanted mother to be proud of her and tell her that she was exceptional. She had never been satisfied with doing the "ordinary," always feeling she should have done better, and "failure" was like a slap to her pride and self-esteem.

Such open preoccupation with sex is rare in primary anorexia nervosa, though in Karol's case it was forced on her by her parents who were more impervious to her feelings than most. Usually absence of any interest is a pronounced feature, or insistence on retaining the preadolescent friendship relations to boys. Sharon (No. 13) was aware that she was attractive and she had many boys as friends, but she did not want anyone to be close to her. There was a strong feeling that nobody would really want her, that she must not respond. When she began her dieting a young man was paying attention to her, but she felt he was adding just one more girl to his lists of conquests. When it became apparent that he was truly fond of her personally she did not dare to respond. Her fear of being heavy was associated with the fear of not being attractive and popular, although she realized that this boy had paid attention to her when she was at her heaviest, before the reducing began. The idea of gaining weight involved the fear of her belly being larger and that was one thing that she could not possibly tolerate. When the suggestion was made that this might indicate fear of pregnancy she absolutely denied this association or that such an idea would ever have occurred to her. Long before the anorexia began, and in competition with an older slender sister, she had taken special exercises to have a perfectly straight posture, without sticking out in front or behind.

Several girls got married while still anorexic, or during a remission. Christine (No. 19) made an unsuitable marriage, which was subsequently annulled. She had felt that she had to accept the proposal because she was so relieved that there was a man who wanted her, and who did not think of her as ugly. She has since remarried. Nora (No. 4) appeared happy in her marriage; she took pride in her husband and this compensated her for not having pride in herself. Though still amenorrheic, she became pregnant. She experienced the enlargement of her abdomen as something desirable, as entirely different from the hateful fear of her body being big and fat.

I have emphasized the various ways in which psychosexual immaturity and anxiety may interact with the basic issues in anorexia nervosa. There seems to be a tendency to confront patients too early in treatment with specific sexual topics, before they have developed some sense of identity and self-directed independence. Such efforts lead to sterile and threatening discussions and account, in my opinion, for the fact that treatment so often results in a stalemate. I have been impressed by the frequency with which a referring psychiatrist represents his patient as "resisting insight," and that patients, in turn, will speak of their past therapeutic experiences with disdain, ennumerating topics which, they felt, had been forced upon them but did not make sense to them, at least not at that stage in their development.

Psychiatric Differential Diagnosis

There has been considerable controversy about the proper psychiatric classification for anorexia nervosa; some of this was reviewed in Chapters 12 and 13, particularly the need to differentiate between an unspecific refusal to eat and primary anorexia nervosa. As long as the focus was on unconscious conflicts about sexuality, pregnancy wishes, or fear of it, the condition was conceived of as a neurosis. This was the majority opinion until fairly recently. However, as was discussed before, the possibility of an essentially schizophrenic core, with underlying deformation of the ego, had not been entirely overlooked. Even now some will speak of it as a neurosis, and schizophrenic development later in life is considered evidence against the earlier syndrome having been anorexia nervosa. In a survey of 30 patients, observed between 1935 and 1959, Rowland (16) noted that the final diagnosis was a medley of conversion hysteria, obsessive compulsive neurosis, anxiety reaction, schizophrenia (undifferentiated, mixed, and paranoid) and depressive reaction, with schizophrenia being diagnosed more often during the 1950's than during the 1930's. This trend has continued; most of the patients I have observed, at the same medical center during the 1960's, were diagnosed as schizophrenic. However, as was discussed before, schizophrenia with noneating for a variety of reasons needs to be differentiated from primary anorexia nervosa where pursuit of thinness with the singular goal of autonomy is the core issue.

Much of the old confusion was related to the fact that all cases of severe psychological weight loss were lumped together, and that psychiatric diagnostic categories were conceived of as rather fixed clinical entities. Modern psychiatric thinking has undergone many changes. Mental illness is no longer conceived of as a definite disease process which invades an organism, but rather as disturbances in an individual's functioning. Questions like "does a patient have hysteria or schizophrenia," etc., are reformulated today as "under what conditions will he react in a schizophrenic, hysterical, depressive, or obsessional fashion?"

When anorexic patients are followed over many years the interrelatedness of various psychiatric syndromes comes into the open. Not uncommonly an early diagnosis of neurosis needs to be changed to schizophrenia as the illness persists. There has been increasing discontent with schizophrenia as a diagnostic concept, and it has even been stated that no such disease entity exists, that it is fallacious to make a diagnosis by adding up various symptoms, or to deduce it in retrospect from the long-range outcome. It has even been suggested that the concept be abolished altogether, but no new term or diagnostic label has been formulated that would refer to the clinical conditions characterized by disturbances in the symbolic processes with *deficits* in reality testing and self-awareness, and also in psychosocial competence and personality integration.

Changes in the underlying conceptualizations have progressed further in the United States than in Europe, where many psychiatrists still adhere to the old concept of dementia praecox as an organic process. Confronted with the same clinical material, American psychiatrists are inclined to diagnose schizophrenia in patients whom their British colleagues might diagnose as suffering from depressive or neurotic illness, or personality disorders. With these differences in the usage of diagnostic terms it is not surprising that anorexia nervosa is assigned to different classifications by European and American authors.

The development of a frank schizophrenic picture in obese patients has been described earlier (Chapter 10). This may occur when they are exposed to new life situations and tasks which outrange their adaptive capacities, or under the stress of unrealistic reducing programs. By exhausting their conviction of secret power, that by reducing they could set everything right, they come face to face with the bare facts of their problems, which not only are not solved but appear more threatening and distressing. In some a schizophrenic disorganization will occur. Others, however, cling to the hope that further reducing will solve their problem, and will pursue the diet with the determination that results in anorexia nervosa, which in itself is an irrational and unrealistic effort.

In the exploration of the psychological factors in schizophrenia there has been increasing emphasis on the deficits and failures in essential learning in various areas of human experiences. For eating disorders, failure to acquire discriminating awareness of essential body sensations, in particular of hunger, is the outstanding deficiency (Chapter 4). Invariably this is associated with distorted concepts of one's own bodily identity; it may or may not be associated with disturbances and deficiencies in the integration of other symbolic processes. Not all patients with primary anorexia nervosa are overtly schizophrenic or ever progress to that state of disorganization. In the beginning of the illness a variety of neurotic pictures, most often obsessive-compulsive defenses, stand in the foreground. This expresses an effort to ward off confrontation with the false awareness of their own needs, their lack of control over their bodily functions, and the frightening awareness of their complete helplessness in presenting themselves to the world around them, or inability to interpret the intent and actions of others.

The significance of depressive features deserves special evaluation; it may indicate a clinical depression as a primary illness or express the underlying despair of a schizophrenic reaction. Quite often the early manifestations of something wrong, preceding the actual anorexia by months or years, are depressive mood swings. In my experience true depressive illness does occur in anorexia nervosa, but it is rare; one case was described in the previous chapter. After a long illness an affective depressive state is difficult to distinguish from apathy.

It is my impression that one reason for the reluctance to recognize the schizophrenic core in primary anorexia nervosa is an old, uncorrected conviction that this would indicate that the condition was untreatable. I should like to present briefly two cases from the literature of undoubted schizophrenia; careful review of the histories reveals that the long-lasting illness had begun with an anorexic episode. Will (23) described a young woman who had been a psychiatric patient for many years and had received the currently popular treatments with insulin and electricity, not only without benefit, but with considerable worsening. He described movingly her display of anxiety, fear, loneliness, and the corroding effect of social isolation. She was said to have been an amiable, good, and intelligent child, more than adequate as an athlete, an excellent student and participant in social affairs. In her teens she became markedly preoccupied and depressed, and suffered from constipation, loss of appetite, and a persistent decline in weight. The diagnosis of a pituitary disease was made but endocrine medication effected no cure. She was finally hospitalized as a "mental" patient, emaciated, increasingly withdrawn, hostile, and was described in various reports as "empty," "hollow," "unable to love," and "hopeless." She was of slight build, not having eaten freely for many years, and regurgitating food that was given to her. Nevertheless she responded well to a therapeutic approach with emphasis on human relatedness. In response to my inquiry, in 1971, Will wrote: "We stopped work about 17 years ago, after which she finished college, worked, and at present has a busy and as far as I know satisfying life, both personally and professionally."

Another description of what looked like a deteriorated schizophrenic state in a 36-year-old woman was given by Gibson (10). Her illness had begun when she was 12 years old with long periods of refusal to eat. She wasted away to as little as 65 lbs. After many years of various treatment efforts, including hormonal treatment, insulin, and electroshock, but fortunately not lobotomy, which had been strongly recommended, she finally came to psychotherapy. She was exceedingly fearful in therapy; once she dropped her stereotyped complaints to say fearfully that if she lost her illness there would be nothing left—she had no other identity. In spite of the long history of personal and emotional neglect she responded well to psychotherapy, and during the recovery from the psychotic state she reexperienced some of the characteristic anorexia nervosa symptoms. She revealed that she had starved herself in an effort to control indescribable but to her terrifying feelings. Despite her seeming lack of interest in food an underlying voracity was revealed with enormous interest in food and eating, and acquiring a collection of cookbooks. She also began to crave sweets and occasionally gorged herself on candy bars.

None of the anorexic patients I have known had been quite as neglected or exhibited such overt schizophrenic pictures. I have cited these two reports to illustrate that the diagnosis of schizophrenia does not indicate a hopeless prognosis. On the contrary, recognition of the underlying, potentially schizophrenic core is essential for effective treatment. I have seen many anorexic patients where increasing isolation had progressed to apathy and withdrawal into an autistic way of life. Unfortunately I have seen this happen not infrequently while they were in treatment which focused on their so-called conflicts and neglected to deal with the underlying essential problems, the ego deficiencies and incompetence in self-awareness and in human relatedness. In a misguided effort a therapist will "support" an anorexic's increasingly bizarre living arrangements; an example was described in Chapter 4, the case of Gail. Unfortunately she does not stand alone; there were many other situations where a therapist had not only permitted but even encouraged a symbiotic relationship with himself, without helping the patient become more clearly differentiated, and thus he had become a collaborator toward an insidious schizophrenic development.

BIBLIOGRAPHY

1. Bilz, R., Anorexia nervosa, Bibl. Psychiat. Neurol., 147:219–244, 1971.
2. Blinder, B. J., Freeman, D. M. A., and Stunkard, A. J., Behavior therapy of anorexia nervosa: Effectiveness of activity as a reinforcer of weight gain, Amer. J. Psychiat., 126:77–82, 1970.
3. Bruch, H., Perceptual and conceptual disturbances in anorexia nervosa, Psychosom. Med., 24:187–194, 1962.
4. Bruch, H., Anorexia nervosa and its differential diagnosis, J. Nerv. Ment. Dis., 141:555–566, 1966.
5. Bruch, H., The insignificant difference: Discordant incidence of anorexia nervosa in monozygotic twins, Amer. J. Psychiat., 126:123–128, 1969.
6. Bruch, H., Death in anorexia nervosa, Psychosom. Med., 33:135–144, 1971.
7. Crisp, A. H., Reported birth weights and growth rates in a group of patients with primary anorexia nervosa (weight phobia), J. Psychosom. Res., 14:23–50, 1970.
8. Dally, P., Anorexia Nervosa, Grune & Stratton, New York, 1969.
9. Franklin, J. S., Schiele, B. C., Brozek, J., and Keys, A., Observations on human behavior in experimental semi-starvation and rehabilitation, J. Clin. Psychol., 4:28–45, 1948.
10. Gibson, R. W., The ego defect in schizophrenia, pp. 88–97, in Psychoneurosis and Schizophrenia, ed. G. L. Usdin, J. B. Lippincott, Co., Philadelphia, 1966.
11. Hiltmann, H., Urteilsbildung und Affekteinstellung bei magersuechtigen jungen Maedchen und Frauen, pp. 128–138, in Anorexia Nervosa, J.-E. Meyer and H. Feldmann, eds., Georg Thieme Verlag, Stuttgart, 1965.
12. Kazantzakis, N., Spain, trans. A. Mims, Simon & Schuster, New York, 1963.
13. Kelley, K., Daniels, G. E., Poe, J., Easser, R., and Monroe, R., Psychological correlations with secondary amenorrhea, Psychosom. Med., 16:129–147, 1954.
14. King, A., Primary and secondary anorexia nervosa syndromes, Brit. J. Psychiat., 109:470–479, 1963.
15. Richter, H.-E., Die dialogische Funktion der Magersucht, pp. 108–112, in Anorexia Nervosa, J.-E. Meyer and H. Feldmann, eds., Georg Thieme Verlag, Stuttgart, 1965.
16. Rowland, C. V., Jr., Anorexia nervosa, A survey of the literature and review of 30 cases, pp. 37–137, in Anorexia and Obesity, C. V. Rowland, ed., Int. Psychiat. Clin., Little, Brown & Co., Boston, 1970.
17. Selvini, M. P., Anorexia nervosa, pp. 197–218, in The World Biennial of Psychiatry and Psychotherapy, Vol. 1, S. Arieti, ed., Basic Books, New York, 1970.
18. Singer, M. T., and Wynne, L. C., Principles for scoring communication defects and deviances in parents of schizophrenics: Rorschach and TAT scoring manuals, Psychiatry, 29:260–288, 1966.
19. Theander, S., Anorexia Nervosa. A Psychiatric Investigation of 94 Female Patients, Acta Psychiat. Scand., suppl. 214, Munsgaard, Copenhagen, 1970.
20. Thomae, H., Anorexia Nervosa, Huber-Klett, Bern-Stuttgart, 1961; Int. Univ. Press, New York, 1967.
21. Ushakov, G. K., Anorexia nervosa, pp. 274–289, in Modern Perspectives in Adolescent Psychiatry, J. G. Howells, ed., Oliver & Boyd, Edinburgh, 1971.
22. Waller, J. V., Kaufman, R., and Deutsch, F., Anorexia nervosa: A psychosomatic entity, Psychosom. Med., 2:3–16, 1940.
23. Will, O. A., Jr., Human relatedness and the schizophrenic reaction, Psychiatry, 22:205–223, 1959.

15

Anorexia Nervosa in the Male

Anorexia nervosa in the male requires a separate discussion. It is exceedingly rare, occurring conspicuously less frequently than in females, and the literature on it is even more ambiguous and contradictory, with few authors having observed more than an occasional case. Opinions vary widely, and one finds contradictory statements side by side: that typical anorexia nervosa does not occur in the male, and that it is not different from that observed in the female. It has even been doubted whether it was justifiable to make the diagnosis in a male. If amenorrhea is considered a cardinal symptom then males are ipso facto excluded. If one approaches the syndrome in psychiatric terms, as I have done here, then the condition does occur in males and should be diagnosed as such; namely, when one encounters the same psychological constellation and issues associated with severe loss of weight as in females. As in females, anorexia nervosa in the male is not a uniform condition, and both the genuine syndrome as well as the atypical form are observed (3). In the genuine or *primary anorexia nervosa syndrome* the patient is preoccupied with his body size, with a relentless pursuit of thinness. The bizarre misuse of the eating function represents a frantic effort to establish a sense of control and identity, whereas in the unspecific *atypical form* the eating function itself is disturbed with various distortions of its symbolic meaning and thinness is only an accidental byproduct.

Morton (10), who is credited with having given the first distinct medical description of anorexia nervosa in 1689, includes in his treatise the case of a 16-year-old boy:

The Son of the Reverent Minister Mr. Steele, my very good friend, about the Sixteenth Year of his Age fell gradually into a total want of Appetite, occasioned by his studying too hard, and the Passions of his Mind, and upon that into an Universal Atrophy, pining away more and more for the space of two Years, without any Cough, Fever, or any other Symptom of any Distemper of his Lungs or any other Entrail; as also without a looseness, or Diabetes, or any other sign of a Colliquation, or Preternatural Evacuation. And therefore I judg'd this Consumption to be Nervous, and to have its seed in the whole Habit of the Body, and to arise from the System of Nerves being distemper'd. I began, and first attempted his Cure with the use of Antiscorbutick, Bitter, and Chalybeate Medicines, as well Natural as Artificial, but without any benefit; and therefore when I found that the former Method did not answer our Expectations, I advis'd him to abandon his Studies, to go into the Country Air, and to use Riding, and a Milk Diet (and especially to drink Asses Milk), for a long time. By the use of which he recover'd his Health in a great measure, though he is not yet perfectly freed from a Consumptive state; and what will be the event of this Method, does not yet plainly appear.

Gull mentions that the disease may occur in males, though without describing a case (8). The modern literature has paid very little attention to male anorexic patients. If such observations are referred to at all they are mentioned in the form of an appendix or footnote. Dally surveyed 140 females with anorexia nervosa and subdivided the syndrome into distinctly different groups (6). He observed 6 male patients during the same period and noted that anorexia nervosa in the male was a more heterogenous condition and that it was difficult to compare the course and outcome in the two sexes. Selvini (11) based a recent discussion of anorexia nervosa entirely on observations of females, stating in a footnote:

The cases of undereating I have seen in males were cases of pseudo-anorexia. One was a monk who had developed paranoid delusions: by fasting, he thought, he could redeem the corrupt members of his order. Another was dominated by hypochondriacal ideas of a schizophrenic type, centered on the digestive system. The third was the closest to true anorexia, also because of the presence of neuro-muscular hyperactivity. This patient, however, showed atypical signs. In the first place he explicitly declared a longing for food as for a "paradise lost," whereas true anorexia never admits such a longing. In the second place, he exhibited his fasting performances, unlike female anorexic patients, who constantly claim they have eaten a great deal.

It may not be accidental that the few more detailed descriptions on male anorexics deal with fairly young patients. Falstein and his co-workers (7) reported, in 1956, on 4 prepubescent boys whose pathological attitude toward food, the feeding person, and their own bodies and body images had resulted in a clinical state that revealed the classical picture of anorexia nervosa. They considered it the end-result of diverse and multiple contributing factors and that its defense function had a more or less individual meaning in each case; all four boys had been preoccupied with their size. Tolstrup (13) observed 4 males among 14 patients with onset before age 14, and he felt that they showed the typical anorexia nervosa syndrome. Blitzer and co-workers (2) observed three boys among 15 children who "starved themselves" with onset between 11 and 12¾ years. Crisp (5) reported one case of anorexia nervosa in a male of 14 years who suffered from a persistent fear of being too fat. No specific statement is made about the state of pubescence of this boy, but his size (5'8") and the published picture suggest that he was undergoing early pubertal development. Ushakov (14) found the admission rates for anorexia nervosa five times higher for girls than for boys, and that an early onset, 10 to 13 years, is more common in boys.

Among the 70 anorexic patients whom I observed between 1942 and 1970, there were 10 male patients (14%) in whom at the time of their illness the diagnosis of anorexia nervosa had been made. Not included are patients in whom it had been recognized that the marked weight loss was incidental to schizophrenia, depression, or some other well-defined psychiatric condition; some of them were briefly mentioned in Chapter 13. The chief descriptive data for the 10 male anorexics are summarized in the accompanying table (Table 15–1). By focusing on the core dynamic issues and by clarifying the whole life pattern, interpersonal experiences, emotional conflicts, and psychological deficits, it was possible to define a syndrome of primary anorexia nervosa and to differentiate it from a condition where the refusal to eat and the cachexia were incidental to some unspecific psychiatric disturbance. The need to differentiate between different forms of anorexia nervosa was recognized only with growing experience. It forced itself into the open when Nathan (No. 3)* and Eric (No. 5), with dramatically different dynamic constellations, were observed on the same service at the same time, between 1959 and 1961. Four patients were rated as showing the *atypical picture*, and six as exhibiting the *primary anorexia nervosa* syndrome. Two of them developed atypical symptomatology which in Edgar (No. 6) expressed a progressive schizophrenic deterioration, and in Everett (No. 10) a frantic effort to camouflage the underlying problems of a persistent primary syndrome.

Atypical Cases

I shall present the atypical cases first. It is probably accidental that they were the ones who were observed first; at the time of their illness they were considered examples of the classical anorexia nervosa picture.

Eli (No. 1) was 27 years old when he became nervous and fearful and lost his appetite, about 1 month before the birth of his first child. A few months later he developed persistent vomiting, progressive weight loss, and suffered from severe fatigue. There were several hospitalizations without evidence of an organic disease. During all these examinations his general condition became progressively worse, with frequent vomiting and poor sleep. His interests became more and more self-centered, he lost his desire for marital relations and was increasingly annoyed and irritated by the baby. His increasing weakness made any work impossible. He was referred to the Psychiatric Institute 1½ years later, in 1944.

He was the youngest of 8 children of Jewish parents who had immi-

---

* Nathan (No. 3) and all other names and numbers in this chapter refer to Table 15–1.

TABLE 15-1

Anorexia Nervosa in Ten Males

NUMBER NAME	PUBERTY	ONSET YEAR	ONSET AGE	WEIGHT HIGH	WEIGHT LOW	LOSS LBS	LOSS %	CONSULTATION YEAR	DURATION (YEARS)	LAST INFORMATION
				ATYPICAL						
1. Eli	Mature, married, 1 child	1942	27½	150+	97	53	30	1944; 1948	6	1948 Died
2. Ira	Beginning	1954	14	125	85	40	32	1955	2+	1960 State hospital, schizophrenic
3. Nathan	No	1954	13	91	60	31	34	1955	6	1968 Recovered, restricted
4. Ervin	Mature	1963	24	158	118	40	25	1963	n. i.*	n. i.*
				PRIMARY						
5. Eric	No	1952	12	91	45	46	50	1959	8	1970 Recovered
6. Edgar	No	1957	12	105	75	30	28	1961	4+	1963 State hospital, schizophrenic
7. Bert	No	1960	12	110	68	42	38	1961	2	1971 Recovered
8. Elliot	No	1963	13¾	115	86	29	25	1963	⅓	1963 Died
9. Newton	No	1963	12½	100	67	33	33	1965	4	1970 Recovered, restricted
10. Everett	Beginning, after endocrines	1968	13½	119	75	44	37	1970	2+	1971 In residential treatment

* n.i. = no information.

grated to the United States as young adults. The father had died several years earlier of rectal cancer. The mother was 61, an energetic woman and very much in the picture. His six older brothers were doing well whereas his only sister was described as thin with many nervous complaints. Even as a child Eli had been exceedingly shy. He felt isolated as an adolescent and did not date girls. At age 24 he married the first girl he ever dated, against the expressed opposition of his mother.

After admission he continued to vomit and had no appetite and his weight fell to 97 lbs. He was treated with subcoma doses of insulin and with psychotherapy. He stopped vomiting and regained his appetite, with a weight increase of 43 lbs. He began to enjoy his visits to his home and became attached to his child. For the next 18 months he seemed to be doing well; while still a resident at the hospital he had obtained a good paying job, commensurate with his skills.

Then he began to complain again of increasing tension, nausea, vomiting, and despondency, and of his wife being unsympathetic and resentful. He spent the next winter in Florida, with his mother, where he attempted several jobs but each time gave up after a few days because he felt too weak and the work made him nervous. On his return from Florida his wife greeted him with the announcement that she planned to divorce him.

Even before he had learned about his wife's divorce decision he had planned to return to the Psychiatric Institute for further treatment, having lost 30 lbs. His weight on the second admission (1948) was 109 lbs. He was obsessively preoccupied with his gastrointestinal symptoms and was afraid of having an ulcer or cancer. No organic reason for his ill health was found. Insulin injections were tried again; this time with little effect. He complained about extensive fatigue more than he had during his first admission. His weight remained approximately 105 lbs and he had frequent episodes of vomiting. After three months he had a short febrile disease, without localized findings. He continued to vomit for the next week and there was increasing distension and weakness, again without adequate findings. He was seen by a medical consultant and was in good verbal rapport with him. During this consultation he suddenly turned over; after brief tonic spasms he was dead within a few minutes. An autopsy was performed revealing no abnormal findings except for a remarkably distended and enlarged stomach. The patient's relatives accepted his death and insisted that he died because he had no wish nor will to live.

Ira (No. 2) was 14 years old in 1954 when he developed the first symptoms during the summer before entering high school. He complained of headaches, became depressed and moody, was irritable and became even more withdrawn than before. His eating became irregular and this progressed to the point where he was unable to take anything except liquids. He was fearful that when he swallowed the food would go to his lungs, causing him to choke to death. He talked about this quite often before he actually became afraid to eat. Gradually he became so phobic about swallowing that he refused to eat. There was rapid weight loss (30 lbs within 5 months) and he was unable to attend school. Extensive medical and neurological work-up failed to reveal any organic abnormalities and he was referred to the psychiatric service.

He was the only child of a tense and anxious mother and a passive and taciturn father who never had wanted children and remained distant to his son. The family constellation resembled in many ways what has been previously described (Chapter 5) as characteristic for the family of fat children. Food and eating had always been extremely important. There had been two brief periods of refusal to eat in early childhood, but on the whole his appetite had been large, "as if he couldn't get enough," and he had been quite obese.

At the hospital he attended the school but did only borderline passing work. He was seen in psychotherapy where he appeared irritable and depressed until he finally verbalized that the therapist was not helping him enough and there must be something more that could be done for him than just talking. After this he appeared less depressed and had fewer complaints and began to explore his underlying fears. He went home during the Christmas holidays and decided, with agreement of his parents, not to return to the hospital but to seek private psychiatric treatment. In spite of the marked schizoid picture the main diagnosis at the time of hospitalization was psychoneurosis, conversion hysteria. Five years later, in 1960, an effort was made to contact the patient, and it was learned that he had been admitted to a state hospital with the diagnosis of schizophrenia.

Nathan (No. 3) began his noneating regimen following his bar mitzvah (1954). He felt he had not done as well as was expected of him, had not deserved the lavish celebration because he had brought shame on his family. There was considerable loss of weight, from 91 lbs at his thirteenth birthday to less than 60 lbs 8 months later. Simultaneously many other changes in his behavior were observed. He expressed mystical ideas and would get up in the middle of the night to say his prayers, or he would check the water faucets and keep on tightening them so there would be no drip. He explained that the significance of the bar mitzvah was expressed in one sentence: "Now you are a man." This meant to him that he himself, no longer his parents, was responsible for his sins. He became increasingly concerned with his sins and how to atone for them. Since the Day of Atonement in Jewish ritual is a fast day, fasting became for him the leading means of self-punishment and expiation. Throughout his illness there was a constant intermixing of fasting with doing other rituals for atonement, noneating for having done them incorrectly and more rituals and more refusal to eat. At no time did he express concern about his size or fear of fatness.

Nathan was the second of three children of Jewish parents (not orthodox) in their early thirties, of lower-middle-class status. His older brother was retarded and demanded his mother's complete attention. Nathan was left to the care of his grandmother, an invalided rigid woman who dominated the household with her superstitions and anxieties. She was in the habit of beating herself whenever her children or grandchildren misbehaved, in particular if they did not eat all the food she offered. There was a sister 5 years younger who seemed to be doing well; much of her care had been entrusted to Nathan after his mother had taken a job to contribute to the family's finances.

When admitted to the psychiatric service Nathan looked like the victim of a concentration camp; not only was he emaciated but he was covered with large bruises, mainly on his forehead. Whenever he did something he felt he was not supposed to do he would beat his head against the wall. To protect him against injury he was given a football helmet which he wore with pride. He stayed at the Institute for nearly five years and was a star performer at innumerable conferences and an expert on Board examinations. There must be a whole generation of American psychiatrists who associate the concept of anorexia nervosa with a disheveled cacheticlooking boy in a football helmet. He looked very sick and regressed in his behavior and he was unable to take care of himself and too weak to take part in activities. He would spend many hours standing instead of sitting or lying down. This was not an expression of hyperactivity as is observed in true anorexia nervosa but was one more form of self-punishment.

He was the first male anorexic patient whom we observed after a systematic study of anorexia nervosa had been decided on. The many deviations from the classical picture were recognized and explained as different manifestations in the male. In a way the error of our interpretation was clarified by another male anorexic, Eric, who himself was quite an expert, having survived 6 years of analytic psychotherapy, when he was admitted at age 18. Eric's reaction to his fellow anorexics was startling: He said he would rather eat than be tube fed. He explained later: "I took one look at him. Man, that scared me. He was weird!" By that time Nathan had been on the ward for over 3 years, had been exposed to our whole repertoire of psychiatric regimens (including, when first admitted in 1955, a course of insulin shock therapy) and had been tube fed for over three years, debating at each feeding whether it was "harder" to eat by himself or to be tube fed. He was articulate and argumentative in his psychotherapeutic sessions. The leading theme was guilt and atonement, and he used the noneating in this context. His many other bizarre rituals served the same purpose. He would sleep on the floor because it was "harder" than sleeping in his bed, or he would wet himself instead of going to the toilet with the same explanation. He would feel guilty for causing so much trouble and extra work for the staff, and then would devise new rituals and prescribe more fasting to atone for this. At no time did he give another explanation for his noneating than the need for atonement and self-punishment.

There were brief periods when he would eat. Once he began eating when a nurse put food into his mouth and he swallowed it. He later said he did not have any intention of eating but since the nurse shoved it in he ate it. He explained:

I got so fed up with everything so I started to eat. I wanted to make myself feel better. I had no intention of eating. I did it because I was so fed up and was so far behind in my rituals that I decided I would do it. I wanted to wait for the doctor but I was also fed up with waiting. So I forgot about the doctor and thought that I might just as well eat. It was nonsense to wait. There was no reason why I should not eat.

He was also impressed by the nurse's attitude. "She made me swallow it. She said that it was her job to make me eat. She was strict about it. I didn't get a feeling of love. She wasn't interested in whether I ate or not. If she loved me, she would have encouraged me."

He added that taking food was a pleasure, but when he feels guilty he can't have the things he enjoys. If he can get enough reasons together for eating he sometimes can do it, for example, when he can convince himself that by eating he can save other people a lot of trouble (tube feeding), then he can eat; but then he no longer needs to eat because he has saved some people some trouble. These arguments illustrate the ruminative quality of his thinking. Except for the area of his morbid preoccupations, he was rational and precise, kept well informed on events and was somewhat of the ward philosophizer. A certain competition developed between him and Eric (No. 5) but he decided to continue tube feeding "because it was harder." One day, two years to the day after his grandmother's death, he declared he wanted to leave the hospital and would eat because he wanted to finish his education. He did exactly that. He has maintained himself on the outside, living a rather restricted life, but is self-supporting having acquired some semi-professional training. His weight has stabilized at a reasonable level (135 lbs when 28 years old) without food fads, except for rigid adherence to Jewish dietary laws.

Ervin (No. 4) was 24 years old when he applied for psychiatric treatment after having lost nearly 40 lbs during the 8 preceding months (1963). A medical hospitalization had failed to establish evidence of an organic reason for his weight loss. He was a student in professional training and had been doing well in his academic work. His eating difficulties began when he had to meet clients. He became rather tense and anxious, in particular when he had to face a client and instructor at the same time. He had difficulties in concentrating and also began to withdraw from his normal social activities. There was a progressive loss of weight, from 158 lbs to 118 lbs, though he did not notice any particular change in his feelings about food or in his eating habits. He did not have full awareness of the weight loss except for an increasing looseness of his clothes. He neither had a feeling of being empty or full, nor was he particularly interested in his weight.

Psychological tests were in agreement with the clinical impression of a man who had grave doubts about his masculine identity and who felt too passive and dependent to stand up in a stressful situation where he had to function in an authoritative role. In contrast to his excellent performance on intelligence tests, the quantity and quality of his responses in projective tests was below what one would expect in a person of his intellectual capabilities. There was indication of anxiety with strong tendency to withdraw, to rationalize, and to deny problems. The impression was that of a psychoneurosis but there were some unusual verbalizations reflecting a slight disruption in his thinking, particularly regarding his masculine sexual identification.

Since he could not be accepted for psychotherapy he was referred to another psychiatrist and no follow-up information was obtained.

Except for the weight loss and noneating these 4 patients have little in common. They were diagnosed as suffering from anorexia nervosa on the basis of the outer picture with emaciation of the same order of magnitude as that observed in the true syndromes. However, there were no similarities in the underlying patterns of life and in the circumstances precipitating the loss of appetite or food refusal. Two of them, Eli and Ervin, were adults who suffered from true loss of appetite which had developed in response to what they experienced as overdemanding life situations. Though of good intelligence both had been "underachievers," performing below the level of their capacities. Eli suffered from severe anxiety about his symptoms, in particular about the weight loss, whereas Ervin was pathologically indifferent. Both complained of fatigue and were unable to work.

Ira developed a phobic fear of swallowing, that the food might get into his lungs and he would suffocate, and these anxieties about his body and its functions coincided with his pubertal development. He had been an only child and somewhat obese, always clinging and dependent on his mother. There was no intent to change his body size and by the time he became a psychiatric patient he was frantic with fear about the weight loss and his other symptoms. In Nathan, fasting was one among many rituals to "atone for his sins" and was associated with complete indifference for his body and his appearance. Fatigue was not complained of by either boy, but there was definitely no hyperactivity, and they both had stopped going to school soon after the symptoms developed.

None of these 4 patients had been in psychiatric treatment before this illness, but there had been many recognized difficulties: complaints about their poor achievement, disturbances in their attitude toward food, overt social anxieties, and the families on the whole appeared overtly disturbed.

The psychiatric diagnosis ranged from psychoneurosis to schizophrenia, with little relationship between the diagnostic classification and the final outcome. In Eli the diagnosis was consistently psychoneurosis, but he relapsed after remarkable improvement and finally died. Ira was initially diagnosed as suffering from psychoneurosis, and showed satisfactory improvement, but at age 20 years he was in a state hospital with a frank schizophrenic picture. Nathan, on the other hand, had been recognized as schizophrenic when the illness became manifest; he did fairly well and at age 28 was active and employed, though somewhat restricted in the range of his social activities.

Many of the male patients reported in the literature seem to belong to this group of atypical anorexia. Bliss and Branch (1) included in their report 3 male patients, 21, 28, and 32 years of age who had nothing in common except the weight loss and a certain degree of "give-upitis" (defeatism). Dally (6) emphasized the heterogeneous picture among his 6 male patients, 5 of whom were adults with age range from 19 to 42 years who exhibited various atypical pictures. One of his patients, a 14-year-old boy, "dieted" because he resented being called "fatty" and seems to represent the primary picture.

Just as in my series where each patient when first seen had been considered a representative of the "classical syndrome," many reports in the literature deal with atypical patients who are presented as "classic" anorexia nervosa. To give just one example: Kuenzler (9) discussed at the Goettingen Symposium a male patient with anorexia nervosa and emphasized that his patient showed "characteristic" features. This young man had been well advanced in pubertal development when he fell in love with a girl. He became frightened about closeness when she responded to him. He tried to avoid contact with her, left school, and withdrew to live at home. During this time he developed abdominal pains, then disgust for food, began to vomit and suffered from constipation. His symptoms are quite different from the primary picture which will be described in the next section.

Primary Anorexia Nervosa

In contrast to the divergent atypical pictures the primary group has many features in common and the psychological issues are similar to those described for girls with primary anorexia nervosa (Chapter 14). Relentless pursuit of thinness appears to be the leading motif with vigorous defense of even severe cachexia as "not too thin." It occurs in youngsters who seemingly were doing well but whose accomplishments were a facade, an expression of compliance, and not of self-initiated and self-directed goals. In their desperate struggle to become "somebody" and to establish a sense of differentiated identity, they become overambitious, hyperactive, and perfectionistic. Manipulation of their own body through noneating and weight loss is a late step in this development but it produces the desperate picture that draws attention to their plight and finally when they refuse to accept anything from anyone, brings them into treatment.

Eric's illness (No. 5) became manifest at the time of his twelfth birthday (1952) when the family moved to a new house and to a neighborhood which was superior to their old quarters. Eric was afraid he would not make new friends and that he might no longer excel in baseball. In order to be fit he took long walks, did calisthenics to the point of exhaustion, and then refused to eat because he felt "too fat." His weight dropped from 91 lbs to 57 lbs within 6 months. From the beginning there were episodes of bulimia followed by self-induced vomiting. Hyperactivity and high performance in school work persisted throughout his illness, which lasted more than 8 years, and during which his weight dropped as low as 45 lbs. Eric was the older of 2 children and had always been considered a particularly competent boy, very bright in his academic work, and excellent in athletics. He graduated from high school in spite of continued illness when he was 17½ years old.

Psychological tests when he first became sick suggested the possibility of beginning schizophrenia, or that of a "borderline case" with compulsive features, with his overt behavior more bizarre than his thoughts. He appeared well aware of what he was doing and could think along generally accepted lines. The psychological evaluation when he was 19 years old revealed an equally ominous picture, with paranoid overalertness to environmental cues, and considerable guilt and anxiety disrupting potential intellectual and social function. The diagnostic impression was that of a schizophrenic process with marked paranoid features behind a fairly well preserved "front" of acceptable responses to the structured tests. The projective drawings supported this impression in their peculiar emphasis on certain body parts, their immaturity and their general inappropriateness, but he still possessed certain definite assets with fairly well-preserved intellectual abilities. His verbal I.Q. was 126, performance I.Q. 103, indicating a potentially superior intellectual capacity that had been impaired by an undoubtedly psychogenic and probably schizophrenic disturbance.

For many years Eric appeared to be resistant to all treatment efforts. There were repeated hospitalizations for medical reasons, at times as a life-saving measure, and also continued psychiatric treatment. At age 18½, after he had been sick for over 6 years, he was admitted to the New

York State Psychiatric Institute, weighing 49 lbs, 49 inches tall, and without any signs of pubertal development.

It was recognized early that Eric offered unusual psychological difficulties; he was either completely negativistic in his psychiatric interviews, or pseudo-intellectual, speaking of self-experiments to study nutrition, and he expressed a desire to "function like a statue or automaton." He felt it was more important not to be touched than having any contact with people, and his sense of security depended on following *his* plans, *his own* technique, quite rigidly and to perfection. Clinically there was increasing withdrawal, reluctance to participate in activities he had formerly valued, suspicion of everybody, excessive concern with his body, and constant motility. It was recognized from the beginning that his attitude toward food and eating was an expression of much more profound problems; the noneating was only the mechanism through which he tried to solve his underlying anxieties.

Eric did exceptionally well under a treatment regimen that was directed toward correcting the underlying sense of ineffectiveness; details about his treatment will be presented in Chapter 17. Throughout his illness pursuit of thinness was the outstanding motif, expressing a frantic effort to establish his sense of separateness from his parents, to prove that he himself was "somebody," not needing anything from "them." He stayed in the hospital for over 2 years. On his twentieth birthday, after there had been marked psychological improvement, and after extensive endocrinological work up, treatment with depot testosterone was instituted, to stimulate his growth and pubertal development. When last heard of (1970) he was 30 years old, finishing his Ph.D. thesis. He was sexually developed and showed an outgoing interest in girls, though he was concerned about being aspermatic. There were no food fads; he weighed 135 lbs and was of short stature, but not conspicuously so.

In Edgar (No. 6) the dynamic constellation initially resembled that of primary anorexia nervosa but after three years atypical symptomatology became dominant. The illness began with his superimposing a reducing regimen on his dog who he felt was "too fat" and not "frisky" enough to win when racing against the dogs of other boys in his neighborhood. Edgar became so insistent and anxious about reducing his dog and made such frightful scenes when his parents tried to feed it that the dog finally was given away. Edgar became quite depressed about losing his dog and now worried that he himself was too fat, went on a diet, and then stopped eating. He also would run by the hour until he was so exhausted that he could not stand up. This was about the time of his twelfth birthday (1957). An upsetting event occurring at that time was that Edgar changed from the neighborhood school to a large junior high school where he met for the first time boys whom he considered "tough" and of whom he was afraid.

He was the younger of two children in a middle-class family. His sister was 5 years older and was described as very quiet. In comparison to this "easy" girl, the mother had considered Edgar to be demanding, tense, and hyperactive and had been inconsistent in handling him.

The family was slow in recognizing the abnormality of Edgar's behavior and did not take him to a physician until he had lost nearly 30 lbs, going from 105 to 75 lbs. Then there was a series of medical and psychiatric hospitalizations, most of short duration. Only at one time, in 1958, did he stay long enough in one hospital to derive some benefit, and he gained weight to a nearly normal level. After discharge he was sent to a summer camp where he felt unhappy and lost weight. On second admission to the same hospital he responded well in the beginning but left prematurely.

After coming back to the city he complained about a postnasal drip, noted a pseudo-medical advertisement about X-ray treatment for this condition, and forced his mother to take him to this place. He received some sort of radiation therapy, woke up the next morning complaining that his throat was dry and his appetite was gone altogether. He became depressed again, was unable to attend school, and lost weight. When admitted to the Psychiatric Institute in 1961, at the age of 16½, he was conspicuously small, prepubertal, and cachectic, weighing only 65 lbs. He complained about dryness in his throat, and many other, often changing, physical symptoms which had delusional character. He expressed distress about being so short and undeveloped, not like other boys of his age, but denied any concern about getting fat. He absolutely refused any therapeutic approach that dealt with "himself." An effort was made to work with the parents to help them see Edgar's problems in more realistic terms. Once they returned him after he had run away from the hospital, but would not do so the second time. Two years later (1963) he was in a state hospital with the diagnosis of schizophrenia.

Bert (No. 7) began to cut down on his eating at or around his twelfth birthday (1960), when he weighed 110 lbs. Eight months later when he was seen in consultation, his weight was 68 lbs, a loss of 42 lbs. His mother had first noted that he did not spend the money she gave him for lunch. He complained about being too fat and would throw up at times. He was admitted to a medical service where he would walk back and forth in the hallways all day long afraid that he might not burn up his calories.

The parents were Orthodox Jews who had survived war-time Europe. Bert was born 3 months after their arrival in the United States. The parents spoke with pride about him as the healthiest of their 3 sons, strong, exceptionally bright, well liked, and unusually good looking.

The onset of his illness was related to a complaint from the Hebrew teacher about Bert being too fresh and not listening, and the father's admonishment: "I want you to be the best in this class." These reproaches precipitated a marked change in Bert's behavior; until then he had received only praise and admiration. He studied intensely and achieved the highest grades at the end of the term. But from having been carefree and bright he became more and more depressed, irritable, and resentful, spending more time on his homework, and refused any food until everything was finished to perfection. Finally he declared, "I do not need to eat," and would take only a small piece of melba toast.

He responded well to a therapeutic psychiatric regimen. In response to a follow-up letter in 1971, the father reported that Bert, now 23 years old, was doing well, was happily married, had one child, held a position in his father's business, and was finishing his college education. The illness had lasted for over 2 years during which time Bert continued to attend school though depressed and emaciated. After he resumed eating, he developed well and was now 6' tall and well nourished.

Elliot (No. 8) was 13¾ years old (1963) when his family moved from a crowded section of New York to a suburban town. In the city Elliot had always excelled in school and was in an advanced section of his class, with high prestige because of his academic achievement. In the new school tremendous importance was attached to athletic activities and social skills. He resented that he was referred to as "fatty" when he tried the wrestling team. Until then he had not been concerned about his weight of 115 lbs which made him somewhat chubby. He decided to go on a reducing regimen and at first there seemed to be nothing abnormal about his doing calisthenics and being conscientious about his diet.

After he had lost the planned amount it became apparent that reducing had become a fixation with him. He became exceedingly calorie conscious and increased the amount of exercise. He had a strong emotional reaction to the assassination of President Kennedy in November of 1963 and stopped eating altogether. He also refused fluids and became severely dehydrated. On his fourteenth birthday he fainted in school and was hospitalized; he was severely depressed and intensely preoccupied with eating. A week later, in the beginning of December, he was referred to a psychiatric hospital because he had absolutely refused to eat and had continued to lose weight. His weight was down to 86 lbs (height 5'2"). Extensive clinical and laboratory examinations had failed to disclose any organic abnormality, except signs of starvation and dehydration. Elliot himself requested psychiatric consultation because he felt mixed up and upset.

Elliot was an only son, with two younger sisters, in a family of mixed religious background, with close ties to both background families. Much love and attention had been lavished on him as the first child and grandchild and his two sisters had been comparatively neglected. Concern with weight had played a role in this family, with continuous talk about reducing and dieting.

Immediately after admission to the hospital Elliot began to keep a diary which he addressed to his parents, mainly his mother. It is a jumble of detailed enumeration of medical procedures, of his various complaints, of plans for his and his family's future, of celebration for the coming Hanukkah and Christmas holidays, and of every bite of food as it was served to him, and increasingly of his mental confusion. He refused any solid food and insisted that his parents bring him dietetic drinks, the only fluids he would take. When there was further drop in weight he was transferred to the infirmary where glucose was given intravenously. Occasionally he would take fruit juices or some regular food.

The intensity of his preoccupation with food and fear of fatness, and also his mental confusion and thoughts about death, are reflected in his diary. A few sentences were cited in the previous chapter. They and the following sentences were selected from many similar statements.

Whether I really want food or would rather be content without it, I keep on thinking that I am saving calories for one day over the Rainbow and I will gorge myself to death. I keep on opening the trays, smelling and admiring the stuff. I get exceptional pleasure from watching others enjoy food but I can't touch it.

I feel now that suicide would be very easy but I am so obsessed with food that I couldn't even eat a death meal for fear of being overweight on death. Oh God, I'm mixed up.

I look at recipes to find the one that will finally satisfy me.

If they fatten me here I go mad at home and starve myself. Maybe I am trying to punish myself. I don't know!

I think of quick death to end it all, and then slow death to have your love while I am dying. Oh, mom, and dad, help me.

I am so mixed up in a logical unlogical way. . . . So much runs through my mind, I feel like a ticker tape hours behind.

I don't think I'll have the power to fast any more. Food is so good. Now I am worried I'll surely gain weight. I think that it is terrible; it is just like mental spite work.

I want to save all my gaining for when I come home. Where I can be spoon fed by you and you only.

The psychiatric diagnosis initially was anorexia nervosa in connection with an adjustment reaction of adolescence. The increasing bizarreness of his preoccupation suggested a schizophrenic reaction, paranoid type.

He became convinced that he would die and refused all food and took very little fluid. Two days before Christmas a slight distension of his abdomen was noted and was relieved by rectal tube. Fluid was given intravenously. When he attempted to take fluid by mouth he vomited it. During the following night he vomited dark material. For the first time there was a rise in temperature to 102°. An hour later he suddenly vomited large quantities of brown fluid and was dead within a few minutes. Heart massage and other attempts at resuscitation were unsuccessful. An autopsy, not including the brain, revealed acute congestion of the lungs and aspiration of vomitus and early peritonitis. The findings were not felt to be entirely sufficient to explain his sudden death.

Newton's (No. 9) illness was triggered by his going to camp when 12½ years old, weighing approximately 100 lbs (1963). He was homesick and asocial, ate little, and lost 10 lbs while at camp. He was glad about this because he had wanted to be thinner, like his friend who was thin and wiry. After this summer he appeared changed in his behavior, clung to his mother and was exceptionally helpful around the house and with cooking. A month later his weight loss was so severe that he was admitted to a medical service where he continued to lose to a low of 67 lbs in December, a loss of 33 lbs in 6 months.

Newton was the second child in a financially successful family, with a sister 14 months older. The father came from a prominent family and was outstanding in his own career. He had married a woman of foreign background whose parents had been in the diplomatic service. Newton was a healthy and active child, "normally aggressive" and busy with activities and his friends. He had one close friend from whom he became separated when the family moved to a new home 1 year preceding the camp experience.

Newton became involved in psychotherapy and continued with the same therapist when he left the hospital after 5 months. He had gained some weight and was able to maintain it at home, and then gained some more during a vacation trip, mainly by eating pancakes. By the time he was 16 his weight and height were normal and puberty development had begun. At times he worried that he was getting too fat again, but his weight did not exceed 120 lbs when he was 18 years old. Though he continued to be in treatment until 16, he resisted dealing with the underlying problems, though the need for this was recognized by him. He graduated from high school when 18 and planned to go away to college. He returned home after one term because he felt too lonely and homesick. He felt he was "ugly" and became preoccupied with various facial features as undesirable and consulted plastic surgeons to correct these imaginary defects.

In Everett (No. 10) the anorexic picture developed at age 13½ when he was sent to an Eastern preparatory school. He felt that sending him there was an arbitrary decision in which he had not participated. His parents had felt that his superior intelligence deserved the best educational opportunities, more than was offered in the private schools in the Southwest. Everett did not enjoy his stay at the school, did not make any friends, and showed his resistance by poor academic performance during the first year. He also lost some weight which was not considered undesirable since he had been a rather pudgy child. There was considerable criticism about his having done so poorly and when he returned to school for the second year he was determined to "show his mother" that he could do the work, and he did well academically. But he became a recluse, withdrew to his room and refused to eat; he would vomit what little food he took. In response to his desperate pleas his mother went to see him at his school, found him in such poor physical condition, weighing only 75 lbs, that she removed him. He had kept the vomiting a secret and its extent was recognized only after he had been home for quite some time.

Everett was the third of four children born into a family of great wealth. During the early years the parents had had a very active social life with much and extended traveling. A considerable portion of his care during the first year was provided by a nurse to whose departure, when he was 1 year old, he reacted with some depression. She was replaced by another nurse who played a significant role in his care until he was 11 years old. "Nanny" exercised authority by giving or withholding food. Everett was her favorite and she would punish any misdeeds by restricting food, but when he recanted she would shower him with affection and stuff him with specialties. There was considerable rivalry for her attention but Everett remained her favorite and he grew obese from her overindulgence. When the nurse left he was 11 years old and weighed 119 lbs which, combined with a very short stature, made him feel ridiculously fat. At that time his mother took over his care and supervised his diet. This was a period of real closeness between them. He gradually lost weight and stabilized at about 100 lbs. He still was shorter than the other members of his family, but he looked well proportioned.

Everett was nearly 15 years old when he returned home, cachexic, quite depressed, and at loose ends. He ate very little and the vomiting became more pronounced. He was seen by an endocrinologist who gave him some endocrine injections (APL) to correct hypogonadism and to induce puberty. There was only a minimal response, and further endocrine treatment was withheld lest his growth potential would be shortened. Everett became increasingly depressed and less inhibited in showing his anger. He repeatedly threatened suicide and would walk out with a loaded gun, or would raid the bathroom cabinets in their very large home, collecting whatever pills he could find. On two occasions he swallowed these pills, but then ran for help and was taken to the local hospital for gastric lavage.

Increasingly he expressed dissatisfaction with his body, his short stature, and delayed puberty. The one thing about which he could do something was his weight, and he continued to eat sparingly and to vomit. This he explained as due to his gastric discomfort. He also began drinking alcohol and taking drugs. He would insist "there is something wrong with my stomach," and would refuse to discuss any personal problems unless he was promised he would receive pills for relief of his discomfort.

It was at this time that he was seen in consultation with the question of possible need for residential treatment. He was very resentful about the idea of being sent away from home again and saw it as arbitrary as having been sent to the boarding school. He was frantically preoccupied about having damaged his body and was afraid that he might never get well, made great declarations and gave promises that he would eat what was correct, would never throw up for the rest of his life, and would not get sick, drink, or use drugs. The extent of his hypochondriacal concern was reflected in his Rorschach responses where he saw "the insides of a polluted up body with the lungs and intestines rotting away," or "demons having a lot of fun on the body—here comes the spine and a part of the liver which they have destroyed." In spite of his best intentions he was unable to control his eating and vomiting, or to stay away from drugs, and reluctantly agreed to residential treatment since he had to admit that he was unable to establish controls from within.

Evaluation of this case was complicated by his use of drugs and alcohol. It has been stated in the past that the slave-like passivity of such patients showed resemblance to what was observed in drug addiction. However, until the late 1960's I did not see any obese or anorexic patients who were drug users. Then there were several who seemed to enter the drug scene in a desperate effort to establish some form of social contact. But only in Everett, whose home was close to the Mexican border, did drug use become a serious problem.

In all six boys the illness began with what looked like a deliberate decision to reduce because they felt "too fat." Only Everett had been obese when 11, but had reduced to a normal weight before he began his drastic dieting. When the planned lower weight had been reached it proved "not enough" because much more than weight loss had been expected. Being and staying thin, a protection against the dreaded fate of being "too fat," became a goal in itself. The real fear is that of not being truly respected, of not being in control but of being a helpless product of "them." Since no manipulation of the body can possibly provide the experience of self-confidence, self-respect, or self-directed identity, the pursuit of thinness becomes more frantic, the amount of food smaller and smaller, and aimless activity, "to burn off calories," becomes more hectic.

This acute sense of dissatisfaction with themselves, expressed as feeling "too fat," had occurred rather suddenly, at a critical period in their lives. In all six cases there was a change of the social setting, be it moving to a home in a new neighborhood, or entering a new school, or going away to summer camp or boarding school. Throughout their lives these boys had received a great deal of praise for being outstanding from their families, and from teachers and peers. The illness became manifest when the assured status of superior achievement was threatened, when they feared they could not obtain the same prestige in the new environment.

In this group the term "anorexia" is a misnomer; there is no true loss of appetite, in spite of the rigid self-starvation, which is endured without definite hunger awareness. Periods of vigorous refusal to eat alternate with eating binges of unbelievable proportions and which are followed by self-induced vomiting. Bulimia with vomiting was present to various degrees in all of them except for Edgar, whose illness was less typical in many other respects, too. Hyperactivity and drive for achievement were remarkable in all, though Everett, under the influence of alcohol and drugs, became a dropout from school for a while; they all had been success- and achievement-oriented before they became sick. Interest in athletics, greatly encouraged by their fathers, had been prominent in 4 cases; even Edgar's father, who had taken little interest in him, was proud of his excellent physique. With increasing social withdrawal the activities tended to become aimless, no longer integrated into athletics and group activities. The drive for superior intellectual achievement persisted; they continued to go to school in spite of the severe emaciation, with some excelling even more than before.

Through psychotherapy it was learned that, in spite of their excellent performances, they had suffered from severe doubts about their adequacy and competence. In spite of the stubborn, aggressive, and violent negativistic behavior, an underlying disturbance can be recognized; namely, an all-pervasive sense of ineffectiveness, the dread of not being in touch with or in control of their own sensations and functions. Rigid control over their weight becomes a magical touchstone, the tangible evidence that at least one's own body obeys his own control. The families appear to be stable and well functioning, but with a transactional pattern in which a controlling adult, usually the mother, superimposes upon the developing child her own concepts of his needs and desires, disregarding the clues originating within himself (Chapters 4 and 5). Since these mothers were fairly stable, well-informed women, what they superimposed was quite reasonable, not contrary to the child's physiological and developmental needs, and the children when young offered the facade of adequate functioning, until life situations arose where they felt lost without the accustomed supports, and where independence, decision-making and self-initiated behavior were expected. The serious deficits were in the area of autonomy and active self-awareness. Various diagnostic labels were assigned to these patients, with a tendency to diagnose psychoneurosis early in the picture and schizophrenia developing later; there was little relationship between the diagnostic labels and the long-range outcomes.

The similarity in the underlying dynamic pictures in males and females with primary anorexia nervosa is great. There is only one point of difference, namely that all cases of primary anorexia nervosa in males occurred in prepuberty and these boys did not develop sexually until recovered. This is consistent with the reports by others who also observed that the typical picture of anorexia nervosa in the male occurs only in young preadolescent boys.

It may not be accidental that the illness becomes manifest when their lifeline is interrupted during preadolescence. Sullivan (12) has stressed the paramount importance of this phase in human development, as the era during which a child forms his first important extra-familial relationships. It is through relationships with his peers and in the intimacy of a meaningful friendship that he can emerge from the family bonds and can develop a more realistic self-concept, and find his self-worth. The interruption of such ties at this critical period proved so traumatic for these boys because their excessive performance had been achieved with constant strain. The spurious nature of their success story was revealed before they had achieved an independent identity, and the weak underlying structure crumbled.

It is an often discussed question why anorexia nervosa is so conspicuously less frequent in males than in females. It may well be related to pubescence itself, to the psychobiological effects of the male sex hormones. If one considers the figures of preadolescence alone, there are 6 boys and 6 girls with primary anorexia nervosa. It is quite possible that the characteristic slave-like attachment of a child to the mother is more apt to develop in a girl, and efforts to solve psychological problems through manipulation of the body are also considered characteristically female. It is probable that it is unusual for a boy to be caught in this developmental impasse. In addition, male pubescence will flood a boy, even one who has this type of attachment, with such powerful new sensations of a more aggressive self-awareness that the event of puberty makes a new self-assertion possible, something he was not capable of in prepuberty. Once they are caught in the vicious cycle of self-starvation and distorted body experience, endocrine treatment appears ineffective, even disturbing, and becomes of value only after the underlying psychological problems have been clarified.

BIBLIOGRAPHY

1. Bliss, E. L., and Branch, C. H. H., *Anorexia Nervosa—Its History, Psychology, and Biology*, Paul B. Hoeber, Inc., New York, 1960.
2. Blitzer, J. R., Rollins, N., and Blackwell, A., Children who starve themselves: Anorexia nervosa, Psychosom. Med., 23:368–383, 1961.
3. Bruch, H., Anorexia nervosa and its differential diagnosis, J. Nerv. Ment. Dis., 141:555–566, 1966.
4. Bruch, H., Anorexia nervosa in the male, Psychosom. Med., 33:31–47, 1971.
5. Crisp, A. H., and Roberts, F. J., A case of anorexia nervosa in a male, Postgrad. Med. J., 38:350–353, 1962.
6. Dally, P., *Anorexia Nervosa*, Grune and Stratton, New York, 1969.
7. Falstein, E. I., Feinstein, S. C., and Judas, I., Anorexia nervosa in the male child, Amer. J. Orthopsychiat., 26:751–772, 1956.
8. Gull, W. W., Anorexia nervosa (Apepsia hysterica, anorexia hysterica), Trans. Clin. Soc. London, 7:22, 1874.
9. Kuenzler, E., Pubertaetskonflikte eines maennlichen Patienten mit einer Anorexia

nervosa, pp. 161–166, in *Anorexia Nervosa*, J.-E. Meyer and H. Feldmann, eds., Georg Thieme Verlag, Stuttgart, 1965.
10. Morton, R., *Phthisiologica—or a Treatise of Consumptions*, London, 1689.
11. Selvini, M. P., Anorexia nervosa, pp. 197–218, in *The World Biennial of Psychiatry and Psychotherapy*, Vol. 1, S. Arieti, ed., Basic Books, Inc., New York, 1970.
12. Sullivan, H. S., *The Interpersonal Theory of Psychiatry*, W. W. Norton, New York, 1953.
13. Tolstrup, K., Die Charakteristika der juengern Faelle von Anorexia Nervosa, pp. 51–59, in *Anorexia Nervosa*, J.-E. Meyer and H. Feldmann, eds., Georg Thieme Verlag, Stuttgart, 1965.
14. Ushakov, G. K., Anorexia nervosa, pp. 274–289, in *Modern Perspectives in Adolescent Psychiatry*, J. G. Howells, ed., Oliver & Boyd, Edinburgh, 1971.

PART IV

Treatment

16

The Practical and Psychological
Aspects of Weight Change

"You can lead someone to cottage cheese but you can't make him shrink," expresses in a nutshell the trouble with reducing regimens. Their number is legion and they are all proved to be effective—for those who follow them. The "how to lose weight" reports range from serious, scientific-minded, well-documented studies to facetious, even unscrupulous publishing adventures and publicity stunts.

Admittedly, changing a person's weight is not an easy task, and it is not compatible with healthy living if one attempts to push the weight below what is appropriate for an individual's body build. Within these constitutional limits, however, lasting weight reduction, though often difficult, is not an impossible enterprise. I shall try to review here some of the factors that make for success or failure, for dramatic but only temporary losses, or for weight stability.

Basically there are two conceptually and operationally distinct therapeutic approaches. One is the mechanics of it: how to manipulate the energy balance so that an obese person expends more than he takes in and thus loses weight (and the reverse in anorexia nervosa). This will be the topic of this chapter. The other approach to losing weight attempts to effect a change in the person himself so that he no longer abuses the eating function in futile efforts to solve other problems of living, and to help him gain sufficient inner strength so that he can face the task of reducing without undue mental strain.

My experience is based on numerous observations of the problems encountered during reducing by difficult obese patients seen in psychiatric consultations or treatment. The inner psychological problems during reducing were recognized during psychoanalytic therapy of severely obese adolescents and adults who had repeatedly reduced their weight, but had been unable to maintain the losses. There have been many references to this before, as it applies to individual cases. This chapter is an attempt to summarize my observations and deductions.

Dietary Treatment

Viewed as a manipulation of energy balance, treatment of obesity should be simple: reduction of food intake and increase in exercise should, and actually do, accomplish a predictable loss in weight. These basic facts have been known since the time of antiquity. It has also been known that this simple procedure often fails to be effective, so much so that doubt has been expressed about whether the laws of conservation of energy apply to obese people. The endless number of new suggestions, special drugs, exercise machines, massage and bath procedures attempt to do away with the cheerlessness of the program. The essence of every advertisement about "easy reducing" is that the follower will not have to suffer the pangs of hunger or exert himself beyond his inclination. No reducing program has yet been devised that accomplishes this, except in the claims of the inventors. Since overweight people who want or need to reduce differ enormously as to the phase of obesity, their life adjustment, and motives and goals of reducing, it should be obvious that no one regimen could be suitable for all; but this is the claim of all new reducing inventions.

Systematic scientific interest in dieting for obesity began in the middle of the last century. When Banting (1) published his "Letter on Corpulence" in 1860 he did so in praise of his physician, Harvey, who himself published a book on obesity (13). The novel aspect of Harvey's diet was the emphasis on meat, "the strong food," which had just been recognized as being less fattening than the "innocent" foodstuffs, such as bread and sweets. Harvey included in his book some notes he had taken while attending Claude Bernard's lectures on metabolism in Paris in 1856. There he had learned that there were two types of foodstuffs, those needed for restoration of body substances (the proteins, which were included in relatively large amounts in his diet), and others for the acute combustion processes (the carbohydrates, which he restricted).

In quick succession other metabolism experts developed their own diets. The new reducing regimens, without the benefit of special waters, represented dangerous competition to the traditions of the European spas. The Congress of Internal Medicine discussed with refreshing frankness the pros and cons of different diets at its meeting in 1886 (15). I quote a few paragraphs because the problems are remarkably similar to the unsolved questions with which we are still confronted today. Three regimens had acquired a certain popularity, the Harvey-Banting diet (high protein content), Ebstein's method (high fat content), and the Dancel-Oertel cure (fluid restriction and systematic exercise). Difficulties had been encountered with all three methods, which were attributed to their "schablonenhaften" (mechanical) application, with neglect of the necessary individualization. In spite of our increased understanding of metabolic processes most of the problems and questions have remained just as unsettled today.

Friedrich Mueller (who later as a professor in Munich was called "Friedrich der Grosse" by his admiring students), mentioned some patients who became extraordinarily tired and depressed while on a diet and he considered loss of protein from the body as the possible cause. It is of interest that in modern clinical thinking this possibility has been denied until quite recently. He also suggested that an intolerable degree of fatigue and depression was produced if a diet was not absolutely adequate, or if one became bored with it. He stressed the importance of secondary psychic reactions to reducing diets, again an amazingly modern argument.

Geheimrath Leyden, the leading obesity authority of his time, stressed that whatever was done to make things more comfortable, there simply was no reducing without imposing certain restrictions. All methods carried the same danger, namely, that overly rigid reducing could result in states of exhaustion, anemia, and cardiac weakness. "There are people to whom it is essential to be fat; they become weak and sick the moment one reduces their fat. Natures are different, and as physicians we have to pay attention to this.

"Not every person can become lean, and if people who feel well only when they carry a certain amount of fat try to reduce, even to a limited degree, then I can only confirm that certain symptoms will appear that have been described by the previous speakers."

He emphasized that helping people reduce was not a new problem in modern times, but had been a challenge to physicians through the ages. We struggle today with exactly the same questions, namely, of evaluating the advantages of different diets so that they are in harmony with the metabolic requirements of individual patients. We know today the essentials for an adequate diet in much more detail and can compensate for anticipated deficiencies with mineral and vitamin supplements. We have a much more exact knowledge of caloric values, but also increasing awareness that the armchair calculations for predicting weight loss are necessarily inexact and are chiefly valuable in providing realistic guidelines for how much can be lost over a given period of time, and how to accomplish weight decrease through loss of body fat only with a minimal breakdown of lean tissue. Emphasis is now on the maintenance of physiological and emotional fitness during the reducing period with avoidance of untoward reactions and, hopefully, the establishment of eating and exercise habits that will help the formerly obese patient maintain his new weight.

The popular emphasis is on excluding carbohydrates, but nutritionists know that they are needed in sufficient quantity to prevent ketosis and to minimize wastage of protein and electrolytes. A well-balanced diet should contain sufficient protein to replace wear and tear losses and to maintain reasonable reserves. A certain amount of fat is necessary to make food more palatable and because diets devoid of fat tend to be bulky and unappetizing. In practice it is virtually impossible to design an acceptable diet that does not derive at least 25% of its calories from fat.

All this is widely known and generally accepted. Every "new" diet uses the hook of offering these essentials in an unexpected, interesting, and convenient combination so that weight-conscious people become curious and follow it for a week or two, and proudly confirm its effectiveness. An important factor in the whole diet game is publicity and packaging; scientifically designed diets are taken over by commercial enterprises and advertising, and then become highly successful. Dole (9) developed during the 1950's a formula diet, low in protein, for metabolic studies, and observed that hospitalized obese people taking this fluid diet lost weight without too much discomfort. Then the "formula diet," advertised as Metrecal, could be obtained in every grocery store: it seemed to promise an easy way of reducing, until the losses were discovered to be just as temporary as with other diets. At this moment a high protein diet which the New York City Health Department had prescribed for years in its obesity clinic supports a million-dollar business by being propagated in fashionable detail by Weight Watchers.

One might expect that people with a rational motive for reducing would do well if given a general understanding of nutrition and that they then would restrict the intake of high caloric foods. This type of self-imposed limitation is effective for people with good inner discipline who gain satisfaction from various activities. They are people who appear slim in spite of a tendency toward overweight because they never permit themselves to gain an extra ounce of weight; they follow such regimens of reasonable self-imposed limitation. I have rarely seen it be successful in those who have permitted overweight to develop.

Once they are overweight, even to a mild degree, most people do better if a definite routine is prescribed; this applies even to experts in nutrition who know all about calories and composition of adequate meals. Detailed individualized instructions and a weekly check of the weight are essential. It seems that giving up one's accustomed eating and living habits implies surrendering one's adult independence. Most people find it easier to substitute the rational authority of another person to freedom of choice with continuous self-denial. Many years ago, while evaluating the possible effectiveness of Benzedrine in children, I observed that weight loss was directly proportional to the regularity of clinic attendance, whereas the medication was found to be ineffective (5). It seems probable that the weekly weigh-ins have as much to do with the success of Weight Watchers as the diets spelled out in detail.

Except for severe degrees of obesity, most physicians seem to prefer moderate caloric restriction (1000 to 1800 calories) and diets that resemble ordinary meals. If prescribed in a definite form, without permitting too much juggling and exchanges, such diets are useful for well-adjusted people. But many fat people, in particular those with personality problems, prefer rather unusual diets that bring visible results more quickly. To them an extraordinary situation appears more acceptable than just a slight change of one's established habits; the great appeal of absurd fads and outlandish diets appears to be related to this. In my work with severely disturbed obese people I have found that rather monotonous, somewhat strange diets are more effective than reasonable restrictions, at least in the beginning of a reducing program. It is my impression that it is the very strangeness that makes these diets effective. If dietary instructions are given in a definite form and in writing after having been figured out with the patient to suit his individual pattern of living—such as where and when he has his meals—he can establish a definite routine. The monotony is an advantage, not so much because the patient will eat less because he gets tired of such a diet (this he does anyhow, with any type of diet), but because he does not need to think continuously of what he is going to eat next, and about how to improve the diet without cheating. With very simple diets like the formula diet or an all-meat diet, there is simply no question about whether any other food is allowed. All the dilemmas of ordinary diets, the social handicap of having to refuse hospitality, or the "this time it won't hurt me" attitude, are done away with.

These types of diets emphasize also something that is often overlooked —that dieting is a serious business which cannot be accomplished in a haphazard way. In difficult cases it is helpful to take dieting out of the realm of ordinary living, remove all the traditional aspects of mealtime and make losing weight something of a nutritional operation. A serious reducing program needs to be approached with the attitude that it is something unusual, outside the normal state of affairs. After a certain weight loss has been achieved, a switch to the more conventional maintenance diet should be made, with emphasis on establishing a new mealtime routine. Severely obese people tend to regain weight unless they adhere to special diets. Obesity, or the potential for it, is a lifelong problem and requires continuous supervision. This is a hard fact to accept, but it is only honest to state the problem in these terms. Eventually a more precise understanding of disturbed metabolic processes will bear fruit in the form of some new medication, enzyme, or what have you, that will keep metabolites from being transformed into depot fats; until that happy day continuous attention to what and how much to eat is a fat person's lot.

Exercise Programs

Though the prescription of "eat less *and* exercise more" is age old, the second half of the formula has been comparatively neglected except by commercial reducing establishments which promise that the fat will be taken away in easy luxury through exercise machines, massages, electricity, mudpacks or bandages, and the unending inventions of new gadgets for fat people to buy that will clutter up their bathrooms or closets. (If they are used at all it is by the slim members of the family.)

The importance of exercise for obesity has often been neglected in medical thinking; it has been objected that the amount of calories spent in exercise would be too small to warrant the effort, or that extra activity would result in an increase in appetite. Both points are erroneous: though not a quick method for weight loss, increased activity is effective in the long run if the fat person sticks to the regimen. Since fat people are not well-attuned to their bodily needs they will not react with increased appetite to being more active. On the contrary, activities distract from the time available for eating, and even more from their preoccupation with it.

It appears that the inner resistance against exercise is even stronger in most fat people than against food restriction. It is much harder to induce a fat person to walk an extra step than make him refrain from eating an extra bite. He will do so if bullied and strictly supervised or constantly encouraged. The unsolved problem is how to change basic patterns of inactivity. It is not so much nonparticipation in athletics or other ways of energy expenditure, but the fat person's whole way of living, the minute but endlessly repeated ways of doing things efficiently with the least amount of wasted energy that add up to enormous savings. And this is the aspect that is difficult, if not impossible, to change. One cannot order a person to become fidgety instead of sitting quietly, or to do things in a complex way when he takes pride in his shortcuts, in not taking an unnecessary step. One of the neatest descriptions of obese inactivity is that of Nero Wolf, in Rex Stout's detective stories. Once Nero has settled down in his chair and has made the necessary adjustments, he will not make one extra move, except to lift a beer glass to his mouth; when he thinks, he sinks into a complete stupor.

At times it is possible to induce a heavy young person to become interested in activities and enjoy them. I have seen plump youngsters become graceful dancers, or efficient in skiing, ice skating, or swimming. Usually this coincides with their having become more secure in their self-concept, with having developed some awareness of their bodily functions. Moderate activities over an extended period of time, such as swimming, walking, horseback riding, etc., are more effective and suitable than competitive sports or those involving brief spurts of great energy. It is my impression that it is not so much the increased energy expenditure that leads to a change in appearance, but the greater attention to the body and its functions. Individual gymnastic programs with emphasis on becoming alerted to muscular tension and other bodily sensations may produce better results than vigorous activity.

In the study of obese children (Chapter 8) the inhibition of activity was recognized as a more fundamental disorder than the overeating. It expresses a disturbance in the total approach to life, a real lack of enjoyment in using one's body, or a deep-seated mistrust in one's ability of mastery. For an effective increase in energy output an individualistic approach is even more important than in prescribing a dietary regimen. One can impose food restriction from the outside, just by not offering it; but doing calisthenics or other exercises always requires a major effort from within.

Medication and Drugs

Throughout the ages there has been the search for the ideal drug that would dissolve unwanted fat. The ancient Greeks, with their preoccupation with the beauty and efficiency of the human body, envied the still more ancient Cretans who, according to tradition, had possessed a potion that permitted them to eat as much as they wanted and still stay slim. The Cretan mosaics, which represent human figures of great slimness with wasp-like waists, suggest that they had achieved the goal of slenderness. Unfortunately, the secret of this wonderful drug has been lost.

The search for such an ideal medicine has continued and a review of the topic would involve writing a history of quackery, in or outside of medical practice. Physicians and patients share the belief that there are pills to be swallowed or something to be injected that would affect weight control. Throughout the many years that I have studied obesity there was no time that patients did not receive from their physicians some form of medication that was supposed to influence their weight. If a physician was honest and stated that there was no such miracle drug a patient would soon find another one who would prescribe or inject something. One is forced to conclude that modern medicine still finds it necessary for practitioners and patients to share their beliefs and attitudes, even if they are proved wrong. This approach to weight control is no less exploitative than outright quackery, though it may be clothed in the up-to-date language of modern medicine. There are many physicians who feel that they have not done their job properly, or have not fulfilled their patient's expectations, if they do not give a prescription.

Many patients have an unshakable belief in the efficacy of injected medications. During the 1930's and 1940's, many parents would not rest until their fat child had received some endocrine injection, even when they had been advised against it because there was no objective indication. In addition, the extracts in use at that time were quite ineffective. Many physicians may give in to the demands of patients, and at least a few may convince themselves of the effectiveness of these medications, real data to the contrary. In earlier chapters I have presented several case histories which showed the harmful effect of such practices. If no direct physiological damage is done, there is the psychological effect; it may confirm the patient's worst fears that there is some basic fault in his make-up.

There are many drugs and household remedies that have been tried in the fight against excess weight. Diuretics have recently gained widespread use and carry the danger of electrolyte imbalance with all its consequences.

I shall limit myself to the discussion of only two such substances that have found so much medical, presumably "scientific," support that not prescribing them was looked on as some form of neglect. I am referring to thyroid medication in its many different forms, and to the amphetamines. Thyroid was supposed to speed up metabolic processes which were assumed to be low, and thus help burn off calories. The amphetamines were credited with inhibiting the appetite and thus making acceptance of a reducing diet easy. Both drugs obtained enormous popularity, and physicians continued to prescribe them long after the fallacious reasoning on which their prescription was based had been documented, or attention had been drawn to the possible dangers of the amphetamines. Thyroid is ineffective because usually there are no objective signs of hypothyroidism except in rare cases where it is then indicated. Its continued administration carries the danger of suppressing normal thyroid activity.

The amphetamines have an interesting history. They were discovered during the early 1930's, and in 1937 Lesses and Myerson (14) recommended their use for certain obese patients with a low type of depressive reaction, a state they called anhedonia, with the rationale that a patient no longer needed to overeat but would lose weight when his mood improved. More recently similar reasoning has led to the prescription of certain psychotropic drugs, with similarly equivocal results. Subsequently amphetamines acquired the reputation of making reducing painless through appetite depression. This they do not, at least not in nontoxic doses. As far back as 1942 I carried out a double-blind study of the effects of Benzedrine sulfate in obese children and adolescents (5). Loss of weight occurred during the first few weeks of treatment on both the placebo and Benzedrine, an unspecific expression of the patients' enthusiasm for a new therapy. The greatest losses were observed in children without medication who attended the clinic regularly.

Some adults report that they feel better and more active when they first take amphetamines, and that they have less desire for food. This effect is short-lived. Dissatisfaction with a stressful life cannot be appeased by an artificially superimposed sense of well-being. After a short time they become tense and dissatisfied again, and the urge for overeating reasserts itself. Frequently this leads to an increase in dosage, and an addiction-like habituation for the drug may develop, associated with restlessness and irritability and a feeling of not being able to function without it. Psychosis-like states following such indiscriminate usages were observed and reported during the late 1940's and increasingly often during the 1950's. Nevertheless, the amphetamines dominated the field of weight reduction until quite recently, when their destructive, even deadly, effect was finally acknowledged. It was only when the young began to misuse "speed" for its stimulating effect that physicians began to examine their role in our pill-oriented society, and recognized that reducing drugs have played a substantial role in encouraging dependence on drugs.

The worst abuse has been perpetrated by certain "reducing doctors," who together with drug houses created a whole industry devoted to "treating" obesity with "rainbow pills," various combinations of drugs which were offered in different colors, to be used at different times of the day. In 1968, following the death of several patients from unjustified and senseless prescription of such diet pills, *Life* magazine published an expose of these practices (16). A reporter, a young girl who had never had a weight problem, consulted physicians in different parts of the country who were nationally or locally known for their "easy" reducing procedures. With monotonous repetition she was either put through a meaningless routine examination or just measured and weighed, and then was given, even by physicians who had declared, "you have no weight problem," various numbers of multi-colored pills which contained amphetamines or other so-called appetite suppressants, in combination with thyroid and digitalis. The outcome of each consultation was the same, namely the recommendation to buy pills at the doctor's own drug counter. There was no consensus among the "fat" doctors concerning diets; some advised that with these pills she could eat anything that she wanted, others offered elaborate restricted diets; nor did they agree on exercise, or on liquid consumption. There was consensus, though, on one point: pills, pills, pills.

Under pressure from a patient a physician may feel forced to give a prescription; he can do so only at the price of feeling that he is perpetrating some form of quackery. Some feel that such prescriptions are justified, that they have a certain suggestive value, or may insure regular visits to the office. It is my impression that unjustified prescriptions are often given to reassure the physician that he is doing something, so that the patient cannot blame him for having neglected anything. This is most likely to happen in conditions where the underlying problems are hidden or poorly understood.

The Setting: Hospital, Family, and Group Efforts

Though the physiological aspects of the best methods for weight change in each individual case are not yet completely solved, enough is known that any obese person could lose the extra weight if he followed the diet and exercise program calculated for him. The difficulty is to ensure his cooperation over a long enough period. Evaluation of the setting in which a reducing regimen is to be carried out is important, in order to ascertain whether it contains elements that will facilitate the task or might provoke insurmountable resistance.

Many obese people are successful reducers under strictly controlled conditions, such as in a hospital or a reducing institution, where they will adhere to a drastic regimen, even total starvation, without too much discomfort, only to regain the weight as soon as they are back in their old surroundings. Some feel that hospitalization is valuable because it provides psychological support and removes the patient from the negative interpersonal influences of the family where the condition had developed. These factors play a role in individual cases, but there are other aspects to account for this paradoxical behavior. As was discussed earlier (Chapter 4), obese people suffer from a deficit in hunger awareness; they do not eat so much in response to nutritional needs but to the promptings of a variety of internal tension states, or of external stimuli, in particular the sight and availability of food. The sterile atmosphere of a hospital where no food is within sight except what is served on one's plate makes it relatively easy to abstain from eating, though there, too, "cheating" does occur. More than one research project has been invalidated by well-meaning friends who smuggled food onto the metabolic ward for a starving subject.

Fat people eat "because it is there," and it is inconceivable to them *not* to eat the platter clean. The most tempting place is the ordinary home and the person most endangered is the one in control of the food supply, usually the housewife, who would not dream of *not* finishing the leftovers from every meal. It is not even necessary to "see" the food; just the knowledge that it is there will act as a continuous stimulus. I have heard more than one overweight friend describe an opened box of candy as the most dangerous object in her home, even those who do not particularly like sweets and candy. As long as the box is in its cellophane wrapper it is safe. But once the cover is broken, with just one piece removed, the lure becomes irresistible. One friend described it, "It is like a magnet drawing me back to the cabinet. It doesn't help if I 'hide' it; knowing that there are some pieces left keeps pulling me. Whatever my plans, I cannot settle down to them until the box is completely empty." An unfinished roast or cold cuts in the refrigerator, or a piece of cake or cheese may exercise the same attraction. This factor needs to be considered in deciding on a reducing program. Such people will do poorly on a regimen that leaves too many decisions to them: they are more likely to adhere to a prescribed diet in which the choices are limited.

Many people are not aware of the continuous attraction of food and their helplessness against it. An important step in therapy is their becoming aware of their own behavior and establishing control over it. Recently Stunkard and his co-workers described behavior modification in the treatment of obesity, which rests on this principle (17). As a preliminary device, they made sure of regular attendance by requiring prepayment for the whole course of treatment which consisted of lengthy weekly sessions over a 3 month period. The first step was to make patients aware of the behavior to be controlled; they were asked to keep daily records of the amount, time, and circumstances of their eating. They also recorded their weight in relation to meals. Then they were asked to confine their eating, including snacking, to one place, to use a distinctive table setting and to make eating a pure experience, unaccompanied by any other activities. Additional steps toward establishing control over the act of eating were counting each mouthful of food during a meal, placing utensils on the plate after each third mouthful, and interrupting the meal for a predetermined period of time. The rationale of this maneuver was to give the patient, as early as possible, an experience of control over one aspect of his eating, however small. Only after a variety of such techniques of self-control had been mastered did weight loss become a major focus. The behavioristic aspect of this approach was prompt reinforcement of the behavior which established control over eating. Such reinforcement was both positive, such as using a point system rewarding control, and negative, namely making favorite snacks unpalatable. The results appear encouraging, with more patients losing significant amounts of weight, though with greater variability, than those in a control group. Six months later the behavior modification group had done somewhat better than the controls. Unfortunately the group was dissolved then and no information about the long-range effect is available.

Many years ago I used a similar approach in the treatment of obese children and adolescents, though without these elaborately detailed steps. Remarkable weight losses were achieved and maintained for a year and even longer. However, when reexamined several years later, most had regained and surpassed their former weight. It was recognized that temporary control over food intake alone was not sufficient if there was not at the same time a valid change in personality structure and in the family interactions.

The pernicious familial interference with a reducing regimen is most readily recognized in obese children and adolescents. Much of this has been discussed earlier (Chapters 5, 8, 9), usually its combination with severe maladjustment. Unavoidably the family is involved in all cases of juvenile obesity. The treatment goal is to stimulate independence and responsibility in these youngsters, but not uncommonly the family takes over and assumes responsibility for the dieting. There must be chubby youngsters who, because their parents handled this problem tactfully, did not grow more obese; but this approach does not seem to be successful very often. When obesity in a child has persisted for any length of time, in particular when there is progressive increase of weight, the question of dieting becomes the focus of violent family arguments. There are many fat children who do not remember ever having felt satisfied with a meal. Such youngsters may develop an attitude of defiant resistance against the very word "dieting," feeling that they are being looked upon "just as a body." They express their bitterness in self-defeating negativism, eating huge quantities to show that nobody can tell them what and how much to eat. It is a fighting back against "this horrible life where the holes on your plate are more important than what is on it and with somebody breathing down your neck with every bite you eat."

Under such circumstances it is necessary to disengage the fighting forces and to make it possible for a youngster to recover sufficient self-respect and develop some sense of independence so that he can accept dieting without the feeling that it is forced upon him. Once he has come to this point he will need the sympathetic support of his physician, who will help him also to adjust his eating habits to his changing needs and activities. For some adolescents the reducing routine is easier if meals are taken apart from the family table. To them it is a way of disengaging themselves from the eternal fighting; however, others would feel rejected and completely isolated.

In prescribing a diet for an obese child it must be kept in mind that many are unhappy and poorly adjusted; depriving them of food will only add to their unhappiness. Dieting should not set a child apart. Commonly the eating habits of the whole family, their methods of discipline, and styles of interaction need understanding, and often, correction. There are situations which require a more permissive attitude toward a child's eating, namely when there is severe emotional turmoil. Fighting over food aggravates the difficulties. Though such grave situations are rare, they serve as a warning that prescribing a diet for a child is not a simple matter of calculating calories.

Such children need help in finding new sources of satisfaction, and even more important, better self-respect. Asking a fat child to restrict his eating places a very hard task before him. Frequent contacts, if possible at weekly intervals, are necessary. Such a child has had little chance to develop self-reliance, and a doctor's friendly and respectful interest can help to supply a confidence which he himself does not feel. If a child does not adhere to the diet it is more helpful to find out what has interfered during that particular week than to show a punitive or disgusted reaction. Thus one learns about the daily problems of a child, his joys and sorrows, and one may be of help in his finding new and constructive outlets for his energies, and in his becoming independent.

Many who had been fat as children or adolescents retain throughout life a negative attitude against "having to go on a diet" or "being told what to eat." This stubborn negativism is not limited to the attitude toward food; passive resistance is a character trait of many obese people. Staying fat may also imply, on the interpersonal level, a continuous plea for love. If people really cared for them it would not matter whether they were fat or thin. In trying to dissuade parents from focusing too intensely on a child's diet, care must be taken lest an emotional vacuum develops. A child's overeating may be his response to emotional starvation, to the lack of real rapport between him and his parents. Though he resents being nagged about his diet, he will feel completely abandoned if they suddenly stop paying attention to it. This to him can mean only one thing, that they have given up on him, that they no longer care, not even about his being fat. Both parents and children must learn and experience that they have things in common which are not related to food, and which prove to the child that his parents enjoy his progress and want his development.

Conflicts about eating may not always be in the open; peculiar eating habits may develop, such as eating on the sly or eating at night. In some it is part of the rebelliousness against all interference, proof that they can eat what they want and get away with it; others literally block out the knowledge of this eating. It is a denial of reality; they act as if food which nobody watches them eat does not count. This mechanism operated in a young woman who was in analysis for periodic depressions, inability to enjoy life, and a feeling of disorganization. She was big and well-built, but too heavy by fashionable standards. Her mother had wanted to protect her against the fate of becoming too fat and, without many words, there had been a continuous stringent supervision of everything she ate. Usually this leads to open arguments; this girl had accepted it in seeming compliance.

This was the characteristic pattern of her childhood which had been described as harmonious. The parents were conscientious and intelligent, and everything was planned with the daughter's consent; there was never a reason for disagreement. Her every wish and need were anticipated, and at no point was initiative, independence, or rebellion necessary or possible. She developed the habit of eating very little at the family table, but then, quietly, ate more afterwards. She continued this pattern even after she was married. Her husband was puzzled about her weight. "It is amazing on how little food she can maintain this size." Eating when nobody was watching had become a necessity for her. She knew it was ridiculous, but she did it with the inner conviction that this food which nobody saw her eat would not be fattening. When she felt the impulse to eat, she reassured herself, "This doesn't matter, this will not count." In this way she avoided feeling guilty for defying her mother; if the food did not count, then she was not really disobeying her. The unquestioning obedience which she had adopted to maintain the superficial harmony had resulted in enormous resentment, completely unconscious before her analysis, about not having been an active participant in living her own life; she had literally been "the fulfiller of mother's perfect plans."

Not only parents and children are involved in such neurotic struggles around a diet; problems may come up in many different ways between married couples. A husband on a diet is at the mercy of his wife. Her solicitous concern may provoke his adolescent rebelliousness against being told what to do, particularly if she comments on every bite he eats. Others complain that their wives are not concerned enough about their weight. Sometimes a husband will turn the complete responsibility over to his wife, even insisting that she check his weight every day. If she forgets he will be furious for being neglected, go on an eating spree, and then accuse her of wanting to be a young widow; by not watching his weight she would be responsible for his early death.

Sometimes the lean spouse will object to dietary restriction, feeling deprived of companionship when enjoying good and rich food. If the marital relationship is strained a wife may prepare diet dishes with less care and the husband will refuse the tasteless diet and prefer her tempting rich meals. She may express contempt for his greed and lack of will power, whereas in reality it is her lack of consideration that sabotages his efforts.

A husband, too, can interfere with his wife's good intentions, either by making fun of all the fuss and foolishness, or through thoughtless remarks about being sure that she can't do it. The obesity and dieting, or more correctly nondieting, may become the source of continuous strain and reproaches between husband and wife. There are husbands who will tactlessly declare: "I have a right to a wife who is slim and well-dressed," and the wife will blame him for her obesity, saying that it is his cruelty that drives her to overeating.

In situations like this, just as in juvenile obesity, treatment is doomed to failure unless the partner becomes involved in a therapeutic effort and is willing to cooperate. With adolescents one can work actively toward their moving away from home; the involvement of marriage partners is more confining unless they are heading toward divorce. Usually there is too much satisfaction in this mutual combat for divorce to be seriously considered, although talk about its possibility is a recurrent threat. The constant fighting about dieting between adults may make even greater demands on the skill and patience of a physician.

Dieting has always been a dreary and rather lonely business. There was the tradition of the famous European spas that, in addition to the healing waters, rested on changing the living habits to make them conducive to reducing. In the atmosphere of the spa, the overweight person would find congenial companions, all of whom were working toward the same goal. This custom has been revived, American style, by obese women who had struggled in vain with their weight and who formed self-help groups to learn about diets and to give each other support in their efforts. One group, Weight Watchers, turned commercial and became a corporation, and with good organization and an excellent press is now the leader in the field. If its commercial success is a measure of its effectiveness then the weight problem of the stable overweight adult seems to be solved. Its success is based on many factors. One is the fact that the clients are self-selected volunteers who come on their own initiative, or with the encouragement of a friend. The dietary advice appears to be sound, and is given in sufficient detail and with interesting variety that some of the boredom has been taken out of dieting. Frozen prepared meals are available, relieving the housewife of preparing separate meals, and eliminating cheating. The main feature, keeping close control on an individual's progress, is the weekly weigh-in and class, which has been described as combining "the atmosphere of a religious revival meeting and a high school pep rally" (10). Those who have been taking off pounds are loudly applauded; those who have gained are sympathetically counseled to renew their efforts. Stunkard has made a study of one of the self-help groups (TOPS) where the participants were chiefly overweight women, average age 42 years, and average weight excess 58% (21). The meetings seemed to be based on the same principles. Stunkard commented on the variability of the results, but found that they compared favorably with contrasting groups from medical clinics. Emotional control is a central virtue in the TOPS philosophy; overeating and consequent overweight are viewed as due to defective emotional control. Members regard each other as intelligent persons who have the power, if they so desire, to overcome their emotional problems and to establish self-mastery. Making reducing a group enterprise relieves many of these women from the isolation of their lives and the cheerless frustration that dieting usually implies.

There is so much optimism and enthusiasm about these enterprises that I regret to report that my own impression of the results is less favorable. Admittedly, my experience has come mainly from dealing with obese people with complex psychological problems. Earlier several individual case studies have been cited where weight had been lost this way but was immediately regained, as it was with other methods. It is not likely that figures about the long-range results will ever be published. In recent years almost every patient who consulted me had at least considered going to Weight Watchers, or had gone to one of their meetings but had found them too unsophisticated and had felt turned off. Some who had attended for a period and had regained the lost weight would speak with a certain embarrassment about having taken part in the meetings and their childish ways of praise and blame. It seems that people with a more secure self-concept accept these naive rewards and punishments as helpful for the immediate goal, namely for achieving weight loss, and for them these group efforts seem to offer a helpful solution.

The Physician's Problems

Treatment of obesity has always confronted the physician with many baffling problems. Consulting a doctor is based on the assumption that he has special knowledge for the treatment of an illness. But everybody has special knowledge about reducing diets and the recent success of the group enterprises has found wide publicity. The physician is consulted by two types of obese people, those who have failed in their previous efforts, and those who have thus far been indifferent to their weight but in whom some other medical condition makes reducing a necessity. More than in any other illness, the physician is called upon to do a special trick, to make a patient do something—namely stop eating and be more active—after he has already proved to himself that he cannot do it or is not interested in it.

The uncooperative fat patient is a trial to his physician. He provokes feelings of helplessness and frustration. Many doctors try to make their patients confess that they have cheated, and foolproof systems and calculations have been devised to convince a patient that he cannot get away with it. More often than not a patient will break off treatment when he feels trapped or because he recognizes the doctor's frustration. There are many physicians who consider fat people the most boring and uncooperative of patients. One summarized it succinctly: "All they ever lose is the sheet with the carefully calculated diet." Many patients complain about their physician's indifference, in contrast to the supportive attitude in the group approach.

An emotional attitude is expressed also in a doctor's preference for one or the other theory and treatment method. Roughly two main streams can be recognized, the broader one of naive simplistic optimism, a "do as I tell you," promising health and slimness as reward, and a smaller trickle of fatalistic hopelessness, that nothing can be done, except having slim ancestors. The literature is full of reports of the marvelous successes to be achieved by this or that *new* diet, medication, starvation regimen, behavior modification, or psychotherapy. It is easy enough to achieve a dramatic loss in weight through practically any method as long as the patient cooperates. The trouble is that these mechanically induced results are not lasting. Our whole concept of the treatment of obesity would change radically if patients who do not cooperate were not excluded from such reports, and if only long-term results were considered worthy of being published.

There is need for a decisive change from the conventional pseudo-activity to a meaningful new action. This implies communicating to the patient that one accepts his problems as serious and recognizes that they are not his fault, and that he deserves help with them, not ridicule. Detailed knowledge about living habits is necessary, not to trap the patient into confessing that he is lazy and greedy, but to diagnose specifically the extent of his difficulties. Only on the basis of such a nonreproachful approach is it possible to examine together with the patient the advisability and prospect of dietary and other changes in living habits, and to recognize environmentally conditioned disturbances and conflicts. Some of them the physician may help to remove or solve, particularly those that are apt to interfere with a reasonable reducing regimen. Sometimes it will appear advisable to postpone reducing to a more appropriate time; in other cases one might want to discourage reducing altogether unless the underlying serious personality problems can be resolved.

Care must be taken that an encouraging attitude does not lead to excessive praise. Obese patients want and need the feeling of personal interest from their physician, but too much praise and admiration should be avoided because a patient might misinterpret it as erotic interest, even as a sexual advance; they may make corresponding demands on the physician and become depressed when rejected. Two cases, one of a woman who became psychotic because she misinterpreted her physician's admiration this way, and of another who developed an anorexia nervosa-like picture in a similar situation were described in Chapters 10 and 13. Other patients may become frightened and break off treatment if they feel that they cannot live up to the doctor's expectations. Under favorable circumstances a constructive, dependent relationship develops, with the patient knowing that he can rely on his physician to help with the new problem. The tendency to gain weight must be recognized as a life-long condition for which a patient needs help whenever he faces difficulties.

The difficulties in the relationship between physicians and their obese patients is not a one-sided proposition. The notoriously poor cooperation of fat people is often the outer manifestation of an underlying hostility against physicians who by virtue of their job are supposed to change their faulty ways. Obese patients are in the habit of consulting a great many doctors, and they transfer to each new contact not only the emotional attitudes of their own family but also of past treatment situations. Thus we are faced with patients who come to a new physician with an "I dare you" attitude. Increasingly there are physicians who look upon the problem of fat people with respectful consideration instead of with moralizing condemnation. The progress in physiological research, even though it has scarcely been applied to human obesity, has the great merit of demonstrating in scientific terms that fat people are not just bad, blameworthy children who should be branded as weak-willed and self-indulgent, but that they offer interesting problems that challenge the skills of any physician.

Readiness for Reducing

Among the many factors that need to be evaluated before a reducing regimen is prescribed, there is probably no aspect more important than the patient's motive for wanting to lose weight, or conversely, for not being interested in it. Quite recently Crisp and Stonehill (8) reported their experiences with the treatment of severely obese patients and emphasized that detectable "neuroticism" at the behavior level might frequently be absent or denied, but that severe depressions might become behaviorally evident when reducing is carried through. Stunkard (20) reported earlier on the untoward responses to weight reduction among certain obese persons, chiefly middle-aged women; he observed a startlingly high number of patients (50%) with psychological symptoms when reducing was enforced.

Even without such serious underlying depression, many middle-aged people show little motivation for losing weight. However, the same patient who had not been able to diet just for appearance sake, will do it consistently and seemingly effortlessly when confronted with a problem of health, such as diabetes, circulatory difficulties, or orthopedic problems. Yet even with such strict medical indications there are some who cannot accept the need for food restriction. I give as an example the story of a 38-year-old woman, the wife of a successful executive. She came from a family with a tendency to overweight and diabetes on both sides. She had been heavy all her life and took pride that she was active and successful nevertheless. When she married at age 20 her weight was about 150 lbs. She gained with each pregnancy and thus her weight had gradually risen to over 200 lbs. There had been several efforts at reducing but she would immediately regain and said she felt and functioned better when heavier. She described herself as happily married and in addition to running a large home she was interested in many community affairs.

Even though she had known all her life about the diabetic inheritance, she experienced the diagnosis of the illness as a blow to her pride and competence. She suddenly felt completely unable to control her weight and gained rapidly. Her physician referred her for psychiatric treatment but this was unacceptable to her because it implied that something about her life needed changing. She had always run things and told other people what to do and the idea that her way of life could be improved upon was an insult. Though she refused therapy, the evaluating conferences accomplished something—she stopped gaining weight.

Yet eagerness to reduce does not in itself foretell a good prospect for long-range results. It is among people who clammer for quick reduction and who appear most eager to cooperate that the baleful cycles of drastic losses and rapid regaining occur. I have observed this particularly among adolescents with severe personality problems who are desperately unhappy about being fat (6). They are particularly gullible and easily exploited by all the advertised commercial establishments, trick diets, and make-it-easy contraptions which promise the magical transformation of a drab and miserable life to a glamorous existence. It is important for the physician to recognize the underlying unreasonable expectations. "Dieting" to such patients is not what it appears to be in physiological terms, but it becomes a magic tool that will bring fulfillment of impossible aspirations. Without a corrective reappraisal of their fantastically high aspirations they are bound to be disappointed and will regain the painfully lost weight. If the distortion of the sense of reality is severe they may suffer a breakdown, or go on with reducing to the bitter end with anorexia a tragic, though fortunately rare, outcome.

The very process of reducing without emotional readiness is as much an expression of sickness as the overeating. Such merely mechanical reducing is carried out for various lengths of time, sometimes for a few days only, more commonly for approximately three or four weeks. Then the whole system just collapses—"something breaks"—and one single "step off the diet" suffices to destroy the whole ritual. It may be "just one cookie," or a word of concern by a parent, or more commonly the realization of the hopelessness of the procedure, that the daydreams will not be fulfilled, that life will be as common, plain, and bleak as they had always experienced it. Once the diet is broken, the old craving for food returns, the painfully lost weight is regained in a short time, often surpassing its previous level.

Psychiatric referrals come chiefly from this group of fat people with severe interpersonal problems and unrealistic expectations. Therapy must be directed toward the problems of living that have resulted from being fat, and the circumstances which have brought them about. If and when a patient feels ready he is referred to a physician experienced in handling the medical aspects of reducing. My comments about how difficult obese patients react to reducing programs are based on observations which I have made in the role of an actively interested spectator. Many of these extremely discouraged patients, as their psychiatric difficulties improved, were able to carry through a reducing regimen and to keep their weight under control even through periods of emotional upsets and crises. Few obtained the petite sylph-like figures they or their mothers had dreamt of during their worst periods, just as their dreams of unheard-of success without effort could not be achieved. They became slender appropriate for their build and were able to concentrate on worthwhile achievements in realistic terms.

Medical Management of Anorexia Nervosa

Whatever the problems encountered during reducing of obese people they are insignificant in comparison to the panic and upheavals that surround the management of anorexia nervosa. The central importance of psychological and situational factors in its treatment has been recognized since its description 100 years ago, and there have been continuous debates on how to accomplish the seemingly impossible task of getting food into a patient who is stubbornly determined to starve herself. The discussion has extended to what food to offer, how to feed it, where to do it, and what medication to use. The writings often reflect exasperated frustration, the helpless feeling of being involved in a battle of wills. The physiological principles are very simple: increase the food intake and slow down these hyperactive cachectic patients. The question is how to persuade, trick, bribe, cajole, or force a negativistic patient into doing what he or she is determined not to do.

It is virtually impossible to draw conclusions from the medical litera-ture about the effectiveness of various regimens. The case material is ex-tremely heterogeneous, with patients at different stages of their illness. Medical services usually see patients relatively early, with the picture not yet complicated by the serious secondary problems and symptoms which are outstanding features in the patients seen on psychiatric services. One reason for the confusing reports that is rarely openly stated is the fact that the authors frequently have little experience themselves in handling such patients. Rowland's survey (18) is based on the study of the case records of thirty patients who were observed at the Columbia Presbyterian Medi-cal Center between 1936 and 1959. The figures indicate that about one patient was observed per year in different sections, and that there was no senior physician with seasoned knowledge supervising the therapeutic re-gimens. Needless to say the survey reflects something like chaos; nothing was applied with any consistency. A variety of methods were used, such as frequent small feedings of special preparations, or, in contrast, coercion to eat the regular hospital food, or tempting choices from special trays, or feeding by gastric tube or threat of it.

Similarly discouraging is a survey by Browning and Miller (4) who reviewed the records of 36 female anorexic patients treated at the Univer-sity Hospitals of Cleveland between 1942 and 1966. They concluded that hospitalization did little to improve the course of the disease, and that there was no difference in the outcome whether the patient was on the medical, surgical, or psychiatric service. A puzzling conclusion is their statement that "very few of the patients died"; three deaths out of 36 patients represent a mortality rate of 8%, a regrettably high figure con-sidering the fact that these are young people who had been in good health before the anorexia developed. All three had died while hospitalized, which is reported with the implication that vigorous treatment might have hastened the fatal outcome. This fact might be interpreted differently, that hospital admission is postponed until patients are in such debilitated states that they are beyond help. This was the situation in three of the five patients about whose deaths I have detailed information, and where there was delay in deciding on tube feeding. Treatment of a condition so rare that only one or two patients are seen per year even in a large hospital is necessarily frustrating unless there is a nucleus of senior staff with suffi-cient experience to direct the treatment.

An example of good treatment results is Berkman's report (2) from the Mayo Clinic based on his extensive experience over many years. A definite treatment regimen was developed which consisted of a frank discussion of the whole treatment plan with the patient, including possible discomfort she might suffer when 300 calories were added in slow steps to the amounts she had eaten before, until the daily intake was up to 3000 calories. Treatment results are reported as good, but no information on the long-range development is given, nor does Berkman differentiate between cases of true anorexia nervosa and some other functional disorder of eating. At one point he refers to "patients who have dogged resolution to get well," a description incompatible with the denial of illness and the frantic determination not to gain weight characteristic of true anorexia. Not explicitly stated is that these good results were obtained on a service where the whole staff had developed great skill in handling the problems of such patients. One may wonder whether the same method could be carried out as successfully in a hospital with less charisma than the Mayo Clinic, by personnel without the special skills.

An individualized but experienced approach is of the greatest importance; detailed evaluation is necessary not only of the patient's condition and problems but also of that of the service, its facilities, and treatment philosophy. Brief admissions to a medical service without special experience in the management of the condition can create as many problems as it attempts to solve. The personnel are as helpless and inconsistent in dealing with the deceitfulness and cunning of the patient as was his family, and are apt to react with anxiety, frustration, and angry coercion. Thus a hospital stay may be characterized by the same type of frantic emergency situations that led to the hospitalization in the first place. Whether hospital admissions are helpful or not, in reality the situation is that most patients, long before they are seen by a psychiatrist, have had at least one hospitalization. Early in the disease the focus is on diagnostic procedures to recognize or exclude possible organic factors. Later on hospital admissions are considered essential, often as a life-saving measure, when there has been considerable emaciation with progressive decline, or when the tension of the whole family has risen to panic levels.

Increasingly it has been recognized that the acute danger to life does not come so much from the emaciation but from serious disturbances in the electrolyte balance, in particular in patients who use vomiting, laxatives, and diuretics which they continue to do even after they have become painfully aware of the dire consequences. Under such conditions rather heroic methods of correcting the electrolyte balance through intravenous infusion may be necessary. In one of my patients this help came too late; extreme calcinosis had led to widespread irreversible changes, with cardiac and renal failure the cause of death.

Even if there is no immediate threat to life, anorexia nervosa is such a serious, anxiety-provoking condition that sooner or later the question of hospitalization will come up. There has been considerable controversy about the merits of hospitalization going back to the time of Gull and Lasègue who held different views in this matter. A tradition has developed that it is best to treat these patients away from their families, but in my experience short-term hospitalization to enforce a weight gain without attention to the underlying problems is useless, if not harmful. But treatment in the home setting is possible only if the whole family becomes involved in therapy. Otherwise, admission to a psychiatric hospital for long-term therapy is essential. The success, of course, will depend on the facilities and therapeutic philosophy of the service. It has been objected that psychiatric admission is superfluous, that weight gain could be accomplished on a medical service and that psychotherapy could be carried out on an ambulatory basis. This reflects an outdated concept of the function of a psychiatric hospital. It is true that these patients do not need custodial psychiatric care, but great benefit can be derived from the experience of living in the hospital "milieu" when the interaction with other patients and staff are made integral parts of the therapeutic experience. Details about this and its integration with individual psychotherapy will be discussed in the next chapter. Psychiatric hospitalization is indicated when the effort to resolve the endless and destructive struggle between the patient and his family has failed in an ambulatory approach.

Recently Stunkard and his co-workers (3) described a method of behavior therapy for anorexia nervosa, namely permitting freely chosen activities as immediate reward for gain in weight. The patient is restricted to bed rest but on any day that she has gained ½ lb she may get up and exercise as much as she wants. Faster gains in weight were achieved than with any other method. However, the results with 4 patients tell dramatically that weight gain in itself is not a cure for anorexia nervosa. One patient who gained weight satisfactorily committed suicide after discharge.

The success of ambulatory treatment depends on the pertinence of the psychotherapeutic approach, and, to a large extent, on the resolution of the pathological family interaction. Though difficulties in family relationships had been recognized early—Lasègue gave an insightful description —systematic therapeutic involvement of the families has not been discussed until quite recently. Traditionally a patient was admitted to a hospital to make her gain weight, by force if necessary, and then returned to a family setting in which nothing had changed. In younger patients with onset before puberty, the need for therapeutic work with the parents was more readily recognized. While the young patient is hospitalized on a pediatric or child psychiatric service, the parents are in treatment so that by the time the child comes home there has been a rearrangement in the psychological interaction in the family. In fresh cases, before secondary problems have become entrenched, young patients may do well at home and can continue in school while the patient as well as the parents are in therapy. The intensity of treatment for each member, the focus, and its length vary considerably. Recently efforts have been directed toward reaching the whole family as a unit. I have been impressed with the enthusiasm of some of these reports, in which a few dramatic sessions supposedly do away with the problem of anorexia nervosa. No follow-up information on such cures has been reported. Selvini (19) speaks of the promising results of intensive work with the whole family, but observed that families of clinic patients accept joint therapy more readily than those seen in private practice.

As to the medical regimen, individualization is essential. A firm attitude that eating is necessary, combined with the reassurance "we won't let you die," is a prerequisite. Some find it useful to prescribe certain definite amounts of high protein, high-caloric liquid nourishment which is offered as "medication," and to leave eating ordinary food to the patient's choice. Usually such a program is reinforced by instructing the patient that the alternative to this will be tube feeding. In my experience a psychotherapeutic approach with focus on the underlying personality structure that deemphasizes the psychological importance of the noneating is often accompanied by resumption of normal eating.

The use of various medications reflects changing concepts of the etiology of anorexia nervosa. When Berkman (2) stated that neither insulin nor thyroid had been used it was in contrast to the common practice at the time of his report. Insulin was given to stimulate the appetite. Prescription of thyroid was based on the assumption that a "low" basal metabolic rate indicated deficiency. This practice was continued even after it was known that the low metabolism was an expression of undernutrition which would correct itself with weight gain. It is not unusual even today to see an anorexic who has been receiving thyroid for many years and would not think of giving it up, because the patient is convinced that it helps her keep her weight down. As long as anorexia nervosa was considered of pituitary origin, it was a matter of course to prescribe some glandular extract, or even to implant pituitary glands from animals.

Endocrine products have a legitimate use in the treatment of amenorrhea, where it is possible now to produce regular bleeding. In males with delayed puberty testosterone may be useful, but only after the condition is sufficiently corrected that its administration will not stunt a patient's growth. In a case to be discussed in the next chapter, testosterone had been attempted early in the picture with untoward emotional reaction, but with good response later after considerable progress in psychotherapy. In recent years the anabolic steroids have been used as adjuncts in the rehabilitation of long-standing cases, with impressive weight gains and a greater sense of well-being. However, as far as I know, no controlled studies have been made.

The psychiatric problems have also been treated by somatic methods. Both insulin and electroshock therapy have been used; in my observation, only with very temporary results. Psychotropic drugs have also been used, sometimes under drastic conditions. Frahm (11) reported a treatment approach which consisted of isolating the patient, feeding through an inlaying gastric tube, and giving high doses of phenothyazine. Immediate weight increase was satisfactory, but there is no report on the long-range results of this treatment regimen in which personal problems are completely neglected.

I should like to close this chapter with some reports by parents about their experiences. In a letter to the *Lancet* (May 1, 1971) the father of a 13-year-old girl wrote that his daughter had been unsuccessfully treated in England where she was permitted to move at her own pace, without any consistency or strictness about the way she was fed. When he heard about a French professor (name not reported) who had almost total success in treating anorexia nervosa, he took his daughter to this man's clinic, where she was given treatment which he described as

largely confined to very strict and consistent discipline, bordering at times on harshness. —The strictness involved a locked room, an absence of hot baths, and eating meals with a very high starch content under firm supervision and against the clock until every morsel had been consumed. The harshness depended on the degree of resistance of the patient.

Nine weeks later he collected his daughter to find that she had gained 2 stones in weight and he considered treatment "triumphantly successful."

A mother tells in a book (12) the story of her 13-year-old daughter, Kathy, one of 4 sisters. She had felt unhappy and suffered loss of appetite and then increasing weight loss. There followed a pilgrimage from one doctor to another, with increasing dissatisfaction with the diagnosis and recommendations, and increasing desperation of the family about the progressive weight loss. When things were at an absolute low, the mother took Kathy to Florida where she herself had spent happy years. There a small-town physician diagnosed what had been "missed" by all the extensive studies in New York, namely, "thyroid deficiency." Miracle of miracles, within 24 hours after the first thyroid pill had been given the pulse rate had climbed from 44 to 84! And Kathy laughed for the first time, felt nice and warm and enjoyed every bite she ate, determined to gain weight as fast as possible. After 4 weeks she left the hospital happy and plump, went home, and, according to the book, lived radiantly happy ever after. Through contact with other patients I learned about the subsequent progress of this young girl, when she was 20 years old. It seemed that she still suffered from enormous anxiety about eating and had many other neurotic problems.

Unfortunately, this less glamorous outcome is more in agreement with observations on the long-range course of patients who had so-called spontaneous recoveries with weight gain, even resuming menstruation. Cremerius (7) studied the late development of patients who had refused psychiatric treatment and found that weight gain alone was not a sign of cure but was often associated with serious maladjustment and personality disturbances. My own observations on the long-range course of seemingly spontaneous recovery are equally dismal, although some were quite miraculous sounding.

BIBLIOGRAPHY

1. Banting, W., *Letter on Corpulence, Addressed to the Public,* 4th ed., Mohun, Ebbs and Hough, New York, 1864.
2. Berkman, J. M., Anorexia nervosa: the diagnosis and treatment of inanition resulting from functional disorders, Ann. Intern. Med., 22:679–691, 1945.
3. Blinder, B. J., Freeman, D. M. A., and Stunkard, A. J., Behavior therapy of anorexia nervosa: Effectiveness of activity as a reinforcer of weight gain, Amer. J. Psychiat., 126:77–82, 1970.
4. Browning, C. H., and Miller, S. I., Anorexia nervosa—A study in prognosis and management, Amer. J. Psychiat., 124:1128–1132, 1968.
5. Bruch, H., and Waters, I., Benzedrine sulfate (Amphetamine) in the treatment of obese children and adolescents, J. Pediat., 20:54–64, 1942.
6. Bruch, H., Psychological aspects of reducing, Psychosom. Med., 14:337–346, 1952.
7. Cremerius, J., Zur Prognose der Anorexia nervosa (13 fuenfzehn-bis achtzehnjaehrige Katamnesen psychotherapeutische unbehandelter Faelle), Arch. Psychiat. Nervenkr., 207:378–393, 1965.
8. Crisp, A. H., and Stonehill, E., Treatment of obesity with special reference to seven severely obese patients, J. Psychosom. Med., 14:327–345, 1970.
9. Dole, V. P., Treatment of obesity with a low protein calorically unrestricted diet, Amer. J. Clin. Nutr., 2:381–383, 1954.
10. "Fortune from Fat," *Time,* February 21, 1972.
11. Frahm, H., Ergebnisse einer systematische durchgefuehrten somatisch orientierten Behandlungsform bei Kranken mit Anorexia nervosa, pp. 64–70, in *Anorexia Nervosa,* J.-E. Meyer and H. Feldmann, eds., Georg Thieme Verlag, Stuttgart, 1965.
12. Fryer, K. H., *Kathy,* E. P. Dutton & Co., New York, 1956.
13. Harvey, W., *On Corpulence in Relation to Disease: With Some Remarks On Diet,* Renshaw, London, 1872.
14. Lesses, M. F., and Myerson, A., Benzedrine sulfate as an aid in the treatment of obesity, New Engl. J. Med., 218:119, 1938.
15. Mayer, J., *Ueber den Werth und die Resultate der verschiedenen Entfettungsmethoden,* Reimer, Berlin, 1886.
16. McBee, S., "Diet Pills," *Life,* 64:23–28, 1968.
17. Penick, S. B., Filion, R., Fox, S., and Stunkard, A. J., Behavior modification in the treatment of obesity, Psychosom. Med., 33:49–55, 1971.
18. Rowland, C. V., Jr., Anorexia nervosa. A survey of the literature and review of 30 cases, pp. 37–137, in *Anorexia and Obesity,* C. V. Rowland, ed., International Psychiatry Clinics, 7, Little, Brown & Co., Boston, 1970.
19. Selvini, M. P., Anorexia nervosa, pp. 197–218, in *The World Biennial of Psychiatry and Psychotherapy,* Vol. 1, S. Arieti, ed., Basic Books, Inc., New York, 1970.
20. Stunkard, A. J., The "dieting depression." Incidence and clinical characteristics of untoward responses to weight reduction regimens, Amer. J. Med., 23:77–86, 1957.
21. Stunkard, A., Levine, H., and Fox, S., The management of obesity. Patient self-help and medical treatment, Arch. Intern. Med., 125:1067–1072, 1970.

17

Evolution of a
Psychotherapeutic Approach

Psychotherapy with individuals suffering from eating disorders aims at helping them achieve a more competent, less painful way of handling their problems of living. As was discussed before, neither obesity nor anorexia nervosa presents uniform characteristics, and individual patients will differ in what interferes with their efficacy. I shall focus here on the problems encountered in the treatment of developmental obesity and primary anorexia nervosa, both of which have a potential for schizophrenic development. They may represent only a small percentage of those with disordered weight regulation, but they are the largest group seen by psychiatrists. They are the patients in whom the disordered weight and allied symptoms appear to be related to core problems of their whole development. The intrinsic task of psychotherapy aims at effecting a meaningful change in the personality so that a constructive life becomes possible without the misuse of the eating function in bizarre and irrational ways. The problem is how to achieve this.

Psychotherapy as it is known today is in such a process of flux that nearly any interaction between two people or groups is referred to as "therapy." The term is used as unspecifically as if one were to speak of "surgery" when referring to opening an abscess, or setting a bone, or transplanting a heart. The various methods and techniques of therapy and the essential nature of the therapeutic process have all been disputed, and there is no definition that has found general acceptance. I shall attempt to review here what I have found useful and effective in the treatment of severely disturbed people suffering from developmental obesity or primary anorexia nervosa. Patients suffering from these two conditions have in common certain basic deficits in their functioning due to the absence of appropriate responses to expressions of their needs (Chapter 4). They suffer from an all-pervasive sense of ineffectiveness, and in this lies the link to schizophrenia, where passivity, lack of volition, and a conviction of being influenced by others are cardinal symptoms. Like schizophrenics, these patients experience themselves as being the helpless product of others without an active self-awareness. Quite often this is expressed in a patient's speech patterns; he always presents himself as passive and helpless, someone to whom things happen (1).

Evoking awareness of impulses, feelings, and needs originating within is considered the essential step in helping a patient to develop a sense of competence in areas of functioning where he had been deprived of adequate early learning. Through the therapist's alert and consistent confirming or correcting responses to any self-initiated behavior and expression, the patient can become an active participant in the treatment process, and thus eventually capable of living his life as a self-directed, competent individual capable of enjoyment.

This formulation is the outgrowth of continuous reevaluation of the therapeutic process, in particular of difficulties and failures encountered over a period of 30 years. I shall review some of the problems in some detail, because they seem to be similar to those that continue to be encountered by others.

Psychoanalysis has undergone marked changes since the early 1940's, and many of the modifications I gradually developed, with emphasis on evoking a better functioning self-concept in the patient, are now widely accepted and in agreement with current psychotherapeutic practices, particularly in the treatment of schizophrenia, borderline states, or narcissistic personalities. However, I find it useful to be explicit in stating the changes in the old concepts because with all the progress in psychotherapeutic principles, the approach to obesity and anorexia nervosa, even of many experienced therapists, seems to have remained tied to old and outmoded models and concepts. The more the psychological disorder is conceived of as expressions of oral dependency, incorporative cannibalism, rejection of pregnancy, etc., the more likely that therapy will follow the classical psychoanalytic model. The concept that the abnormal eating is a late step in the development of the illness, a frantic effort to camouflage underlying problems, or a defense against complete disintegration has only recently been formulated for anorexia nervosa, and is not widely known. With this new orientation the therapeutic focus is on the failure in self-experience and on the defective tools and concepts for organizing and expressing the patient's own needs, and on his bewilderment in dealing with others. Instead of dealing with intrapsychic conflicts and the disturbed eating function, therapy will attempt to repair the underlying sense of incompetence, conceptual defects and distortions, isolation and dissatisfaction.

In my own work I approached the problem at first in the optimistic expectation that "insight" into the unconscious conflicts and the symbolic meanings would lead to a cure. But improvement was often followed by relapse, not only among my own patients but also among those analyzed by others, some of whom had been reported in the literature as treated successfully. It looked as though they had remained unaffected by the analytic experience.

The literature on the value of psychoanalysis for the treatment of eating disorders is hopelessly inconclusive. There was a flood of publications on psychoanalytic treatment of neurotic obesity during the 1940's, but subsequently considerable doubt has been expressed about the efficacy of psychoanalysis, or of psychotherapy in general. In anorexia nervosa psychotherapy has been referred to as useless (6), or conversely, psychoanalysis has been praised as the best approach (12), an attitude not shared by therapists with extensive experience in the field. Authors who feel that a psychotic core underlies the overt clinical picture, such as Eissler (3), and Meyer and Weinroth (10), have expressed doubt about verbal forms of treatment resulting in meaningful change in a condition that presumably develops during the preverbal period. Selvini (11) feels that in anorexia nervosa the body is used concretely and serves as a tool in the struggle for an acceptable identity; she found traditional psychoanalysis ineffective, but a more pertinent understanding of the condition was accompanied by increasingly better treatment results.

My own experience goes in the same direction; I feel that obese and anorexic patients appear singularly unresponsive to traditional psychoanalysis. This, however, does not render them untreatable, but psychotherapy must be modified to meet their personality problems. They need help because of their lack of the sense of autonomy and for their disturbed self-concepts and self-awareness. The aim of therapy is to assist them in developing a more competent, less painful, and less ineffective way of handling their problems. Changing their abnormal eating patterns becomes possible only when at least some of the underlying problems have been resolved. It is then the visible expression that some improvement has taken place.

Disappointing treatment results led to my reevaluation of these patients' needs, and I felt it necessary to examine the question of to what extent the traditional model had failed to fulfill them. In spite of gaining insight, some basic disturbance in their approach to life remained beclouded and untouched, or was even reinforced in the traditional psychoanalytic setting where the patient expresses his secret thoughts and feelings and the analyst interprets their unconscious meanings. This represents in a painful way a repetition of the significant interaction between patient and parents, where "mother always knew how I felt," with the implication that they themselves do not know how they feel. "Interpretation" to such a patient may mean the devastating reexperience of being told what he feels and thinks, confirming his sense of inadequacy and thus interfering with his developing true self-awareness and trust in his own psychological faculties.

Under a fact-finding, noninterpretative approach, seemingly unanalyzable patients who were filled to the brim with useless, though not necessarily incorrect, knowledge of psychodynamics, began to change and improve. This was achieved by paying minute attention to the discrepancies in a patient's recall of his past, and to the way he misperceived or misinterpreted current events, and often responding to them in an inappropriate way. Hiding behind expressions like "compulsive eating" or "food addiction," patients will uncover, when held to a detailed examination of the when, where, who, and how, real or fantasized difficulties and emotional stresses of which they had been completely unaware. Inability to identify bodily sensations correctly is a specific disability in eating disorders; other feeling tones, too, are inaccurately perceived or conceptualized, and often associated with the inability to recognize the implications of interactions with others. They suffer from an abiding sense of loneliness, or the feeling of not being respected by others, or of being insulted or abused, though the realistic situation may not contain these elements. The anticipation or recall of real or imagined insults may lead to withdrawal from the actual situation and flight into an eating binge. The process of exploring and examining alternatives in such situations eventually leads to the patient's experiencing himself as not utterly helpless, or the victim of a compulsion that overpowers him.

For many this close collaborative work with the therapist is a new type of experience; his *being listened to*, and not being told by someone else what he "really" feels or means, is important because his own contributions are being treated as worthwhile. Lidz and Lidz (8) described many years ago that schizophrenic patients can achieve self-esteem only through the realization that their own desires and impulses count, that their beliefs and opinions can have value as a guide to living. The therapist who presumes to know the answers plays into the patient's beliefs that somebody else knows the way and will care for him magically.

Examining their own development in this way becomes an important stimulus for the patients' acquiring thus-far deficient mental tools. It leads to a repair of their cognitive distortions and they learn to rely on their own thinking; thus they can become more realistic in their self-appraisal. Clarification of what a patient is saying is best carried out in a manner that can be followed step-by-step by himself, rather than by giving summarizing explanations. Many approach seemingly realistic goals in a distorted way, and though articulate, many think in a peculiar unclear way. These minor distortions, if not recognized and clarified, result in a good deal of meaningless verbal exchange during treatment, something I have called "counterfeit" communication. Psychiatry has paid a great deal of attention to the understanding of the disturbed language of patients, particularly of schizophrenics. Less attention has been paid to what the patient *hears* when the psychiatrist talks to him. In the course of this fact-finding exploration, it became apparent that a seemingly rational patient may understand something entirely different from what the therapist intended to convey. Much of what is termed "resistance" may be the result of discrepancies in meaning and verbal usage, even though it may sound like ordinary words being exchanged. This makes a demand on the therapist that his communication be simple and unambiguous, free of professional jargon.

These patients' sense of not knowing how they feel and of not being in control of their sensations is not a figure of speech but a literal expression of faulty self-awareness, as was discussed in detail in Chapter 4. The core problems, their profound sense of ineffectiveness, their lack of awareness of their sensations, not feeling in control, of not even owning their body and its functions, were recognized as related to deficiencies in the mother-child interaction, the absence of the experience of a regular and consistent appropriate response to child-initiated behavior, resulting in a gross deficit in initiative and active self-experience.

These considerations led to a reformulation of the therapeutic task. For effective treatment it is decisive that a patient experience himself as an active participant in the therapeutic process. If there are things to be uncovered and interpreted, it is important that the patient makes the discovery on his own and has a chance to *say it first*. The therapist has the privilege of agreeing or disagreeing if it appears relevant. Such a patient needs help and encouragement in becoming aware of impulses, thoughts, and feelings that originate within himself. Only in this way can he learn to discover his undeveloped and untapped resources, and become alert and alive to what is going on within himself. These are necessary steps for his developing autonomy, initiative, and responsibility for himself.

This approach implies a definite change in the therapist's concept of his role, and to make these changes is not always easy. It involves suspending one's knowledge and expertise and permitting a patient to express what he experiences without immediately explaining and labeling it. Some of the current models of psychiatric training emphasize early formulation of the underlying psychodynamic issues. Such early formulations may stand in the way of learning the truly relevant facts. A therapist who assumes that he understands the patients' problems is not quite so alert and curious in unraveling the unclear and confused periods. He may be tempted to superimpose his prematurely conceived notions on the patient.

I have called this fact-finding treatment approach *the constructive use of ignorance*, using the word *ignorance* in the way a scientist might use it who regardless of what discoveries have been made is always ready to ask: "What is there that I do not know?" Patients respond well to this objective fact-finding attitude when they recognize that the therapist regards them as true collaborators in the search for unknown factors, and feel that the therapist does not have some secret knowledge which he holds back from them. It is important that the therapist recognize meaningful messages in seeming generalities that are often labeled as evasive. Never having experienced confirmation for anything he expressed, such stereotyped complaints frequently reflect the patient's state of profound bewilderment.

The therapeutic goal is to make it possible for a patient to uncover *his own* abilities, *his* resources and inner capacities for thinking, judging, and feeling. Once the capacity of self-recognition has been experienced, there is usually a change in the whole atmosphere of involvement. Minor events may indicate this. One young girl suffering from anorexia nervosa entered the office, her face shining as if something great and exciting had happened. She announced: "This afternoon (after school) I took a shower because *I wanted to*." Thus far she had done it because it was a required routine. There was a good deal of elaboration of how new and different this feeling was. Another patient, an obese young girl, appeared with a similarly happy expression on a gray and rainy day. She had made the great discovery that she put galoshes on to keep *her feet dry*, and not to keep *mother* from making an angry face.

It may happen that during this transitional period, when there is growing awareness of one's own impulses and resources that are not yet modified by sufficiently maturing experiences, certain delinquent behavior may occur. This phase makes treatment very difficult, and may even result in premature interruption. Having been encouraged to discover his own feelings and needs, a patient, not aware of the immaturity of his desires, may assert his independence by following all kinds of impulses, and accuse the therapist of interfering with his freedom of decision. If the therapist has been careful to differentiate between the appropriateness or inappropriateness of a reaction, and if he has been honest in labeling misconceptions and errors of a patient's thinking, then the foundation has been laid for a constructive handling of this period of transition. If, on the other hand, the therapist has maintained an uncritical supportive attitude of "I am on your side," a true impasse may develop, and a change in therapists may be indicated.

If the deprivation of early learning has been severe or complete, a function can become organized later in life in a limited way only. In obesity with onset early in childhood the eating function rarely becomes truly automatic and self-regulatory. Patients with this background, after discovering initiative and self-directiveness in other areas of living and becoming more effective in their interpersonal relations, love experiences, and professional achievements, no longer need to abuse the eating function to camouflage other conflicts and stresses. They can exercise, without suffering undue strain, conscious control over this function, even though it may remain inaccurately conceptualized. At first they need supervision so that they learn how to control their food intake. When other areas of self-awareness have been effectively developed, this conscious "dieting" may become so matter-of-fact that it comes to resemble true autonomy.

In anorexia nervosa, too, in particular in long-standing cases and those with eating binges and vomiting, some patients will continue to resort at times to abnormal eating patterns, though functioning well in other respects. A young woman whose illness had lasted for over 10 years, who had recovered after a radical change in the treatment approach, reported 5 years later about her happy and busy life but added, "My eating is still wacky." But she explained that she was so busy with the realities of her life, in particular with taking care of two children, that there was not enough time to indulge in a neurosis.

I should like to illustrate how systematic eliciting of feelings of awareness and of trust in her own psychological effectiveness resulted in a decisive change in the patterns of experience during a brief period of treatment for a young anorexic girl, with weight loss of recent origin. She is the only anorexic patient I have seen in whom there had been no previous psychiatric or medical treatment.

Olga was 12 years old when the weight loss began, and she was still in prepuberty. She was unusually short, 4'5" tall, and looked slightly plump at a weight of 70 lbs. She had been on cortisone for several years for a serious eye disease (uveitis and iritis). Since age 10 she had been practically blind though she could differentiate light and dark. In spite of this handicap she had been an excellent student, with her mother acting as her "seeing eye." Olga was popular with her classmates, quite athletic, and had received prizes for horseback riding.

She was the youngest child with a considerably older brother and sister. When she was 10 years old, her divorced sister came to live with the family with her 3-year-old son, who was taken care of by Olga's mother. The sister stayed 2 years until she obtained a college degree. It was noted that Olga paid no attention whatsoever to her nephew; she was never mean to him but she seemed to resent that he took attention away from her. After the older daughter left, the mother, feeling that Olga was doing well and no longer needed special help, looked forward to having time for herself and to pursue her own interests.

It was at this time that Olga's weight loss began. At first it looked all right but then it became apparent that she ate almost nothing, and that she had become conspicuously thin. She was restless, slept poorly, would get up at 5 in the morning and pace around. When her weight had dropped to 50 lbs she still felt "too fat." She had always been an excellent student but now she became upset about having "failed" when she made 93 on a test, saying that her grades were no longer "perfect." She also became socially withdrawn and refused to go to parties. However, she liked to cook and would bake cakes for the other girls, and also prepared rich desserts which she insisted her parents eat. She loved to go to the grocery store, to feel and smell the food. After taking even the smallest amount she would immediately complain that her stomach was full, and accuse her mother, saying, "You give me too much—you try to make me fat again."

When Olga was seen in consultation 5 months after she had begun her dieting, the most disturbing factor appeared to be the mother's extreme tension and anxiety. There was one treatment session in which all 3 family members were seen together. The mother accepted the recommendation that it would be better if she were not present at meal times, and she was encouraged to pursue her plans for more adult activities. Olga's care was taken over by her father, who was much less anxious about the weight loss and her behavior, and they had their meals together. Olga was referred to another therapist, who, making use of his musical talent, helped her in becoming aware of her sensations and feelings by whistling different tunes. They talked about the feeling tones expressed in various melodies. Olga became fascinated with searching out her feelings and showed a widening spectrum of emotions. Food and eating were never discussed. After a while she began to report dreams in which colors represented different emotional and feeling tones, and she eloquently described them: "Gold discovery and purple determination floated lazily across the pulsing surge, dipping and diving in and out among the abandoned patches of blackness, and yellow sorrow wove itself narrowly between the happy colors, trying to choke out their joy."

After this there was rapid symptomatic improvement; within a few more sessions she announced her decision to terminate treatment, saying that she was now able to tell how she felt and she knew what she wanted and what she did not want. She promised to contact the therapist if she were to feel insecure again. The mother reported about Olga's progress. Three months later she could write that Olga's old confidence had been restored and that she again took part in group activities. She was more relaxed in school, less grade-conscious, and had revived her former interest in riding horses. A year later Olga was described as her old outgoing self again, agreeable in her attitude; she looked well, loved to eat, and had continued to gain weight, but not excessively. Two years later the picture sounded equally good.

Several factors seem to have contributed to the recovery in a relatively short time. The fact that the mother's unusual closeness to Olga had been determined by the necessities of the child's blindness and not by her neurotic need to dominate, and also that she had wanted to lead a more independent adult life, were considered favorable signs. Encouragement toward self-initiated behavior through the explicit and consistent emphasis on developing awareness of her own feelings and needs effected a change in Olga's attitude toward herself and the family. Her eating was advisedly left out of the discussion. It is the area in which initiative cannot be developed during the acute stage of the illness.

The following is an example of inadequate therapeutic intervention, though the downhill weight loss was interrupted by appealing to the patient's desire for autonomy. It concerns a 17-year-old girl who had become anorexic when 15 but who had maintained herself sufficiently to graduate from high school. After graduation the situation deteriorated with further weight loss, to a low of 70 lbs. Family tensions increased and the situation in the home became untenable. The mother felt at the end of her own control, and lived in terror of her daughter, who had taken over the kitchen and overwhelmed the family by forcing food on them. The father, a professional man, tried to be tolerant of the daughter's behavior but he felt guilty for feeling actually repulsed by her. Psychiatric help was not sought until a month or two before graduation. Hospitalization appeared necessary because of the increasing turmoil in the family and also to prevent further weight loss, since the muscle tissue had begun to waste.

A psychiatric consultation was requested at that time, and it was suggested that the treatment of the psychological problems and the medical regimen needed to be separated. The patient was given a choice between tube feeding and eating on her own, but there was no debate on the necessity to improve her nutrition. It was explained that therapy would focus on her lack of self-confidence, her fear of losing control, and her difficulties in decision-making. This very bright girl grasped both points and put them together in her own way, thereby dominating the treatment situation. When vanilla-flavored Sustagen was given by gastric tube she asked the nurse whether she could let her drink it, since it smelled so good. The next morning she awakened ravenously hungry with the thought, "Why not eat delicious things instead of receiving them by tube?" When the intern made rounds he responded to her request for a sweet roll like the one her roommate was eating by pulling out the tube and ordering a full tray. For the first time in nearly 3 years she drank orange juice and milk.

When seen by her psychiatrist later in the day she was ecstatic about her decision, talking at length about every aspect of it, with the recurrent theme, "I have done it myself. I decided to live for myself, to eat what I feel I need." She began to gain weight and when she was discharged 3 weeks later, she weighed 87 lbs. But it was obvious that not all was well. She had been overexcited and had subjected the entire staff and fellow patients to manic talking streaks about her eating problems; she had needed tranquilizers to quiet down. The parents had not become involved in therapy, and there was concern that the symptoms would recur at home. For the next two months the girl was seemingly doing well, was less obsessed with food, and was planning to go away to college at the end of the summer.

As it turned out, no real change had occurred in spite of the weight gain. By assuming "autonomy" in the feeding situation but excluding everything else from discussion, the underlying disturbances in her self-concept had remained unchanged. She did well academically, though she was not happy at college. She made few friends and went home practically every weekend. Now her uncontrolled eating became the object of concern. Her weight rose rapidly, reaching 140 lbs less than a year later. The mother expressed her disgust with her daughter's fat appearance by referring to her as "the fat lady in the circus."

This story vividly illustrates that correcting the weight loss in itself is not a solution. Not infrequently a therapist shares the belief that something lasting has been accomplished when an anorexic patient begins to eat, stops losing weight, or even more when he gains. Though treatment emphasis should be on a patient's ability to recognize his needs and to make decisions about them, the abnormal eating is not the area in which this can be explored. The goal is to help a patient become aware of his participation in other areas of his functioning, in particular in his relations to others, so that the eating function no longer needs to be misused as a pseudo-solution.

Family Involvement and Milieu Therapy

Psychotherapy is not a process that takes place in a vacuum. Very few of the patients I have here described lived alone. Most stayed with their families, or, when severely sick, were hospitalized. In either case therapeutic work needs to be done with the people with whom they are in daily contact.

Since my earliest work with obese children I have been impressed with the intense involvement of these patients with their families, and how this close bond interferes with their developing a sense of separate identity. This is so glaring, even extreme, in some cases, that I cannot conceive of successful therapeutic work without changing the noxious interaction. Whenever I have succumbed to pressure to accept a patient without involving the family, or when the outer circumstances seemed to suggest that the patient was well on the road toward independence, I have come to regret it. The two brief histories which were just outlined showed the difference in outcome dependent on whether or not the family had participated in the therapeutic process. As another example I should like to give the history of an unmarried young woman who had been sick for nearly 6 years and was 23 years old when she came for treatment. She had lived away from her parents' home for several years, had an apartment of her own, was able to work as a model, and was at least partly self-supporting. She was phobically preoccupied with her weight; periods of starvation alternated with enormous eating binges and vomiting; she was depressed about the constant lying and deceitfulness which her efforts to keep her illness a secret made necessary. Her parents, who lived in a different city, absolutely refused to be involved with the treatment process, or even to stop their control through frequent telephone calls and unexpected visits. In their opinion it was their daughter who was sick and needed to change; they did more than their duty by paying for therapy.

In spite of this handicap she seemed to be progressing well. Increasingly she felt she acted on her own initiative, and she seemed to develop a better sense of her own identity. She expressed the task ahead of her as "release the hand that clutches you" and made valiant strides in that direction. With greater inner freedom she established a meaningful relationship to a man, with increasing openness and honesty on her part. There was much indication of a maturing love relationship, but she feared he would not accept her if he knew about the severity of her illness, particularly about the eating binges and vomiting. She felt upset when he criticized her for eating so little when they went out for dinner, though he took pride in her being glamorously slim.

At this point, the "clutching hand" interfered. Though she felt definitely not ready for it the parents insisted on a formal announcement of an engagement, and also on keeping the illness and symptoms a secret from her fiancé. Since I expressed concern about this course of action they also terminated treatment.

More commonly dissatisfaction is expressed by family members of an obese or anorexic patient about the fact that the abnormal weight has not changed in the desired direction, leading at times to premature interruption of treatment, or, under more favorable conditions, to a consultation. Relatives are usually quite explicit in expressing their discontent; sometimes it is the physician who supervises the medical regimen who feels that progress is unsatisfactory.

Not uncommonly difficulties can be traced back to the beginning of treatment, namely, when therapeutic goals have not been clearly stated or defined. When accepting an obese patient for psychiatric treatment there is need for a negative statement: psychotherapy does not amount to persuading, tricking, or bullying a fat patient into using a mysterious will power so that he will lose weight. Quite often, this assumption underlies the referral of an "uncooperative" patient to a psychiatrist, and this point needs to be clarified early in the relationship, to the patient as well as to the family.

However, quite often dissatisfaction expressed as concern about persistent fatness substitutes for the tension and upheavals that come into the open in a family when one member is in intensive therapy. Usually these "interferences" occur when there is good therapeutic progress manifested by the patient making his first steps toward emotional separateness and independence. From unexpected termination when things seemed to be going well in therapy, I gradually learned that this occurs when parents have not been offered the support and help that they needed. Intensive emotional involvement with the parents, particularly with the mother, plays an outstanding role in obesity as well as in anorexia nervosa. Therapeutic efforts are directed toward loosening these ties, with encouragement of the patient toward independence. It is not sufficient to engage the cooperation of the parents, which often amounts to nothing more than a recommendation not to interfere. Even though parents may complain about a child's immaturity and lack of independence, they need help in truly permitting a change and in finding new satisfactions for themselves so that they can let go of the child they had held so closely.

How best to accomplish this depends on individual circumstances and the willingness of parents to be involved. Though unhappy about the situation, many parents absolutely refused to be "blamed"—as they interpret a recommendation of working with them. This particular difficulty arises often in obesity which the family considers a shameful nuisance for which the patient is to blame, or in long-standing cases of anorexia nervosa when the acute anxiety and frenzy about the danger of the condition have subsided.

Family therapy has acquired in recent years a certain status of independence, as being a distinct treatment technique. I have not been able to convince myself that conjoint family therapy, which means seeing all members together for the whole treatment period, offers any advantages or is even feasible for these serious disorders. There are reports of successful intervention at the point of crisis; unfortunately they do not contain information about the long-range results. They deal with young patients, in the 12- to 15-year-old range, who were seen shortly after the onset, the optimal time for effective intervention. In my experience it is not the one or the other technique, but the clarification of the disturbed patterns and the stimulation to greater autonomy in the child that bring about a favorable course of events. Temporary weight gain can be achieved through many different methods, and is not a valid measure of true inner changes. In severe eating disorders, the patient is not just "a scapegoat" who could drop his symptoms when the patterns of family interaction change, though such changes are of the utmost importance. Whether this can best be accomplished through individual family sessions or through conjoint family therapy depends on the total situation. When difficulties have existed over an extended period and faulty self-awareness dominates the picture, individual therapy is essential to help a child learn to differentiate between his different needs, and for the development of inner guideposts, and trust and confidence in his own psychological abilities.

Treatment of a difficult anorexic patient, in particular when the illness is of long standing, requires the facilities of a modern psychiatric service where he is exposed to many experiences. Here too, experience in the handling of such patients is needed, otherwise there is the danger that the personnel and the other patients will become overwhelmed by the anorexic's constant demands and complaints. In spite of the severe weight loss these patients are rarely so sick that they cannot participate in the whole ward routine. The activity programs, particularly when oriented toward milieu therapy, offer the chance for interaction with many people, and these experiences can then be explored in individual therapy. I have found art work, and also dream reports, particularly useful, not so much for their unconscious symbolic content but as aids in evoking a patient's self-awareness, as illustrating his own patterns of experience, and of his way of expressing his concepts of his functioning and interaction with others. Art work and dreams serve to convince him that he does not function only under the influence of others, but that there are things which are truly his own, originating within him, expressing in his own imagery what goes on within him.

The contributions of other treatment modalities, group sessions and milieu therapy, vary in individual cases. Generally they serve an auxiliary function, often providing the setting for the daily events which are examined in the patient's individual therapy sessions. In some cases the milieu experience appears to be the more important factor for the improvement.

An example was reported by Mesnikoff (9). It concerns an anorexic patient who had been in intensive psychotherapy on the outside and had shown beginning signs of true self-awareness, but whose progress was handicapped by unmodifiable interaction with her family.

Naomi was an identical twin (see p. 260) whose illness had begun six years earlier, when her co-twin, the "executive," began to lead an independent life in college. When her twin became engaged Naomi completely disorganized. She had been in treatment, including a lengthy hospitalization, in a different city for 5 years before she was seen in consultation and accepted for psychotherapy. She was panicky about not being able to maintain her low weight, and suffered from enormous eating binges, 3 or 4 a day, followed by vomiting. She was well-educated and capable of supporting herself, and lived in an apartment of her own. Whenever she felt upset, usually late at night, she would go to her parents' home, eat enormous amounts, and then vomit. Each visit created a family crisis and it was felt that no progress could be made unless this pattern was interrupted.

Naomi appeared comfortable and asymptomatic, without eating binges, when first admitted. She reacted with a feeling of triumph that the capable sister had failed when she learned that her twin had separated from her husband. Within a few days her elation gave way to anxieties and depression and guilt over her hostility toward her twin. All her old fears reappeared—dissatisfaction with her body, conviction of her incompetence, and feelings of general unworthiness—and the compulsive eating and vomiting recurred. She organized other patients to bring her food and criticized the staff as incompetent when they could not stop this traffic.

In conferences with the other patients and the nursing staff it was recognized that the attacks on the staff occurred when Naomi was intensely preoccupied with her own incompetence. Subsequently it was brought into the open that she had always compared herself unfavorably to her twin sister. She had felt inferior and had presented herself to others as a "sick" person who needed special attention. The treatment program focused on her reaction in rivalry situations, her doubts about ever succeeding, and then gradually focused on exploring her ego capacities. In the controlled and supportive hospital setting she was able to work out her jealousy and fear of failure without resorting at the slightest disturbance to her old symptoms, and she began to test out her abilities and to establish a sense of independence.

After her discharge she married her boyfriend, who was deeply devoted to her and fully informed about her illness. Until then she had not been willing to commit herself. She has functioned well in this marriage to a very gifted man who advanced rapidly in his career, which involved repeated moves to different cities. They subsequently adopted two children and Naomi proved herself a loving and capable mother.

Weight Change and Food Intake

Though psychotherapy with obese and anorexic patients should focus on their personality problems and not on their eating behavior, the fact that food plays such an active role in their psychic economy is a complicating factor. Psychotherapy always involves facing unpleasant and painful issues, and obese people have resorted, throughout their lives, to eating as a defense against anxiety, awareness of rage, or depressive feelings, and they will continue to do so for quite some time while in therapy. Instead of working through their problems, they are apt to overeat when anxiety arousing issues come to the surface. At the same time they become impatient when there are no quick results, and weight is such a visible symptom that it is often conceived of as a measure of success or failure. Anorexic patients, by the time they come for psychiatric treatment, have developed elaborate rituals to maintain their low weight, while the families are frantic about the lack of progress. Therapists themselves often become discouraged by the tenacity with which their patients cling to the abnormal weight.

I am in the habit of informing new patients and, if necessary, responsible family members, of the possibility of an initial weight increase when the usual pressures to enforce dieting are relaxed in the more accepting climate of psychotherapy. Yet there is usually an angry, even desperate, outcry that treatment could not possibly be helpful when a fat patient gains more weight. In the psychotherapeutic encounter many will experience for the first time the highly unpleasant sensations of anxiety which until then had been camouflaged by their eating behavior, and they may react with the conviction of getting worse, saying that they never felt so miserable before. Once they have gained some understanding of the underlying problems and of the masking role of abnormal eating, they can no longer blame the obesity as the cause of all their troubles. Painful as this period is, it is an unavoidable part of growing understanding and self-awareness. During this phase, a strong bond to the therapist is essential.

The family also needs support to gain some understanding of their own problems so that they can permit the patient to develop more independence.

At this moment, with the beginning of some awareness of competence and independence, some patients will decide to go on a diet which they use as a demonstration that all is well, that they no longer need treatment, and they work through the difficult problems. Invariably this premature effort is short-lived and is followed by renewed weight increase, which reveals this "acting out" as what it is, a precocious declaration of independence from the parental figure to whom they had clung until now, or an act of defiance against the therapist who has confronted them with the painful issues.

Invariably the question will come up whether and when to institute a reducing program. To be effective, this should include more social activities and exercise in addition to controlled eating. These patients have failed with innumerable reducing programs before they ever consulted a psychiatrist, and will resist changes in their social and activity patterns. Reducing should not be introduced as an issue until some understanding has been gained of the underlying problems, of the abnormal attitudes and tensions. They need to learn discriminating awareness of their various needs, and how to distinguish between physiologic and emotional discomfort, confusion about which is such a basic symptom. Theoretically one might say, a patient is "ready" when he can look upon a reducing regimen as a rational task which will result in weight loss, but not as a form of magic which will solve his life's problems; and when his concept of what represents his "ideal weight" is realistic and in harmony with his constitutional make-up, and does not represent fashionable emaciation.

Except in very disturbed patients, I find it useful, for practical and also therapeutic reasons, to encourage efforts at reducing before this theoretical ideal has been reached. When dieting is attempted during psychotherapy, many problems come into the open that had been masked by the obese state. Such efforts can contribute to a more distinct recognition of the perceptual deficits and disturbances in bodily awareness, and help to clarify the many ways the eating function has been misused. It is necessary to refer patients to another physician for management of the reducing program so that the therapist himself does not become involved in the struggles over its details.

Patients who are severely disturbed and grossly obese, in particular those who have been fat since early in life, will find that they function more competently at a higher than average weight. For them, it represents a healthier attitude to accept a stable degree of overweight instead of exhausting their life's energy in futile, recurrent cycles of "stuff and starve." During therapy their weight will usually stabilize at an acceptable level, which they can maintain when they stop being preoccupied with their weight in this frantic way.

It is not uncommon that a therapist, in his enthusiasm about psychological understanding, conveys to a patient the feeling that once his problems and conflicts have been solved, the fat will just melt away. This it does not. Regardless of what understanding a patient achieves, reducing is still a difficult task. But he can master it without becoming discouraged and depressed when he has developed better self-awareness and no longer indulges in overly optimistic fantasies. Treatment may be unnecessarily prolonged if this aspect is not clearly understood, or a patient may withdraw in angry disappointment and give up the gains he has made when the implied promise does not come true and the fat does not disappear. Avoidable difficulties may be created through an overly permissive attitude toward eating and the obese state. I spoke before of weight gain during the early part of treatment; in my observation this rarely exceeds 20 to 25 lbs. In consultation I have heard of weight gains of up to 100 lbs or more, without the therapist having challenged the patient's provocative surrender to eating binges. This is apt to happen when the therapist himself has a fatalistic concept of the whole disorder, such as eating addiction, and thereby reinforces a patient's concept of his complete helplessness. In seriously disturbed patients who require psychiatric hospitalization, being in a hospital usually serves as a curb on the eating; food is not as continuously available as when they lived at home. Rarely, if ever, is a prescribed diet indicated; it may be of help when a patient is ready for discharge and wants to lose weight.

A wait-and-see attitude, an unrealistic expectation that the weight will correct itself after the psychological problems have been solved, may be harmful, even fatal, overoptimism in the treatment of anorexia nervosa. One cannot do meaningful therapeutic work with a patient who is starving. As was discussed before, so-called "anorexic behavior" is the direct expression of the state of starvation. A certain degree of nutritional restitution is a prerequisite for effective therapy. I have been impressed by the fact that if the therapeutic focus is on a patient's self-doubts, lack of self-confidence, and fear of losing control, and not on the symbolic meaning of the food refusal, he will accept truisms like "one must eat to live," and assume responsibility for eating voluntarily as an autonomous decision, instead of being tube-fed while hospitalized. Severe and long-standing degrees of emaciation, with weights below 60 or 70 lbs, rarely, if ever, can be handled in the home where the condition had developed, and where parents are as angrily set in their ways as the patient is in his rituals. These patients need the well-integrated efforts of a hospital with an attitude of medical responsibility, while the therapist encourages autonomy after clarifying the underlying problems. The judicious management of the medical problems requires close collaboration with the physician supervising them. If these problems are not attended to, they will complicate and interfere with the intrinsic task of psychotherapy.

Consultations

In my efforts to reevaluate various treatment problems I was greatly aided by the many physicians and psychiatrists who requested consultations for patients with unsatisfactory progress, and who frankly described the difficulties they had encountered in their treatment approach. Many had analytic training, at different times and in different "schools" of psychiatric and analytic thinking, but their therapeutic problems showed definite similarities. Usually they had focused on the abnormal eating and its symbolic significance, instead of on the underlying developmental distortions and misconceptions. It seems that anorexia nervosa and obesity, which lend themselves to ready explanations in psychoanalytic language, can often seduce therapists into being more tradition-bound, foregoing the broader, more dynamic concepts with which they usually operate. These patients' overconformity also makes them absorb a therapist's utterances, encouraging him to continue in an unproductive and ineffective direction.

Kolb (7) has drawn attention to the fact that little has been published on psychiatric consultations on patients of other psychiatrists, and mentions that only 12% of his consultations had come from other psychiatrists or psychoanalysts for an opinion on the therapeutic progress of their own patients, and that these requests usually came from the "wiser and more experienced members of our profession." In obesity and anorexia nervosa, a much higher percentage, as a matter of fact the majority, of consultations were on direct request by other psychiatrists. As Kolb had observed, the more experienced therapists were more specific in reporting and formulating the treatment problems on which they expected an opinion. To me such consultations have been one of the most important of my learning experiences. They require evaluation of the interactional processes between patient and therapist and examination of the therapeutic relationship in the nexus of interaction with the patient's family and other associates; in eating disorders the reality demands of handling the somatic picture create special problems during psychotherapy. Invariably, I was stimulated to reappraise parallel problems I had encountered with my own patients.

Some consultations were requested in anticipation of therapeutic and management problems in such an unusual psychiatric condition. Since they came from the most experienced colleagues they offered me the most stimulating learning experiences. To give one example: probably the best-known account of the treatment history of a fat schizophrenic girl, *I Never Promised You a Rose Garden*, was written by the patient herself (5). I am sure I do not divulge a professional secret when I mention that Dr. Fried, the therapist in the story, was Dr. Frieda Fromm-Reichmann. Never having treated a fat adolescent she asked me to stand by as a consultant, and to meet her young patient. The book scarcely mentions that the heroine, Deborah, was extremely obese, nor are there any references to the symbolic meaning of her eating, nor that any restrictions on her eating were imposed. At that time I had already learned from my own work that exploration of the motivational and symbolic significance of the eating disturbance was therapeutically ineffective. Accordingly it was decided that the eating should not be singled out for any particular attention. The therapeutic focus was on Debby's inner problems, her dissatisfaction in all her human relationships, her confusion about her self and her identity, and the extreme isolation from which she had tried to escape into a fantasy world. Without going into details, the repeated opportunity of reexamining and comparing my observations and deductions with those made by a leading expert in the treatment of schizophrenia was an important step in formulating my own concepts. Many years later, Fromm-Reichmann, as was her custom, reviewed with her patient what she herself had considered most helpful and significant in her recovery (4). This artistic girl expressed it as a simple image, "The We experience," her awareness, even at the time when she was most distraught, that her therapist considered treatment as something in which they would work together. This is what I have tried to describe here as a decisive aspect in the treatment of these difficult patients, and what I have called, more clumsily, "making the patient an active participant in the treatment process."

More commonly consultations deal with the question of why treatment progress appears unsatisfactory. Some of the repeatedly encountered problems were discussed earlier in this chapter. I should like to mention here two recurrent constellations that seem to perpetuate the condition instead of curing it. One is adherence to outmoded psychodynamic concepts, spending endless treatment hours, year in and year out, in the exploration of unconscious conflicts, oral dependency needs, incorporative and cannibalistic fantasies, and "specifically" in the search of fear of oral impregnation. As late as the time of this writing, patients will summarize their previous treatment experiences as "he tried to convince me that I was in love with my father and that I would not get well unless I admitted this," or "that I wanted a baby but was afraid of pregnancy," or something along this line. I doubt that any therapist had pushed such a single-minded interpretation; the important point is that this is what the patient had understood—and the fact that they were seen in consultation suggests that something had miscarried.

The other complication, and one which is more difficult to correct, is having permitted the therapeutic relationship to develop in such a way that it is controlled by the patient's anxiety and threats of disintegration. Like an overanxious parent the therapist conceives of the patient as extremely fragile and, by offering "his strength," a symbiotic relationship develops to which both cling. In a mistaken concept that such "support"

would offer the patient a chance to mature through the relationship, the
therapist becomes a collaborator in maintaining the illness by condoning
bizarre living arrangements and absurd eating rituals. Gail's story, which
was presented in Chapter 4, is an example of what bizarre situations may
develop. Unfortunately, her story is not unique. I continue to be consulted
about interminable treatment situations where a patient's increasingly eccentric demands and rituals have been condoned. When the parents are
asked why they had permitted such disorganization of their home life,
they will invariably answer: "We are completely buffaloed—but her doctor told us to go along and do what she wanted." There is no simple
solution for changing such difficult, abnormal therapeutic relationships.
Usually the situation requires interruption through hospitalization. If the
difficulties are based on an erroneous theoretical orientation, a change in
treatment approach, in particular in consultations with experienced therapists, is usually rewarded by resolution of the impasse.

I should like to describe one such consultation in some detail. It began
in December with a letter of inquiry from the therapist, and included the
patient coming to Houston for 2 weeks in April and an exchange of
letters during the next 5 years.

Felice was the younger, smaller, and less assertive of a pair of identical
twins, briefly referred to in Chapter 14 (Table 14–1, No. 33) who had
become anorexic when her co-twin asserted her independence from the
twinship in college. The illness began when she was 18 years old, and she
had been in psychiatric treatment since that time, though with several
lengthy interruptions. While in therapy she was able to finish college,
attempted to live away from her home town but had a relapse, and
returned home and resumed therapy. When the consultation was requested Felice was 29 years old and had been sick for over 11 years. Her
therapist reported that during the first few years of treatment the focus
had been on her sexual problems, that an alleged rape had preceded the
onset of the symptoms, and that the relapse had been triggered by an
unhappy love affair. About a year later she left treatment abruptly when
fantasies centering about oral impregnation began to emerge. During in-
patient treatment of 7 months duration, she showed considerable improvement but on discharge her bizarre eating rituals returned in full
force. Before resuming treatment her therapist sought consultation from a
senior member of the local psychoanalytic institute, who recommended
that emphasis should be on the ego aspects of her personality, with few
interpretations of unconscious content. Felice had been able to function
on a high level professionally, and had left her parents' home to move
into an apartment of her own.

During the past year a puzzling problem had developed: she claimed to
eat practically nothing but her weight remained stable at about 110 lbs.
Her internist was at a loss to explain this, and a hospitalization for

endocrine studies gave negative results. Her psychiatrist assumed that she ate during episodes of tremendous anxiety and dissociation. He felt the central problem was her intense need for symbiotic attachment, her feeling that she could not control herself unless she could cling to someone. She had expressed the problem as: "Either you believe as I do about myself (that she is grotesque and animal-like), or I must believe what you think and have no thoughts of my own, or we are so far apart that there is no hope of communicating."

A report of her illness was requested from Felice herself, and she wrote that she felt that she had made some progress as far as insight went. "However, the remaining symptoms surrounding food and eating have *not* improved." Her twin sister also cooperated by sending a lengthy report of their childhood, and her observations on Felice during the years of her illness.

The consultation was undertaken with the explicit understanding that an attempt would be made to find out whether some awareness of initiative and participation in the therapeutic process could be evoked, since her conviction of helplessness and nonidentity had stymied the previous efforts. Her illness seemed to express in an exaggerated form the all-pervasive sense of ineffectiveness which is an essential aspect in severe eating disorders. Extensive psychological tests, including the Rorschach and TAT, had suggested that therapeutic benefits would be limited by her immaturity and very strong dependency needs, that she would structure therapy in terms of these demanding dependency needs, and that she would strongly resist interpretative activity in those areas most threatening to her. The question was whether these "demanding dependency needs" were deplorable but unalterable traits or whether this conviction of helplessness could be challenged during the consultation.

Felice was first admitted to the metabolic service to study the metabolic mystery. The admission weight was 110 lbs, and metabolic signs of acute starvation were absent. She was given the amount she claimed to have taken during the preceding period, namely one can of liquid diet, (225 calories); within 4 days she lost 5 lbs and developed signs of ketosis. This clarification was of the utmost importance. Instead of a metabolic puzzle beclouding the issue a psychiatric fact was established, that she misinterpreted her own bodily states and misperceived the reality of her behavior and actions.

She was then transferred to the psychiatric service where she received a prescribed 1200 calorie diet. The dietitian planned this with her participation, and during the second week, on her own request, the choice of food was left to her. She expressed great concern about gaining too much weight and was rather disappointed when this did not happen. She complained about stomach pains, panic attacks, and "blackouts," even saying that she had forgotten how to handle a knife and fork. Nothing unusual was observed and she settled down to eating her meals and even seemed to enjoy them. On discharge, 2½ weeks after admission, she weighed 111 lbs, and looked and acted as if there had been a general increase in her well-being.

During the 16 days of her stay she was seen 12 times in psychiatric interviews. Rapport appeared to be good from the beginning; she was eager to talk about her problems and the exchange was at all times animated and lively, at times breezy, jovial, and even jaunty. She was vivid and articulate in talking about her enormous anxieties and eating problems. When she selected her own menus, she spoke about her indecisiveness, the horror of "making choices," and the "blackout reactions," when there was the slightest error, when what was served did not fulfill to the letter what she had "chosen." When these dramatic descriptions were given for the first time, they were listened to, and some episodes were explored. Then she was advised to write about these anxiety experiences as they occurred, but that we would spend the consultation time on other issues, on her responses and reactions to people and events. She produced many pages of well-written notes which when typed amounted to more than 70 pages. Some of her descriptions of disturbed bodily experiences were presented in the chapter on body image. Only if something truly novel or unusual occurred was it taken up in our conferences.

It was explained to her that symptoms that had persisted for such a long time tended to lose their original dynamic meaning and needed to be understood in operational terms, namely as expressions of current interpersonal problems. When she felt her "choices" were in the slightest way disobeyed, she experienced "blackouts," instead of emotional reactions, which eventually were recognized as enormous rages. Such transformation seemed to occur frequently, and she would complain of enormous anxiety and then become preoccupied with food. She tended to repeat the description of her symptoms and to enlarge on them with enormous facility. When she grasped the connection she began to pay attention to the underlying feeling tones of her experiences. The dramatization of her bizarre food habits was systematically labeled as camouflage for the underlying feelings which she seemed to deny before she had even identified or acknowledged them to herself. Something else became apparent during these discussions, a rigid determination not to give up her power of negation, and a readiness to sacrifice her own life to a vengeful demonstration that she had been wronged.

Her twin sister had mentioned in her report that even as a child Felice would dwell on some injustices and could not understand how her sister could go about her business after some upsetting event. From reconstruction of her past attitudes, and from the minute exploration of her current reactions, it was shown to her that she acted as if her whole life was devoted to being a monument to the faults and failures of others, and that the increase of symptoms during the past few months could be understood as a vengeful message to her therapist that he, too, had failed her. During our exploratory talks her immediate response to whatever theme came up had been a nihilistic demolition of any new idea, that she "knew" it already, or that "it" had been tried and failed. It also appeared that she had a uncanny knack of making collaborators out of people who took an interest in her, maneuvering them into the position of sharing or being dominated by her anxieties.

As long as she used treatment to demonstrate that nothing and nobody could be of help to her, continuation in any form would be futile. Whether or not she should continue with her former therapist was a question to be worked out between the two of them. A detailed report had been sent to him, which focused on her active role in keeping her symptoms alive, pointing out that she was not as "helpless" as she presented herself. After many pros and cons on her part, she and her therapist decided that she continue treatment with him, and they did so along the lines that had been initiated during the consultation. Three months after her discharge she wrote:

I am managing to eat fairly well (a task easier for me to plan than to accomplish), but my "shenanigans" (an expression repeatedly used during the consultation)—obsessive preoccupation with food, exaggerated fear of gaining weight, and periodic episodes of destroying food—are still frequent. I am encouraged, however, by my growing ability to tolerate this anxiety and to refuse to let it deter me from trying to confront the real roots of the problems face to face.

About a year later she was happy that she could write about excellent progress. "First and most importantly, things are—and have been quite consistently for some time now—going very well. So well, in fact, that I plan to terminate my work with Dr. X very soon." She had advanced in her job and had an active social life with many close friends and acquaintances.

What about my symptoms? Well, I see now they are indeed the "red herring" you once called them, and though I still detect their "odor" in my life, it is not nearly so pervasive as before. I feel considerable confidence that I shall not always have to express my feelings (of anger, loneliness, fear of losing control, or whatever) by means of ritualized or erratic eating, or compulsive daily "weigh-ins." Actual starvation and self-induced vomiting have all but disappeared from my "repertoire of desperation."

Often in the year since I have consulted you I have thought of some of the things you said to me; recently, I feel that I *understand* as well as *remember* them. I recall with particular clarity four things you said: "Self-starvation is *not* autonomy"; "Felice, you *can* make choices—don't waste them on trivia like food"; "Passivity is the greatest form of manipulation"; and "The choice is between living to show the world what terrible parents you had, or going ahead with living your own life." What a long time it has taken me to truly *hear* those things after having merely *listened* to them! It seems unnecessary—impossible, though I sometimes think of trying—to specify in words the things I have learned that have enabled me to overcome the severity of my anorexic symptoms. However, if I were to do so, I surely would include the above four things near the top of my list. Yes, the *real* issues are—and always were—those to which your words referred; autonomy, decision-making, manipulation and vindictiveness! It is insight into this which now serves me as a kind of "tool kit" from which I very often can select the instrument I need to work out my everyday hang-ups. And every day is simply *filled* with opportunities to choose to use it!

These are only a few sentences from a long account of the changes she felt had occurred. Her therapist agreed with her that a turning point in her illness had occurred at the time of the consultation.

The next year she went through with her long-postponed decision to move to the West Coast. She became engaged and then married a man whom she had met during her socially active period and both found satisfactory professional positions. The following year she noted in a very long letter:

I see that it contains more of "events" than of "feeling" type things. That is somehow fitting, I suppose, as my life these days very little time is spent in introspection—I am far too busy living.—I seem to be doing just fine even without all of the pre-planning and deliberation that used to precede every act (remember when "what to have for lunch" was a major issue?), so I guess I shan't try to change that.

I don't want to let you believe that everything is just "perfect" now—I DO occasionally find myself having to stop and look at some of the old relics that I carry around in a deep, "hidden back pocket" of me still. But each time that happens, I seem to be able to rather quickly "dust off" the relic, clean it of the rationalization of fears or angers or doubts that make it seem "a valuable possession" and then retire it to its pocket again. There have been times—happily, very few, however—when my food symptoms have recurred.—I remember your saying once that every one had souvenirs of their illness if they had been ill such a long time, but that I "had *too many* souvenirs."—I guess what it comes down to is that I have acquired a feeling for "who I am" and a certain amount of pride in that "who."—I can live even with the idea that such disappearance (of all symptoms) may never happen, and the *best* thing is that I only VERY rarely even waste my present life comparing it to my past! It is too short, and too good and too full to spend that way! It isn't, therefore, even a matter of thinking of myself as "better" than x-number of years ago, it is a matter of thinking of me as *me*!

The long-range value of a consultation depends, of course, on the open-minded readiness of the consultee to utilize suggestions in a constructive way. As Kolb pointed out, special difficulties are encountered when a consultation is requested, under family pressure, by an unwilling therapist. To give an example: A patient appeared for the consultation, though the requested report had not been forthcoming, and stated that in her therapist's opinion she did not suffer from anorexia nervosa, but had an obsessive-compulsive neurosis and he knew how to treat that. This was an out-of-town consultation which had been requested by an experienced psychiatrist; it turned out that he had already been a consultant and felt that the problem was so serious that he wanted another opinion. The actual therapist had agreed rather unwillingly. In spite of this negativistic attitude, the patient, a 19-year-old girl, was eager for an exploration of the ongoing difficulties. Until recently, in spite of the serious medical complications, she had been able to pursue her studies; now she suffered from fatigue and an inability to concentrate.

The anorexia, which had lasted now for over 4 years, was complicated by diabetes. Not only had she drastically reduced her food intake to one restricted meal at midnight, she had also reduced the prescribed insulin so that she would not assimilate what she ate but would spill part of it. The illness had developed when her parents were divorced, and the seemingly intractable illness was a source of continued conflicts. There had been frequent changes of therapists though she had been in treatment during all these years. She used her present therapist as an ally in her fight against both parents. The mother was also in treatment, but a situation had developed in which mother and daughter quoted their therapists in mutually hostile exchanges.

When the various components of the complex situation and how they interacted and influenced each other had been clarified, she agreed to the recommendation of hospitalization on a psychiatric service with extensive experience with anorexia nervosa so that she could begin to lead her own life instead of exhausting her energies in family struggles and absurd eating behavior. With her agreement, arrangements were made accordingly. Six months later, in a frantic telephone call, the mother requested new recommendations, saying that her daughter's condition had deteriorated, with further weight loss and decompensation of the diabetes. Her therapist, having persuaded her not to enter the hospital, felt now he could no longer handle the situation. The service with whom arrangements had been made was now unable to accept her.

As was mentioned before, such reluctant consultations are rare in eating disorders. Therapists seem to recognize the special nature of the complicating factors in obesity and anorexia nervosa, and most make constructive use of whatever clarification has been achieved.

Supervision of Psychotherapy

In my efforts to formulate my therapeutic experiences I was greatly influenced by my work as a supervisor of psychotherapy of psychiatric residents. Patients coming to a teaching hospital are apt to be sicker than those seen in office practice, and arrive there often as a place of last resort, after other treatment modalities have been exhausted. A few cases treated under these conditions will be presented as illustrative of how general principles are applied in an individual way.

Supervising other therapists eliminates the element of personality and special experience. It also necessitates spelling out in detail to the therapist as well as to the patient what the changes in orientation imply. In this approach the emphasis is on a patient's own role in the way he has lived his life, and on his assuming responsibility for more effective self-discovery. Some of the young therapists felt that the different focus in this approach, with its emphasis on the structure of one's comments and the patterns of interaction instead of on the content, represented a challenging enrichment of their therapeutic awareness, while others felt it interfered with their acquisition of analytic knowledge. Through this ongoing exchange with students I felt stimulated to examine and reexamine my concepts, and to state them in as clear and unambiguous language as possible.

The first example is the treatment history of Gail who was presented in Chapter 4. Gail was unusually clear in describing her predicament, namely that of being unaware of hunger sensations and unable to control how much she ate while insisting on maintaining her weight at a low level. She was 21 years old when she was admitted and had been in treatment with several competent psychiatrists for nearly 10 years. When the treatment approach was changed she had been at the hospital for over a year but so little progress had been made that she was considered "untreatable." During this year her overall behavior had been exceedingly irritating. She could easily have been called the best-hated patient in the hospital. She demanded that a physician be called whenever she felt anxious or panicky, something she experienced at the slightest discomfort. When her first physician left the hospital she greeted her new therapist with sarcastic accusations which persisted through several sessions. He felt discouraged, not without justification, and requested an evaluating conference in which the social worker participated. Though Gail had been in the hospital for over a year, her relationship to the parents had remained unchanged. She would fight with them practically to the point of hand-to-hand combat; interruption of this interaction appeared to be essential. To explain this to Gail and her parents a joint conference was held in which the therapist, social worker, and supervisor participated. There was much mutual accusation and expression of guilt, but a number of rather remarkable statements were made, presented in Chapter 4, in which Gail expressed her despair about her parents having created and raised her in the wrong mold.

It was arranged that Gail and her parents would not communicate directly, but that all messages would go through the social worker, who would also see the parents regularly. Much was accomplished in these conferences, particularly with the mother, who started them with remarks like: "Look, what can you do about this? I hate my daughter, I have always hated my daughter, there really isn't any more I have to say about it." These statements were accepted as "it might or might not be so, but this did not constitute an excuse for not trying to find out why she hated her, if this indeed was the case, and whether they could not get along better in the future." This mother had attempted to superimpose her "body image" of what her child should be on her daughter, as was discussed in Chapter 6.

An effort was made to evaluate the previous therapeutic efforts. The psychiatrist who had been her therapist for several years before hospitalization, and on whom she had been extremely dependent, expressed himself freely about his thinking and attitude. His picture of the parents was entirely negative, and he conceived of his role as providing support to Gail to the fullest. Thus he had stood by when the parents were forced to move out of the house, and when the fantastic arrangements about Gail's meals were made with the parents bringing three meals a day in exactly measured amounts. He had recognized the abnormality of all this, resented that the parents had allowed themselves to be pushed into this weak position and had set no limits to the girl's aggression, but he took no stand because *he felt helpless* in the situation. He saw his therapeutic task as *giving her strength* through his faith in her, that in this way *he could mobilize her*, that *she might draw from him the strength* to go to work and thereby gain more self-confidence. When he finally recognized his inability to make a dent in her terrible panic and fears he advised hospitalization. There, too, her therapist tried to mobilize her by encouraging her to go to work or to resume her studies, though he felt stymied by her direct aggression and her negativistic rejection of all suggestions.

In formulating a new treatment approach Gail's concept of being the product of her parents' incompetence was taken as a clue. The concept that she was the helpless product of her parents' activities had permeated all her actions. Violent as her behavior appeared, it was recognized as expressing her despair over her helplessness and incompetence. Paradoxically, her seemingly uncontrollable aggression had been the outcome of an underlying fear of utter helplessness and inefficiency. Throughout her life she had felt unhappy about being a "bad child" whom everybody disliked, and she had tried to force her parents to change so that they could raise her better. She tried to obtain a sense of identity and independence by manipulation of her body. Since her mother had wanted her to be plump, *being thin* was to her a declaration of her independence.

She assigned to her psychiatrist the role of being her savior and perceived his attitude that through faith and confidence in him she would gain strength as confirmation that somebody else would make her over and mold her fate. As long as this misconception was unrecognized it was unavoidable that she would be terrified when there was a change of physicians; each time she was in danger of getting a doctor who might not be able to work this special magic. She attacked and belittled a new therapist, then tried to influence him in such a way that he would recreate her in a better mold.

The task was to outline a therapeutic approach that permitted her to develop a concept of initiative within herself and to make it clear that her therapist was not a magician who would make her over. Several sessions were used to reconstruct what might have gone on in this family where

Gail had developed this dramatic helplessness, without sound body concept, and with the inability to identify her own needs correctly. There was much evidence that she felt just as helpless in her relationships to other people; she feared they influenced her or that she might influence them. She had been an excellent student in high school by the simple method of studying hard and absorbing what other people had said. There was little evidence of her having any trust and confidence in her own thinking. This had also become apparent on the ward, particularly in group sessions, where she might be exceedingly talkative in voicing complaints, but was absolutely silent when opinions were exchanged.

I have gone into such details about the underlying thinking because this appears to me the most important step for an effective change in the therapeutic approach. Once these considerations had been spelled out the therapist could use his inventiveness in putting them into action. He was open and direct in telling Gail that he would approach her problems differently, without talking about the motives for her fighting and other forms of misbehavior, but wanted to listen to *what she had to say*, and thus help her discover *what she herself felt*. She reported many small episodes, usually complaints, and they were discussed from this angle, namely, that she experienced herself as being ineffective, that she was "a nothing," to use her term. She began to pursue this concept of "being a nothing" because it was meaningful to her; it expressed what had troubled her all her life. Gail and her physician began to explore her previous treatment experiences, of which she said now they had meant "nothing," with one exception. When she was in the boarding school, there had been a psychologist whom she described as being "the first adult who ever listened to me, who tried to understand me, who was willing to sit down and take the time and *listen to what I had to say*." She felt now that she should not have left the school; that he might have helped her.

It was rather surprising how quickly a change took place; within a month the frantic night calls to the physician on duty stopped and she no longer used treatment time for complaining. She now wanted to find out what was wrong in the way she had viewed herself. Being less belligerent, she suddenly found herself an accepted member of her age group. She would take part in discussions or listen and come to her sessions with comments and questions: "What does such and such mean?" Her physician accepted it as such, without efforts at interpretation, but explained what might have been said by the other patients. Gail herself made this the formal treatment approach: "Do you care if I ask you some of these things when I'm uncertain?"

At first, the questions she asked appeared somewhat disconnected or even irrelevant, and her therapist needed support to pursue the line that the important point was that Gail would develop trust in identifying what *she* felt was troubling her. Shortly thereafter she appeared one Monday morning in a session saying that she had enjoyed the weekend, that the whole group had watched a TV performance of *Macbeth*. When asked,

"How did you like it?" she became flustered and extremely embarrassed, and then admitted "I didn't like it." The source of her embarrassment was that the *New York Times* had given the show an excellent review. It was around the discussion of this difference that she finally stated clearly that she had never known, throughout her life, whether she liked or disliked anything unless she heard the opinions of others. When asked about details she explained she was dissatisfied with the integration of voices and background images during the fantasy scenes. Her physician was alert in helping her recognize how sensitive her observations were, but also how ready she was to let such a minor defect detract from her enjoyment of the whole production.

Beginning with the rather vague approach of finding out whether she had any thoughts and feelings of her own, and of encouraging her to express whatever she felt, she now began to focus on definite points, such as her inability to trust something as spontaneous as her feeling of "liking" or "not liking" people, things, or experiences. She also began to relate what was going on in the present to how she had felt about her own life. She asked directly: "I have been in treatment so long—is there any hope for me?"

Without any direction on her physician's part, her themes gradually changed to personal matters, and she started to talk about body functions and sensations. What became apparent was that she felt as if there was nothing about which she had the right to feel that it belonged to her. She brought up many details that had conveyed to her that her mother was omnipotent and knew everything, with the conviction, "I cannot do anything or develop in any way unless my mother changes first." It took considerable alertness on her physician's part and his being openminded to whatever occasion offered itself to point out to her that each human being has an independent life, that her progress toward health could be achieved through her own efforts, and that this was not dependent on her parents' changing first.

At that time she suddenly began talking about her father, and it became clear that she was acutely embarrassed about having had feelings of tenderness and affection for him in the past. This had stopped when at age five she was hospitalized for a mastoid operation. Much time was spent in reevaluating and finding the possible sources of misunderstanding in relation to this event. Apparently as a child she had misinterpreted her whole hospitalization as punishment for having been more affectionate toward her father than toward her mother. Due to the hospital rules, visiting hours were so arranged that the father could not come until the weekend; by that time she was so convinced of its punitive meaning that she refused to see him when he came to visit. The same episode was reevaluated with the parents, and it was now learned that this child, though not as plump as her mother desired, actually had been a responsive child. The unreconcilable fighting and arguing had developed after the operation and hospitalization.

The emphasis shifted now to recognizing other possible misunderstandings of events in the past. Approximately 6 months after the initial joint conference there was another one in which the parents participated to discuss misunderstandings within the family in general terms, and which helped to dissolve to a considerable degree the atmosphere of mutual blame and the conviction that things could never change that had permeated their life. How much all members had dreaded this continuous fighting may be illustrated by the fact that the mother, following a conference where Gail's improvement was obvious, had a panic attack. She visualized Gail coming back into the home and the whole struggle beginning all over. She was reassured that the long-range treatment plan was that Gail should *not* return to the parents' home. This is exactly how things worked out. Gail planned to continue her education (which she did not carry through), but first took a job to learn to feel more at ease living on the outside. She lived at first in a residence club for young working women, later in an apartment of her own. Her rapport with the parents remained somewhat strained, but they saw each other regularly without the violent fighting.

Nothing had been said about what happened to the eating difficulties. No direct attention was paid to them. As Gail became more confident in handling her life affairs, she no longer felt so passive in relation to eating. While in the hospital her weight stabilized at about 150 lbs; she did not particularly like being somewhat plump, but had to admit that she felt more comfortable when not manipulating her weight. When her therapist left the service, and also the city for several years, she would not work with someone else but preferred to wait for his return. She could not maintain her weight at the stable level and gradually gained to about 200 lbs.

The other example of lasting improvement with change in the therapeutic approach after many years of illness and downhill course is Eric, whose history was given in Chapter 15. In his case psychological tests had revealed a rather ominous picture. His previous physicians and hospitals cooperated by giving reports on their findings and treatment approach, which had involved the parents. From the enormous amount of often contradictory information, the leading patterns of family interaction were reconstructed to learn what had miscarried in Eric's development and also why the previous therapeutic efforts had remained ineffective. This became the leading theme during Eric's treatment, in conferences with his parents and in conjoint family sessions.

Previous Psychiatric Approaches

Eric's first psychiatrist had stayed in the picture for 4 years and had arranged for several hospital admissions and his going to a boarding school. He found Eric exceedingly hostile and evasive, willing to go along as long as "deeper issues" were avoided. He felt that the basic problem was Eric's struggle with his mother, an issue he would never face. He tried to show him how he was out to torture and destroy his mother through his symptoms and general attitude. He also saw the parents and was of real help to the mother.

Eric's second psychiatrist, when Eric was hospitalized at age 17 weighing only 45 lbs and in extremely poor physical condition, reported that the primary concern was with the very real problem of keeping Eric alive. Interpretations were made regarding his bizarre eating habits as self-destructive and suicidal, and also as attempts to punish his parents. Later in therapy the expression of unconscious material was not encouraged but certain fantasies recurred; a frequent fantasy was one of being cut up and eaten; it was pointed out to him how his thoughts interfered with his living, especially his eating. When there was no progress, Eric was referred for long-term residential treatment, at age 18½, weighing 49 lbs.

His first physician at the psychiatric institute focused on Eric's interpersonal difficulties, in particular on his aggression and manipulative power struggle. Feeling that Eric needed another battleground for his hostility than that of food, he attempted a direct approach to his aggression. When he discontinued treatment he considered Eric a master of the technique of "divide and conquer." Eric had remained withdrawn, hostile, and suspicious of his therapist, but when he learned that he had been assigned to another therapist he decided to sign out of the hospital.

Much later when Eric had made good progress, he spoke freely about his previous treatment experiences. He complained that he never had felt that his other doctors understood him, and that he did not know what they wanted from him. He had resented the first psychiatrist because he seemed to be in league with his parents and had sent him away to a boarding school. At the same time he felt guilty that he was fighting all the way. He described his second doctor as having let him talk until he became frightened by the things he said; as Eric remembered it, this doctor never said a word. About his other previous therapist he said that he had tried to make him angry and Eric had resented that.

Change in Therapeutic Approach

Eric had been admitted to the general service where he had done poorly. It was suspected that he vomited whatever little food he ate. After 2½ months his weight was only 50½ lbs and he was transferred to a smaller service with more intensive nursing care. This had been avoided when he was admitted because it was felt it would be discouraging for a new patient to meet another anorexic who had done poorly thus far and who received tube feeding twice a day. This patient, Nathan, was a schizophrenic whose refusal to eat served as "atonement for his sins"; he was also discussed in Chapter 15. Eric diagnosed his fellow anorexic correctly as different from him and he decided to eat—just enough to avoid tube feeding. As he explained later: "I took one look at him—Man, that scared me. He was weird." His weight rose to approximately 65 lbs in 3½ months, without a change in his attitude and behavior. At this point, 6 months after his admission, a new therapist took over, and he asked for my supervision.

The first task was familiarizing him with the change in orientation, pointing out that anorexics do not refuse to eat or vomit to show their hostility, or to be destructive, and that "pointing out" such conclusions was damaging because it put the patient in the position of somebody else knowing more about him and his feelings and inner functioning than he himself did. Several supervisory sessions were used to evaluate Eric's background, his relations to his parents, and his behavior in the hospital and in psychotherapy, *not from the angle of aggression and hostility*, which were glaring and obvious, but *in order to recognize the underlying lack in self-confidence, effectiveness, and competence*, and the perceptual and conceptual deficits that had resulted in this misinterpretation of his place in life.

When 10 months later a change in therapists became necessary, Eric attended the briefing conference with his new physician. He had objected that he did not want to start "from scratch" and refused to repeat "these nonsensical things." He had withdrawn again into responding to any question with "I don't know." When it was explained to him that he still needed help and he began to understand the task, he relaxed and was able to give an example confirming the basic thesis, that he needed help to become clearer and more decided about his own wishes, that he needed to discover errors in his thinking and to correct deficits in his experiences. He recognized that if he became active in this process, he had a chance of making the necessary corrections.

Several conferences with the social worker were aimed at a reappraisal of the approach to the family. Like Eric, the mother had experienced previous interpretations as accusation and humiliation. She was depressed, pessimistic, and hostile in her attitude toward Eric whom she described as "my supreme disappointment," and toward psychiatry which had completely failed her family. The shift here too was away from pinpointing the one or other shortcoming and trying to come to a new awareness of the subtle misunderstandings that had distorted their conscientious and devoted efforts at being good parents into something that had stymied the development of their son. This same line was pursued in the joint family conferences, with avoidance of fixing blame and emphasis instead on recognition of mutual misunderstandings, or of misinterpretations of well-meant efforts.

In therapy with Eric interpretations of any one specific problem were avoided. Concrete situations in the present were used to help him recognize when and how he failed to exercise his basic right of being a person with feelings, wants, and needs of his own. It was essential not to get involved in his virtuosity of engaging other people in a struggle for power and control, and equally important to avoid vague permissiveness or inconsistent giving-in.

The situation at the time of transfer offered an opportunity for his new physician to convey to Eric this different philosophy of treatment. Eric had signed out of the hospital and refused to see his doctor, but he knew that his parents did not want him home. Since he had no place to go he was forced to withdraw his letter but he was concerned about "losing face" on the ward. His doctor took the stand that this was an irrelevant point as compared to the important issue: the regard he owed himself and his chance of getting well. Eric acted as if he did not truly think of his own life as important, as not rating it higher than what other people thought. If he did not value his life, then this needed to be recognized as an important sign of his illness. The leitmotif of the new treatment effort became that he not only had a right but also an obligation toward himself of which he did not seem to be aware. This was the one point where his doctor could be of help to him, namely in finding out how it happened that he approached life with this tremendous error of not really respecting himself.

It is, of course, impossible to say whether this aspect had been touched on by his previous psychiatrists. Eric's positive response suggests that this was the first time that he heard this message, and that he experienced his doctor's interest not as an intrusion but as benevolent support. The problem of his eating was not included in the discussions. He had the choice of taking food himself or being tube-fed (and he had decided on eating himself), but it was the hospital's responsibility that he would receive sufficient nourishment. By chance he saw his first psychiatrist (who was teaching at the institute) about 2 months later, and told him that he was now doing well, that he had not understood his problem at all and that he should have sent him to this hospital immediately. This was the first time he had a physician who understood his problems and had helped him to come to the point of *wanting to get better*. Until then he had been so enraged at all doctors that he had only wanted to get sicker.

There was gradual improvement which could be recognized in many areas. I shall discuss here chiefly the changes in his relationship to his family, in his attitude toward his body, and in his self-concept. Changes could also have been illustrated through his ward behavior, and in his attitude and relationship toward his physician. Eric was encouraged to report dreams as something that truly originated in him and expressed how he felt. They were used mainly to bring to his awareness how difficult it was for him to see the world in realistic terms and to trust his own abilities, and how he both wanted and hated to stay dependent on others. Only a few examples will be given.

Interaction with the Family

When Eric came to the hospital his attitude was one of bristling hostility in his relationship to the family and also toward the hospitalization, which he resented. He expressed this during the first few months by continuous criticism of every rule and regulation, by making sarcastic demands for his convenience, and rejecting any effort by his fellow patients or on the part of the staff at making contact with him. He objected to any form of examination, be it for medical evaluation or psychological tests, but then would gradually cooperate, always bargaining for special considerations, and using refusal of food as a threat. Noneating alternated with periods of voracious eating which was followed by vomiting.

His relationship to his family was openly hostile, particularly to his mother. They had not seen each other alone for nearly two years because there was too much mutual hatred and accusation. The mother felt "he fouled up our whole lives." When she heard that he was gaining weight and improving she responded: "But I had been led to believe there was no hope." Eric was equally outspoken in his hatred and in accusations of how his mother had ruined his life, always telling him what to do and never permitting him to do what he wanted. As he gained confidence in his new physician he was puzzled that his younger sister had been able to stand up against the pressure and that only he had become sick. This was the first indication of his being ready to reexamine his past development not with accusations against his mother, but in an effort to differentiate between what she had done and what he had experienced.

During the early months of treatment there was little contact with his parents. His first visit home was for Christmas Day, 9 months after coming to the hospital and 3 months after beginning work with the second therapist. When he came back he reported in detail what he and his father had done and how his sister had reacted, but only when questioned did he speak of his mother as having been "hospitable," not warm. The only good thing he could say was that they had not bickered. During January his mother went on a vacation and Eric became upset when she brought him a present. It was a cigarette lighter. She knew that he did not smoke and suggested: "You can light cigarettes for other people—it looks so gallant." He was enraged; that was the trouble with all her gifts, they were always something that she wanted him to do, never what he wanted. That's why gifts were disturbing to him: "I would rather have nothing. I cannot accept it with thanks—but I feel I have to use it." He went on to explain why he never wanted gifts from her; there had always been problems in relation to clothes. "As a child mother always told me what to wear. I had to wear knickers because she had bought them but I hated them. I could not stop the clothes I had to wear, but I could stop the food."

After considerable improvement he requested to be transferred to the open service. He told his mother on the phone and had another outburst, because she expressed skepticism. "Maybe she is scared I will come home." It did upset him that *he could never please his mother*. This was made the starting point of many discussions, that he did not live to please others, but was entitled to pursue his own life. He began to notice how much this had played a role in his relations to all people. When the head nurse one day noticed that he looked "happy" he was torn between pleasure that she had paid attention to him and indignation that she had dared to tell him how he felt. She was just like mother who had always done that.

A few weeks later, after a visit home, he felt for the first time that his mother was *warm*. "She brought me back to the hospital, she did not need to do so. It showed she cared." He was aware also that he could accept her care now because he felt more independent, more of a self and a person.

By now he was actively interested in therapy and his obsessive waivering over small decisions often became a starting point for clarification of underlying important issues. He discussed with many pros and cons the question of going home for the holidays. His father had offered to pick him up by car, but Eric hesitated because he did not feel he had the right to impose upon them. If the situation were reversed and he was supposed to pick them up, he would do it without hesitation. "I would be honored, because they are my parents and I owe them something. *I am their property*—that's why I owe them willingness to do things for them."

When the word *property* was singled out, he at first wanted to dismiss it, saying that he had used the wrong expression, that of course he was not their property. But then he took it up in detail: "Everything I have and own comes from them. I feel guilty that I have nothing to show for it. I keep taking and taking from them.—Only after I have shown that I can make something out of myself, then I can feel that *I am myself* and that things I have belong to me."

With his now nearly passionate interest in his own development it was rewarding to review his past history. This could be done in more objective terms because by that time the parents had good rapport with the social worker. It could be learned that from age 8 or 9 Eric had been exceedingly concerned about his fitness and manliness. He had become a star athlete and would not only test the traditional biceps for strength but repeatedly examined the muscles of his thighs to see whether they were developing well enough. In his behavior at home the word No appeared more and more often, as if he were trying to prove himself as an independent individual.

He finally did go home for the holidays, and his father came to pick him up by car; to Eric's great amazement his father seemed to be eager to do it. During this weekend the family had a meal in a restaurant and he was indignant when observing that among other parents and children together the children were making difficulties for the parents. He recalled how he had been an inconsiderate child, quite apart from the paradox that his illness and his striving for independence had disrupted the family life in a most traumatic way. When he was 8 or 9 they had planned a winter vacation in Florida. He was afraid of flying and thus the family went by train. Now he felt acutely guilty for having forced a long train ride on them just because he was afraid.

The social worker who was in contact with the parents noticed that they had changed during this winter, had become much more aware of Eric's inner problems, and were dedicated to helping him. It was felt that a joint family conference might help to clarify what really had taken place in this family, how it came that Eric had felt from earliest childhood on that he was an intruder, someone who was not doing his part of the bargain in return.

Though Eric felt so much better about his family, he strenuously objected to a conference. "Do I have always to repeat the things that made me sick? I will not go through that hell again—I did it once. It was just one attack on me." At first he refused to come, then he was obsessively concerned with hurting his parents by what he might say, or with causing them new worries by not talking. His mother, too, appeared reluctant to participate and was at first very defensive. It was helpful for Eric to hear his parents talk about their efforts on his behalf; it was the first time that he had listened seriously to what they had seen in him and how they had felt they had encouraged him and hoped for a good future for him.

Eric remained in the hospital and in intensive treatment for another year, went home regularly for holidays and gradually for whole weekends. Finally it was felt he was functioning with an adequate sense of self-reliance and appeared ready to leave the hospital. It had taken many detailed discussions before he could accept that the life ahead was his own and not something he had to produce in order to satisfy his parents. Before discharge another joint family conference took place where Eric participated as an equal, though he had been concerned whether he would understand what was going on and could express himself well enough. The general atmosphere was one of mutual pleasure in his progress and of hope for the future. The practical question was whether he should live at home. In this conference the subtle ways in which the parents stymied him through well-meaning planning on his behalf were revealed. When the question was raised whether it would be advisable to move to a new neighborhood to spare Eric the embarrassment about having been in a mental hospital, he was finally able to say, "If you want to move to a new house—then move. Do it because you don't like the neighborhood or for whatever reason, but don't blame it on me and make me feel guilty."

The parents' greater alertness to their tendency to superimpose their plans on Eric made it possible to formulate what to avoid and how to meet problems that lay ahead. It had become apparent how much anxiety and tension had been mutually infectious. Eric was particularly sensitive to and intolerant of any signs of anxiety in his mother, and felt that he had to fight back. He felt more prepared now to let her be anxious without becoming involved in his old negativistic way. The mother accepted that Eric was under no obligation to live his life according to her often exaggerated expectations.

When Eric left the hospital he went to live with his family while attending college, and encountered fewer difficulties at home and in new social situations than he had anticipated. He found he had become quite tolerant of his mother's perfectionistic overconcern. He reported to his therapist, after a visit to old friends, that he was "surprised how unbothered I was."

Changes in Body Awareness and Self-Concept

Like other anorexics, Eric had violently denied that he was too skinny or that he needed to eat. In his struggles and fights he had often stressed: "It's my life. If I don't want to eat, why should my mother make a fuss over it," or, "It's my life—I have the privilege to destroy it." In the new approach, this disregard for his life, his not valuing it, was focused on as the essence of his illness. Gradually changes in his self-concept were observed and a few will be pointed out here.

His eating habits had been quite bizarre. There was angry refusal of food, often days of complete abstinence, but also, from the beginning, eating binges with subsequent vomiting, which had been interpreted by his former psychiatrist as expressing his intent to torture his mother. When he was first admitted to the large ward where he ate but did not gain weight, efforts were made to weigh him weekly, but he made such scenes that for many weeks his weight was not taken. This was one of the first points Eric's new physician, discussed with him. He was aware that his reaction to being weighed was abnormal—"like a phobia." He felt the scale was his enemy who would give him away and reveal that there was something wrong with his body. His fears had begun as "fear of the hospital" and then "fear of the tube," but now it was "fear of the scale." "I feel I get evaluated by it and then I am panicky of what they will say on rounds." Or, "If I gain they are so proud—it is always somebody else's business."

Then he began to speak about his dreadful concern with what was "natural" for his body. He was particularly afraid of endocrine treatment; it indicated both that there was something wrong with his body and that he would be forced to change and to catch up "too fast." His real fear was that he had permanently damaged his system. He was reluctant to acknowledge that the starvation had brought about severe growth retardation, that, in a way, he had "made time stand still." Everybody's concern had focused for so long on his weight that he could not truly accept that his progress now was not rated in pounds. A change began to occur when he started to differentiate between his mother's overpowering good intentions and his violent and fearful reaction to them.

At that time he had a dream that a tiger was loose. The people behind him were killed by the tiger; the ones ahead of him were running, and he, too, ran to the safety of his home. There he hid in the basement fearing that the tiger would invade the house. The dream meant to him that the dangers were on the outside but also that he had become aware of dangers within himself. The therapist took the attitude that his concept of danger was exaggerated, that life was neither as threatening as he felt, nor was he himself such a hostile and aggressive person. Many realistic situations were used to help him recognize to what extent he had misinterpreted happenings and suffered from unrealistic fears.

When he was transferred to the open floor, on his own request, there was a decided change. He encountered many of the patients who had met him when first admitted as a "nasty kid"; there was general surprise about his change, about his willingness to participate in the ward life. During the first week Eric gained 5 lbs and continued to gain from then on, though at a slower rate. His first reaction was fear of getting sick again; it had all started with his feeling too heavy. "I don't know whether to gain any more—how much more can I take." But he could also look at it with humor: "Me of all things to have to watch my weight!" He expressed the feeling: "I am free—*I own my body*—I am not supervised any more by nurses or by mother." He became more active in gym and showed interest in others.

At that time he had a dream that he had an electric shaver—and that he was going to give himself a haircut. He felt that this expressed his optimism that he was going to be all right. He even went ahead and bought an electric razor, "I use it now to trim my hair while waiting—but there is a definite expectation that I will need it."

His attitude toward his weight and eating underwent a complete change. He felt even if he gained too much weight, he could no longer follow a diet. "I have controlled myself so long—now I want to enjoy food." While extensive dental work was done and a soft diet was prescribed he greatly resented it; now that he had given up his starvation regimen, he did not want to be left out. "Now if I lose weight it makes me feel sick, that I am losing something that is mine. If they are serving something I like, then I feel I am missing something." Even if he felt like not eating, he would still eat. "I would make myself do it." He also recognized that eating was a release: "It is a real pleasure—*now I want to eat*."

Increasingly he showed concern for his body instead of attacking it, and even became angry with other patients who he felt did not care properly for their health. "My body was not my own. It was my parent's concern. By neglect I would get back at my mother. Now I am willing to treat my body well. I won't take it out on my body any more. Now I know it is *my* body."

With this change in attitude he began to express a feeling of responsibility for his body, acknowledged that he had mistreated it, had let his teeth rot and decay, and stymied his growth. He now cooperated with an endocrine study. When collection of a 24-hour urine specimen was requested he became alarmed that his body did not produce well enough; he thought that he passed less urine than on a similar test, several years ago. He became also concerned that the medical consultant was slow in making a decision.

He could review his mother's concern with his health in a different light. "When I was a little kid she cared for me—she did things for me, mainly when I was sick. But now I know she helped me." His attitude toward his mother had changed after the anorexia developed. He particularly resented her taking him to doctors. "She did not act the way as when I had chicken pox. That was not my fault, but then they began to act as if it were all my fault. She sees now that I am not hopeless, that something good is coming out of me." At that time he needed extensive dental work, and also an eye check-up. He was touched that his father made arrangements for him to be seen by private physicians. This to him was proof that they really cared and saw something worthwhile in him.

His deficit in feeling differentiated from his parents, in particular from his mother, came up in many other ways. It had been rather puzzling that a boy as bright as he showed so little intellectual interest. It became apparent that his good school performance had also been something expected of him, without true curiosity or eagerness to learn. Gradually he began to develop an interest in reading. He became aware to what extent he wanted things planned for him, how little he relied upon his own initiative. When choosing a book he would ruminate: "What would my mother say—shall I please my mother when I read or am I pleasing myself?" He recalled that his mother had always suggested what he should read and he never had the feeling that he was reading for his own enrichment.

When endocrine treatment was instituted he began to pay attention to his bodily sensations and talked about "feeling different," without vocabulary on how to describe sexual feelings. Sex had never been discussed at home and during the years when other boys acquired sex knowledge he had been sick. He was constantly amazed that his sister, who was dating at this time, was doing so well.

He had a dream in which the head nurse asked him to go to the river and bring frogs. He came back with tadpoles. In his reaction he waivered between pleasure about having been singled out and trusted to do this special job, annoyance at being used as a servant, and discontent with himself for not doing the thing correctly. He could also see a connection between frogs in the undeveloped form and his own life, that he himself was still undeveloped and faced with the problems of becoming a mature person who had clung to being immature. The dream reflected also his ambivalent attitude about his relationship to others, his hypersensitive fear of being taken advantage of. This had expressed itself repeatedly in his objections to being interviewed by medical students, one of the accepted routines for patients at a teaching hospital. He objected that since he was not benefitting from it he would not cooperate. This fear of being taken advantage of was made the focus in his next session, until he finally had to admit that he had "learned" something from this experience, and therefore it had been to his advantage.

With progressive improvement the need to consider the future became more imminent. He now clung to the fact that he was of such short

stature as an insurmountable obstacle, and became obsessively preoccupied with his size. He alternated between feeling guilty for having ruined
his valuable body, and thinking of his body as the enemy who kept him
from taking his role in the adult world. He would refer to himself as a
teen-age dwarf. It was not altogether undesirable that his first physician,
who was very tall, left the service at this time and Eric began to work
with a new therapist. He again objected but, in a common conference,
treatment problems could now be defined as including the problem of
living in the adult world with a shorter than average stature.

He was finally willing to talk about his preoccupation with money; he
was aware that he was stingy and that *hoarding money* had been the *very
first sign of his illness*. He had a dramatic reaction when a parallel was
drawn between his attitudes toward money and food. He recognized that
he tried to live as a closed system, as an island to himself. Many episodes
in his behavior on the ward had shown to what extent he was afraid of
being cheated, or felt he was not treated as an equal, or feared that unjust
impositions were made on him.

Eric's attitude became one of waiting, of feeling that he could not
concern himself with anything until he had grown. Endocrine treatment
was instituted on his twentieth birthday. He was eager for it, though
afraid that it might "hurt" his body. He anxiously watched for new sensations, particularly sexual feelings, and was disappointed when there were
no immediate, marked reactions.

His failure in taking any initiative became more and more apparent.
Though he had spent years accusing his parents for having done too many
things for him, he now became increasingly aware that he was quite
unable to start anything, and was constantly trying to get directions about
the simplest decisions. This was a difficult period for his new therapist
because his repetitious complaining was a temptation to supply him with
"motivation," thereby depriving him of the need to decide for himself. In
the initial conference with his new physician he had accepted, at least
intellectually, that the remaining therapeutic task was a paradoxical one,
namely, that he himself had to take an active part in discovering errors in
his thinking and deficits in his experiences. The more active he was in this
process the greater the chance of his making the necessary corrections.

As he began to note some effects from the endocrine treatment, growth
of an inch, a change in the hairline, nocturnal erections and beginning
interest in girls, there was a gradual change. When he felt sure about his
development he decided that he wanted a job and used his father's connection to obtain a desirable position. His behavior at work showed how
little understanding he had for other people's behavior and of the impression he made on others. But now he could ask for help with his problems.

By the time Eric was ready to leave the hospital he had become a much
more self-reliant person. He stood quite securely on an island of realistic
awareness of his participation in his own life, not only in the most biological sense, but also with greater awareness of his needs and sensations, and

with vastly improved self-esteem and sense of effectiveness, and with more discrimination and sensitivity in interpersonal relations.

Only a few of the areas have been presented in which there was visible and describable change during this development toward personhood. It will have been noted that there was not only no specific exploration of the disturbed eating function, but also little discussion of sexual issues. When the patient brought up sexual questions they were discussed in context, but not specifically pursued. When endocrine treatment became effective in Eric, with nocturnal emissions and new sensations and his beginning interest in girls, he was eager to discuss these problems with his therapist. Gail suffered from severe sexual anxieties and misconceptions, but they were subordinate to her overall feeling of nothingness, of being a helpless product of her parents.

It is my impression that a premature focusing on the sexual issues hinders instead of fosters the development of an integrated self-concept. Under favorable treatment conditions a patient will examine such doubts at times when they become relevant. I quote from the history of Karen, where one might have expected that sexual anxieties stood in the foreground of her concern. She had become anorexic at age 16 after her menses had been pharmacologically induced. Two of her sisters had married when they were pregnant, something the family had deceptively denied until it was obvious. The emotional message could only have been that to grow up and become a woman was a disaster. The delayed menstruation after she had been pubescent since age 14, might well be interpreted this way. Induction of her menstrual periods provoked considerable unrest. Her weight at that time was 105 lbs; 6 months later it was 74 lbs. Her parents had considered Karen to be a warm, grateful, untroubled "perfect" child; her mother rewarded her for being "unlike the others," for not dating and not causing her parents worry. Karen delusionally denied that she had breasts or rounded buttocks, and defiantly repeated this literally hundreds of times. Unawareness of all her functions was extreme. She was unable to recognize who she was bodily, and would assume the identity of whoever she was around, and had "people eat for her." Treatment (by a resident psychiatrist under supervision) focused on her differentiating herself from the people around her and on becoming aware of her own sensations. She herself recognized her tendency to regurgitate whatever ideas and suggestions others expressed, in particular what she felt her therapist implied or wanted to hear. She wrote letters to set the record straight, feeling that when she was alone she might express more clearly what troubled her.

Since I have a tendency to completely void myself of feeling and the ability to express myself in your office—merely saying—"I can't think or feel" seems to be a slump I constantly fall in to rid myself of any responsibility of communicating with you how it is I really feel.—If I haven't eaten, I keep my mind eternally preoccupied with what size I am, always hoping it will become

smaller. *Nothing* interests me except getting skinnier and I can't give that up.
—Is there any hope of change? Especially when there are no feelings, like no
FEELINGS?

When she enrolled in college Karen was intensely pursued by men, and
because of her passivity was not able to ward off their advances. Whenever a man attempted to "demand" responses from her erotically, her
original symptoms were exacerbated, often with frantic "sizing" of other
people, and efforts to become "smaller." When her sexual anxieties were
taken up in therapy, Karen protested in a letter.

I feel that too much of your thinking centers around the feminine and maturation issues. It seems that these are secondary aspects of the underlying insecurity, denial, fear, and pain which has been around longer and has had more
developing time than any "awareness of what it is like to become an adult
woman." From these more basic instruments of forming my life and how I
respond *then* arise such conflicts as "should I be a girl," etc. From the
insecurity comes constant derision of myself: first that I am not as good, cool,
loving, understanding, human, as others—second, that I have no identity of
my own (any affirmation of me by my parents simply told me not to be
around or that I didn't have anything to say that was of the least concern to
them) and since I don't have any identity—I keep trying to imitate others,
accommodate to them, adjust myself to their mood—and then I find myself
confused as to what I think.

In spite of her protests there was visible improvement and when her
physician left the service she went to another city for professional training. Two years later she returned and was in therapy with another resident (also under supervision). She was still very slim but not conspicuously so, weighing 105 lbs. She held a job and lived in an apartment with
several other career girls. She spoke of herself in essentially the same
terms, as having no real personality of her own, saying that she would
mimic the style, mannerisms, and personality traits of other people with
whom she worked. She remained preoccupied with the theme of what was
her and was *not her*, or what was *within* her psychologically or physically,
or whether it was *outside* and somebody else's. "The road from the
outside of me to the inside has never been built." She was now 22 years
old and had become somewhat freer in having dates. She felt terribly
threatened by and fearful of her own sexual desires. She seemed to be
near to acknowledging her own sexual longings and began to become
aware of her inability to deal with them.

She began to recognize that her constant ruminations about food and
fear of getting fat were related to real life situations, interpersonal problems, and also sexual fears. One day she began to feel hungry in the
morning, didn't feel full after eating her lunch and was hungry throughout
the afternoon and looked forward to eating her supper. At that moment
she received a telephone call from a young man who had taken her out
before, and she became upset. Following this she suddenly noticed, "the
hunger went away entirely," and she began to ruminate about not eating
and getting skinny. She also recognized that her enormous tension when

she was with men was related to the way her father had treated her during adolescence, slapping her on the bottom or pinching her hips, saying, "hips are getting pretty fat, aren't they, kid?" She had lewd and disgusting feelings when this occurred, and these feelings recurred in the presence of other men. She could permit herself to experience attraction, but then would be disgusted with herself.

Her weight at this time was 110 lbs which aroused her concern as "too fat." She still felt uncertain about her body sensations. "Hunger and satiation are just words for me, not feelings or sensations.—The closest thing to hunger is dizziness when I haven't eaten; fullness is a vague pain, if anything." When her father died after a period of illness, her reaction was "one of tremendous, unbelievable relief." She noticed great gnawing hunger pains, with great persistence, beginning one week before his death and increasing after he died. There was a weight gain of over 10 lbs and she had to get used to her "fat new body." Shortly thereafter she made several steps toward greater independence, changed her job to something much more appropriate for her intelligence and training, and joined a sailing club where she felt she was respected for what she had to contribute and also felt more relaxed in relation to her fellows. It was in this more relaxed social setting of shared experiences that she could acknowledge sexual desire. She had tremendous feelings of guilt about sex, but no longer repressed it.

This step-by-step clarification of the underlying sexual problems is therapeutically effective in contrast to pushing the issue too early, though because of the repeated interruptions of treatment and change of therapists, it was extended over a longer period than usual. Sexual feelings come within awareness, or are recognized and identified as such, only after experiencing oneself as separate from the controlling forces. The failure in the experience of sexual sensations is intricately interwoven with other developmental disturbances. If one wishes to put this in terms of cause and effect, I am inclined to consider the sexual inability as part of these primitive overall disturbances, not the cause of them.

Comment

Though this approach has been developed in the treatment of severe eating disorders, it is in no way specific for them. Anorexia nervosa and developmental obesity, in spite of the dramatic manifest pictures, are in their underlying structures not specific but resemble other disorders of adolescence. In anorexia the noneating is a very late step in an overall defective development. Some adolescents in the same predicament will resort to overeating as a defense against their sense of "emptiness" and "nothingness"; some will alternate between phases of bulimia and anorexia. The great majority adopt other ways and means that do not involve the eating function in their search for selfhood.

One may call the struggle for a distinct identity with awareness of and control over one's functions an essential task of adolescence. The fear of being influenced from without, or of being empty and ineffective, can be recognized as the core issue in schizophrenics and in borderline cases, and in many others who are seeking deviant avenues toward self-differentiation.

The treatment approach I have described has been used successfully in many other conditions characterized by "weak ego" or "diffuse ego boundaries" or "narcissistic character." It has been particularly useful in the treatment of borderline states and schizophrenia, and in other patients who are considered poor candidates for classical psychoanalysis (2). This approach represents a modification of the analytic process, with explicit and consistent emphasis on the patient's developing awareness of thoughts and impulses originating in himself.

BIBLIOGRAPHY

1. Bruch, H., Some comments on listening and talking in psychotherapy, Psychiatry, 24:269–272, 1961.
2. Bruch, H., Psychotherapy with schizophrenics, International Psychotherapy Clinics, 1:863–896, Little, Brown & Co., Boston, 1964.
3. Eissler, K. R., Some psychiatric aspects of anorexia nervosa, demonstrated by a case report, Psychoanal. Rev., 30:121–145, 1943.
4. Fromm-Reichmann, F., personal communication.
5. Green, H., I Never Promised You a Rose Garden, Holt, Rinehart and Winston, New York, 1964.
6. Kay, D. W. K., and Leigh, D., The natural history, treatment and prognosis of anorexia nervosa, based on a study of 38 patients, J. Ment. Sci., 100:411–431, 1952.
7. Kolb, L. C., The value of consultation, pp. 122–132, in Evolving Concepts in Psychiatry, P. C. Talkington and C. L. Bloss, eds., Grune & Stratton, New York, 1969.
8. Lidz, R. W., and Lidz, T., Therapeutic considerations arising from the intense symbiotic needs of schizophrenics, pp. 168–178, in Psychotherapy of Schizophrenia, E. B. Brody and F. C. Redlich, eds., International Universities Press, New York, 1952.
9. Mesnikoff, A. M., Therapeutic milieu for the seriously disturbed, International Psychotherapy Clinics, 1:891–910, Little, Brown & Co., Boston, 1964.
10. Meyer, B. C., and Weinroth, L. A., Observations on psychological aspects of anorexia nervosa, Psychosom. Med., 19:389–398, 1957.
11. Selvini, M. P., L'Anoressia Mentale, Feltrinelli, Milano, 1963; Chaucer Publ. Co., London, 1972.
12. Thomae, H., Anorexia Nervosa, Huber-Klett, Bern-Stuttgart, 1961; International Universities Press, New York, 1967.

18

Outcome and Outlook

The leitmotif of this book has been the theme that eating and weight regulation are highly complex functions, with many different factors acting and interacting to various degrees in individual cases. This view is in agreement with that expressed by other investigators, but little of this progress in delineating the variety of disturbances is reflected in the evaluation of treatment results, which continue to be reported in terms of pounds lost or gained, and not of correction of the various underlying factors. Even modern authors recommend their approach, whether it is a physiological or psychological treatment method, on the basis of the speed and magnitude of the weight change. It has been known for a long time that it is relatively easy to effect short-term weight changes, both in obesity and anorexia nervosa, and that this can be done by practically any method. The real problem is whether this represents a lasting improvement. Absence of reports on long-term treatment results, and with due consideration for relevant individual factors, is probably the most remarkable deficiency in the obesity literature.

Medicine's fight against overweight as dangerous and undesirable is based on the statistical evidence of its association with higher morbidity and mortality rates. However, such figures, dealing mainly with the stationary obesity of middle-age and its association with heart disease, contribute little or no information on the course and treatment prospects of the unusual cases of early onset, or weight instability and obesity associated with severe personality disturbances. The main concern of this book has been the fate of such difficult and unusual individuals. The various treatment histories that were given in some detail were intended as illustrations of the many individualistic factors that determine the long-range outcome and need to be considered. No one factor has been isolated that might have been applicable to all cases as indicative of a good or poor prognosis in the long run. If there is a general conclusion, then it is that there are no generalizations.

Even for the same age group no general statements can be made. This was discussed in detail for childhood obesity (Chapter 8). Fat children seen in a pediatric clinic varied widely in the pictures they offered as adults. Those with a good self-concept and a well-integrated body image had a decidedly better prospect of a healthy adaptation later in life, including ability to control their weight, than those with early signs of the emotional disturbances, invariably related to intrafamilial problems. The poorest outcome, that of progressive obesity and severe mental illness, was observed in those who had been exposed to the most active therapeutic attacks, with various, often changing, methods, including enforced reducing. This was recognized as being related to the rejecting and confusing family climate rather than to the detrimental effect of one or another therapeutic approach, though extensive endocrine treatment served to confirm a child's conviction of being defective in his basic make-up.

Obese patients who come for psychiatric treatment are almost by definition people who have been therapeutic failures in conventional approaches, who have undergone repeated reducing regimens but have been unable to maintain the weight loss, or who have become emotionally disturbed during such efforts. With some psychotherapy has been tried but felt to be unsuccessful. In view of this negative selection, the long-range treatment results of the patients with whom I have been concerned have been surprisingly good, much better than might have been expected. This was discussed in some detail in the chapters on adolescent obesity and schizophrenic development (Chapters 9 and 10). These patients had become obese early in life, something usually considered a poor prognostic sign. Progress was evaluated not only in terms of weight stability, which was achieved by most, but even more in terms of the adequacy of their living. Those who stayed in therapy until at least some of the underlying problems were clarified achieved a high level of functioning, often finished their education and were successful with their work. They married and functioned adequately as marriage partners and as parents. They raised their children so that they grew up slim, with the ability to control their eating and not burdened by the weight excess from which the parents had suffered as children or adolescents. None achieved "automatic" weight control, but they owed their slim or slightly plump figures to "eternal vigilance" about what they ate. In this regard they did not appear different from the ordinary weight-conscious person in our culture. A few found they functioned better at a higher than normal weight, without, however, suffering from the hopeless and helpless fluctuations that had formerly interfered with their lives.

These positive findings stand in contrast to the many pessimistic reports about the therapeutic prospects of adolescent obesity and the value of psychotherapy. As was discussed in Chapter 17, there is probably no other method as poorly defined as "psychotherapy." I am inclined to conclude that unsatisfactory therapeutic results are related to inadequate conceptualizations of the underlying problems. These patients suffer from deficits in self-perception and inner controls, and they need help with these underlying issues; conventional psychotherapy, with its focus on intrapsychic conflict, fails to correct these conceptual distortions and inadequacies in self-perception.

In contrast to these good results, obese youngsters with severe personality problems who remained untreated, or who broke off treatment prematurely, uniformly had an unfavorable course, usually with increasing obesity; they were apathetic, leading indolent lives. A few escaped into compulsive reducing and developed the complications and various forms of maladjustment and inner restrictions described in the chapter on thin fat people (Chapter 11). The extreme of this course is the disaster of anorexia nervosa.

Intensive psychotherapy with obese people admittedly is not simple, but it appears to be the only way of helping such disturbed youngsters achieve the competent adjustment that makes a constructive life possible. The follow-up inquiries, up to 35 years later, have brought evidence that improvements achieved this way are lasting. Effective treatment offers people with distorted development the chance of clarifying the errors and misconceptions of a whole lifetime and of replacing them with realistic new concepts. Like the physician who supervises a reducing program, the psychiatrist may feel pressured into producing quick results, or may become involved with a patient's fantastic goals which often resemble realistic ambitions. Thus he may be tempted to try to achieve results quicker than is possible in view of the deep-seated disturbances, and he and the patient may become discouraged when the impossible cannot be done.

There is a widespread assumption that psychiatric treatment is a costly and self-indulgent alternative to reducing. This it is not. Psychological support is a necessary part of every reducing regimen, and it is the domain of the physician and nutritionists. It has found probably its best execution in the group approaches, such as Weight Watchers or similar enterprises. Psychotherapy is a treatment method for those with strict psychiatric indications. As in other fields of medicine the indication should be made on the basis of a positive diagnosis, the assessment of the personality structure, and the potential for schizophrenic disorganization or depression—not on the basis of the scale. The generalization that every fat patient is in need of psychiatric examination and treatment is not only unrealistic but also without justification. Psychotherapy can help certain obese people approach life in a more mature and realistic way. Its influence on weight control is only indirect; the solution to underlying emotional problems by opening up alternative ways of experiencing satisfaction may remove the basis for the excessive eating. In its very essence psychotherapy is a process of inner growth which cannot be hastened beyond the innate rhythm of the individual in treatment.

In contrast to obesity, where reports on long-range treatment results are practically nonexistent, there have been various efforts to evaluate the outcome of anorexia nervosa. There is general agreement that it is a serious condition and that cases seen by psychiatrists have a poorer prognosis than those treated on medical services. This reflects the simple fact that most, if not all, patients who eventually come for psychiatric treatment are those with whom medical treatment efforts have failed. Evaluation of the prognosis on the basis of the literature is more confusing than enlightening. One reason for this is that all cases of psychological weight loss are lumped together. Often an inaccurate, even misleading picture is presented; records of anorexia nervosa patients seen at large medical centers over many years are culled. Not uncommonly the reporters themselves have little experience with the condition and are not equipped to evaluate the various pictures which have been approached in a variety of ways by different physicians.

Information about the later outcome is usually based on letters which report the weight only, and not on personal contact or evaluation of the whole life situation. Cremerius (2) evaluated some of the older reports and took issue with considering weight gain alone as presenting a "spontaneous cure." He attempted to observe the "natural history" of the untreated illness and to assess the factors influencing the prognosis. He personally reexamined 12 out of 13 cases, 15 to 18 years after his first contact with them, or 21 to 28 years after the onset. These patients had come for consultation after several years of illness, after they had been exposed to a variety of conventional medical approaches that included endocrine products, periods of hospitalization, gastric intubation, etc. In all cases psychotherapy had been suggested. It was refused in 5 cases and was of such short duration in the other 8 that he considered them as untreated.

He found that 5 had developed a chronic picture of anorexia nervosa, still markedly underweight though to a somewhat milder degree. Another who had died of an intervening illness would have belonged to this group, and one had become manifestly schizophrenic. In 5 others the eating disturbance and weight loss had improved, and some had even lost the amenorrhea. However, they had either developed new symptoms or their life style was seriously disturbed and restricted, with various persistent or new neurotic manifestations. All patients were still living with their parents, even the 2 who were married. Cremerius concluded that there was no spontaneous recovery though 5 might have been rated as recovered if weight alone was used as criterion. His efforts to relate the long-range outcome to the premorbid personality, special medical treatment, or social influences was without success. He felt he could confirm concerning anorexia nervosa what Bleuler had said about schizophrenia: "The more exact the follow-up examination, the rarer a recovery."

My own observations are similar to this somewhat pessimistic assessment of the course of anorexia nervosa once a chronic picture has developed. I, too, was unable to identify any one factor that could have been predictive of the long-range development except the competence and adequacy of the psychotherapeutic intervention. In contrast to Cremerius' group, most of the anorexics whom I saw in consultation had been in psychotherapy. The approach discussed in the previous chapter has evolved from the evaluation of what had been successful or had failed to be effective in the previous therapeutic efforts.

Even with efforts to maintain contact with patients, it is not easy to obtain complete follow-up information. I shall give here only the figures for the 45 females with primary anorexia nervosa. No further information was obtained in 6 cases beyond what was learned at the time of the consultation, when two had already been anorexic for 5 and 6 years. Twenty-five (58%) were seen or heard of as late as 1970–1971. The last information applied to the condition from 1 to 5 years after onset for 25 cases, and from 6 to 19 years after onset in 20 cases. This represents information about the long-range development for a relatively large number. Contact with these patients ranged from evaluating consultations to intensive psychotherapy carried out over several years.

At the time when the last information was obtained, 4 were hospitalized with the diagnosis of schizophrenia. Four had died, one of an accident and 3 from causes related to the anorexia. Five were chronic anorexics; they were seen in consultation after the illness had existed for many years; one had become obese. In 24 the weight was normal but there were marked differences in the overall functioning. In 11 instances detailed information revealed that they led rather restricted lives, were intensely preoccupied with their weight, and socially isolated or ill at ease. They had been in various forms of treatment which frequently had been interrupted before a satisfactory resolution of the underlying problems had been achieved. Thirteen were rated as recovered; they were well adjusted, not only with regard to their weight but in their whole range of living. Two were still in treatment and appeared to be progressing well. Among the recovered, six were married and three functioned well as parents. In this group eight had become sick before the age of 14, and treatment had been instituted during the first year of illness. The approach had been comprehensive and had included work with the families; there had been good integration of the medical and psychiatric approach. However, a higher age of onset and protracted course are not incompatible with recovery. In five instances the illness had developed when the patients were 16 to 19 years of age; two of them had been sick for 9 and 11 years respectively when the therapeutic approach was changed and resulted in a resolution of the underlying illness. My therapeutic results are in agreement with Selvini's (3) conclusion, that the outcome is entirely dependent on the therapist's capacity to understand the basic problems of the anorexic and to help him find better ways of dealing with them, and that a statistical evaluation, based on weight alone, is not only not informative but may be misleading.

The other groups (atypical and male patients) showed a similarly wide range in outcome. Though early institution of meaningful psychotherapy improves the chances of recovery, long duration is no counter-indication for attempting a different therapeutic approach, as was illustrated by examples in the previous chapter.

Gain in weight is commonly cited as a sign of improvement, whereas in reality it may represent only a temporary remission, often a response to coercive treatment procedures. Several of the patients who came for long-term treatment had gained some weight after the initial episode and had been considered recovered by the family and attending physician until new symptoms, usually compulsive eating and vomiting, or a depressive reaction led to intensive therapy, which revealed that the essential problems had persisted below the facade. The most tragic illustration that gain in weight is a misleading sign of true progress are the histories of 4 patients with fatal outcome who had regained sufficient weight that they had been thought of as recovered. The descriptive information for the 5 patients who died is given in Table 18-1. One boy died within the first few months of the illness, and a man with an atypical picture died after several years of seeming recovery.

I shall give here briefly the histories of the three young women who died. One had developed anorexia nervosa at age 16 and had married during what looked like a spontaneous recovery. Though still amenorrheic she became pregnant. The combination of pregnancy and malnutrition with vomiting led to tetany, which was treated with vitamin D, phosphorous and milk; this caused a disturbance in calcium metabolism, which in turn led to irreversible changes in her renal and circulatory systems. Death occurred at a time when there was marked improvement in her psychological attitude. The autopsy gave a satisfactory explanation for the death, which was considered to have been inevitable even at the time when psychiatric and intensive medical treatment was instituted (1). Psychiatrically, this young woman was probably the least sick of the whole group. She had been able to carry out a sensible reducing program between the ages of 12 and 16, but then became frantically obsessed with her size and appearance and lost to the point of emaciation. There was considerable improvement, physically and psychologically, so that she got married and became pregnant. Despite a progressive deterioration in her medical condition, she remained active and mentally alert to the end. Efforts to correct her condition were made too late, after irreversible tissue damage had been done.

The two other girls had become anorexic at ages 11 and 14 respectively. They gained satisfactorily while in some form of supportive psychiatric treatment, but this treatment failed to deal with their inner sense of incompetence or to effect a change in the very disturbed family interaction. When the relapse occurred, 2 or 3 years later, there was in both instances a fateful delay in arranging for medical or psychiatric treatment. When they were finally hospitalized, inanition was far advanced and did not respond to medical intervention. Their weights were as low as 45 and 57 lbs, and acute infection and circulatory collapse was the immediate

TABLE 18-1

Death in Anorexia Nervosa

CASE	PATIENT	SEX	ONSET YEAR	ONSET AGE	WEIGHT HIGHEST	WEIGHT AT DEATH	PUBERTAL DEVELOPMENT	ILLNESS DURATION	DEATH YEAR	DEATH AGE	CAUSE OF DEATH
1.	Eli	M	1942	27½	150+	105	Mature, 1 child	6 years	1948	33	Gastric distention
2.	Nora	F	1951	18	(140) 115	85	Mature, 1 stillbirth	4 years	1955	22	Generalized calcinosis, renal and cardiac failure
3.	Dora	F	1959	11	95	45	No	5 years	1964	16	Inanition (no autopsy)
4.	Elliot	M	1963	13¾	115	86	No	4 months	1963	14	Distention and infection
5.	Thelma	F	1967	14	110	57	Menarche, at age 12	3 years	1970	17	Inanition and early broncho-pneumonia

cause of death. In one case (No. 5) gross autopsy findings suggested some abnormality of the pituitary gland on the basis of discoloration, but microscopic sections revealed normal glandular structure. The severe degree of cachexia and bronchopneumonia was considered sufficient to account for the death.

There are few experiences that leave one with as haunting a sense of failure as witnessing helplessly the decline and death of a hitherto energetic young person. This whole group of seriously disturbed youngsters provokes the feeling of witnessing unnecessary and avoidable anguish, of their being the victims of the tragic misinterpretation of the cultural exultation of slimness as a goal in itself. Whatever the handicaps and dangers associated with overweight, they are negligible in comparison to the suffering and invalidism that excessive reducing and self-starvation create. The fact that among the many hundreds of fat youngsters there was only one whose death from pneumonia at age 24 (page 145) appeared to be related to his superobese state in contrast to 5 deaths among 70 anorexics, is a sign of the disparity in suffering and illness created by over- as compared to under-nutrition. It may be objected that anorexia nervosa is a rare disease. This is true: but for every youngster who declines to the woeful state of cachexia, there are dozens if not hundreds who waste their efforts and energies in trying to be thinner and slimmer than is natural for their body build or compatible with a healthy, effective life. Our whole society is so preoccupied with slimness that there is a need to draw attention to the fact that many can achieve it only at a great sacrifice of health and competence.

This concern with the undesirable consequences of dieting and under-nutrition runs counter to the tenor of the conventional ideas of prevention with the focus on the penalties of overweight. It is usually approached in terms of "education," teaching people the caloric value of food and the composition of sensible diets. This knowledge is of course important, and imparting information about food values is essential for child care and health education in general. However, the difficulty lies in making people apply such information. We are faced with a paradox: we live in a society of plenty with surplus of food, and a continuous stream of advertising encouraging people to want more of everything; then comes the instruction to "eat less" which runs counter to this whole climate of abundance. For the innumerable millions who are overweight but rarely if ever come to the attention of physicians or nutritionists, dissemination of nutritional information is important, and every effort should be made to supply such knowledge in sufficient and palatable detail so that even the uninformed and uneducated can apply it to their daily lives. But much more than knowledge of calories is involved in changing food habits.

Entirely different issues need to be considered for the patients with intensely personal difficulties on whom I have reported here. Their whole life has centered around the fear of being too fat and they have felt defeated by their inability to control their weight. They know to the last decimal point the caloric value of every bite they eat, and the anorexics who carry blotting paper to take off the last trace of fat are superspecialists in this regard. They have more than enough nutritional knowledge but cannot apply it. They suffer from hopeless fluctuations in weight, expressing a deficit in inner controls. The difficulties of these patients demonstrate that for prevention to be effective, efforts must be directed toward factors that promote inner self-regulation. The conventional approach is too simplistic and misses the real issue.

If there is anything new in the understanding of obesity it is the knowledge that many factors are involved, which means that like other problems in obesity, prevention, too, needs to be approached from different angles. To give just one example: the existence of hereditary factors is often interpreted as condemning one to inactivity, that nothing can be done. Actually, obesity in other members of a family should be a call for greater alertness to prevent the potential of these inherited capacities from becoming a reality by avoiding the environmental influences which would encourage them to flourish. If proper limits are set a child so endowed may fulfill his potential for growth without becoming manifestly obese. That this is more than a possibility but a practical reality has been illustrated by the follow-up observations, in which it was found that formerly obese children and adolescents who had benefited from psychiatric treatment raised their own children in such a way that with one exception, they had not become fat. These children had grown up with good regulation over their food intake and showed signs of self-directed individuality, in spite of the obesity in their immediate ancestry.

This type of prevention must begin early in life and involves attitudes and behavior not directly related to food and eating. Knowledge about the influence of early experiences has become much more definite than it was only a decade ago. The fundamental problems leading to obesity are amazingly similar to those derived from schizophrenia research, and also from studies of cultural deprivation with deficits in intellectual and conceptual competence. Parent education must help to make it realistically possible for parents to become discriminately responsive to a child's expression of his needs, thus encouraging the organization of initiative, controls from within, and positive self-awareness. Some of the child-care recommendations of the not too distant past had the opposite effect. The rigid scheduling in common practice during the 1930's was replaced during the 1940's and 1950's by campaigns urging mothers to express their love by never frustrating their children, but to indulge them. The common error of these seemingly opposite recommendations was their neglect of a child's own expressions of his impulses and bodily needs, which resulted in deficits in their inner controls. Important for the appropriate interaction between mother and child is her readiness to fulfill his needs but also to set necessary limits. A mother must learn to differentiate between expressions of nutritional need and other discomforts, and she must not use food as a universal pacifier, or as reward, or withhold it as punishment. Much more is involved than not overfeeding a child and keeping him from growing too fat. This discriminating attention to his needs is the foundation for the inner organization of a self-directed personality, instead of the helpless passivity so often associated with obesity.

Whatever the inner problems of obese people whose self-regulatory controls are not properly programmed and who feel hopeless and helpless in their struggle to keep their weight within proper bounds, they are compounded and reinforced by the hostile cultural attitude which regards even a mild degree of overweight as ugly and abnormal, and condemns it as a sign of greed and self-indulgence. It is my personal conviction that this hostile attack on weight as a shameful evil has contributed to overweight and obesity's becoming such serious health problems. Whatever the relationship between overweight and life expectancy may turn out to be, there is no doubt that the current campaign against it is damaging in its effect on mental health. It is an amazing paradox that our society, with its emphasis on flexibility and liberal ideas, attempts to superimpose *one* form of body build on those who are differently endowed or whose early experiences have left them without control over the eating function.

Those who suffer from anorexia nervosa represent the most dramatic illustration of the great inner hardship provoked by this cultural attitude. These people condemn themselves to the torture of self-starvation in the futile hope of "deserving respect" and not being despised for being "too fat." Their pitiful emaciation is living proof that losing weight in itself does not solve underlying problems, and that the moral pressure only aggravates inner problems and conflicts. The pressure to be thin seems to be still on the rise, and increasingly often parents condone excessive thinness and fail to ask for help until severe emaciation has developed.

On the whole, the medical profession has shared the condemning cultural attitude and has attacked the weight directly. Increasing knowledge about various underlying physiological and psychological mechanisms has encouraged a more tolerant and respectful approach to the problem. If the irreversible factors are recognized, then it becomes understandable why people with these tendencies will react to life stress with weight increase. In spite of the handicaps of obesity, the most damaging of which are culturally created, to react with overeating in the face of conflicts and difficulties is relatively harmless. It is less destructive personally and less of a social liability than many other abnormal reactions in the face of similar stress, such as hypertension, suicide, neurotic or psychotic breakdown, alcoholism, or, in recent years, amphetamine or other drug abuse. In the liberal approach to drug addiction the emphasis is on the underlying problems of the victim and the social ills that need to be corrected in contrast to the reproachful ridicule to which the obese may be exposed, though the life-long patterns that interfere with weight control are not immediately accessible to change either, except through careful therapeutic reeducation.

It may be too early to expect a change in taste that praises near emaciation as "beauty," but there is beginning to be greater awareness and respect for the rights of minorities. Even fat people may come into their own, so that at least there will be relief from the damage resulting from being despised and rejected. It is a type of social reform in which both the professional and the general public can play an active role. Prevention of obesity calls for social acceptance of human diversity and fostering freedom and initiative in the individual. It repudiates manufactured, stereotyped ways of life and demands instead respect for human individuality.

BIBLIOGRAPHY

1. Bruch, H., Death in anorexia nervosa, Psychosom. Med., 33:135–144, 1971.
2. Cremerius, J., Zur Prognose der Anorexia nervosa (13 fuenfzehn-bis achtzehnjaehrige Katamnesen psychotherapeutisch unbehandelter Faelle), Arch. Psychiat. Nervenkr., 207:378–393, 1965.
3. Selvini, M. P., L'Anoressia Mentale, Feltrinelli, Milano, 1963; Chaucer Publ. Co., London, 1972.

Index